# "I, Too, Am America"

Archaeological Studies of
African-American Life

# "I, Too, Am America"

## Archaeological Studies of African-American Life

Edited by Theresa A. Singleton

University Press of Virginia
Charlottesville and London

The University Press of Virginia
© 1999 by the Rector and Visitors of the University of Virginia
All rights reserved
Printed in the United States of America

*First published 1999*

The paper used in this publication meets the minimum requirements
of the American National Standard for Information Sciences—Permanence
of Paper for Printed Library Materials, ANSI Z39.48-1984.

Library of Congress Cataloging-in-Publication Data
"I, too, am America" : archaeological studies of African-American life /
    edited by Theresa A. Singleton.
        p.  cm.
    Includes bibliographical references and index.
    ISBN 0-8139-1842-1 (cloth : alk. paper). — ISBN 0-8139-1843-x
(paper : alk. paper)
        1. Afro-Americans—Antiquities. 2. Africans—America—
Antiquities. 3. Afro-Americans—Social life and customs.
4. Africans—America—Social life and customs. 5. United States—
Antiquities. 6. America—Antiquities. I. Singleton, Theresa A.
E185.89.A58I15  1999
973'.0496073—dc21                                98-45871
                                                        CIP

Reprinted by permission of the publishers: The poem "I, Too" is from *Collected Poems*
by Langston Hughes, Copyright © 1994 by the Estate of Langston Hughes, reprinted by
permission of Alfred A. Knopf, Inc., and Harold Ober Associates Incorporated. Chapter 3
by James Deetz first appeared as "American Historical Archaeology: Methods and Results,"
*Science* 239 (1988): 362–67, © American Association for the Advancement of Science.

*I, Too*

*I, too, sing America.*

*I am the darker brother.*
*They send me to eat in the kitchen*
*When company comes,*
*But I laugh,*
*And eat well,*
*And grow strong.*

*Tomorrow,*
*I'll be at the table*
*When company comes.*
*Nobody'll dare*
*Say to me,*
*"Eat in the kitchen,"*
*Then.*

*Besides,*
*They'll see how beautiful I am*
*And be ashamed—*

*I, too, am America.*

Langston Hughes

# Contents

## Part II: Plantation Contexts

## Part III: Beyond the Plantation

## Part IV: Epilogue

# Illustrations

## Tables

# Acknowledgments

M ANY PEOPLE have played a role in bringing this volume to fruition. I would like to thank first the contributors to the volume for their excellent essays. They have exhibited great patience throughout a lengthy review and manuscript preparation process. I am particularly grateful to Warren Perry and Robert Paynter for writing the epilogue as well as providing useful comments on the individual essays in the early stages of this project. I also appreciate the comments provided by the anonymous reviewers, who reviewed both the prospectus of book and the final manuscript.

I am very grateful to Mark Bograd, Brian Crane, Abdul-Karim Mustapha, and Tom Ormsby for their assistance on various aspects of this project. They helped with some of the more mundane tasks such as proofreading, checking references, and rekeying. A special thanks goes to Marcia Bakry, illustrator of the Department of Anthropology at the Smithsonian Institution, for generating several of the line drawings.

My heartfelt appreciation goes to Ronald Bailey for inviting me to co-organize the conference "Digging the Afro-American Past: Archaeology and the Black Experience," held at the University of Mississippi in May 1989. That conference provided the impetus for organizing this collection of essays on African-American archaeology.

Acknowledgment is due to the National Endowment for the Humanities for funding grant RX21117-89, which provided the financial support to host the conference. Acknowledgment is also due to the National Museum of Natural History, Smithsonian Institution, for providing a subsidy to assist with some of the production costs of this publication.

Several individuals at the University Press of Virginia have greatly contributed to the success of this project. John McGuigan, formerly with the Press, was instrumental in getting this publication started. Richard Holway made sure that this project stayed on course. I am indebted to the editorial assistance I received from Jessamy Town and Boyd Zenner. Finally, I am eternally grateful to my family and friends for their continued support in all of my endeavors.

# "I, Too, Am America"

Archaeological Studies of
African-American Life

# 1

# An Introduction to African-American Archaeology

*Theresa A. Singleton*

THE ARCHAEOLOGICAL STUDY of African-American life has become a well-established research interest within American historical archaeology. Referred to as African-American archaeology or the archaeology of the African diaspora, it is no longer seen as simply an effort to capture unrecorded aspects of black history or to bring attention to the heritage of a neglected community. Many archaeologists recognize a message of Langston Hughes's poem "I, Too": you cannot fully understand the European colonial experience in the Americas without understanding that of the African. This heightened appreciation of African-American archaeology is transforming its goal from the study of a forgotten people to the study of the formation and transformation of the black Atlantic world. Archaeologists engaged in this research are increasingly concerned with issues such as the analysis and representation of cultural identity, race, gender, and class; cultural interaction and change; relations of power and domination; and the sociopolitics of archaeological practice.

This collection of essays epitomizes the changing vision of African-American archaeology and reflects the broad spectrum of studies that characterizes this research. The purpose of this volume is to identify promising areas of research that can lead to new ways of looking at the archaeological record of African-American life.

## Moral Mission to Social Action

As a research interest initially set in motion by black activism, the first studies of African-American archaeology emanating out of the 1960s and 1970s (Ferguson 1992:xxxv–xxxix; Singleton 1995:120–21; Singleton and Bograd 1995:14–15) had a moral mission: to tell the story of Americans—poor, powerless, and "inarticulate"—who had been forgotten in the written record. Although this characterization of potential archaeological subjects included more than African Americans, it was perceived as being particularly applicable to the black experience (Ascher 1974:11; Deetz 1977:138; Fairbanks 1974:62) and became the rationale for pursuing the study of that experience.

Moral mission archaeology sought to interpret the everyday lives of African Americans from their own perspectives using the remains of housing, foodways, and personal effects recovered from excavations. It succeeded in giving a voice to the voiceless, but many of the interpretations were overly simplistic. African-American communities were perceived as bounded, insular enclaves (as was the case in nativistic approaches in cultural anthropology) capable of reproducing material aspects of African culture. This view of African-American life ignored the complex social relations involved in the formation and maintenance of the cultural identity of any group and was particularly unsuitable for the study of African Americans who were forced to occupy a subordinate social position. Further, by choosing African survival rather than its demise or reconfiguration as a research focus, moral mission archaeology established a research precedent that still stalks African-American archaeology today: the search for cultural markers linked to Africa as the most significant aspect of African-American material life.

Efforts toward analyzing social complexity in African-American archaeology began in the mid-1970s (e.g., Handler and Lange 1978; Otto 1975). Its application to the study of African-American life was perhaps best articulated in Robert Schuyler's edited volume *Archaeological Perspectives on Ethnicity in America: Afro-American and Asian American Culture History*, the first attempt toward synthesizing archaeological studies of African-American as well as Asian-American sites. Using a cultural evolutionary framework, Schuyler stated that "ethnicity had little meaning until complex structures arose based on political domination" (1980:vii). He specifically chose to examine African and Asian Americans because they represented "distinct cases of subcultures being incorporated into Anglo-American society" (1980:vii). Although not all the studies in his edited volume examined social complexity in their discussion of ethnicity (some of them were, in fact, moral mission studies), the volume paved the way for the inclusion of African-American archaeology under the more general study of ethnicity, the process of group identity formation that can be either self-ascribed or ascribed by others.

Widespread adoption of ethnicity as an approach to understand intergroup difference de-emphasized or replaced race as a social construct in analyses of cultural phenomena. Yet the use of ethnicity has often failed to specify the conditions under which social groups subordinated as "racially" distinct emerge and persist (Harrison 1995:48). In archaeological literature ethnicity is often equated with race (see chap. 15 for a discussion of this point); therefore, the essential differences between European-American ethnic communities and "racial minorities" have not been adequately addressed (cf. Scott 1994). For example, the authors in Schuyler's edited volume recognized that the experiences of African and Asian Americans were different from ethnic communities of European descent; but how those differences framed the experiences of African and Asian Americans, making their lives different from many European-American ethnic groups, did not establish the context within which the archaeological data were evaluated.

Leith Mullings (1978) distinguished ethnic groups for whom ethnicity is symbolic, manipulable, and voluntary from historically oppressed ethnic groups (e.g., African, Asian, Latino/Latina, and Native Americans) for whom ethnicity is not just symbolic but is also used by the dominant group to rationalize and structure oppression. Such structured oppression limits the extent to which ethnicity can be utilized situationally or mobilized (1978:19). For this reason some scholars declare that ethnicity is inappropriate for the study of groups designated as "minorities," while others have shown how ethnicity and race (as a social construction) are interrelated and why the examination of one should consider the other (Harrison 1995:49). In chapter 8 Epperson explores how the historical and social construction of racial difference is discernible in landscape design and architectural space on Chesapeake plantations. Through his careful analysis of contemporary accounts and archaeological findings, Epperson shows how plantation space was manipulated to create "difference" or "otherness." More significantly, his argument supports the position that race, not ethnicity, is the proper starting point for archaeological considerations of African-American identity.

Class, another analytical category like race, may inform ethnicity but is not equivalent to ethnicity. In African-American archaeology class has more often been an organizing principle in discussions of external relationships between blacks and whites and has been used less often to examine internal relationships within African-American communities. Some archaeologists, however, have attempted to identify material differences perceived to be related to class (e.g., Crader 1990; Parker and Hernigle 1990), but such efforts are misguided because the criteria used to designate class differences are suspect. Additionally, these interpretations of class or status tend to support perspectives taken from the dominant culture rather than those of African Americans (see Singleton and Bograd 1995:17–18).

John Otto (1975, 1984) introduced class to the archaeological study of African-American life in order to investigate how cultural differences between African and European Americans are reflected in the archaeological record and to distinguish material differences of ethnicity from those of socioeconomic class. Other archaeologists have followed this line of inquiry and have refined Otto's approach to plantation social structure (e.g., Orser 1988a). Focusing upon white resident artisans of Monticello, Thomas Jefferson's plantation home, Barbara Heath (chap. 9) examines the social position and power relationships of white artisans within plantation labor. Her comparison of the archaeological record of white artisans with that of skilled slave artisans reminds us that plantations were also arenas of struggle between slaveholders and nonslaveholding whites.

Class, for the most part, is an underdeveloped area of archaeological analysis in

African-American studies. This may be partially related to the greater emphasis and visibility given to the study of African-American communities occupying the lowest socioeconomic strata (slaves, tenant farmers, wage laborers) of American society than to other social classes. Few studies have been undertaken on African-American communities that are equivalents of present-day middle class, who own land and other property (e.g., Blomberg 1989; Catts and Davy 1991; Muller 1994). Archaeologists are beginning to explore these diverse groups of African Americans, and the future of such studies should shed light on material manifestations that integrate African-American identity with social class.

Studies of race, class, and gender (e.g., Muller 1994; Wilke 1996; Yentsch 1994) in African-American archaeology are emerging, but these topics are presently secondary to the study of cultural interaction and change. Practitioners of African-American archaeology are interested in the role that cultural interaction between African and European Americans played in the construction of African-American identity. Over the past two decades, several conceptual apparatuses have been utilized to understand this interaction, including: (1) acculturation (e.g., Otto 1975, 1984; Wheaton and Garrow 1985); (2) creolization (e.g., Ferguson, chap. 6; Mouer 1993; Mouer et al., chap. 5); (3) relations of power and domination (Epperson, chap. 8; McKee, chap. 11).

Anthropologists formulated the concept of acculturation long before the advent of ethnicity studies, but it initially shaped the application of ethnicity in archaeology (see Staski 1990). Acculturation generally refers to "those phenomena [cultural traits or complexes] which result when groups of individuals having different cultures come into continuous first-hand contact, with subsequent changes in the original cultural patterns of either or both groups" (Herskovits 1941:10). Melville Herskovits, a pioneer in acculturation studies, conducted the first comprehensive studies of African-American acculturation, and modified versions of his African survival-acculturation model have been applied to archaeological studies of African-American life.

Acculturation studies assumed that the simple replacement of African-influenced items with European items was an indication of cultural change and a loss of cultural identity. Although archaeologists seldom conduct such studies today, they point to a persistent interpretative problem in African-American archaeology. This is the assumption that the acquisition and use of mass-produced or other European-American objects meant the same to African Americans as these objects meant to European Americans. This "from the top down" perspective reflects the view of the dominant and is disappearing with studies that seek to understand how African Americans appropriated the material culture of the dominant and created new meanings for it (e.g., Brown and Cooper 1990; Ferguson 1992; Howson 1990; Orser

1992; Paynter 1992). Within this volume several authors offer alternative and/or multiple readings of material culture. Emerson (chap. 4) and Ferguson (chap. 6) search for African meanings and uses for Chesapeake pipes and colonoware that might lead to alternative interpretations of these artifacts. Epperson (chap. 8) considers the audiences for plantation landscapes and the multiple ways in which they were read. Armstrong (chap. 9) shows how enslaved African Americans responded to the imposed European spatial norms by transforming house-yards into community-defined activity areas. McKee (chap. 11) contrasts slaveholder perceptions of food provisioning with those of the enslaved people.

Dissatisfaction with the Eurocentric biases inherent in acculturation studies gave rise to concepts capable of analyzing multidimensional changes in multiethnic social environments (Lightfoot 1995:206). Creolization is one of those concepts. It is defined as a process involving multicultural interaction and exchange that produces new cultural forms (Ferguson 1992:xlii). In African-American archaeology it allows for the study of social action, wherein African Americans are seen as active agents engaged in the production and reproduction of their world. Several authors in this volume incorporate creolization in their discussion, but Ferguson (chap. 6) best articulates its usage: "In creating their American culture, African Americans drew elements from African, European, and Native American culture and combined these into a new and unique way of life." Comparable to creolization is *cultural transformation*, the term Armstrong uses to identify the process that resulted in African-Jamaican lifeways. Both concepts provide for the interpretation of artifacts, architecture, and spatial plans originating from another culture, as these were appropriated, used, and perceived by African Americans. Perry and Paynter (chap. 15), however, critique creolization (and related concepts) for its lack of explanatory power. They argue that the concept fails to explain how or why certain characteristics, and not others, become part of the new creole culture, or why the new culture "takes on a specific form or color."

Analyses of power relationships enhance our understanding of cultural interaction by providing a context that presumably reflects the character of most black-white relations. In this way the study of power can provide access to the lived experiences of African Americans. Archaeologists often frame their discussion of power as a dialectic between domination and resistance (e.g., Miller, Rowlands, Tilley 1989): the examination of how dominant groups exert their power and how subordinate groups resist such power.

African-American resistance is a growing area of archaeological research. Both its overt forms like maroonage (e.g., Agorsah 1994; Orser 1994b, 1996) and its covert, day-to-day forms are being studied (e.g., Ferguson 1991; Hall 1992:385–86; McKee 1992; Singleton 1995:128–30). Numerous examples of covert resistance are found in the following chapters; some of these have been alluded to in the previous discussion. Deagan and Landers's study (chap. 13) of the black settlement at Fort Mosé is the only case study of overt resistance in this collection.

Fort Mosé, though technically not a Maroon community, was established for black settlers who fled from enslavement in British colonies to Spanish Florida. The Spaniards granted them their freedom and gave them a town of their own in return for defending the Spaniards from the British. Deagan and Landers examine how these African-American settlers manipulated the British-Spanish conflict to their own advantage, thereby providing insights into African-American agency. Fort Mosé clearly illustrates Eric Wolf's notion of structural power: the forces that constrain, inhibit, or promote what people do (1990:587). In resisting British enslavement the Fort Mosé settlers established alliances with the Spaniards, but they had to comply with the new terms of Spanish hegemony. Thus, power relations are multifaceted and must not be studied using simple, binary approaches but with ones that provide lenses into the complexities of social interactions.

Having reviewed the analytical frameworks used in African-American archaeology, particularly those in this volume, I now examine the themes and questions raised in each of the following chapters.

## African-American Identity and Material Culture

The relationship between material culture and cultural identity is a long-standing and reemerging problem in archaeological interpretation. Recent efforts are attempting to better define how the two are intertwined (e.g., Graves-Brown et al. 1996; Jones 1997; Shennan 1994). For example, Shennan (1994:18) defines ethnicity as "self-conscious identification with a particular group." The association with material culture unfolds "once some aspect of style [symbols, forms, and underlying value orientations (see Royce 1982:147)] has an ethnic reference"; "it is by definition 'emblemic,' since it has acquired a different and specific value" (1994:18). Shennan further states, "Ethnicity is a specific and contingent phenomenon, the product of particular situations . . . which may involve new uses for old styles . . . [it may also] be a rather special group identity associated with the appearance of states" (1994:19). The question that this definition poses for archaeological analysis is: How are references to ethnic style or a special group identity determined archaeologically?

Archaeologists have approached this problem in African-American archaeology in two essential ways. The first approach relies upon making artifact identifications with African cultures, and it is the subject of chapters 2–7. In the second approach, types, quality, or percentages of artifacts (not associated with Africa) are used as a point of departure for making inferences to one of the following conditions: the social position African Americans held in white America (inexpensive ceramics, cheap cuts of meat); ethnic style (e.g., foodways, hair-care products); both social position and ethnic style. This second approach frames the discussion of African-American identity in chapters 13 and 14.

In chapters 2–7 the authors consider how archaeologists assign cultural affinities to material culture and examine whether or not artifacts can provide insights into the cultural identity of its makers. Focusing upon handcrafted earthenware pottery and pipes recovered from sites once occupied by African Americans, they address several questions: Did African Americans participate in the production of these wares? What is the evidence of their participation? Whose artistic and pottery traditions are reflected in these objects? How does the study of these artifacts provide insights into understanding African-American life? What archaeological approaches are best suited to understand African-American culture?

In debating the answers to these questions, these authors engage in a reexamination of a larger question that has dominated the study of African-American life for most of this century: To what extent was African-American culture derived from an African heritage? That Africa was the source for black American culture figured prominently in the writings of many black scholars (e.g., Martin Delaney, W. E. B. Du Bois, James Weldon Johnson, and Carter Woodson) long before this idea received serious attention in mainstream scholarship. The reluctance to accept the possibility of African origins for African-American culture stems largely from the widespread acceptance of catastrophism: the belief that all vestiges of African culture were destroyed during the Middle Passage and subsequent enslavement. Eager to suppress racist arguments that people of African descent were innately inferior to Europeans, antiracist scholars, including many blacks, embraced catastrophism. They argued that black Americans, deprived of their African culture, had fully assimilated into American culture (Cerroni-Long 1987).

Melville Herskovits was the first anthropologist to challenge catastrophism. During his fieldwork among African-American communities in Haiti, Brazil, Suriname, and Trinidad, he observed striking similarities in their customs and practices with those of African societies. He coined the term *Africanism* to refer to the presence of what he believed to be African-derived cultural traits. In the *Myth of the Negro Past* (1941), Herskovits argued for the existence of a distinct African-American culture tradition that had resulted from an African heritage. His work immediately provoked controversy both within and outside of anthropology (Joyner 1986).

Although Herskovits's work inspired the research trajectory that now seeks historical or archaeological evidence of an African heritage in the Americas, there is a critical difference between his work and that of more recent archaeologists and historians. Herskovits and his followers were making claims that present-day social and cultural forms represent direct continuities from Africa. This is not the same as the investigation of African influences in the formative years of African-American history (Mintz and Price 1992:55) or their role in the shaping of colonial American life as a whole—reasons why archaeologists search for Africanisms.

The archaeological search for "Africanisms," however, has been fraught with numerous problems. First, like many other archaeological efforts seeking evidence of cultural identity, the primary purpose is to recover ethnic markers and not to examine the social complexities that affect why these ethnic markers emerge, persist, or change. This is what Upton refers to as "static" ethnicity (1996:1). Another problem is that it is very difficult to establish a specific cultural provenance for many African-American practices (see Posnansky, chap. 2, and DeCorse, chap. 7). Finally, as DeCorse discusses, it is unlikely that African practices, objects, or symbols had the same meanings in the Americas as they did in Africa, because Africans were unable to reproduce the social systems of which they were a part.

These problems present significant challenges to the archaeological investigation of African influences in the Americas, but they are not sufficient, either singularly or cumulatively, to dismiss all efforts that pursue this line of inquiry. The abundant revisionist scholarship of the last three decades has eroded catastrophism (though vestiges of it can still be seen in some scholarship) and has demonstrated that an African heritage contributed to the development of African-American aesthetics, craft practices, folklore, language, music, and religion. Some studies also have examined the impact of African culture or technology upon the development of American culture as a whole (e.g., Carney 1993, 1996; Philips 1990). Today, most students of African-American life in the United States agree that African Americans form a culturally distinct community with its own heritage (Abrahams and Szwed 1976:137). What remains unclear is: How was this cultural identity constructed in specific settings and how can it be interpreted from archaeological resources?

Merrick Posnansky (chap. 2) opens the discussion of associating materials recovered from African-American sites with African culture by stressing the need for Americanists to understand African archaeology. Through a summary of archaeological work in West Africa relevant to African-American archaeology, he suggests ways archaeologists can better understand the African-American past. He offers two specific recommendations for African Americanists: first, they should incorporate a broader knowledge of African ethnology in their studies; second, place greater emphasis on grappling with the dynamics of the slave trade. These two issues are critical to making credible connections between Africa and the African diaspora.

In chapter 3 James Deetz advances the argument that colonoware (a term used by archaeologists to designate earthenwares recovered from sites in the United States) from sites in Virginia was made by enslaved Africans, not Native Americans. This essay, first published in 1988, lays out Deetz's argument for the production of this ware by Africans in seventeenth-century Virginia. Deetz's interpretation is based on the recovery of colonoware from five of eighteen sites at Flowerdew Hundred, a plantation established on the James River drainage in 1619. Blacks were at Flowerdew Hundred as early as 1619, but colonoware only occurs on sites dating between 1680 and 1720. This period corresponds to the institutionalization of racially based slavery in Virginia, when the numbers of enslaved Africans significantly increased in the region. Deetz suggests that the pattern of colonoware occurrence is related to changes in the social and residential patterns of blacks during the seventeenth century.

Since 1988 Deetz has reaffirmed his commitment to this interpretation (1993: 79–90). Acknowledging that there can be no definitive answer to the question of who made colonoware, he asserts that the evidence "points strongly to slaves as the makers of this pottery" (1993:81). Deetz further sets forth what he perceives as the weaknesses in arguments that support Native American manufacture of these wares: too much reliance upon the early observations of scholars whose studies were inconclusive; the lack of well-dated archaeological contexts to support Native American production of these wares; the appearance of surface treatments, such as cob-impressed pottery, that occur on Indian-made pottery only during the historic period when it was possible that Native Americans learned this technique from runaway slaves; the increase in the quantity of this pottery at the time when the Native American population was decreasing and the enslaved African population was growing (1993:79–90). Finally, he suggests that attribution of colonoware to Native Americans is partially an accident of history: it was first identified as an Indian ware, but someone else could have arrived at another conclusion.

Related to Deetz's interpretation of colonoware is Matthew Emerson's study of Chesapeake pipes (chap. 4). Emerson posits that certain decorative patterns and motifs on seventeenth-century Chesapeake pipes may be of African origin. Emerson opens his discussion by arguing that the insights into this craft have been hampered by limited archaeological evidence and written documentation on Chesapeake pipe making. Next, he examines individual characteristics of Chesapeake pipes— bowl forms, decorative techniques, and motifs—and discusses their occurrence in Chesapeake Indian, English, and West African decorative arts. From this examination Emerson identifies a stylistic pattern consisting of the patterned use of decorative lines and stamps highlighted with white-clay inlays that he asserts "describes much of the decorative essence of Chesapeake pipes." He believes this style to be an African aesthetic because of its widespread use in West Africa predating the mass shipment of Africans to the Chesapeake, and because an examination of seventeenth-century European and Chesapeake Indian artifacts has "failed to reveal a similar stylistic history using stamped characters, decorative lines, and white inlay." He further supports his argument through illustrating the use of identical African motifs, executed in this stylistic pattern, on Chesapeake pipes.

A counterargument to Deetz's and Emerson's interpretations of African influences in colonoware and Chesapeake pipes is offered in chapter 5, by L. Daniel Mouer, Mary Ellen Hodges, Stephen Potter, Susan Henry Renaud, Ivor Noël Hume, Dennis Pogue, Martha McCartney, and Thomas Davidson. They review the evidence used to attribute the production of colonoware pottery and Chesapeake pipes to Native Americans from archaeological, ethnological, and documentary sources. Opening their discussion with the claim that American historical archaeologists have overlooked the role of Native Americans in colonial America, they proceed with separate treatments first for pottery, then for pipes, detailing a research trajectory covering several decades that argues for Native American manufacture of these artifacts. The case they build for pottery is based upon three observations: first, technological similarities between colonowares and comparable wares of the late prehistoric and early contact period; technological similarities between colonoware with ethnological descriptions and specimens of wares made by the Pamunkey and other Native American communities in the nineteenth and early twentieth centuries; third, historical references to Indian pots and pipes in traveler accounts, probate records, and other documents.

In their review of pipes, they examine the presence of individual characteristics of the pipes—pipe bowl forms, decorative techniques, and motifs—in pre-Columbian Indian and, occasionally, European decorative arts. From this investigation they observe that two essential characteristics of Chesapeake pipes—the pipe form and *pointillé* decoration—were in use by Native Americans at least 1,000 years before European contact, and that many of the decorative motifs can be found in both Indian and English decorative traditions.

They conclude with a recommendation and a question, both of which offer important considerations for the archaeological study of ethnicity in colonial North America. Archaeologists should critically evaluate historical references suggesting that Indian populations had vanished. In the Chesapeake (and possibly elsewhere), these documents were written as propaganda to ease potential colonists to America from their fear of Indian uprisings. They raise the question: Can or should archaeologists assign ethnic affiliations—based upon modern ethnic categories—to the makers of artifacts in a creole society like the seventeenth-century Chesapeake? Their response is that they cannot, but for them the evidence is clear: seventeenth-century Virginia was a creolized culture highly influenced by Native American customs, values, and practices.

An underlying assumption in the arguments over colonoware is that the production of artifacts, more than their use, embodies ethnic style. Who made colonoware pottery and pipes may never be known, but all three groups—Africans, Europeans, and Native Americans—presumably used these artifacts. In a creolized society such as the seventeenth-century Chesapeake, new uses undoubtedly arose for old styles, as Shennan's definition of ethnicity suggests. In view of the assessment of seventeenth-century Chesapeake society by Mouer and his coauthors, it is very likely that Africans adopted and reinterpreted old "Indian" styles that may have become emblematic of African identity in colonial America. African manufacture of these artifacts, however, should not be ruled out, particularly for the pipes. Locally made terra-cotta pipes are associated with Africans during the seventeenth and early eighteenth centuries at sites found throughout the Americas. In all these contexts these artifacts curiously disappear after that time (see discussion in Armstrong, chap. 9; Orser 1996:123–29).

From the Chesapeake, the discussion of colonoware moves to South Carolina. By the 1740s a majority black population exerted its influence on the cultural landscape of South Carolina and created a distinctive African-American culture (Wood 1974, for detailed discussion). Leland Ferguson (chap. 5) situates his analysis of localized incisions and scratches found on some colonoware vessels within this cultural milieu. This essay is an elaboration on his interpretation that these marks exhibit similarities to cosmograms found in the Bakongo culture of West Central Africa (Ferguson 1992:110–15). After ruling out the possibility that these marks are either makers' or owners' marks, he explains the significance of crosses and circles in the Kongo religion. Support for his thesis that similar symbols were important in the religion of African Americans comes from the work of art historian Robert F. Thompson (1983) and historian Sterling Stuckey (1987), as well as the oral testimony of a former slave from Georgia.

From this discussion Ferguson builds a case for the ritual use of these vessels based upon several observations, including: demographic evidence showing Congo-Angolan people dominated the areas where these vessels are found; the importance of circles in African-American ritual—here he posits that bowls may have been selected for their circularity in rituals; and the significance of water in Kongo cosmology and the fact that most of these vessels were recovered from underwater contexts, a finding that suggests bowls were purposefully placed in the water as part of rituals.

In chapter 7 Christopher DeCorse, an Africanist archaeologist, critiques African-American archaeology with specific comments on previous chapters in this section. He begins by identifying what he sees as the central problem in studies that search for African continuities in the Americas: the lack of familiarity with African material culture and the tendency to generalize about African cultures and their practices. From there, he surveys pertinent archaeological and historical studies that provide a context to understanding the Atlantic slave trade and the cultural diversity of the people who were enslaved.

DeCorse evaluates the individual strengths and weaknesses of Deetz's, Emerson's, and Ferguson's arguments. While noting that there are African parallels to these artifacts, he discusses some problems inherent in these and similar investigations. He concludes his review by asserting that these studies and others (particularly those that utilize artifact pattern recognition) may provide evidence of the contribution of Africans to American life, but they offer limited insights into African-American culture. He recommends that archaeologists make more use of cognitive approaches in archaeology to examine the emergence and transformation of African-American culture.

## Plantation Contexts

Central to the emergence of African-American archaeology is an evolving research area of plantation archaeology. Through time, this interest has produced new findings, paradigmatic shifts, and engaging, as well as regressive, critiques within historical archaeology. At first the plantation was approached for its perceived functionality in "the world the slaves made," versus the world that was created and controlled by planters. Archaeologists continue to explore this area with increased enthusiasm for using material culture to lead to alternative histories.

Using a variety of conceptual approaches, the authors of chapters 8 through 12 consider several themes. The first is that of power relations, an approach to archaeological study of plantations that continues to develop and that frames all or part of the discussion in each of these essays. A second theme is representation, a growing concern for the archaeologist who, as interpreter of plantation histories to the public, negotiates the past with the present. Transcending and encompassing both representation and power relations is the theme of historiography, specifically how historical interpretations generated solely from written sources compare with those that incorporate analyses of material culture. The essays by Terrence Epperson, Douglas Armstrong, Barbara Heath, Larry McKee, and Edward Chappell encourage us to see that race ideology, architectural and landscape design, slave housing and use of domestic space, craft production, labor stratification, and foodways all fit together in the study of plantations.

In chapter 8 Terrence Epperson sets the stage for analyzing power relations in the plantation studies that follow by examining the social construction of racial difference within both Christian theology and plantation architectural and landscape space. The common thread that ties theological and architectural practice together is the contradiction between the need to incorporate the oppressed within a unified system of control and the need to create distance, difference, and otherness. Slave conversion to Christianity was seen as a means to incorporate and enhance control over the enslaved, yet they were excluded from being treated as Christians through the refusal of theologians and the plantocracy to recognize enslaved people as spiritual equals. The tension between the exclusionary and incorporative aspects of domination in the spatial realm is explored through four vignettes derived from written accounts and archaeological and architectural studies of Virginia plantations. These sources are used to provide insights into the manipulation, multiple meanings, and significance of plantation space, in which domination was most apparent but which also formed the nexus for slave resistance.

Douglas Armstrong provides in chapter 9 a comprehensive overview of plantation archaeology conducted in the English-speaking Caribbean. His essay is organized around several themes for which archaeological inquiry is an important interpretative tool. The first is the examination of how an African heritage was retained, modified, or merged with other European and Amer-Indian traditions in the Caribbean. For example, Armstrong observes that African-Jamaican wares were derived from African practices and technology, but they incorporate elements of European potting technology. A second theme is the study of cultural transformation in which cultural change is viewed as an active rather than a passive response to the social, historical, and environmental conditions that gave rise to African-American communities. In illustrating this process he expands upon Epperson's notion that the manipulation of plantation space formed the nexus for slave resistance. Armstrong shows how the house-yard, which had its origins in Africa, was a form of resistance to European spatial patterns. House-yards were not only important during slavery and in the early years of emancipation; even today "yards" are culturally symbolic among African-American communities in the Caribbean (e.g., Mintz 1974:225–50) and in the southern United States (Gutherie 1996:75–76; Westmacott 1992). Power relations, social structure, and economics are further discussed under what Armstrong labels as critical analysis—an investigative process that can lead to the redefinition of questions and their solutions. Additional topics include: bioanthropological studies of human remains, the public interpretation of archaeological findings, and future directions of African-American archaeology in the Caribbean.

Barbara Heath (chap. 10) adds a neglected dimension to understanding planter hegemony through her study of resident white artisans. She compares their economic and social position to that of skilled slaves within Thomas Jefferson's plantation community at Monticello. Because white artisans have received little attention in archaeological studies, she begins with a detailed discussion of the artisans— William Stewart and Elisha Watkins—and their material world derived from documentary and archaeological sources at Monticello. She proceeds with a comparison of artisan and slave assemblages using two questions to frame her analysis: (1) Can the degree of individual choice be determined in each assemblage? (2) Was the private material life of the artisans comparable to their public material life embodied in the house provided for them by Jefferson? Through this comparison she provides insights into how Jefferson categorized his labor force, and how they in turn accepted or rejected Jefferson's authority and constructed their own material lives.

Larry McKee (chap. 11) demonstrates that food was also a significant source of conflict and control on plantations. He challenges the "veterinary" approach to slave diet that only considers food in terms of its nutritional value. In its place he offers a model that presents and attempts to interpret foodways from the perspective of the enslaved and addresses the question: How are subsistence activities reflected and influenced in plantation social relations? The premise for his argument is that food was not just a biological necessity but also had "great symbolic force."

McKee's approach to the study of slave foodways is twofold: first, through an examination of articles in agricultural journals and planters' records from five plantations along the tidewater region of the James River in Virginia (the focus of this study), he establishes a context for understanding the production and management of plantation food supplies. Second, he uses the analysis of faunal remains recovered from slave quarters of three Virginian plantations to shed light on the actual foods that enslaved people consumed and their active participation in food procurement. Together the two sources show the interplay of "ideals, motivations, realities, decisions, and actions of both masters and slaves" within the system of plantation food supply.

Until archaeological investigations were undertaken at slave quarters, little or no attempt was made to develop exhibits on slavery at America's famous sites, such as Colonial Williamsburg, Mount Vernon, or Monticello (Bograd and Singleton 1997). Archaeology has been a fulcrum for the public interpretation of African-American life both at historical sites and in traditional museum displays (see additional discussion on the public interpretation of African-American archaeology in chaps. 9 and 13). Edward Chappell (chap. 12) places African-American archaeology at the heart of contemporary debates on the politics of museum representation. He questions the responsibility of museums in their interpretation of American slavery. His argument addresses three significant issues. First, he examines the limitations involved in the presentation of colonial life through museums. Racism, he argues, influences the biases in these presentations, because museums often operate on a double standard as to what they accept as valid information for interpreting the slaveholding class and what they accept as valid for the interpretation of enslaved people. Second, he is interested in changing our frame for viewing the past, and he contends that museums have an important role to play in this intervention. Historical memory remains a negotiable and dynamic field that has political and ethical ends. Third, he examines the intentions of museum curators and urges them to create more critical presentations of American slavery.

## Beyond the Plantation

Understanding African-American meanings and uses of material culture is a challenge at all sites, but perhaps even more so in nonplantation contexts. Plantations offer archaeologists the opportunity to observe material manifestations of social relations within discrete components of a well-defined cultural landscape. At sites not part of plantations, these material manifestations will be more varied and possibly more obscure than on plantations. Moreover, archaeologists are just beginning to contextualize African-American life within these diverse settings (e.g., Agorsah 1994; Askins 1988; Bower 1991; Cressey 1985; Paynter 1992; Orser 1994b, 1996; Yentsch 1994). These efforts, however, represent only a limited number of potential possibilities for elucidating the relationships between sociocultural, economic, or political factors and the archaeological record of African-American life.

In keeping with most African-American archaeology, the two case studies that examine life beyond the plantation in this collection are primarily concerned with identifying material expressions of African-American identity. They also reveal how social relations in these settings differed from those of plantations. The Fort Mosé example was discussed earlier. The study of the Elmwood site (chap. 14) suggests how white racism played a role in the demise of this settlement and the historical memory of it. More significantly, both case studies show how archaeology can be a powerful corrective to the erasure of African-American stories in local histories.

In chapter 13 Kathleen Deagan and Jane Landers recount the history of the Gracia Real de Santa Teresa de Mosé, a fort and settlement located just north of St. Augustine, Florida. Verification of the site's location became a major objective for the Mosé project because over the years doubts about the actual site arose. This public amnesia toward the site's location and history, in addition to St. Augustine's "troubled history of race relations," generated some hostility toward the project. Moreover, that free Africans Americans contributed to the defense and culture of St. Augustine was a difficult idea for many residents of the city to accept. These circumstances became the impetus for developing educational materials, popular publications, and an exhibition of Fort Mosé which is still traveling around the country.

Deagan and Landers provide a description of African-American life at the site based primarily upon a rich archive of Spanish colonial records that contrasts with those available for the study of African Americans in many other former European colonies. Archaeological research contributed less than documentary sources to this reconstruction, primarily because the archaeological evidence of actual occupation is ephemeral and the sample size extremely small compared with other contemporary sites in St. Augustine. Yet the material assemblage at Mosé is very different from other St. Augustine assemblages in two important ways: it has a lower proportion of aboriginal materials and a higher proportion of non-Spanish-European wares. Whether these observations are indicative of ethnic style or reflect socioeconomic variables are issues to be tested in future investigations.

All of the case studies in this volume, with one exception (chap. 14), are concerned with colonial and preemancipation African-American history. Beverly Bastian's study of Elmwood demonstrates that archaeology is equally important in the study of the recent past. She unravels the reasons for the abandonment of Elmwood, a short-lived African-American settlement in Michigan's Upper Peninsula. The apparent victims of a land scam, the black settlers moved to Elmwood from Chicago in 1926 to farm and cut timber on a worthless twenty-acre tract land. By 1930 the settlers had abandoned the site and returned to Chicago. Through archival research and oral history, Bastian pieces together the sociopolitical climate and the sequence of events that led to the site's abandonment. But she also confronts conflicting depictions of African-American life at the settlement. Local newspapers and white informants indicated that the blacks could not adjust to the cold climate, were destitute, and resorted to producing illegal alcohol to make a living. Two former black occupants of Elmwood painted a different picture—that families kept gardens, livestock, hunted and fished, had plenty of firewood to keep them warm, and drank illegal alcohol but never made it. Although the archaeological evidence did not resolve the conflicting accounts, it brought more credibility to the memories of the former African-American occupants than to the depictions by the white informants or the newspaper accounts.

## Conclusion

In the final chapter of the volume, Warren Perry and Robert Paynter critically analyze key issues and themes raised in the preceding chapters. They evaluate African-American archaeology within the global political economy of colonialism, thereby supplying the theoretical capstone for the volume. From this framework Perry and Paynter argue that the archaeology of the African diaspora is the study of W. E. B. Du Bois's color line. Du Bois ([1903] 1969) coined the term *color line* to characterize the suppression of people of color (Africans, Asians, indigenous Americans, Pacific Islanders, and so forth) resulting from European imperialism and hegemony. Given this definition, the goal of African-American archaeology is to lift the "veil" of the color line (racism) both in the study and practice of African-American archaeology. By bringing attention to related studies in other disciplines, particularly the works of African-American scholars, Perry and Paynter offer future directions for archaeology that can expand its role in understanding the consequences of the African diaspora.

The essays in this volume incorporate diverse theoretical and social-political positions—from Afrocentrism to Marxism, from positivism to postmodernism. These various departures are indicative of the many voices that have contributed to formation of African-American archaeology as a special area of study. Yet through these competing as well as overlapping ranges, one consensus is apparent: African-American archaeology is more than a moral mission or the study of ethnicity. It is a study of the historical and cultural processes that made the African experience unique in the Americas. To ignore the consequences of forced migration, enslavement, legalized discrimination, and racism misses the very essence of how African Americans created their world and responded to that of the dominant culture. African Americans did not simply adopt a world that was created for them, nor was their world insular to those of other communities. The challenge for archaeological research is to pry open places where the material world can inform the analysis of these complexities.

# Part I

# African-American Identity and Material Culture

# 2

# West Africanist Reflections on African-American Archaeology

*Merrick Posnansky*

## Introduction

In recent years historical archaeologists working in North America have become increasingly aware of the African presence, by identifying, classifying, and debating over the question of who produced a class of ceramics first described by Noël Hume as Colono-Indian ware (1962) and later suggested by many scholars to have been made by transplanted Africans. They have sought identifiable African features in patterns of artifact distribution and spatial relations both within settlements and intramurally (Deetz 1977). Linguists, art historians, musicologists, folklorists, and cultural anthropologists have tracked elements of West African language and discovered numerous, though often isolated, elements of African continuity in the New World (Crahan and Knight 1979); but no concerted effort has been made to examine the archaeology from West and Central Africa where the twelve to fifteen million Africans brought to the Americas as slaves originated.

African-American archaeology should be rooted in the study of African archaeology and ethnology. Thus, the purpose of this essay is to provide an introduction to West African archaeology and material culture for archaeologists interested in studying the African presence in the Americas. In the course of this discussion, I identify areas of research in Africa for archaeologists engaged in the study of the African-American past that are also of mutual interest to Africanist archaeologists.

In 1981 I urged American historical archaeologists to take greater cognizance of African archaeology and cautioned against looking for one-to-one parallels between Africa and the New World (Posnansky 1984a). More recently Matthew Hill (1987) and Kit Wesler (1987) have both used their knowledge of West Africa to caution American historical archaeologists about oversimplifying and speculating too freely on superficial evidence. Given the tremendous growth in West African archaeology, Americanists can draw upon the results of African archaeology to shed light on questions concerning African influences in the Americas.

Many archaeological interpretations of African-American life suggest that North American archaeologists have misconceptions about African culture. One major fallacy accepts African culture as monolithic; once described, it can then be identified either in its entirety or in parts within the American context. At the root of this fallacy is the assumption, perhaps based upon the unwarranted belief in the stagnation or backwardness of African societies, that there is a traditional African culture spread over a wide geographical area and over a long period of time. John Picton, the eminent English authority on African art history, has recently launched a spirited attack on the use of the word *traditional*, believing that it robs African culture of its dynamic nature (Picton 1992). *Traditional* implies a mythical time in the past, yet tradition in reality involves the handing down of ideas and ways of doing things from generation to generation. Periodically old traditions are replaced by improved modes of behavior, which in turn become new traditions handed down to succeeding generations. Few scholars would attempt to describe a single European culture which embraced at once Elizabethan and Victorian England or which lumped English ceramics with those of Albania and Finland, yet African slaves were drawn from an area more than three times greater than that of Europe (excluding Russia) and over a period of nearly four hundred years which witnessed some very dramatic changes in African cultures (fig. 2.1).

Americanists also fail to examine carefully the temporal or geographic context of the African data they draw upon to study African influences in the Americas. For example, the archaeological studies by Hill and Wesler rely quite heavily upon information dating from the past hundred years. Such studies would not be very reliable for making connections with American sites dating from an earlier period. The geographic origins of transplanted Africans may have played a crucial role in their ability to maintain certain practices. If members of a savanna or sahelian community ended up as slaves in a hot, humid, heavily vegetated area—for instance, the Guianas—it is obvious that little of their material culture or their cultural tradition would have been appropriate to their new environment and thus would survive. In contrast, if slaves from the Gold Coast (the coast of present-day Ghana) were transplanted to tropical islands such as Jamaica or from Angola and the Democratic Republic of Congo to Brazil, which have a similar hot and humid climate and many plant families in common, then conditions would have been more favorable for human adaptation and a survival of African ways of doing things.

In some cases the cultural and technological milieu was far more important than the environment. For example, seventeenth-century slaves from a humid tropical environment transplanted to a similar environment in the Caribbean, which to the Europeans presented a formidable contrast to the one they left behind, would have been able to apply their experience much more effectively than nineteenth-century slaves coming to the same physical environment but to a cultural environment already heavily impacted and dominated by Europe. The seventeenth-century European settlers were much closer to West Africans in their technology, and even in some ways in their belief systems, than they were to their nineteenth-century descendants, who as a result of the Industrial Revolution were already heavily acculturated to a new technological industrial economy and urban society. The colonial "earthfast" houses identified in the Chesapeake (Carson et al. 1981) that so excited historical archaeologists in the early 1980s are of course very similar in basic construction to very many wattle-and-daub houses of West Africa. Slaves drawn from the coast of West or West Central Africa and taken to the more temperate parts of North America, such as Virginia, where there was an already established European culture, would have found such an environment less conducive to a survival of African ways of life than those taken to the Caribbean.

## West Africa at the Time of the Slave Trade

Africa during the time of the slave trade was in a process of political and technological flux due to contacts from across the Sahara, European influences from the coast, and local indigenous developments. In 1450 there were few well-established coastal societies: the dominant polities lay within the interior, whether in the forest or in the savanna. New societies gradually sprang up along the coast that were receptive to foreign ideas and technology and took advantage of the opportunities for trade. These coastal communities represented a "frontier of opportunity," to borrow a phrase from the late Kenneth Dike (1956). In response to the new trade and foreign contacts, new towns and new classes of wage earners arose (Daaku 1970). These newly established African communities were vibrant, particularly along the Gold Coast and parts of the Nigerian coast. Exploitation by European colonizers certainly existed, but it was not the commonly perceived picture of unremitting European colonizers bent only on collecting slaves.

This African vibrancy produced, for example, the Akan civilization—at its peak in the eighteenth- and nineteenth-century Asante state—and the full flowering of Nigerian art. From recent excavations by Christopher DeCorse (1989a, 1992) at the African town of Elmina in present-day Ghana, which developed as a result of the erection of the Portuguese fort in 1482, it is obvious that African townspeople rapidly acquired tastes for European imported goods ranging from ceramics, bottled alcoholic beverages, and stemmed glassware to beads and associated metal goods. The people of Elmina lived in substantial stone houses in a very congested setting. Though the importation of cheap iron bars depressed the local iron industry and led to the virtual cessation of iron smelting in many areas, the advent of low-cost brass stimulated brass industries from Nigeria in the east to Senegal in the west. It is true that cheap firearms purchased with the most salable commodity available,

slaves, helped fuel a process of state formation and state disintegration and also led
to the rapid spread of both cultural and technological ideas. This is readily apparent to anyone looking at the diffusion of regalia items and of tobacco use or at the
common elements within the narrow stripped textiles of West Africa. Though the
African world of 1850 was certainly very different from that of 1450—and African
society in the later period gave evidence of extensive demographic dislocation and
social disintegration—there was probably minimal technological change at the village level. The problem, however, is that archaeologists do not have the data to make
accurate comparisons between Africa in 1450 and in 1850. There are excellent documentary sources for the coastal communities, but the sources for those in the interior are fragmentary. The oral traditions of the more successful societies provide
little information on the material culture of those they victimized and sold into
slavery.

Though the point of departure for the slaves was the coastal forts, castles (van
Dantzig 1980a), and barracoons (this is relatively well known from the historical
accounts, particularly European trading company records; see van Dantzig 1980b),
the origins of the enslaved Africans usually lay within the interior, hundreds of miles
from the coast. The enslaved were brought principally from the stateless societies of
what is sometimes termed the "middle belt," which lay between the forest states and
the large savanna states and middle Niger towns like Jenne and the Hausa city-states
like Kano and Sokoto (see fig. 2.1). There is a tendency to look to descriptions of the
most buoyant African societies when looking for parallels with African-American
culture. The majority of slaves came not from major states like Benin, Asante, or the
Hausa city-states but rather from weaker stateless societies. The strong states were
engaged in the trade very often as equals to the Europeans.

The strong, self-confident peoples of the African states still retain much of their
rich culture, while many of the weaker groups, such as the Adja-Ewe of the southern Republic of Benin and Togo, were the most receptive to European colonialism
and often provided early adherents for Christian missions as well as students for
colonial schools. As a result, less of their "traditional" social structure remains in
an unaltered state. Unfortunately many of these weaker societies were less attractive
to nineteenth-century ethnographers and diarists than were the larger states with
their powerful and flamboyant kings, their colorful courts, their royally patronized
crafts, and their richer, less-altered religious and cultural life. These weaker—and
very often acephalous—societies have also been the more neglected by Africanist
archaeologists, who have concentrated their attention (in their studies of the second
half of the second millennium) on towns like Ife, Benin, Begho, and Kong rather
than on rural communities in the areas chiefly affected by the slave trade. By the time
good ethnographic studies were undertaken in the twentieth century on the peoples
affected by the slave trade, these cultures already had been displaced and were in

defensive situations in hills or in similar marginal areas. They were mostly no longer in their original locations or in the social and economic environment from which the slaves were originally wrenched.

It is important to know that slaves in the Americas were a mélange of very different peoples. This was both in part a conscious policy of divide and rule, aimed at destroying old familial and societal relationships, as well as linguistic and religious ties, and in part the inevitable result of a trade that involved many areas of supply and demand. Throughout the four hundred years of the slave trade, Africans were taken from a number of markets along a 3,000-mile coastline from Senegal in the northwest to Angola in the south. African culture became diffused in the Americas except when a consistent pattern of trade from a particular West African region to a particular area of the New World existed for a sufficient time to ensure dominance of a single ethnic group. Examples of this phenomenon are the prevalence of Gold Coast peoples in seventeenth-century Jamaica, of people of Senegambia in parts of the Carolinas in the late eighteenth century, and of Slave Coast peoples in northeastern Brazil in the nineteenth century. Just as historical archaeologists in America have an obligation to research all the available local documentary sources before beginning excavations so that their research can be better informed, so must the archaeologists of the African-American past search all the available information on the origins of the transplanted Africans who occupied a particular region of an archaeological site. Such research efforts call for collaboration with the growing number of historians of the Atlantic slave trade on examination of the West African trading company records as well as on the history and archaeology of African-American communities in the Americas.

Identifying the ethnic origins of New World slave populations is a very difficult task. For a long period of the seventeenth and eighteenth centuries slaves were characterized as "Cormantees" or "Eboes" depending on whether they came from the Gold Coast (where Cormantin was an early Dutch and English trading station) or from the stations on the Bight of Biafra in Nigeria (where Igbos are dominant). Quite a number of different ethnic groups from a variety of ecological zones were thus subsumed under these general ascriptions on the basis of their point of departure. If one can pinpoint a specific, as opposed to a general, area of origin, as well as a specific point of departure, and demonstrate the dominance of a certain ethnic group in that area, then one can gather information on the cultural and material background of the group and be alert for specifically related crafts, proxemics, and physical features among the black populace of the region in the Americas where they ultimately labored. Then, and only then, can the researcher legitimately turn to specific archaeological reports to acquire familiarity with ceramic sequences and settlement patterns, knowing that such reports are pertinent.

## Archaeological Research in Western Africa

The archaeological examination of western Africa has developed very rapidly in the past twenty years (Posnansky 1982). Regional reviews by McIntosh and McIntosh (1984) and by de Barros (1990) and Kense (1990) in Robertshaw (1990) clearly indicate increasing interest in relatively recent periods hardly investigated in the 1960s. There is still a concentration of activity on the great states of the savanna and forest, from which have come most of the famous art pieces of terra-cotta, copper, bronze, and brass, the elaborately decorated ceramics, and the large and extensive earthen walls that surround the capitals of important states. Nevertheless, one of the most encouraging aspects of West African archaeology in the past twenty years has been the growing emphasis on ethnoarchaeology (Atherton 1983; Agorsah 1990), both for the insights it offers into past behavior and as a way for archaeologists to understand the processes of change, adaptation, and life in general in the areas in which they are working.

Several studies of whole villages have been undertaken in Ghana (Agorsah 1983a, 1985a, 1988), as has research on building methods and the decay of mud-walled structures (McIntosh 1974, 1976). These investigations are proving useful in the interpretation of sites with mud architecture. Sophisticated studies that examine stylistic and functional relationships between ceramics and other objects (including buildings) and explore the cultural and metaphysical aspects of form and design are providing a new dimension to our understanding of material culture. Particularly important for its implications for the interpretation of archaeological data has been the work of art historian Marla Berns (Berns and Hudson 1986) in the middle Benue area in the Gongola region of Nigeria and that of Nicholas David and his team from Calgary (David, Sterner, and Gavua 1988) in the grassland area of Cameroon.

Many archaeologists of West Africa began to undertake their own ethnographic studies because they felt that the kind of ethnographic information needed to examine archaeological questions—material culture change, spatial relations, or site formation processes—was missing in anthropological reports. Similarly, it might be necessary for archaeologists of the black experience in the Americas to undertake research in Africa to discover the nature of the societies that slaves left behind and to identify areas from which slaves came to specific American localities. Such studies would shift the archaeological focus to the weaker societies and to the periods when slaves were actually transported and would avoid the pitfall of overreliance upon more recent ethnographic studies or upon the more plenteous works on those societies (such as the Asante) whose members were enslaved in very small numbers, if at all.

The field of West and West Central African archaeology has grown in the past twenty-five years from less than twenty archaeologists (scattered among less than a dozen museums, universities, and antiquities services in only six of the more than twenty countries from which slaves were transported) to over seventy archaeologists in at least fourteen countries. However, there are still at least half a dozen countries without any resident archaeologists, and many archaeologists in the other countries work on minuscule budgets, with virtually no equipment, in an area much larger than the United States east of the Mississippi River. Only minimal work has been done in the Democratic Republic of Congo and Angola, which between them contributed more slaves than any other African region. As a consequence of the economic depression in Africa of the early 1980s, cultural research has assumed a very low priority, and the pace of research has slowed down considerably. Archaeological investigation in Africa has become even more dependent than it previously was on foreign expeditions—largely from France, the United States, and Canada—for the larger programs of regional research.

## West African Material Culture

### Housing and Spatial Arrangements

When seeking a benchmark to use for purposes of comparative archaeology, it is necessary to distinguish between basic West African elements common to a large number of slave-producing African societies and elements that are ethnically or environmentally significant. One basic West African element comprises houses made of either solid mud or wattle and daub. Housing variation is the result of different ethnic, economic, and environmental factors and is expressed in the building shape—whether square, circular, or rectangular—and by the houses' configuration in courtyards and room alignments.

There is no one single universal measure that can be used to recognize African buildings, though in the case of rectilinear layouts in domestic buildings, rooms are seldom wider than 3–4 meters. Room size may be determined as much by the building methods and transport limitations as by anything else. Since roofing timbers were individually hand carried, limitations on timber weight and length related directly to the builder's strength. A further feature of African housing (though it must be pointed out that this is really a general feature of many preindustrial societies in different parts of the world) is the ad hoc nature of many structures. Additions or individual units are readily built.

Whereas there is often a very clear definition in European material culture between the technomic, sociotechnic, and ideotechnic functions of a given object or group of related objects, the distinctions within African material culture are much less clearly defined, largely as the result of undifferentiated behavior patterns. For example, all crafts, all agricultural practices, and all social occasions have religious dimensions. One of the most fascinating features of African material culture is the ideotechnic function of objects: village layouts, houses (Griaule 1965; Blier 1987), iron furnaces (Goucher et al. 1986), and pottery (Berns 1986) may all have an anthropomorphic aspect that should not be overlooked by archaeologists. Among the Tamberma of Togo, the village interspatial relations are also anthropomorphized, so that a settlement (in plan) has a human form (Blier 1987).

The presence of shrines—normally outside but close to the structure's walls—is a common feature in much of West Africa. Shrines are particularly important in craft activities. The process of iron smelting has a deeply metaphysical meaning; it is an act of creation and has to be treated that way. The same is true, to a lesser degree, with ceramics. To the outside observer many shrines might be difficult to recognize as such, consisting as they do of a broken pot with offerings, or a heap of earth with a piece of metal protruding from it, or a group of bloodstained stones, or a forked stick supporting a bowl with hair clippings. Nevertheless, there is a pattern to the locations of shrines which can clearly differentiate a shrine from casual heaps of broken pots. But the pattern varies from ethnic group to ethnic group even though the practice of making household shrines is widespread.

Virtually universal also is the practice of using rooms largely for sleeping, storage, and occasionally for shrines but not for cooking, eating, or craft activities except on an occasional basis (such as during rainy season). As a result, activities take place away from the house: in the courtyard, against the wall of the house, occasionally between houses, on the farm in shelters (Posnansky 1984c), under shade trees, or on the edge of the settlement. This extramural use of space is possibly the most important and pervasive aspect of West African life, and there is no reason to suppose that it was very much different in the past.

Hearths, too, are distinctive. In many areas they consist of three stones or of three specially made upturned hearth pots with holes in their bases. Other hearths are made of molded clay, though in urban environments, for example, Notse in Togo or Elmina in Ghana, special coal pots were used. Unfortunately no study has been made of hearth forms. Hearths are usually situated within the center of compounds, though they are occasionally located against the walls of outhouses or in open-faced rooms.

Normally gender-related activities are also strictly separated, with women being more inclined to work within the house compound and men away from the house. For instance, potting and the spinning of cotton—designated as women's activities—are pursued within the courtyard or sitting on an outside step, whereas most men's activities—including ironworking, basket making, and weaving in those societies in which men weave—are extramural. In Nigerian societies in which women weave, however, the activity is conducted either in the courtyard or in an open-ended room. One technical reason for this latter distinction is that the men's narrow strip looms utilize warp threads stretched out for up to thirty more feet.

Though activity areas are clearly demarcated and thus should be accessible to archaeological recovery, a further relatively universal habit is for West African house-wives and children to sweep compounds and the areas immediately in front of their houses constantly with grass whisk brooms. This means that many women's activities may not be as visible in the archaeological record as some of the men's activities. Some figurative brass gold weights—hundreds of thousands of which still survive from the seventeenth, eighteenth, nineteenth centuries—depict sweeping and brooms, clearly indicating that the practice is far from recent. A further problem is the ephemeral nature of the apparatus for many of these activities. Basket making and weaving leave little or no trace; all the apparatus is made of organic material, the weaving shed is largely a shade for the weaver, and there are no load-bearing uprights, so that even postholes are difficult to locate only weeks after a shelter has been moved. Similarly, open firing of pots leaves only superficial traces, and with the West African practice of recycling, wasters are used for countless purposes, from water troughs for small animals to retainer walls for the hearth's open-fired pottery.

Before considering ceramics in detail, it is important to consider the possibility of other cultural items being transferred from West Africa to the Americas. I have argued elsewhere (Posnansky 1984b) that apart from a few waist beads, minor ornaments of little value (such as thin wire bracelets or earrings that slaves might have worn), the occasional pipe (such as the one associated with the obeah man's burial at Newton plantation in Barbados; see Handler 1982), and not more than twenty types of seeds or plants (Grimé 1979), there was no significant transfer of tangible items. Though one can make a generalized statement that assumes continuities in behavior and patterns of belief and can speculate about the transfer of mental blueprints, the reality is much more complicated. Patterns of rural life in West Africa differ greatly over relatively short distances: there is a bewildering diversity of ceramics, iron tools, and house forms. Even plant usage varies regionally, as a quick perusal of Irvine's *Woody Plants of Ghana* (Irvine 1961) reveals. The impact of the slave trade, the arrival of the European administrators and colonizers in the nineteenth century, and the spread of urban industrial life in the twentieth century all had their effect on rural continuities and have to be taken into account. A visit to the wonderful display of the exuberant varieties of Nigerian pottery in the museum of Jos, well illustrated by Sylvia Leith-Ross (1970), will provide a caution to anyone who thinks that a study of a single West African society can provide easy interpretations for the material culture of the heterogeneous slave communities of the New World that was homogenized under the cultural dominance of the European slaveholder.

## Ceramics

Pottery within any West African society is not only a craft but an integral part of rural culture. Though the potter is an individual, potters work in groups within traditions that are often relatively circumscribed by convention. Pottery is generally made by women in West Africa except for specialized items made by men, such as spindle whorls and tobacco pipes, which arrived within the community after the ceramic tradition was firmly established. Master potters, as well as dyers, weavers, and other skilled craftsfolk, are usually mature persons occasionally as young as twenty-five but normally much older. Several facts can be gleaned about the slave trade from the abundant statistics in company records and shipping manifests. There was an emphasis on securing young healthy individuals, and males exceeded females by a proportion of between 3:1 and 3:2, depending on the area to which they were being shipped. Women were normally taken at a younger age than men. The enslaving African society retained valuable females slaves, particularly farmers (Kiple 1984:48–49) and craftswomen such as potters. All these factors militated against the transference of sophisticated ceramic skills.

In a most perceptive paper, Matthew Hill (1987) highlights some of the problems of discriminating between the cultural influences of Africa, or specific areas of Africa, and those of other regions of the world when the ceramics studied exhibit both a rudimentary technique (as indicated by low-temperature, open-fired pottery) and stylistic simplicity (as expressed in very basic forms with little decoration). I remember that when I first encountered Far Eastern and Polynesian ceramics in 1966, I was struck by the same problem: how to distinguish sherds of undecorated and not very diagnostic pottery from one major region of the world from those of another except by fabric analysis. We have no evidence as yet that any of the colonoware was made from other than American clays.

African traits certainly were retained through the transmission of individual potters' skills rather than that of their social structure. The new social structures created in the Americas combined African elements with European and American elements. It was in this milieu that the occasional potter worked. Hill (1987:138) points out that in such contexts "a lack of shared symbols across populations of disparate origins, coupled with the irrelevance of most of the messages traditionally carried by pottery decoration, spelled a quick demise of sociotechnic aspects of pottery making. It is this which resulted in the decoratively impoverished (and thus ethnically undiagnostic) character of most colonowares." I would agree, based on the small number of colonowares I have seen illustrated, with Hill's central conclusion that "colonoware is remarkable . . . not for being distinctively African, but for being distinctively non-European" (Hill 1987:138).

It is almost certain that individual Africans were making pottery styled on the mental images they brought with them, but these were generalized images. Some of the potters may have been people with a knowledge, but not necessarily a mastery, of a tradition of potting in West Africa. This is a far cry, however, from the assertion that "West Africans have a long tradition of producing the early forms of Colono-

Indian ware" (Ferguson 1980 quoted in Lees and Kimery-Lees 1979:1). West Africans did have a long ceramic tradition, but it is probable that the colonoware tradition in the Americas was born out of the necessity of producing a limited range of relatively simple vessels for a culturally impoverished population. Because of the exigencies of slavery, the makers almost certainly did not constitute the tightly knit community of female potters that characterizes the typical West African potting village.

Colonoware pottery was basically utilitarian. Wesler (1987) has made the interesting suggestion, based on his own fieldwork, that in many relatively recent Nigerian societies it was the imported wares, with their greater sophistication, that provided the sociotechnic element. It could well have been the same in certain slave societies, with favored slaves possessing wares given to them by the planter, thus indicating their higher status in the planter-imposed hierarchy. The problem is of course to decide which wares provided that status. One could surmise that some of the American-made, low-fired earthenwares may well have played an ideotechnic role, in the sense that they represented a knowledge held separately from that of the planter and thus reflected an African sense of accomplishment.

As a group, tobacco pipes constitute a more diagnostic ceramic artifact than utilitarian pots. Men made pipes. Pipes in a slave society were evidently prized and are among the significant grave goods at Newton plantation in Barbados (Handler and Lange 1978). Because there were no centuries of tradition behind their forms, their manufacture represents individual rather than group skills; requiring less raw material and lighter manufacturing equipment than potting, the skill was easily carried over to the New World. Emerson (1988; chap. 4 in this volume) has indicated a very strong African flavor for earthenware tobacco pipes from seventeenth-century sites in the Chesapeake. Though they have a distinctively African feel, they do not directly match any specific West African pipes, yet many of their decorative motifs are not uncommon in West Africa. In West Africa the lack of a pipe-making tradition meant that style and motifs were not governed by the artistic canons and conventions that provide the conservatism of ceramics. Exhibiting a bewildering variation of form and decoration, pipes in West Africa reflect the greatest changes in fashion of any item of material culture. Certain scholars have claimed that Ghanaian smoking pipes can be used to date sites within a fifteen- to twenty-year range.

## Functional Substitution, Coping, and Recycling

The concept of functional substitution, discussed in a musical context by Kwabena Nketia (Nketia 1977, 1979), is important in any consideration of African material culture. It is most easily demonstrated in music (with hand clapping substituted for drumming, the metal container for the wooden drum, or the glass bottle for the iron gong) or in the botanical realm, in which the tree calabash replaces the vine calabash (Posnansky 1984a). A quick glance at Edward Ayensu's two volumes on the medicinal plants of West Africa and the West Indies (Ayensu 1978, 1981) indicates how plants from the same families are used in a similar fashion on both sides of the Atlantic. This does not mean that West Africans were necessarily the first to utilize such plants in the Caribbean, but it does mean that they were able to assimilate the knowledge of their Indian predecessors rapidly, grasp the potentialities of the plants on or near the plantation, and integrate this new information with their own considerable knowledge of plants and the pharmacopoeia of the obeah men and women.

Almost certainly we have to look for functional substitution in such crafts as basketry. The use of different grasses and reeds and alternatives to palm fronds and other familiar African materials would have led to slightly different end products but ones with stylistic and form similarities. The timeless adaptability of the West African—regarded here as "coping" (Posnansky 1986) in the language of modern rural economists—must be appreciated if we are to interpret African-American sites correctly. In the West African context, coping implies a measure of innovation rather than conservatism, of experimentation rather than meaningless repetition of time-honored practice, and of the use of an extensive latent knowledge of useful plants and animal products. West African farmers, in villages away from urban areas, may have a latent knowledge of five hundred or more useful plants and may draw upon this knowledge in their quest for medicines, building materials, soaps, foods, and relishes. These rural people are similarly familiar with animal life.

Coping was particularly marked during the droughts of the 1970s and 1980s, when crop failure made it necessary for farmers to find food to eat. They drew upon their inherited knowledge of plant and animal life—a store of information dating back to the later Stone Age—and experimented with drought-resistant plants. Of all the early "second" Americans, the Africans were the most adaptable. They adapted to the Caribbean root crop, manioc, and to European farming tools, although in the process they altered the long-handled hoe and English billhook to conform to more familiar West African models. Remembering African trapping techniques, they managed to supplement the inadequate and monotonous rations provided by their owners. Additionally, their hardiness enabled them to cope with both the diseases of the Tropics and those introduced from Europe.

When I visited Haiti for the first time in 1980, I saw dispersed compounds in the hinterland. No simple detail of the construction was really West African, yet somehow the overall effect was uncannily so. This can be attributed to the combined effects of similar spatial relations, similar functions for subsidiary structures, similar uses of raw materials, crops, and attendant weeds. There was also the same clutter of familiar household utensils, earthenware and recycled metal, ceramic and wood.

Constant recycling is a very West African feature that may be found even in prosperous African societies. A broken pot serves as a chicken coop if large enough, or as a basin to hold seeds, or as an eating dish or water tray for poultry. If it is the right shape, it may be used as a lid for another pot. On archaeological excavations large sherds need to be examined for residues and wear patterns, and their locations carefully considered in order to determine whether a secondary function is conceivable. Cutlasses may have been whittled down to make knives; broken querns may have been converted to sharpening stones or stool seats to drag sleds for the weaver's warp. Other natural stones, particularly waterworn pebbles, are still used as hammers, pounders, and crushers. As late as the 1970s, strike-a-lights were made in Ghana from unmodified chunks of quartz, as they must have been in slave communities; Douglas Armstrong found evidence of this practice at Drax Hall in Jamaica (1990a). With the arrival of Europeans in West Africa, this recycling phenomenon became even more pronounced. Bottles were rarely thrown away except in the more wealthy town sites; they were—and are—continually reused for storage of oils, honey, alcoholic beverages, and water. Even relatively inexpensive imports, such as clay pipes, were adapted for West African use, with long clay stems being replaced by more practical, cooler, and renewable reed stems. A whole host of products were used as ornaments, from buttons used as beads to broken brass coffin handles and countless other scraps of brass used as gold weights (Garrard 1983). Even in the present day, few products are wasted: grass is used for bedding, thin roots for scouring pots, seeds for rattles and beads, and strings of beads to burnish pots. Natural objects are frequently pressed into domestic service, as exemplified by the three-legged stool made from the part of the tree trunk from which the main branches diverge or the large stone used as an anvil or a seat.

## Burial Practices

Those seeking to identify African continuities will find them readily apparent in burial customs, a topic explored by Handler and Lange (1978) and Emerson (1979). Unfortunately, little work has been undertaken on West African burial practices of the slave trade era. Burial sites have been found incidentally as part of excavations, as my own experience at Begho in Ghana attests, but no one has brought together the material manifestations of West African mortuary customs, though Goody (1962) has assembled a series of studies on the social aspects of death using twentieth-century ethnography. It is apparent, however, that there is a great variation in burial practice within West and West Central Africa. Some societies bury grave goods, others do not; some societies—such as those in the Congo, the Democratic Republic of Congo , and parts of West Africa—place pots or other markers above graves, a feature illustrated by Vlach (1978) and Thompson (1981b) in comparisons of Congolese graves with those on the Sea Islands. Many societies have consistent patterns of orientation, others do not; individuals are positioned in contracted and flexed burials as well as extended burials. Some societies, such as the Kabye of Togo, use relatively deep shaft pits and have multiple interments; while others, like the Akan of Ghana, have or used to have L-shaped pits, with a ledge on which the body was laid forming the horizontal part of the L. At one time burial within houses and compounds was widespread and occurred in African households of Elmina during the slave trade (DeCorse 1987). It is obvious that the variety present in pre-twentieth-century burial customs should provide some points of reference for both slave and postemancipation burials in the Americas.

## African Continuities and Demography in the New World

It is apparent from the few examples offered here that any study of the African-American past needs to be as firmly rooted in African cultural anthropology and archaeology as in American archaeology. In the same way that the historical archaeologists of the white experience in early America are turning to postmedieval archaeology in Europe—and particularly England—for insights into the interpretation of their sites, so must specialists of African-American archaeology turn to Africa for similar insights. Archaeologists interested in the African-American past have specific questions they wish to ask of their material, and the answers can come only from an understanding of the black experience, which includes the African past. It may well be that the answers to many of these questions cannot be provided by a reading of selected African excavation reports or ethnographical accounts but will necessitate research in Africa by the American archaeologists working in close collaboration with their African colleagues.

The African picture, which portrays a wealth of culturally distinct ethnic groups, is much more complex than is often realized. We have seen that there is some divergence of interest between the Africanist archaeologist—concerned with urban archaeology and major industrial and craft activities (for example, iron and brass working)—and the concerns of the Americanists interested in the economic and cultural background of those Africans transplanted to the New World. The element of African continuity is less marked in North America than in the Caribbean for several good reasons. These include the lower percentage of blacks to whites in the North American population; the absence of large Maroon populations that kept African ways alive; the lower rate of importation, which facilitated the gradual acculturation process; and the elapsed time between the effective end of the slave trade and the date of emancipation, which meant that at the time of emancipation there were very few slaves in North America who had actually been born in Africa, in contrast to such countries as Haiti and Brazil. Continuities do exist and have been discussed by many authors, but a true appreciation of them can only come from an exposure to African studies.

## Historical Archaeology in Africa

One major area of convergence between Africanist archaeologists and archaeologists of the African-American past concerns African historical archaeology. African historical archaeology was neglected for many years, and what little work (Posnansky and DeCorse 1986) was undertaken concentrated on validating the existence of European trading posts and the restoration of forts. In recent years, both in South Africa (where Deetz and Schrire [1994] are working in the Cape area, along with a very active group of South African archaeologists; see Abrahams [1984]) and in West Africa (where DeCorse excavated Elmina, a town with an occupational sequence of four hundred years [1989a, 1992], and Kelly [1995] has investigated the seventeenth- and eighteenth-century towns of Savi and Ouidah in Benin), archaeologists have provided information on African and European interaction. Evidence suggests in both cases that Africans were becoming acculturated to European conditions. In West Africa there were both free Africans who moved into towns because of the commercial opportunities of proximity to major European trading centers and domestic slaves working in households and small craft shops. In South Africa many aspects of slavery were similar to those in North America; an opportunity is thus provided for comparative study, already undertaken to advantage on the historical material (Frederickson 1981). Other useful studies aimed at assessing general aspects of slave culture might involve a comparison of slave plantation archaeology in an African state like Dahomey (now part of the République du Benin) with that in the southeastern United States or the Caribbean.

One neglected branch of historical archaeology is that concerned with the sites of African Americans who returned to Africa—in particular, to Sierra Leone, Liberia, and Libreville in Gabon—in the early nineteenth century. This is a research topic in which the expertise of the archaeologist of African-American life, trained in American historical archaeology, would be of fundamental importance. In Liberia, for instance, there still remain many mid-nineteenth-century buildings modeled after antecedents in Maryland and the Carolinas, from which states the American Liberians came (see Herman 1988). Modern Monrovia, however, will soon spread and destroy all the sites of an exciting chapter of African-American archaeology. The destruction wrought by the civil war of 1989–91 means that vast areas eventually will need to be rebuilt. Once peace is fully restored, there will be an urgent need to rescue what little remains, as in London and many other European cities after the

1939–45 war. An opportunity will exist to excavate before the deep foundations of modern structures destroy the palimpsests of the early and mid-nineteenth-century African-American settlers. However, there are no active Liberian archaeologists.

Among the early returnees to Sierra Leone were the Jamaican Maroons who fought the British in the late eighteenth century, were sent to Nova Scotia, and finally were shipped to Sierra Leone. It would be interesting to see how the African slaves— some hailing from West Central Africa—who were captured at sea by the anti-slave trade patrol acculturated to a foreign African society dominated by ex-slaves from the Americas. But again, in Sierra Leone there is no modern archaeological tradition; there is no established department of archaeology at Fourah Bay College, the oldest modern university in West Africa; and few archaeological missions have been undertaken by foreign scholars. The opportunities for collaborative fieldwork between West African and American, and particularly archaeologists interested in African-American archaeology, are unlimited.

## Recommendations for the Future

In conclusion, I cannot help but reiterate my plea for a greater involvement in African studies by archaeologists interested in the African-American past. Most of the major centers of African studies in the United States are not centers for the study of African-American archaeology, and vice versa. Unfortunately, most of the superb collections of African material culture in the United States are associated with large museums or academic programs in African Studies rather than with Black Studies programs. Though African ethnographic arts have been subjected to the exploitative collecting activities of American collectors and dealers in the last twenty years, the common material—the everyday pots, the agricultural implements, the kitchen utensils, the craft paraphernalia—that are of vital interest to archaeologists normally do not figure in such collections, yet they should form the basis of teaching collections.

There is a need to incorporate African anthropology and African archaeology, particularly that of the Iron Age and later periods, into the curricula of students who will be involved in African-American archaeology. Atlantic programs (area study programs that examine the history and culture of people on both sides of the Atlantic Ocean) should be established that comprise in their studies a knowledge of the three axes of the triangular trade. There is a need for historical archaeologists to appreciate the milieus of the dominating European culture, the slaves, and the Africa that the slaves left behind. It makes much greater sense to study African ethnography and preindustrial technology in Africa rather than conduct elaborate replication studies in America as part of experimental archaeology. Let students participate in potting, building mud and wattle-and-daub houses, and blacksmithing in Africa as part of summer fieldwork programs. These are existing village activities. Examine food procurement techniques, building technologies, culinary practices, and household equipment in an African village setting technologically closer to the era of the slave trade than to twentieth-century cities of West Africa. Study West African proxemics firsthand and experience the interdependence of economic, social, and religious traditions within a village community. Tap the latent wisdom of village elders and absorb some folklore that may put hitherto unexplained features of an African-American site excavation into perspective or illuminate the relevancy of an otherwise arcane slave or contemporary African-American custom. Compare the vernacular names of ordinary everyday objects from the American South with those from a range of African ethnic groups. Linguistic syntax disappears much more rapidly than individual terms, and those terms that do survive provide the best clues to activities and customs that endured the Middle Passage and the dark days of slavery. In African studies there has been an expanding interest in historical linguistics, and historians have collected many detailed word lists for metalworking, potting, and other crafts.

These are lean days in Africa, and most African countries would welcome the opportunity to hold joint field-training programs. Good instruction should involve student-to-student interaction. For many West African students, brought up in towns, preindustrial technology is as much a mystery to them as it is to their American counterparts. The University of California at Los Angeles for many years has been engaged in African study programs with a field experience component and has discovered both the cost-effectiveness and the educational relevance of such programs. In Africa there is as much misinformation and ignorance of American slavery as there is in America about Africa. Joint programs would be of mutual benefit and certainly would provide a firm foundation for the future of African-American archaeology.

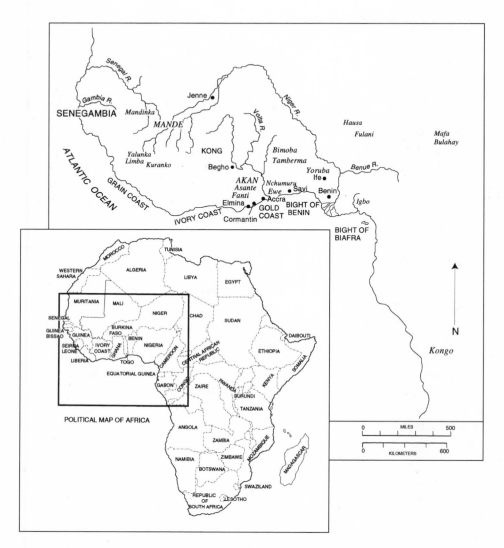

2.1. Map of Africa showing places, ethnohistoric groups,
and historic sites referred to in chapters 2, 4, and 7.
(Drawn by Marcia Bakry)

# 3

# Archaeology at Flowerdew Hundred

*James Deetz*

Eᴏᴏ STABLISHED in 1619 by Sir George Yardley, Virginia's first governor, Flowerdew Hundred was one of a number of "particular plantations" established in the James River drainage. These plantations were private operations, in contrast to those that were established by a company of shareholders, and their granting was done as a way to encourage success through the free enterprise of the owners. Flowerdew Hundred has been continuously occupied since its founding and is today a working farm.

The settlement history of the plantation is complex, involving a large number of individual owners, either of the original 1,000-acre grant or of smaller portions of it. In its broadest outlines Flowerdew Hundred began as a single large landholding, gradually was divided into smaller and smaller sections with different owners, and late in the eighteenth century underwent a process of consolidation, with three owners dividing the property by 1810. By the 1820s a single family owned the full 1,000-acre property, and it has remained intact since that time. Intensive site survey has located over sixty archaeological sites on the property, with the earliest occupation attributed to Paleo-Indians in the tenth millennium B.C. The prehistoric sequence is a full one, with Archaic and Woodland materials in abundance. Some thirty of the sites recorded are from the period of European settlement and provide an unbroken sequence from 1619 to the present. Extensive archaeological investigations have been carried out at nine of the historic-period sites by archaeologists from the College of William and Mary and the University of California at Berkeley. These sites have been selected to provide a set of sites with overlapping dates representing the occupation from 1619 through the early twentieth century.

In addition to those sites that have been fully excavated, collections have been made from the surface of all other sites on the plantation. It is highly unlikely that any sites have been overlooked in the bottomlands along the river, although the survey in the more wooded area on the western edge of the property has not been as thorough. As far as is known, all sites that date to the first hundred years of occupation are located in the bottomlands.

This pattern is partly due to the river's importance as the primary route of transport and communication before the development of efficient overland roads and partly to the fertility of the bottomland soil, which would make siting a house near the fields a logical choice. The first settlement away from the river, along a low ridge a mile from the shore, seems not to have taken place until the latter part of the eighteenth century. All three plantation houses representing the early nineteenth-century three-part division of the land are located on this ridge.

Eighteen sites along the floodplain date to before 1730. Of these, six have been excavated, and the remaining twelve are represented by large surface collections made during spring plowing when the newly turned earth and rain make artifact location efficient. In working with these collections a number of obvious questions are asked, including the determination of the artifact types present, the nature of architectural evidence, density of artifactual material as indicative of the location of features beneath the surface, and, of course, the dating of the site as accurately as possible. Data such as these make site selection for excavation more informed and permit the formulation of tentative research questions.

## Pipestem Chronology and Flowerdew Settlement

One of the most frequently used dating techniques in seventeenth- and eighteenth-century historical archaeology is based on the diameter of the bores of English white clay smoking pipestems. Harrington has shown that, over time, the average diameter of stem bores underwent a rather linear reduction between 1590 and 1800, from $9/64$ inch to $4/64$ inch, a rate of approximately $1/64$ inch every thirty years (Harrington 1954). Although there is some disagreement as to the precision of the method, most workers would agree that given an adequate sample of stem fragments, reasonable dates can be produced, particularly from after the mid–seventeenth century until the latter eighteenth. However, if discrepancies exist, these would not seriously interfere with the use of the method for dating sites relative to each other, even if the actual chronometric date might be inaccurate, since the factors causing the possible error would be present in all samples.

Deriving a date by this method is quite simple. A graduated set of drill bits is used to measure all stem fragments in the sample, and a histogram is prepared showing the percentage of each diameter in the total sample. Thus a site that dates between 1620 and 1650, the time when diameters of $8/64$ inch were typical, will show a high percentage of $8/64$-inch bores and a small number of bores of both $9/64$ and $7/64$ inch. Theoretically, sites from later in this thirty-year period would show more $7/64$-inch bores than those of $9/64$ inch, and to some extent this effect can be observed. Furthermore, the sharper the peak exhibited by the histogram, the briefer the occupation. Sites of occupation duration exceeding sixty years would produce stems with bores varying in diameter as much as $4/64$ inch, and thus each increment of diameter would be represented by a smaller percentage of the total sample of stem fragments. Thus the technique not only provides a reasonable piece of dating evidence for the site from which the sample was taken, but some indication of the duration and nature of the occupation.

Histograms were prepared for the eighteen sites on the Virginia floodplain site that predate 1730. When compared with each other, these graphs provided a pattern that strongly suggested that the sites could be grouped into three discrete sets exhibiting a high degree of similarity within each group and a distinct difference from those shared by the other groups. Sites of group one all produced histograms that peak sharply in the period 1620 to 1650 and fall off quite sharply after the middle of the century. Group two sites exhibit histograms with a much flatter profile, indicating a more prolonged occupation than that of group one sites. Sites of group three are distinguished by histograms with peaks as sharp as those of group one; in this case the peak corresponds to the period between 1710 and 1750. The rapid drop at the end of this period is the result of the withdrawal of almost all settlement on the floodplain, removal to the ridge to the west, and the use of the fertile bottomlands almost exclusively for farming. The only site on the floodplain that postdates the mid–eighteenth century is the remains of a structure that probably housed a person charged with running a nearby ferry service.

Having established a clear-cut pattern in the artifactual evidence, the next step was to look to the historical record to see if events took place in the region that might in some way explain the observed pattern. Two major events suggest themselves as accounting for the site groups. The first was the severe depression in tobacco prices that occurred during the third quarter of the seventeenth century. All seven sites in group one appear to have been abandoned by 1675, with pipestem bores of $8/64$ inch being in the majority. Associated artifacts, particularly datable ceramics, support this date. Four sites in group one have been excavated, and all show earthfast construction. These sites are obviously the remains of farmsteads established by the early seventeenth-century tobacco entrepreneurs; and with the depression in tobacco prices, settlement slowed, and the farms were abandoned. Since the documentary record for Flowerdew Hundred is scanty, it is not possible to determine where the occupants went after leaving their homes.

The second major event in the history of the Chesapeake region that has bearing on the groupings of sites was the full institutionalization of racially based slavery during the last twenty years of the century (Morgan 1975). At this time the numbers of slaves arriving in the region increased dramatically, and the pattern that was to mark the economy of the region until the Civil War was set. Occupants of farmsteads represented by site group three were probably among the emerging class that would form the elite of eighteenth-century Virginia, although their material culture does not suggest any marked affluence at the time of their life at Flowerdew Hundred. If they were slaveholders, the number of slaves at each farm was probably quite small, perhaps as few as the two or three typical of small freeholds of the period (Morgan 1975). In contrast to sites of groups one and three, sites of group two were occupied for a longer period of time, beginning late in the period of site group one occupation and overlapping the settlement of group three sites in its earlier years. It can be suggested that the former occupants of these sites represent a group with a stronger commitment to staying in the area than that of their predecessors. Although there is no documentation for the fact, it could well be that these farmsteads were based on somewhat more diversified crop production, following the arguments advanced by Carson and his coauthors (Carson et al. 1981).

The delineation of three distinct sets of sites, each tentatively related to different aspects of seventeenth-century Chesapeake history, forms the basis of a research design for the archaeology of seventeenth- and eighteenth-century Flowerdew Hundred. This research is still in its initial phases, but significant patterns already have begun to emerge. Once the site groups were defined, the locations of the sites in each group were investigated, and a clear pattern was apparent. Sites of both groups one and three are evenly distributed along the bottomlands. But during the period of group two sites, settlement can be seen to be restricted to either the northernmost or southernmost sections of the plantation. Just what this difference signifies is unclear, but the fact of its existence further strengthens the significance of the groupings. Since the shoreline along most of the eastern boundary of the plantation is cyprus swamp, with a depth of a quarter of a mile, settlement on this shoreline would have been impossible. The group two sites are located in those areas where easiest access to the river would have been possible, and the five sites of groups one and three that are centrally located are farther from river access than their location would suggest.

## Colonoware at Flowerdew Hundred

When the artifact assemblages from sites in each of the groups were compared, another important difference was observed. All five sites in group three produced significant quantities of colonoware, a locally produced, handmade, unglazed pottery in a variety of European shapes. No sites in either of the other two groups produced this type of ceramic. Formerly termed Colono-Indian ware, this pottery was long thought to have been made by local Indian groups and traded to the colonists. Gray-brown in color, fired at a low temperature, and tempered with either grit or shell, it shares certain characteristics with coastal Algonquian pottery. However, its distribution in time and space raises certain problems with such an attribution. It does not become common until the last quarter of the seventeenth century, and it increases in quantity through the later part of the eighteenth century. During this same time the native population was undergoing a severe decline. The Beverley census of 1703 lists 612 Indians for all of Virginia, and the decline continued unabated during the eighteenth century (Feest 1978:257–58, 262). Furthermore, colonoware is found only from the Chesapeake southward into South Carolina and Georgia, those areas where slave populations were large and often settled at a distance from the houses of the planters.

Most scholars working with colonoware now agree that it was made and used by slaves, with its roots in a generalized West African ceramic tradition (Ferguson 1980). Whether found in Virginia or South Carolina, it is remarkably similar in its technological attributes, although there are significant differences in the shapes of colonoware from the upper and lower South. Colonoware from the Chesapeake was made in a wide variety of shapes, closely copying English prototypes, including punch bowls, porringers, pipkins, and handled drinking cups. Colonoware from South Carolina exhibits a much more restricted set of shapes, primarily large and small globular pots and shallow bowls. It will be seen that these differences in form are probably the result of different patterns of planter-slave interaction in each region.

The presence of colonoware in all group three sites at Flowerdew Hundred strengthens the identification of these sites as those occupied by small-scale holders. However, it raises a new problem in turn. If colonoware was made by slaves, why do we not encounter it on sites that predate the 1680s? Flowerdew Hundred had a small black population at its very beginning. Fifteen of the first twenty-five blacks to come to English North America were owned by the first two occupants of Flowerdew Hundred, George Yardley and Abraham Piercy. The muster of 1625 lists seven "negroes" residing at Flowerdew Hundred. While there is no further reference to blacks at Flowerdew Hundred until the eighteenth century, it is very likely that there was a continuous African-American presence there throughout. But whether the presence of blacks in the Chesapeake was continuous or not, the fact remains that they were there from 1619 on, and yet colonoware seems not to have been produced until quite late in the seventeenth century.

It was the association between colonoware and a specific group of sites at Flowerdew Hundred and its absence from sites of the other two groups that prompted the formulation of the question above. An answer to this question, as well as an explanation of the difference in shape between Virginia and South Carolina colonoware, is suggested by Upton's study of the relation between servant-master social interaction and house size in seventeenth-century Virginia (Upton 1982). Upton's research is based on an analysis of room-by-room probate inventories from seventeenth-century Virginia. Taken for tax purposes, probate inventories are detailed listings of the contents of houses and their conditions and values. Not all

probate inventories were taken on a room-by-room basis, but a significant number of them were, and they provide important data on house size based on room
number. Although most houses throughout the seventeenth century were quite
modest structures of two or three rooms, houses of eight to eleven rooms were not
uncommon. These larger houses, built by more affluent members of the society,
were initially occupied by both the planter and his indentured servants.

Between 1640 and 1720 houses in the eight- to eleven-room category exhibit an
interesting trend. They steadily increase in number until the 1680s and then decrease,
reaching their 1640 level by 1710. The reason for the gradual increase in number of
larger houses comes as no surprise. Indentured servants and masters lived under the
same roof; the increase reflects the growing number of individuals who could afford
servants, whose rooms were included in the inventories. However, after the 1660s
there was growing strain between masters and servants, reflected in a sharp increase
in litigation over servants' rights or unrealized expectations on the part of the masters. This time was also a period which saw a number of attempted servant uprisings. The result of this alienation was to restructure the arrangement of living space;
separate quarters were constructed for the servants apart from the main house, and
the main house became smaller. It is particularly noteworthy that this change pre-
dated the major influx of slaves at the end of the seventeenth century, so that the
model for slave settlement had already been established. What were to become slave
quarters already existed in the form of separate servants' quarters. Contemporary
descriptions of plantations of this time clearly delineate the situation (Durand Du
Dauphiné [1687] 1934:119–20): "Some people in this country are comfortably housed.
. . . Whatever their rank, and I know not why, they build only two rooms with some
closets on the ground floor and two rooms in the attic above; but they build several like this, according to their means. They build also separate kitchen, a separate
house for the Christian slaves, one for the negro slaves, and several to dry the
tobacco, so that when you come to the home of a person of some means, you think
you are entering a fairly large village."

## Results and Conclusions

The significance of the relation of the shift in architectural arrangements to the pattern of colonoware occurrence in time is potentially great. If blacks as well as whites
lived in the same household as did the planter before the establishment of separate
quarters, then they would have access to the material goods of the household as well.
Not only would it not be necessary for them to manufacture their own pottery, but
they would have been familiar with both the shapes of English pottery and its function in the preparation and consumption of food. The historical record shows that
black servants or slaves and white indentured servants regularly shared living space

before the last quarter of the seventeenth century. Many blacks paid taxes and also appear in numbers of court actions on a par with their white contemporaries. As Edmund Morgan has noted, "There is more than a little evidence that Virginians during these years [before 1660] were ready to think of negroes as members of or potential members of the community on the same terms as other men and to demand of them the same standards of behavior" (Morgan 1975:155). During this time some blacks were fully enslaved, some served as indentured servants, and not a few were free.

It was not until the end of the century that race became the predominant criterion for slave status, and slavery as a full-blown institution emerged. When Morgan wrote, Upton's study had not been done, and the implications of their conclusions could not be perceived in their relation to colonoware. A closer degree of social interaction between black and white in the years before 1660 made the production of colonoware unnecessary. Once blacks were settled separately and made to produce their own utensils, pottery would be among the most basic of necessities, and it was produced in the range of English forms with which its makers were familiar. When the situation in South Carolina is compared with the patterns seen at Flowerdew Hundred, this explanation also sheds light on the differences in pottery shapes found between the two areas. Blacks arrived later in South Carolina, and when they did, they came in great numbers and from the first were settled apart from the planter's house, often at a great distance. There was little or no opportunity to become familiar with either English pottery forms or English foodways. The limited inventory of shapes found in South Carolina colonoware reflects comparable African forms, and these fit into African food preparation and consumption practices (Ferguson 1980). The large jars are for cooking the starchy foundation for a meal, manioc or cornmeal. The small jars are for preparing the meat, fish, or vegetable relish that is served over the carbohydrate, and the shallow bowls are used in food consumption. This stronger retention of prior African cultural elements among South Carolina blacks is also to be seen in basketry, language (the Gullah dialect), woodcarving, and other crafts. There are no counterparts for these in the Chesapeake, almost certainly because black and white interaction took place over a longer period and on closer and different terms.

In the nonexperimental sciences (if archaeology is indeed a science), precise certainty is rarely achieved. Rather, research takes the form of a gradual refinement of explanation, as more and more factors are incorporated into the construction of the past that one is attempting to create. In historical archaeology this refinement is best accomplished by maintaining a balance between the documentary and material evidence, being always mindful that to be a productive exercise, the results should provide a more satisfactory explanation than would be forthcoming from either set of data alone. To be sure, the conclusions arrived at here could have been arrived at by a different route than that taken, but regardless of the precise set of steps involved, it would be necessary to incorporate both material culture, in this case a discrete type of pottery, and documentary evidence to obtain the explanation provided. The pattern of distribution of colonoware in time and space cannot be understood in the absence of documentary support. However, once this explanation has been provided, a dimension of black and white relations in seventeenth-century Virginia has been made more clear than it would have been if the archaeological data were not taken into account. This is particularly true in the context of pre-1660 Virginia, since the documentary record for this period is thin and there are numerous ambiguities regarding the status of blacks and the way in which they and the white community related to each other.

It is easy to project the better-known eighteenth-century pattern of relationships into the past in an uncritical fashion, but studies such as ours tell us that to do so would run a high risk of error and that every bit of evidence, from both history and archaeology, will be necessary if we are ever to reach a better understanding of what truly was taking place. It may well be that historical archaeology's greatest utility is in contexts such as that of Virginia in the first half of the seventeenth century. In these contexts there is sufficient documentary evidence to inform the archaeology, but not in such a quantity as to make archaeological analysis a weaker component in the total research design.

# 4

# African Inspirations in a New World Art and Artifact: Decorated Tobacco Pipes from the Chesapeake

*Matthew C. Emerson*

ARCHAEOLOGISTS studying ethnic groups in America's past are generally concerned with two questions. Can artifacts be used to identify specific groups of people? What can we learn about those people and the social context in which the artifacts were made and/or used? This chapter offers evidence identifying the activities of one specific group of people through an assemblage of artifacts. Although the artifacts discussed here are not described in the surviving written record, some may be the earliest surviving evidence of black craftsmanship in North America. Seventeenth-century decorated clay tobacco pipes reveal some interesting insights into cultural interactions in the Chesapeake.

## Introducing Chesapeake Tobacco Pipes

While individual tobacco pipes made from American clays have been found at archaeological sites ranging from Maine to Florida, the greatest concentration of locally made tobacco pipes is found in late seventeenth-century plantation deposits in the Chesapeake Bay region. These locally made tobacco pipes are orange to brown in color and thus are easily distinguished from the white clay tobacco pipes that colonists imported from England and Holland during the seventeenth century. Although archaeologists have referred to these earth-tone tobacco pipes as "colono-pipes," "terra-cotta pipes," "local pipes," "Virginia-made pipes," and/or "aboriginal pipes" (Henry 1979), here they are designated *Chesapeake pipes* because they are made from Chesapeake clays and because they were not exclusively made by one group of people. Chesapeake pipes may be generally described as either hand- or mold-made, and many are decorated with abstract designs and representational motifs (figs. 4.1, 4.2). While fragmentary documentary and archeological evidence indicates that English colonists and Native Americans were involved in pipe making, an analysis of a set of decorated Chesapeake pipes demonstrates that many were made by seventeenth-century African-Americans.

Amateur and professional archaeologists have been unearthing Chesapeake pipes from colonial settlement areas in Virginia and Maryland for the past century. My study began with the investigation of a seventeenth-century site at Flowerdew Hundred farm near Hopewell, Virginia. During the excavation of a small seventeenth-century home lot and its outbuildings, hundreds of broken Chesapeake pipestems and pipe bowls were unearthed (Emerson 1987). I decided to examine these and other locally made pipes recovered from sites throughout the Chesapeake.

Collections of Chesapeake pipes are stored at a variety of federal, state, and private institutions throughout Virginia and Maryland. I examined pipe collections at Flowerdew Hundred Foundation, at Colonial Williamsburg, at the Colonial Historical National Park in Jamestown, and at the Virginia Research Center for Archaeology in Yorktown, Virginia. In Maryland the St. Mary's City Archaeological Commission laboratory provided an opportunity to look at Chesapeake pipes recovered from northern Chesapeake sites. The collections studied contained pipes from documented and undocumented archaeological deposits representing twenty-six archaeological sites within fifteen settlement areas (see Emerson 1994:36). Archaeologists have dated these pipe-bearing deposits or sites from the 1630s to approximately 1730 (table 4.1). These determinations have been made on the basis of surviving documentary references to land patents or occupational sequences of settlements, the presence or absence of English ceramics (South 1977), and/or English pipestem-dating methods (Harrington 1954; Binford 1962b; Deetz 1985).

When possible, I examined the total number of pipe bowls and fragments from an entire site assemblage. In many instances, however, this was not feasible as some site assemblages were in permanent storage or not yet completely processed. In the latter cases I examined pipe type collections that had been previously assembled by the host institution. As a result of these varying conditions of curation, I selected a qualitative sample of specimens in order to study Chesapeake pipes as one region-wide assemblage of artifacts from the seventeenth-century Chesapeake.

From among thousands of whole and broken pipe bowls, pipestems, and pipe fragments, I selected six hundred complete pipe bowls and two hundred fragments for my study sample. I recorded and closely examined a subset of this sample containing two hundred distinctly different decorated pipe bowls and fragments. In addition to a physical analysis of Chesapeake pipes, I studied excavation records and site reports and consulted with other archaeologists about the archaeological context and dating of Chesapeake pipes (Emerson 1988). I began my study of Chesapeake pipes with the following questions in mind. Where were Chesapeake tobacco pipes manufactured? Was there regional variation in Chesapeake pipe production? How and why were Chesapeake pipes decorated? What was the significance of Chesapeake pipe art? As a result of this study, some of the origins and inspirations for

Chesapeake pipe art have been revealed. Decorated Chesapeake tobacco pipes disclose information on the cultural origins of people about whom little can be learned from the surviving written record. These people were Africans.

## Looking for Archaeological Evidence of Chesapeake Pipe Making

Archaeologists have had difficulty finding physical evidence for pipe making at seventeenth-century sites. Some have expected to find deformed and unfinished pipe bowls and pipestems and possibly the kiln sites and related kiln furniture used in ceramics firing. In fact, small lumps of fired clay called wasters have been found in domestic deposits (Cotter 1958:145–47; Emerson 1987; Mitchell 1983:31; Outlaw 1985), but their number is extremely small, limiting any conclusions about the extent or longevity of pipe-making activities at particular sites. Moreover, at the few seventeenth-century pottery kiln sites that have been discovered in Virginia (Cotter 1958:66; Hudson 1975; Noël Hume 1975:170–74; Kelso and Chappell 1974), no conclusive evidence for pipe manufacture has been uncovered. The prospect of identifying the source locations for Chesapeake pipe clay is also problematic. Potential clay strata are abundant in exposed riverbanks and open gullies, as well as in cleared fields that are adjacent to or part of settlement areas. Given the abundance and convenience of these clay deposits, it is unlikely that only one source area would be found or that trace-element-identified locations would tell us much about the people making tobacco pipes.

Archaeologists might also expect to find parts of pipe molds and finishing and decorating tools. To date, nothing of the kind has been recovered from plantation sites. Considering the frequent recasting of metals on plantations, it is unlikely that metal pipe molds will ever be found, or that pipe molds made of perishable materials would survive. Similarly, pipe-decorating tools made of natural materials such as wood, bone, and shell are unlikely to survive. Miscellaneous fragments of metal or sherds of ceramic or pipestem may also have been used in pipe making. Although one object known to be a pipe-decorating tool has been recovered from an archaeological site (MacCord 1969:41, fig. 5), and another tool, a signet ring, evidently was used by a pipe decorator (Mouer 1991b:57), many small pipe-making tools may not have survived, while others may be difficult to identify by archaeologists.

It is possible that the individual steps of pipe making— digging and cleaning clay; molding, decorating, and firing pipes—may have taken place in as many as three different locations such as at an exposed riverbank, an outbuilding, and an outdoor fire pit. Or perhaps it was the occasional nature of pipe making in one location coupled with the use of in-house fireplaces that may explain how domestic pipe making was undertaken. Overall, Chesapeake pipe making has not left an obvious impression in the archaeological record because of the modest skill and participation involved, the simple tools used, the recycling of molds, and the abundance of workable local clays.

The failure to address the relative archaeological invisibility of Chesapeake pipe making coupled with the lack of descriptive information from the extant written record has limited archaeological insights into this craft. Decorated Chesapeake pipes themselves, however, are a rich source of information not only on one plantation activity but on the people and cultural milieu in which they were made. A brief examination of Chesapeake pipe forms and decorative art reveals that Chesapeake pipes were made by many individuals expressing themselves through this folk craft.

## Examining Chesapeake Pipe Forms

Chesapeake tobacco pipe bowls were fashioned into many different shapes. My study sample indicates that there were at least two hundred different bowl forms—including obtuse-angled, elbow, and faceted pipes (see fig. 4.1)—used during the brief period that Chesapeake pipes appear in seventeenth-century settlement deposits (Emerson 1988). Before firing, some pipe makers modified their molded pipe forms with polishing or bending or by cutting facets in the clay. The diversity of both decorated and undecorated hand- or mold-made pipe bowls found in plantation deposits suggests that many individuals were involved in occasional pipe making at approximately the same time.

The range of different pipe forms in archaeological collections may be a reflection of the number of seventeenth-century European pipe makers arriving in the Chesapeake. Two emigrating English pipe makers are mentioned briefly in the documentary record, and it is certain that some English pipe makers produced pipes on Chesapeake plantations. The number of different pipe forms may also be a reflection of the molds that these pipe makers brought with them. Using a mold to fashion a pipe is easy, and molds could have been used and mold styles copied by English, Indian, or African pipe makers. Without written documentation, it is clearly impossible to prove the identity of a pipe maker crafting undecorated European-style mold-made tobacco pipes.[1]

Indian craftsmanship can be identified by the traditional hand-made Indian pipe forms that are found in plantation deposits. These traditional obtuse-angled conical pipe forms and tulip-shaped pipe forms are distinctive. They are also rare, compared to the number of European-style forms I observed in site assemblages. At least one seventeenth-century chronicler commented on the creativity of the Indians and the fact that they made pottery and pipes (Du Dauphiné [1687] 1934:153). With documentary references and the archaeological presence of traditional Indian pipe forms in plantation deposits, there can be no question that Chesapeake Indians made tobacco pipes.

A central debate in Chesapeake archaeology concerns whether or not Indians produced pots and pipes in their villages or on plantations for sale to colonists throughout Virginia and Maryland. There is no evidence to suggest an organized production of pipes by Indians for a plantation clientele, and evidence of pottery sales to colonists appears to be an isolated phenomenon in the Chesapeake, reflective more of local Indian relations than of a regionwide demand for local pottery. Although a few Europeans visited Indian villages (Du Dauphiné [1687] 1934), and pipes may have been traded or collected by colonists, most Indians involved in plantation life were wards, casual employees, or occasional visitors. There is no evidence to suggest that they were part of the small craft systems that plantations lived by.[2] This scenario probably varied widely from plantation to plantation around the Chesapeake Bay region, but it does account for the continued, although limited, presence of traditional Indian pipe forms in plantation deposits.[3] However, some other Chesapeake pipe forms and much of the decorative art on European-style mold-made pipes strongly suggest the presence of another group of pipe makers, one who lived permanently on English plantations throughout Virginia and Maryland and whose participation in pipe making is unknown from surviving written accounts.

### Africans, Pipe Making, and Seventeenth-Century Tobacco Pipes

Although Africans were introduced to Virginia as early as 1619 and to Maryland in 1634 (Craven 1971a; Franklin 1980; Vaughan 1972), American historians have little documentary evidence and limited insight into the origins of the Chesapeake's seventeenth-century Africans (Minchinton, King, and Waite 1984:ix–x). Historians have suggested that many of the slaves brought to the Chesapeake in the seventeenth century were not shipped directly from Africa but transported to the West Indies and later reexported to other colonial colonies (Curtin 1969; Kulikoff 1986). The homelands of the Chesapeake's earliest slaves may be extremely difficult to identify given the patterns of slave transportation around the Atlantic basin and the terse manner in which blacks were recorded in early colonial documents. Although the majority of Chesapeake slaves probably came from coastal and inland states of West Africa (Curtin 1969:122, table 35), some Africans from Central Africa, the Congo, and Madagascar probably were shipped to the Chesapeake as well (Curtin 1969:125). Although individual ports on the West and Central African coastline served as principal exporting stations for slavers, many of the people who were quartered at these stations were removed and enslaved from a variety of hinterland areas and cultures. Therefore, it is not surprising to find strong antecedents for some North American traditions, ideas, behaviors, and artifacts in the cultural traditions of the diverse groups who have historically occupied present-day Senegal, Ghana, Togo, and Nigeria and the hinterland areas of Mali and Burkina Faso (see fig. 2.1). Insights into any connections between the New World and West Africa, however, are limited by the survival of artifacts from these areas and the extent of archaeological investigations. In some areas of West Africa, few museums and collections exist documenting seventeenth-century life, and there is a lack of published archaeological research from which the New World researcher can draw information and insights. As a result, many of the conclusions and comparative examples illustrated here are taken from a number of specific culture groups within a geographically and culturally diverse region in West Africa. Nevertheless, it is important to begin any discussion of the African contribution to Chesapeake pipe making with preliminary information on the history of tobacco use and pipe making in West Africa.

The origins and early history of tobacco use in West Africa are basically unknown. While a few written records indicate that tobacco use was introduced by Europeans to some areas of West Africa early in the sixteenth century, it is unclear how the practice became widespread in an area that is geographically and culturally heterogeneous. European travelers commented on the use of smoking pipes in isolated coastal areas as early as the first decade of the seventeenth century (Copes Tobacco Plant Office 1895:52–54; Iobson 1968:122). While written records have not been informative on the subject of local pipe making in West Africa, archaeology and collections of clay pipes may provide some insights into some of the areas of West Africa.

Archaeologists working in modern-day Ghana have uncovered some European-style pipes and a variety of decorated locally made clay smoking pipes (Emerson 1994: fig. 3.4). Preliminary research has identified at least one local pipe-making industry rising in Ghana in the seventeenth century (Ozanne 1962). Ghanaian pipe collections contain a variety of reed and stem smoking pipes that represent attempts to copy North African metal trade pipes in clay (Ozanne 1964:23: Ozanne and Shinnie 1962:97). The tobacco pipes from Ghana are significant because American archaeologists have discovered an identical reed and bowl tobacco pipe at a plantation site in the Caribbean. Archaeologists working at the Newton plantation on Barbados unearthed a decorated fluted reed and bowl tobacco pipe from an eighteenth-century black grave (Handler 1982:130). Although the pipe from Barbados and those from Ghana are clearly different in form from Chesapeake pipes, they evidence a material connection between a New World plantation and an African homeland.

Archaeologists working in Mali and other areas of the middle Niger River valley have recovered seventeenth-century faceted tobacco pipe forms that are nearly identical to Chesapeake pipes found on seventeenth-century settlement sites in Virginia and Maryland. Both Malian and Chesapeake pipes have faceted sides or flutes cut into the sides of the pipe bowl and sometimes down the length of the stem (fig. 4.3). Faceted Chesapeake tobacco pipe forms have no antecedent in European or Indian pipe-making traditions, and yet decorated and undecorated faceted tobacco pipes have been recovered from almost all of the settlement areas in my sample. Similarities in tobacco pipe forms across the Atlantic, however, are only a small part of the evidence for an African contribution to Chesapeake pipe making.

These faceted pipes and other Chesapeake pipes appear in plantation deposits at approximately the same time that Africans arrive in significant numbers throughout the Chesapeake-tidewater region. These concurrent factors may explain not only the variety of pipe forms in plantation deposits but the sudden and prolific appearance of decorative art on many Chesapeake pipes. An analysis of Chesapeake pipe art reinforces this hypothesis by providing a body of evidence that suggests strong African inspirations in Chesapeake pipe making.

### Chesapeake Pipe Decorations: A New World Folk Art

Chesapeake pipes are embellished with a variety of decorations. These decorations may encircle the lip of the pipe bowl, cover the body or middle part of the pipe bowl, decorate the front, back, or both sides of the pipe bowl, and may even extend down the pipestem (see figs. 4.1, 4.2). Decorations were incised, stamped, and/or punched into the soft exterior of the pipe before firing. Decorations on Chesapeake pipes may include a range of geometric, figural, and zoomorphic motifs as well as abstract geometric designs. Chesapeake pipe art is characterized by three separate decorative effects that reflect a set of techniques. Seventeenth-century Chesapeake pipe makers may have used a variety of tools and techniques to obtain these decorative effects.

Approximately 51 percent of the Chesapeake pipes in my study sample were decorated with stamped characters. These decorative characters reflect a number of stamping tools (fig. 4.4). However, 5 percent of these stamped pipes are decorated solely by a stamped maker's mark on the heel of the pipe bowl (see fig. 4.4).

Most decorated Chesapeake pipes are embellished with decorative lines. Although very few of the tools that produced these lines have been recovered, the line drawings reflect some different techniques, often used to achieve the same effect. The effect is described here as *pointillé*—decoration by impressing denticulate lines or lines of dots. Although many Chesapeake archaeologists describe pipe decorations as simple rouletting (incised lines created by the use of a rolling, toothed wheel),[4] a study of Chesapeake pipe art indicates that pipe makers also used stationary hand-held tools to make individual impressed punctates in a line and rocker-stamping tools to impress denticulate lines into the pipe clay.[5] In fact, there are

Chesapeake pipes that have been decorated with the same design scheme without using the same technique. Cord wrapping was also used to produce bands of incised lines, but it is technically distinct from the denticulate line decorations described here. In my study sample cord wrapping was observed on less than 1 percent of the pipe specimens.

Denticulate lines were applied to the lip, body, and heel-stem junction of the pipe bowl as well as on the pipestem. Pipe makers used denticulate lines to define pipe surface space on the tobacco pipe as well as to depict abstract geometric designs and individual motifs in this space. Chesapeake pipes are decorated with vertical line decorations, repeating characters, decorative bands, multiarmed stars, and motifs depicting ships, boats, tobacco plants, hearts, individual geometric shapes, people, and animals.

About 87 percent of the pipes in my study sample exhibited a third decorative effect. These Chesapeake pipes had their stamped, incised, and impressed denticulate line decorations filled in with white clays to highlight the design or motif. In some cases the white clays that had been rubbed into pipe decorations are only visible through low-power microscopy. It is likely that many other decorated pipes once had this white-fill decorative effect but do not exhibit it today because it can be easily washed out after burial in the ground.

Determining exactly when and where this new folk art began in the Chesapeake is difficult. The diversity of Chesapeake pipe forms and decorations testifies to the fact that many hands were making and decorating tobacco pipes at or near the seventeenth-century settlements in the Chesapeake Bay region. Some Chesapeake pipes are simply decorated with one or more encircling lines. Many pipes, however, exhibit a decorative complexity that includes the use of more than one tool and reflects a set of decorating steps. While some of the motifs on these pipes are instantly recognizable as depictions of plants, animals, boats, initials, and stars, the identity of the Chesapeake pipe maker is not obvious. Some of the techniques of decorating and motifs seen on Chesapeake pipes are common in more than one decorative art tradition. It is only by examining the integration of these motifs with other decorative elements that the origins of, and inspirations for, these decorated pipes can be revealed.

## Decorative Art as Text: Tracing Inspirations and Origins

It is tempting to look back into the past and try to identify people and their residences by artifacts, particularly decorated ones. However, tracing the origins of, and inspirations for, a particular Chesapeake pipe-decorating effect or technique, design or motif can be a problematic task. Before this task can be undertaken, a method for comparing decorative arts across time and space must be devised. The following example demonstrates the need for carefully examining Chesapeake pipe art as a complex body of evidence that takes into account the historical and cultural influences of the context in which it was created.

One distinctive decorative motif found on Chesapeake pipes is a quadruped motif. Quadruped motifs are also found on a piece of Indian clothing collected by an English colonist in 1608 (fig. 4.5). Known as "Powhatan's cloak" or "Powhatan's mantle," the garment bears quadruped motifs that have been generally compared to the quadruped motifs decorating some locally made pipes found in Virginia and Maryland. The visual similarities in the embellishment of pipes and cloak make it tempting to conclude that all artifacts decorated with quadrupeds were made and used by Indians. It has been suggested that Virginia white-tailed deer were one of the original inspirations for this motif, and thus, some Chesapeake pipes have been colloquially described by Chesapeake archaeologists as "deer pipes." The problems with this visual conclusion are numerous.

Quadruped motifs on Chesapeake pipes are drawn in many different ways, suggesting many hands and perhaps different original inspirations for the motif. Quadruped motifs are also found on some seventeenth-century English glassware (Ramsey and Edwards 1956:84, pl. 46c) and European ceramics (Arneberg 1951: pls. 86, 87). Spurious arguments for West African inspirations for this quadruped motif also could be proposed based solely on the visual comparison of West African artifacts decorated with quadruped motifs similar to those found on Chesapeake pipes. The fact that these motifs are found on a wide variety of different Chesapeake pipe forms at sites that are hundreds of miles apart may illustrate the degree that the motif was shared by Native and non-Native people throughout Virginia and Maryland. The quadruped motif as a symbol might also be rich in symbolic meaning to one group and merely imitative by another. We may never know its significance to different smokers.

Another problem with the conclusion that pipes and cloak are the product of a single decorative tradition is posed by the historical context. Although both were created in the Chesapeake, the cloak predates quadruped-decorated pipes by a half century. Unfortunately, little evidence has survived suggesting the common use of quadruped motifs on Algonquian artifacts during the seventeenth century. A significant amount of Indian pottery from Virginia and Maryland has also been unearthed, none of which is decorated with quadrupeds.

Comparisons based on simple motifs are not sufficient for tracing the origins of decorative ideas and the inspirations in Chesapeake pipe art. Moreover, some of the decorative effects described may be pancultural. Some Chesapeake tobacco pipes may reflect the syncretic nature of decorative art, demonstrating the incorporation of influences and inspirations of more than one culture group.

The difficulties of tracing a single motif demonstrate the need to take a cautious approach in tracing the inspirations for Chesapeake pipe art. A close examination of some Chesapeake pipe art reveals that it was applied, and therefore subconsciously thought out, in a patterned way. Its execution involved a systematic use of space and the organization of decorative characters into that space. It reflects a mental competence that has clear antecedents in a generalized decorating tradition in West Africa. Thus, along with specific pipe forms, the style and subject matter of Chesapeake pipe art make up a body of evidence, or text, that enables one to uncover some of its inspirations and trace the origins of some Chesapeake pipe makers.

## Tracing Chesapeake Pipe-Decorating Techniques

The three characteristics of Chesapeake pipe art—decorative stamping, line decorations, and the use of white fill—are decorative effects whose seventeenth-century origins are difficult to trace. Examining decorative effects and techniques and identifying them with ethnic groups is a weak approach to identifying people with their art. Nevertheless, each decorative effect and technique must be individually considered here as the vocabulary in the text of Chesapeake pipe art.

The variety of punched and stamped decorative characters on Chesapeake pipes reflects many different tools and perhaps many different pipe makers. The small number of Chesapeake pipes that are decorated solely with "makers' marks" may represent either a transplanted English pipe maker or the imitation of marks seen on contemporaneous European pipes. Stamped decoration has a long tradition in European pottery, metalwork, and leather crafting. Some of the simple punctates decorating Chesapeake pipes are also similar to those found on Algonquian pottery. For example, prehistoric Townsend pottery is often decorated with individual punctate stamps produced with a reed. Many stamped decorations on pipes, however, reflect sectional stamping tools that are very common in the decorative traditions of culture groups in West Africa. A range of surviving historic-period West African artifacts are stamped with decorative characters that are identical to those found on Chesapeake pipes. Although this decorative effect is common in English and Native American decorative art traditions, the only seventeenth-century stamp-decorated clay pipes observed come from areas of West Africa.

Line decorations are pancultural. An exhaustive survey of seventeenth-century European artifacts reveals very little evidence for the regular use of *pointillé* line decorations. Line decoration as an effect is not uncommon in the English decorative tradition, as is exhibited by wriggle work on seventeenth-century English pewter (DeCorse, chap. 7 in this volume). However, a closer comparison to Chesapeake denticulate lines is found on thirteenth-century English pottery (McCarthy and Brooke 1988). These *pointillé* line decorations represent a closer match in technique, but not time. Some precontact- and historic-period Algonquian pottery and pipes also are incised with individual encircling *pointillé* lines. Rocker stamping or impressing dentate lines is a technique that has been identified with several North American Indian groups.[6] Chesapeake pipes recovered from plantation deposits that are simply decorated with one or more encircling denticulate lines may reflect either Native or non-Native individuals. The use of *pointillé* line decoration is also widespread in West African decorative arts. Embellishment of this kind has a long history in some areas of West and Central Africa, and some groups continue it today with modern materials (Wolff 1987). In the absence of written documentation, it is impossible to identify the makers of European-style Chesapeake pipes with single *pointillé* line decorations. Thus, line-decorating techniques alone are not conclusive evidence for the participation of any particular group of people in seventeenth-century Chesapeake pipe making.

Many Chesapeake pipes recovered from plantation deposits have white materials rubbed into their decorative lines and stamps. The idea of highlighting incised and impressed decorations is not an exclusive decorative technique of any particular culture in the New or Old World. The Iroquois used decorative shell inlays in some of their wooden objects, and medieval Europeans used ceramic inlays in tiles for intaglio effect (Rutsch 1973:86). The particular use of white clay fill inlays, however, is widespread in West African decorative arts traditions. White clay, chalk, bone, ash, and a variety of other white substances were and still are used to highlight decorated calabashes, pottery, tobacco pipes, wooden artifacts, and human bodies in West and Central Africa. In some West African societies, white decorative materials are often associated with a range of medical, social, and spiritual ideals (Cole and Aniakor 1984:62, 216). The concept of whiteness is a common denominator of some West African cosmologies and is strongly conserved across time and space as a decorative expression. While this decorative effect could be easily adapted by non-African Chesapeake pipe makers, it is probable that this decorative idea came to the Chesapeake from West Africa.

An examination of each of the decorative effects and techniques used to decorate Chesapeake pipes makes it apparent that no one decorating technique identifies seventeenth-century pipe makers or tells us much about their cultural origins. However, although decorative lines, stamped decoration, and highlighting fill are found independently in the decorative arts traditions of many cultures, their combination defines a decorative style that uniquely characterizes Chesapeake pipe art.

### Comparing Chesapeake and West African Pipes

Some West African tobacco pipes and ceramics demonstrate a strong decorative affinity with seventeenth-century Chesapeake tobacco pipes. Seventeenth-century Malian pipes not only are formally similar to some Chesapeake pipes but exhibit the same combination of decorations as well (see fig. 4.3). Decorations on clay pipes (Daget and Ligers 1962: pl. C5) and pottery (Stobel 1984:232–35) from Mali demonstrate a similar technical application of decoration, including *pointillé* lines, stamping characters, and white inlay identical to those found on Chesapeake pipes. Archaeologists also have recovered decorated tobacco pipes from seventeenth-century sites in Gambia. These pipes share with Chesapeake pipes the combination of decorative stamping and lines, but not the highlighting white inlay (see Emerson 1994: fig. 3; Hill 1989, pers. comm.). Seventeenth-century tobacco pipes from Ghana and the African-style pipes found in Barbados also exhibit the combination of decorative elements that characterizes Chesapeake pipe art. These pipes exhibit decorative stamping, some incised lines, and the use of white inlay (Shinnie and Ozanne 1962:96; Ozanne 1964:20). This particular technique and manner of decorating did not go undocumented; early European travelers to West Africa commented on it (Bowditch 1819:311). Chesapeake pipe art may also have been inspired by the decorative art traditions of other West African areas from which slaves were removed.

### Chesapeake Pipe Art: Defining a Style

In an analysis of Chesapeake pipe art it is not worthwhile to study merely the physical techniques of decoration. The true challenge is in recognizing a stylistic pattern and identifying a past decorative aesthetic. If both technical affinities and similar aesthetic principles between two places can be described and compared, one can demonstrate the transmission or translation of a decorative tradition across time and space. An attempt to identify a generalized decorative style and aesthetic for Chesapeake pipe art is presented here.

Chesapeake pipe art exhibits an interesting patterned use of stamped characters. These characters appear singularly or in clusters of three or four in bands, positioned at the ends of lines, at line intersections, and, often, surrounding bands or motifs (fig. 4.6). Stamped characters complement line designs and motifs as a rule. The pattern of lines and stamps found on Chesapeake pipes is also found on Malian pottery (Stobel 1984:232–35). Stamps are used to complement zigzag lines on seventeenth-century decorated pipes from the Chesapeake and Gambia. Stamped characters also were used by Chesapeake pipe makers to surround bands and patterns of lines. Nupe pottery from central Nigeria and a few Chesapeake pipes share bands of zigzag lines with surrounding punched circlets (Biedermann 1981:66, fig. 6). Bands of repeating stamped characters that appear on Chesapeake pipes and on Malian pottery (Stobel 1984:232–35) are also found on West African musical instruments (Parrinder 1982:64), modern textiles (Seiber 1972:223), and body art (Cole and Aniakor 1984:46). Single or clusters of stamped characters also complement designs and motifs on Chesapeake pipes (see fig. 4.6). This aspect of decoration also is seen in the pottery, metalworking, and jewelry-making traditions of southeastern Nigeria (Eyo 1979:66, 49; Biedermann 1981:69, figs. 12, 13). Seventeenth-century Akan gold weights from Ghana also illustrate a similar use of stamped characters and lines (Garrard 1973). The articulation of stamped characters complementing line designs is consistently seen on Chesapeake pipes and in a range of West African material culture.

The patterned use of decorative denticulate lines and stamps filled with white inlays describes much of the decorative essence of Chesapeake pipes. Although not all locally made pipes in the Chesapeake are decorated, many of the Chesapeake pipes recovered from plantation deposits share this decorative style. An extensive examination of seventeenth-century European and Chesapeake Indian artifacts has failed to reveal a similar stylistic history using stamped characters, decorative lines, and white inlay. West African artifacts, however, strongly demonstrate a patterned use of stamps, lines, and inlay that is almost identical to the decorative art of Chesapeake pipes. A grammar consisting of rules for the articulation of this style would easily fit examples of West African artifacts and many Chesapeake pipes. This generalized decorative style was widespread in West Africa and predates the mass shipment of Africans to the Chesapeake. The appearance of this African decorative style on seventeenth-century tobacco pipes clearly coincides with the increased visibility of Africans in the Chesapeake colonies. The strength of African inspirations in Chesapeake pipe art is further demonstrated by the appearance of exact African motifs on Chesapeake pipes.

## African Motifs on Chesapeake Pipes

A Chesapeake tobacco pipe recovered from excavations at Green Spring plantation, the home of Governor William Berkeley, is decorated with a distinctive motif illustrated in figure 4.7. It is identical to a motif used to symbolize cattle and herding in Central Africa (Jefferson 1973). Livestock was an important investment for seventeenth-century English and free Africans in Virginia and Maryland; herding was also one of many plantation tasks reserved for slaves (Breen and Innes 1980:81–83). Documentary and archaeological evidence indicates that Governor Berkeley had a number of servants, slaves, and livestock at Green Spring in the middle of the seventeenth century (Caywood 1957:70). It is likely that an African pipe maker at Green Spring made this European-style mold-made Chesapeake pipe and decorated it with this African motif.

Another Chesapeake pipe is decorated with a distinctive line and stamped motif that may be described as two denticulate line lozenges surrounded by stamped circlets (fig. 4.8). This motif is also found on an early eighteenth-century Asante black earthenware pot (see fig. 4.8). The question of who carried these motifs to the Chesapeake raises the issue of gender. Over large and culturally diverse areas of West Africa, like the Akan lands in central Ghana, the making of pottery and its related ornamentation was a skill inherited by daughters from their mothers (Antwi 1976:22). Documentary records indicate that black females were present in seventeenth-century Virginia and Maryland, and it is possible that they directed their individual artistic skills to occasional pipe making. Although there is no published source that documents the significance or meaning of this motif, it is undoubtedly West African and probably was inscribed on a Chesapeake pipe by a slave.

Chesapeake pipes from a variety of settlement sites in Virginia are decorated with a motif that is clearly derived from the decorative arts traditions of Nigeria and areas in neighboring Cameroon. This double-bell or double-gong motif is depicted in a variety of ways on Chesapeake pipes and on some West African artifacts. A Cameroonian clay tobacco pipe exhibits this motif (Gebauer 1979:251). While its New World meaning and social context are unrecoverable, the design, when depicted on a personal object in Cameroon, represents ruling class status and membership in a regulatory society within a community (Gebauer 1979:251–52). The double-bell or double-gong shape is also found in recent Tiv scarification (Bohannon 1956:118), Igbo metalwork (Cole and Aniakor 1984:39), and the Nsibidi ideograms of Ejagham peoples in southwestern Nigeria (Thompson 1983:227–68, 244). Ejagham peoples developed a language that consisted of common and secret gestures, words, and ideograms. The graphic symbols of this language were often reminders of status but also symbolized emotions, places, people, and things. Thompson (1983) has demonstrated that this lexicon of ideograms was reborn among Africans in some New World contexts such as the Caribbean.

An exact replication of a West African decorative motif and design on a Chesapeake pipe is the *kwardata* motif. This distinctive blank diamond-shaped motif in a band is offset on a textured background. It appears in several renditions on a variety of Chesapeake pipes forms and on Nigerian pottery (fig. 4.9). The kwardata motif, when placed on a ritual beer vessel, refers to "the transition from youth to adulthood" in contemporary Ga'anda society (Berns and Hudson 1986:135). Chesapeake pipes decorated with this motif were found at several plantation sites in Virginia and Maryland (fig. 4.10).

## Looking for Meaning in Chesapeake Pipe Art

The decorative style, designs, and motifs of Chesapeake tobacco pipe art are clear evidence that Africans made pipes in seventeenth-century Virginia and Maryland. Unfortunately, there are no witnesses, testimony, or documents from this time or place that can give insight into why Africans decorated their tobacco pipes.

One speculative explanation for pipe decorating involves a consideration of per-

sonal identity and status. Near the end of the seventeenth century, English indentured servants and Africans shared living conditions and tasks on the plantation.
Their individual status and personal identity probably reflected their age, sex, and
work on the plantation. It is interesting to note that English initials, the double-
bell motif, the kwardata motif, and the cattle symbol reflect the identity or status
of a person, a stage in one's life, and possibly an occupation, respectively. In addition, enslaved Africans may have identified themselves with the foodstuffs, clothes,
pipes, and other goods that they produced. Their worldview and status were local
and personal. Thus, personal items such as tobacco pipes exhibit both representational and idiosyncratic decorative art. Some of the motifs clearly reflect the physical environment (i.e., cattle and other quadrupeds, boats, and tobacco plants), and
perhaps the social realities of life on a Chesapeake plantation (i.e., personal identity
[initials] and symbols of occupational identity [herdsman, boatman] and adulthood
[kwardata motifs]). As the number of blacks increased in the seventeenth-century
Chesapeake, their opportunities, status, and identity changed. Chesapeake pipes and
the decorations on them may reflect these symbols and changes.

### Pipe Making and the Plantation Crafting Context

European-style mold-made Chesapeake pipes decorated in an African-derived decorative style may offer material testimony on the interaction of whites and blacks
on seventeenth-century tidewater plantations. The documentary record, however,
provides little direct insight into the lives of seventeenth-century European colonist-
pipe makers or their helpers. Although living conditions varied from settlement to
settlement, smaller planters may have encouraged their servants or slaves to make
certain goods, including pipes, for themselves.

Indentured servants and slaves probably had the least access to imported goods,
and their need for locally produced goods such as clothes, shoes, and tobacco pipes
grew dramatically with their increasing numbers in the second half of the seventeenth century. Servants made shoes, candles, cider, beer, and a variety of other daily
goods for themselves and their masters, who in turn sold these commodities to other
planters (Fleet 1942:99). Documentary evidence suggests that some locally made
products, such as shoes, were made by servants explicitly for servants (Beverley
1947:295). Their desire for, but limited access to, imported pipes was motivation for
indentured servants to participate in occasional pipe making. Making and decorating tobacco pipes was probably a leisure-time practice of these people, who identified more with their local world than with any distant one whose goods they could
scarcely hope to obtain. The arrival of numbers of African slaves in the Chesapeake-
tidewater region corresponds closely with the appearance of many decorated Chesapeake pipes in plantation deposits. Although there is no documentary evidence

identifying black pipe makers in tidewater Virginia and Maryland, the possibility of pipe making by slaves on English plantations can be discussed and evaluated in light of documentary evidence concerning other slave activities.

During the second half of the seventeenth century, Chesapeake tobacco plantations competed for incoming slaves because of a dwindling supply of indentured servants (Breen 1973; Galenson 1981; Menard 1977). Historians estimate that by the mid–seventeenth century blacks constituted approximately 3 to 5 percent of the colonial population. During the next three decades, the number of slaves in the Chesapeake rose dramatically to 2,000 in 1670 and to over 6,000 at the turn of the century (Hening 1809–23:2:515; Donnan 1969:4:6). Living on small farms in numbers of less than ten, mid-seventeenth-century blacks were easily incorporated into their masters' households and into daily plantation tasks (Kulikoff 1986:319). This was a more intimate relationship than that shared between whites and plantation-based Indians. The lives of seventeenth-century blacks varied widely according to the status of their masters, the proximity of other plantations where blacks dwelled, and the everyday interactions of blacks and whites.

Planters employed blacks in a variety of small manufactures centered on the plantation. One description of a mid-seventeenth-century Virginia planter talks of plantation industries and the use of blacks on his plantation. Africans were trained to support cottage industries in cloth, leather, and shoe making and a variety of "trades in the house" (Anonymous 1649:15). The crafting context probably varied from settlement to settlement, and some blacks and whites may have shared or influenced each other with a variety of tangible and nontangible behaviors. Whether blacks and whites worked cooperatively in a venture like pipe making cannot be deduced from written records, but the evidence for sharing motifs and the fact that the generalized style of Chesapeake pipe art was widely spread are testimony to an interactive crafting context and the spread of decorative ideas across the Chesapeake. Although some decorated Chesapeake pipes may demonstrate strongly conserved African symbolism, the appearance of hearts, initials, stars, ships, and other European-inspired motifs drawn and complemented in the generalized decorative style described above may be the only surviving evidence of the sharing and syncretism of European and African cultures that occurred on seventeenth-century Chesapeake plantations.

## Changing Attitudes, Changing Activities

The decline and eventual disappearance of local pipe making in the Chesapeake may be a small reflection of the changes in activities and attitudes on Chesapeake plantations at the end of the seventeenth century. Included in these changes may have been some significant changes in relations between blacks and whites as life in the tidewater changed in response to a devastated tobacco market, the disillusionment of freedmen, and the failure of many small planters.

An architectural study of late seventeenth-century Chesapeake plantations offers the physical reorganization of plantations—the shrinking of planters' houses and the increase in quarters and outbuildings—as evidence of social change (Upton 1979). Indentured servants and slaves who once lived in the planter's house were moved out and away to quarters. The physical and social separation of black slaves from owners and the subsequent decrease of white servants marked the end of any occasional pipe making, and decorated Chesapeake pipes disappear from eighteenth-century plantation deposits.

Legal records document additional changes toward Africans as a race with the institutionalization of slavery. Africans became enslaved for life, and thus their status was legally and socially diminished in the beginning of the eighteenth century. Planters' antipathy toward blacks intensified, and they became increasingly alarmed about the long-distance, interplantation social networks that their slaves maintained. Their response was to limit slave travel, ban slave funerals, and attempt to suppress any vestiges of African tribal identities. While increasing control over everyday activities, planters attempted to provide a new identity for their slaves and themselves by distancing themselves physically, emotionally, and materially from those they held in bondage.

As the number of Africans proliferated and the plantation labor force expanded, the diversity of Africans with different cultural backgrounds also increased. Perhaps along with decorated pipes, descriptive, symbolic, and highly personalized decorative art may have disappeared, reflecting not a lack of skill but perhaps the lack of desire to affect or offend others who although black were culturally different.

Not until later in the eighteenth century, with the tremendous increase in imported slaves, do African-inspired creole traditions become highly visible in the surviving material culture of the American South. Second- and third-generation Africans in the Chesapeake began to develop a new way of life, largely unknown to us, but certainly one that conserved certain links to the past and adapted to the realities of the present.

## Notes

This research was undertaken as part of a doctoral dissertation at the University of California at Berkeley. Excavations conducted at Flowerdew Hundred farm in Prince George County, Va., were sponsored by annual field programs funded by the University of California's University Research Expeditions program, the National Endowment for the Humanities, and the Flowerdew Hundred Foundation. Research on collections of Chesapeake pipes was made possible by grants from the University of California and by the cooperation of staff members at the Colonial National Historical Park at Jamestown, Va., the Department of Archaeology at Colonial Williamsburg, Va., the Virginia Research Center for Archaeology at Yorktown, and the St. Mary's City Archaeological Laboratory at St. Mary's City, Md.

Originally this chapter was a brief presentation illustrating the survival of a generalized West African decorative tradition in Chesapeake pipes. It has been expanded to include additional discussions of the archaeology of seventeenth-century pipe making and the significance of Chesapeake pipe art. It has benefited from comments and suggestions from the members of the Washington Area Seminar for Early American History, University of Maryland, College Park (October 1989), and participants at the "Digging the Afro-American Past-Archaeology and the Black Experience" conference at the University of Mississippi (May 1989). I have also attempted to answer comments received at the annual Jamestown Conference (May 1990) at Popes Creek, Va. I am particularly indebted to Theresa Singleton for her support and invitation to participate in the University of Mississippi conference.

1. Previous researchers have attempted to build typologies of Chesapeake pipes defining them as subtypes of known imported forms (Henry 1976, 1979; Crass 1981), but the result has been numerous and vague subtypes of types answering only the question that Chesapeake pipe makers were aware of imported types.

2. Virginia county court records document that there was a strong local trade between settlements in homemade products such as shoes, clothing, beer, cider, and foodstuffs. Tobacco pipes are not mentioned as a cottage industry.

3. Indian children often were taken in by colonists to be raised as Christians. Adult Indians were hired to carry messages and hunt and fish for the plantation kitchen.

4. Chesapeake archaeologists have tentatively suggested that watch wheels, geared wheels from broken watches, were used to apply denticulate line decorations on Chesapeake pipes.

5. The tool found by MacCord (1969:41, fig. 17) is an example of a rocker-stamping tool. Fossilized shark's teeth may also have been used to rocker stamp denticulate lines on pipes. A rouletting wheel that is held stationary in a fixture or by hand could also be used to create rocker-stamp decorations.

6. Chesapeake Indians and some of their neighbors used dentate stamping on pottery and pipes (Leslie 1970; Schmitt 1965:23).

Table 4.1. Chesapeake pipe collections

| Name of site | County or town | Date |
| --- | --- | --- |
| Flowerdew 44PG77 | Prince George, Va. | 1655–1700 |
| Eppes Island 44CC178 | Charles City, Va. | 1650–1700 |
| Kingsmill: Tenement | James City, Va. | 1620–60 |
| Kingsmill: Littletown | James City, Va. | 1641–1700 |
| Kingsmill: Utopia | James City, Va. | 1660–1710 |
| Jamestown Collection | James City, Va. | 17th cen. |
| Governor's Land: Maine | James City, Va. | 1618–30 |
| Governor's Land: Drummond | James City, Va. | 1648–1820 |
| Governor's Land: Petit | James City, Va. | 1690? |
| Green Spring | James City, Va. | 1646–1790 |
| Mathew's Manor | Denbigh, Va. | 1620–52 |
| Lightfoot | James City, Va. | 1675–1700 |
| Martin's Hundred A | James City, Va. | 1625–50 |
| Martin's Hundred B | James City, Va. | 1625–45 |
| Martin's Hundred J | James City, Va. | 1640–90? |
| River Creek 44Y067 | York, Va. | 1640–60 |
| Bennett Farm | York, Va. | 1625–1830 |
| Knowles Collection | Newport, Va. | 1622–80? |
| Thorogood 44VB48 | Virginia Beach, Va. | 1695–1700? |
| Nominy | Westmoreland, Va. | 1655–1720 |
| St. Mary's City: St. Johns | St. Marys, Md. | 1638–1720 |
| St. Mary's City: Popes Ft. | St. Marys, Md. | 1645–55 |
| St. Mary's City: Country Hse. | St. Marys, Md. | 1635–61 |
| St. Mary's City: Van Swerigen | St. Marys, Md. | 1665–1745 |

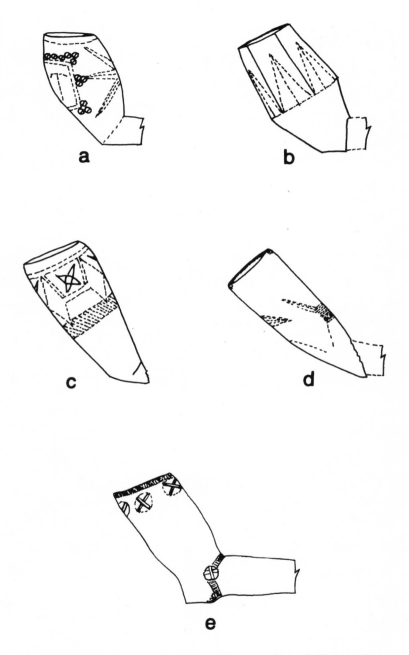

4.1. Chesapeake pipes: (*a*) elbow pipe with star and panel, (*b*) faceted pipe with denticulate line decorations; (*c*) obtuse-angled pipe with encircling kwardata motifs, (*d*) an obtuse-angled pipe with two quadruped motifs; (*e*) elbow pipe with stamped and denticulate line decoration

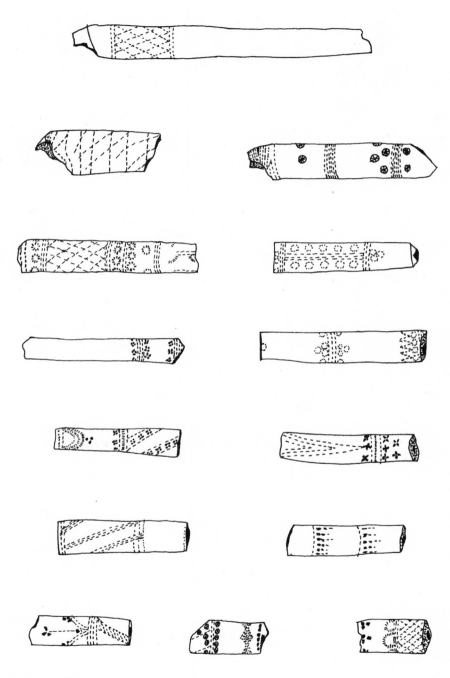

4.2. Decorated pipestems

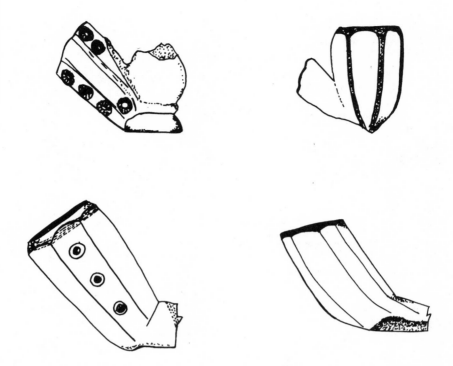

4.3. Faceted tobacco pipes from West Africa and the Chesapeake: (*top row*) seventeenth-century reed-and-bowl pipe fragment and stem decorated with stamped characters, Mali (after Daget and Ligers 1962:38, fig. 10:10), and undecorated seventeenth-century faceted bowl, Mali (after Daget and Ligers 1962:19, fig. 2:3); (*bottom row*) seventeenth-century faceted pipe decorated with stamped characters, Virginia, and seventeenth-century undecorated faceted pipe, Virginia

4.4. Chesapeake pipe art: makers' marks

4.5. Powhatan's cloak. (Courtesy of the Ashmolean Museum, Oxford, Eng.)

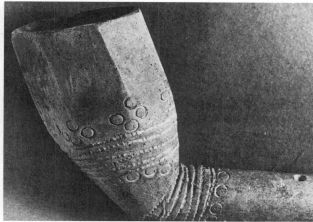

4.6. Two Chesapeake pipes from Lightfoot, Va.

4.7. Chesapeake pipe with motif similar to cattle motifs of West and Central Africa (see Jefferson 1973:187–88)

4.8. Asante black earthenware vessel with lozenge motif and a close-up of lozenge motif (*top left and bottom*; © British Museum); Chesapeake tobacco pipe decorated with lozenge motif from Jamestown, Va. (*top right*)

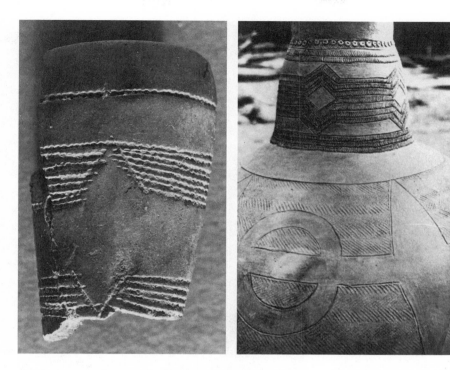

4.9. A seventeenth-century Chesapeake pipe fragment decorated with kwardata motif from St. Mary's City, Md. (*left*), and a twentieth-century Ga'anda ritual beer pot decorated with kwardata motif from Nigeria, West Africa (*right*; photograph by Marla C. Berns, February 1981)

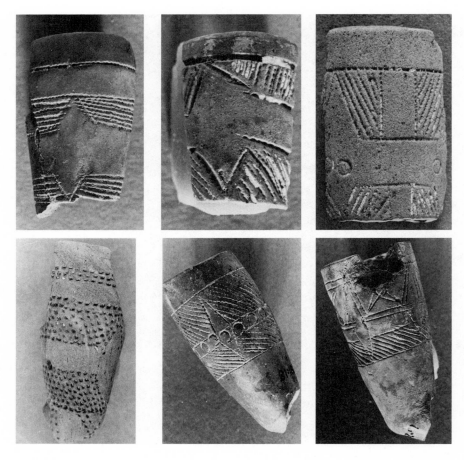

4.10. Chesapeake pipe bowls from Maryland and Virginia decorated with kwardata motifs

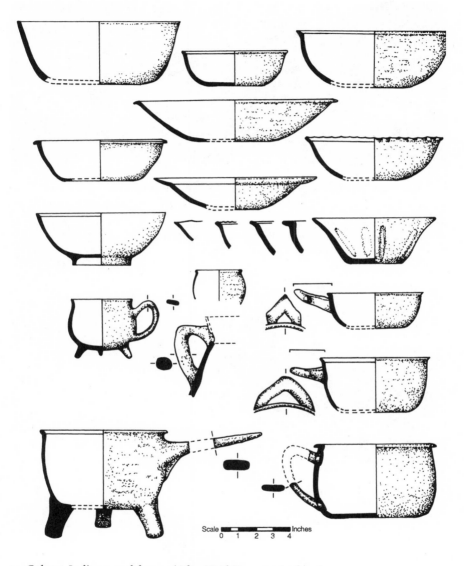

5.1. Colono-Indian vessel forms. (After Noël Hume 1962: fig. 4)

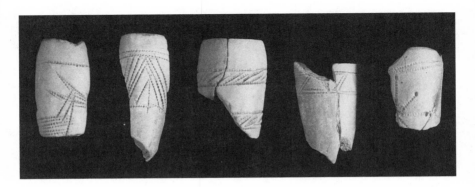

5.2. Rouletted Chesapeake pipes. All bowl fragments from Camden, a seventeenth-century Native American site in Caroline County, Va. One of numerous running deer pipes is at the far left. At right is a common variety of the star motif. (Collections of the Virginia Department of Historic Resources, photograph by Stephen Potter)

5.3. Prehistoric rouletted pipe from the Fout site in northeastern Virginia. (Collections of the Virginia Department of Historic Resources, photograph by Keith T. Egloff)

5.4. Rouletted pipe with running deer motif and white infill, Bowman site, Shenandoah County, Va. (Collections of the Virginia Department of Historic Resources)

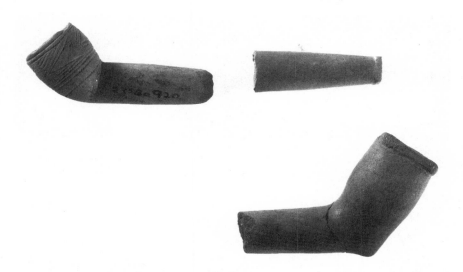

5.5. Prehistoric pipes from Koehler, a Dan River complex site in Henry County, Va. Fragmentary bowl at upper left is roulette decorated with a design very similar to that on pipes from the Great Neck site in Virginia Beach. (Collections of the Virginia Department of Historic Resources; photograph by Keith T. Egloff)

5.6. Tobacco pipe bowl with *pointillé* decoration from middle Woodland context (A.D. 200–800), Great Neck site, Virginia Beach, Va. (Collections of the Virginia Department of Historic Resources, photograph by L. Daniel Mouer)

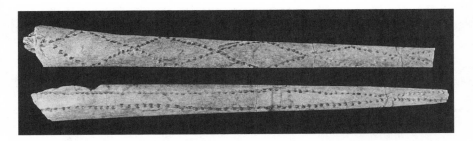

5.7. Bone pins with *pointillé* decoration from middle Woodland context (A.D. 200–800), Great Neck site, Virginia Beach, Va. (Collections of the Virginia Department of Historic Resources, photograph by L. Daniel Mouer)

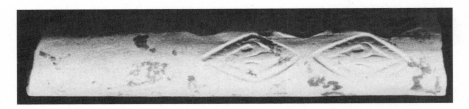

5.8. Fleur-de-lis or trefoil design on a seventeenth-century European import pipestem, Walter Aston site, Charles City County, Va. (Collections of the Virginia Department of Historic Resources, photograph by L. Daniel Mouer)

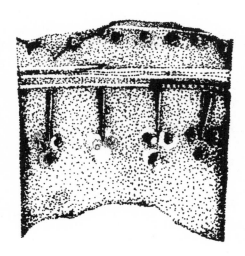

5.9. "Roll-out" planimetric drawing of stamped trefoils or ermines and rouletted bands on a Chesapeake pipestem from Curles plantation site, Henrico County, Va.

5.10. Stamped trefoil or ermine on a ca. 1660 English chest. (Age-croft Association, Richmond, Va., photograph by L. Daniel Mouer)

5.11. Hanging triangles on prehistoric pottery. Townsend incised ceramics of the late Woodland period, Great Neck site (*left*) and Weyanoke Point, Charles City County (*right*). (Collections of the Virginia Department of Historic Resources, photograph by L. Daniel Mouer)

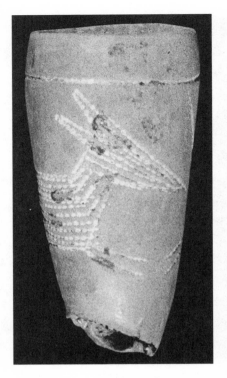 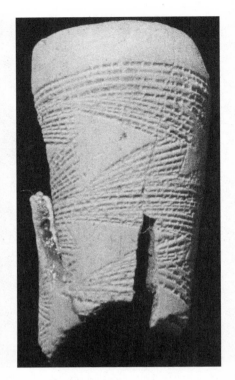

5.12. Chesapeake pipe with running deer, Walter Aston site, a former plantation. (Collections of the Virginia Department of Historic Resources, photograph by L. Daniel Mouer)

5.13. A fourteenth-century rouletted pipe with bands of triangles formed in negative space. This is one of two similarly decorated pipes, Great Neck site. (Collections of the Virginia Department of Historic Resources, photograph by L. Daniel Mouer).

5.15. Chesapeake pipes with English cipher or initials in a panel and typical Chesapeake pipe decorative elements, such as rouletting and small floral stamps, Walter Aston site. Similar marked pipes have been recovered from Jamestown and other sites. The examples at the bottom right are marked "WA," presumably for Walter Aston. (Collections of the Virginia Department of Historic Resources, photograph by L. Daniel Mouer)

5.14. The plume motif on an Oneata pipe and a Chesapeake pipe:
*A* from Gingerstairs Rockshelter, Iowa (after Logan 1976: fig. 81);
*B* from the Thorogood site, Va. (after Emerson 1988: fig. 46b)

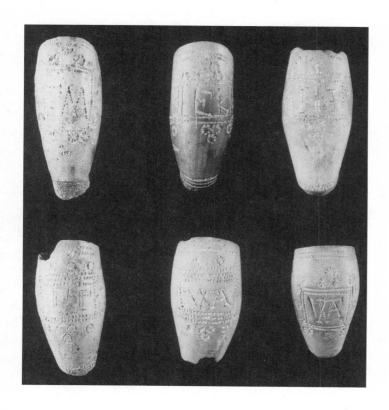

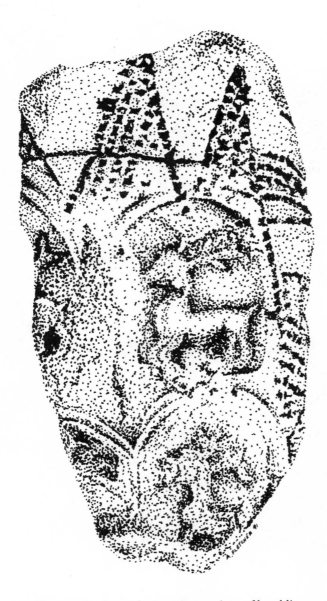

5.16. Chesapeake pipe with signet impressions of heraldic stag standing from Nathaniel Bacon's Curles plantation site of ca. 1675–80

# 5

# Colonoware Pottery, Chesapeake Pipes, and "Uncritical Assumptions"

*L. Daniel Mouer, Mary Ellen N. Hodges, Stephen R. Potter,*
*Susan L. Henry Renaud, Ivor Noël Hume, Dennis J. Pogue,*
*Martha W. McCartney, and Thomas E. Davidson*

## Introduction

IN THIS ESSAY WE ARGUE that a "blind spot" toward Native Americans has characterized some modern historical writings and some recent archaeological interpretation of locally made earthenware vessels and tobacco pipes in the Chesapeake region and elsewhere. The myth that Indian populations disappeared in the face of a massive onslaught of Europeans, Africans, and attendant diseases continues to inform interpretations of United States history and culture (Mouer 1991f).

In an article in *Science* and subsequently in his book *Flowerdew Hundred* (Deetz 1988, 1993; see chap. 3 of this volume) raised a number of points concerning the role of historical archaeology in the study of history and the social sciences and the methods used by historical archaeologists. His conclusions concerning the significance of Colono-Indian ware pottery sparked dissension among historical archaeologists working in Virginia and Maryland. Deetz asserted that "most scholars working with colono ware now agree that it was made . . . by slaves" (Deetz 1988:367). We argue, however, that this statement, as it pertains to the Chesapeake region, is inaccurate. At approximately the same time Deetz wrote this article, Matthew Emerson completed a dissertation asserting that a second class of artifacts—seventeenth-century decorated tobacco pipes regionally referred to as "terra-cotta," "local," "tidewater," or "colono" pipes, but by Emerson named "Chesapeake" pipes—were also the products primarily of African-American servants and slaves (Emerson 1988). Emerson's findings were rapidly reported throughout the country in the popular media, including the *New York Times*, *Washington Post*, and *Archaeology* magazine. Again, we would argue that this conclusion is not widely shared by historical archaeologists working in the Chesapeake.

We believe that the conclusions of Deetz and Emerson are at best premature or overstated. While there has not been sufficient research in the Chesapeake region to establish "colono" pottery and tobacco pipes as items exclusively produced by Native Americans, no evidence has been established that disproves that these artifacts were made by the Chesapeake's Indian peoples for their own use and for trade. This interpretation is not based upon "an uncritical assumption," as Deetz has claimed (*New York Times*, 12 July 1988), but upon sound ethnographic, historical, and archaeological research of more than a century's duration. The explanations given by Deetz and Emerson on the rise and fall in popularity of these artifacts in the Chesapeake region are contradictory and illogical: they serve to rewrite Chesapeake history, muddling rather than illuminating the complex processes of interaction between cultures in contact and in conflict.

## "Colono" Pottery

There has been relatively little detailed research published on Colono-Indian pottery in the Chesapeake since 1980, when Susan Henry completed her master's thesis, including a substantial—if by now somewhat dated—review of the literature and the materials. The term *Colono-Indian ware* was originally used by Noël Hume (1962) to describe locally produced, smoothed or burnished earthenware vessels excavated at Jamestown and Williamsburg and on plantations along the James and York Rivers in tidewater Virginia. The ware is hand-built from local clays and fired at a low temperature in an oxidizing atmosphere, on a clay body that is usually tempered with crushed, calcined shell. This technology matches that used to produce Townsend and Roanoke wares, common among late prehistoric Algonquian Indian pottery types in this area (see Egloff and Potter 1982). Colono-Indian ware was produced primarily in European vessel forms: simple bowls and pots, shallow pans, jugs, chamber pots, pipkins, porringers, and so on (fig. 5.1). Given these characteristics, Noël Hume (1962:4) proposed that Colono-Indian ware was "manufactured by local Indians who were exposed to European influences." This conclusion was reinforced when Noël Hume paid two visits, accompanied by Ben C. McCary (a specialist in Virginia's Indian history and archaeology), to the Pamunkey Indian reservation. At Pamunkey they found both shell-tempered and untempered sherds of Colono-Indian ware in surface associations with eighteenth- and early nineteenth-century European ceramics.

Lewis Binford described similar wares from historic Indian sites in southeastern Virginia (Binford 1964, 1965). Courtland ware, discovered in contexts of seventeenth- and early eighteenth-century Meherrin and Nottoway Indian settlements, was constructed on a clay body with inclusions of fine to very fine sand. Binford noted similarities between this material and Branchville ware, the common ceramic of the protohistoric Iroquoian-speaking groups in this area, although many vessels were made in European forms such as mugs, shallow bowls, and plates. Courtland burnished ware was restricted apparently to the eighteenth century, while Courtland plain pottery was found in late seventeenth-century association with Branchville pottery and rouletted ceramic tobacco pipes, which Binford hypothesized had been decorated with watch wheels acquired by the Indians in trade. Binford also identified smoothed, shell-tempered ceramics made in forms that include flat-based bowls and jars. These were associated with a 1653–67 Weyanoke (Algonquian) Indian settlement in the area and were known as Warekeck ware (Binford 1965:83; Egloff and Potter 1982).[1]

A third study was conducted by archaeologist Howard A. MacCord, Sr., at a late seventeenth-century Native American settlement on the Rappahannock River in northern Virginia (MacCord 1969). Here MacCord described a colonoware pottery type which he named Camden plain, after the name of the site located on Camden farm. Camden plain pottery shows some similarities to, and was found in association with, Potomac Creek and Moyoane wares, the protohistoric and early historic wares of some Algonquian-speaking groups in the Northern Neck area, the peninsula formed between the Potomac and Rappahannock Rivers. Also found at the site were shell-tempered materials similar to Noël Hume's Colono-Indian ware, roulette-decorated smoking pipes, and two serrated lead tools that, MacCord posited, were used to make the pipe decoration. Pipe wasters led MacCord to conclude that the pipes had been produced at the site. There were a few European-made objects as well, which date the site to the period between 1680 and 1710. Not the least of these was a seventeenth-century silver medal engraved to "Ye King of Machotick." In the nineteenth century a similar silver medal engraved to "Ye King of Patomeck" had been discovered on the same property. MacCord concluded that the site was a late seventeenth-century Native American occupation, and that the Camden plain, shell-tempered Colono-Indian ware and rouletted pipes had been made by Indians.

L. Daniel Mouer (1978) identified ceramics similar to Camden or Courtland wares in protohistoric and historic-period Monacan Indian sites in the piedmont section of the James River valley. The pottery was associated with Potomac Creek-like ceramics and, in the one historic-period case, with gunflints and flaked tools made of European wine bottle glass. His conclusion was that these were examples of historic Indian ceramics, perhaps similar to those traded by the Monacan to the French Huguenots at Manakintown at the end of the eighteenth century (Michel [1701–2] 1916).

Work conducted by the Virginia Department of Historic Resources (VDHR) in the late 1970s and 1980s provided further evidence of the association of Colono-Indian ceramics and Native American peoples at the Pamunkey Indian reservation and the Camden site. In 1979, at the request of the Pamunkey Indian tribe, the

VDHR conducted an archaeological survey of the reservation before nominating the property to the National Register of Historic Places. In the course of the survey, a trash-filled pit that had been disturbed by deep plowing was excavated (McCartney and Hodges 1980). Eight of fifteen archaeological sites identified in the survey contained Colono-Indian ceramics. The excavated trash pit was also found to contain an extensive collection of Colono-Indian ware, in association with pearlware and other Euro-American artifacts dating the assemblage to the first half of the nineteenth century. The Colono-Indian ware in the collection is a shell-tempered, plain or burnished ceramic produced in vessel forms similar to those described by Noël Hume (1962) but also including plates, flat-bottomed jars, and a bottle or small jug. Unfired shell-tempered clay was also recovered from the feature.

Following up on work begun by MacCord in 1964, an extensive archaeological survey of Camden farm conducted by the VDHR demonstrated that site 44Ce3 was only one of several similar sites distributed across a long river terrace on the property (Hodges 1986; Hodges and McCartney 1985). Although no further subsurface testing was conducted, these sites appear to represent individual households within an internally dispersed settlement of a Native American village. Archival research associated with the field survey indicated that the complex was situated within a three-mile radius of a seventeenth-century Nanzattico Indian reservation, on the north side of the Rappahannock River. An early eighteenth-century plot of the area identifies the location of the village complex at Camden as "Middle Town," probably a reference to one of the Indian settlements within the Nanzattico preserve. Other Indian groups known to have been living in this part of the Rappahannock Valley during the late seventeenth century include the Portobacco, Mattehatigue, Doeg, Rappahannock, and Nansemond (Hodges and McCartney 1985; Rountree 1990:119–20; Waselkov 1983:27). Of these groups, the Doeg and probably the Portobacco and Mattehatigue (possibly synonymous with Machodoc and Machotick) relocated to the area from precontact territories on the inner coastal plain of the Potomac River. This movement probably would explain the presence of Potomac Creek pottery and a related Colono-Indian ceramic type at the Camden site.

William P. Barse (1985:146–59) has investigated the site of a Conoy Indian settlement in Charles County, Maryland, that included a trash pit carbon-dated to A.D. 1575 +/- 90 (Boyce and Frye 1986:10). This site's inventory comprises sherds of Potomac Creek cord-marked, Potomac Creek plain (the vast majority), Townsend plain, and Camden plain ceramics. Also included are a number of Potomac Creek tobacco pipe fragments including one described as having a European-influenced floral motif; a European ball-clay pipe bowl of a type datable between 1610 and 1640; projectile points of quartz, iron, and brass; and European flint tools and debitage. Again, the association and similarity between the clearly aboriginal pottery and pipes and the "colono" materials, along with the site's location and early seventeenth-century date, suggest that the decorated pipe and Camden pottery were made by Indians.

Beginning in the late 1970s, researchers in South Carolina began an intensive study of low-fired, hand-modeled earthenwares. In the years since the publication of Noël Hume's original article, in which he noted the presence of ceramics similar to his Colono-Indian ware along the South Atlantic coast, numerous additional examples have been identified (Baker 1972; Fairbanks 1962; Lees and Kimery-Lees 1979; South 1974; Scurry and Haskell 1979). The discovery of these ceramics in particularly high frequencies on plantation sites in the low country of South Carolina led Leland Ferguson (1980) to investigate whether African Americans may have produced some of these wares. To acknowledge this possibility, Ferguson (1980:23–24) proposed that the term *colonoware* should replace "Colono-Indian Ware."

With the publication of the South Carolina research, there have been increased attempts to identify possible African-American origins for the pottery in the Chesapeake region. The assemblage from a seventeenth-century tenant's or servant's quarter at Kingsmill, excavated by William Kelso, was briefly studied by Matthew Hill, a specialist in West African archaeology and ceramics (Hill 1987 and pers. comm.). He concluded that the pottery probably was not made by Africans. Chesapeake colonoware lacks specific technical and decorative attributes typically found in West African pottery of the period. Henry (1980), who made an extensive study of Colono-Indian ware attributes in a sample from twenty-three sites in Virginia, surveyed some of the West African archaeological literature and discovered that several formal and decorative attributes were shared by archaeologically recovered Colono-Indian pottery (and historic Pamunkey Indian pottery, discussed below) and some West African wares. She concluded, however, that such parallels were rare, and that attributes associated with West African pottery also were found among late prehistoric Indian wares of the region. While clear Native American and English influences could be seen in Chesapeake Colono-Indian wares, potential African derivations remained unclear.

Chesapeake Colono-Indian pottery has now been well documented in archaeological records ranging from the 1630s (Mouer and McLearen 1991) to the mid–nineteenth century (Parker and Hernigle 1990; Ryder 1990) and from ethnographic sources into the twentieth century.[2] The ware is nearly always a small part of the assemblage and is frequently associated with servants' and slaves' quarters. This observation led Noël Hume (1962; 1963:149, 283; 1966:45) to conclude that the pottery was a relatively cheap ware made on the Pamunkey Indian reservation and purchased primarily for servant and slave use.

## Ethnographic Background

Samples of Colono-Indian pottery have been collected for more than a century by ethnographers and archaeologists and by Pamunkey and Mattaponi Indians on and around the Virginia reservations; examples can be found in collections at the reservation museums, the Heye Foundation Museum of the American Indian, and the National Museum of Natural History. The manufacture of shell-tempered and non-tempered smoothed or burnished pottery by the historic Pamunkey is not a newly discovered phenomenon. Nineteenth- and early twentieth-century ethnographers described Pamunkey pottery and the potters' techniques of construction and firing. The Reverend E. A. Dalrymple visited the Pamunkey in the nineteenth century and returned with examples of their pottery, their potting clay, and the calcined mussel shells they used for temper.[3]

In 1877 Otis T. Mason wrote, "The most interesting feature of [the Pamunkey Indians'] present condition is the preservation of their ancient modes of pottery making. It will be news to some that the shells are calcined before mixing with the clay, and that one-third of the compound is triturated shell" (1877:627). Pollard also described Pamunkey pottery-making procedures: "Until recent years they engaged quite extensively in the making of pottery, which they sold to their white neighbors. . . . The clay used . . . is taken from the Potomac Formation of the geologic series, which yields valuable pottery clays at different localities in Virginia and Maryland" (Pollard 1894:17–19).

The preferences that Pamunkey demonstrated for Miocene marl clays and mussel (rather than oyster) shell for temper were traditions begun at least as early as A.D. 200–300 in this area (McLearen and Mouer 1989). In addition, Pollard described the pounding and sieving of clays; the burning, grinding, sieving, and mixing of mussel-shell temper; and the finishing, stone burnishing, and firing of the pots. Harrington (1908:406, cited in Henry 1980:22A) mentioned Pamunkey pottery making as well, stating that "the grandmothers of the present generation . . . made and sold large quantities of ware for domestic use to their white and negro neighbors." The pottery "was tempered and shaped by native methods, but the forms are evidently of mixed or European origin."

Six Pamunkey ceramic vessels held by the Smithsonian Institution's National Museum of Natural History were illustrated by Holmes (1903:152, pl. 136) in his monograph *Aboriginal Pottery in the Eastern United States*. The dates of manufacture of three vessels—two bowls (catalog numbers NMNH 31853, 31854) and a pipkin with lid (31851)—attributed to the Dalrymple collection are unknown, but someone noted on exterior surface of the pipkin that Dalrymple collected the vessel from the Pamunkey in 1861. Two of the vessels that can be positively attributed to Pollard's collection—a tripodal cup (165453) and a sora house (165460)— were made specifically for the Smithsonian, which registered them in 1892. The sixth specimen, a two-ended cup (167520), is labeled "Bradley," possibly indicating that it, too, was collected by Pollard from Terrell Bradby, one of his informants.

One of the present authors (Hodges) has examined all of these vessels except the sora house. Each of the three vessels from Dalrymple's collection was tempered with moderate amounts of mussel shell, burnished, and fired to a relatively hard body with a tan to light orange color. These vessels are very similar in paste, surface finish, and form (except for the pipkin lid) to the shell-tempered Colono-Indian ceramics described by Noël Hume (1962). The later specimens, the two different cups, were also tempered with mussel shell, but were only smoothed—not burnished—and were fired to a softer body of a brighter orange color.

The earlier vessels from the Dalrymple collection, however, suggest continuity between some seventeenth-century Colono-Indian ceramics from archaeological contexts and the Pamunkey-made wares collected in the nineteenth century. The pipkin, for example, is similar to a piece of seventeenth-century Colono-Indian ware from the Utopia Quarter site at Kingsmill (Kelso 1984b: fig. 130) and also resembles another vessel (now in collection of Colonial Williamsburg Foundation) excavated from ca. 1770–80 contexts at the Anthony Hay Cabinet Shop site (see fig. 5.1, bottom row, left). Furthermore, it is worth noting that Thomas Pettus, owner of the Utopia Quarter site, also owned at least one Indian slave (York Deeds, Wills, and Orders 2:130).

Frank G. Speck, the redoubtable ethnologist of the Eastern Woodland Indians, collected artifacts and oral histories from the Pamunkey reservation and surrounding community in the 1920s. He referred to early historic Pamunkey pottery as "Smooth ware," to distinguish it from the more typical stamped and impressed ceramics of the prehistoric period that were abundant in the area. He described "Smooth ware" as a smooth, clayey-paste, mussel-shell-tempered material and noted "numerous angular bottoms, parts of curved handles or lugs, legs and knobbed lids, together with evidence of flat bottoms and the exclusive lipped rim style, [which] are indications of a modification in form, bringing them [these vessel forms] into correspondence with the common European forms. . . . Comparing this material with the [19th-century] Pamunkey ware, we are forced to conclude that the later archaeological material [the "Smooth ware"] is transitional, forming the link between the pre-European and the modern pottery" (Speck 1928:402–4).

Speck's information on the nineteenth-century pottery was derived not only from collections in the Smithsonian and from publications such as Holmes's but from twentieth-century Pamunkey informants who had been involved in the manufacture and sale of the pottery in the previous century. Speck made note of the similarities between the "Smooth ware" and historically collected pottery and pottery found "from South Carolina to Delaware." He also detailed manufacturing methods, describing vessel-forming techniques that were identical to those used by the late prehistoric ancestors of Virginia's Indians (Speck 1928:411).

In the early 1940s the Pamunkey were visited by Theodore Stern, another ethnographer interested in their pottery manufacture who discussed the industry "as far back as the traditional memory of informants will go" (Stern 1951:iii). According to Stern, the traditional potting methods "may be considered as having been stable in practice from about the end of the eighteenth century to recent times." He described the vessel-building techniques in great detail, indicating that different building methods were used for different types of pots. He also described the making of "plugged" handles, a common feature of Chesapeake Colono-Indian ceramics. Wheaton, Friedlander, and Garrow (1983:229) have noted one attribute that differentiates what they called Yaughan (African-American) from Catawba (Native American) colonoware types from South Carolina: the application of handles. The handles are affixed to the surface of vessels in the former and inserted or plugged into the vessel wall in the latter.

Stern cataloged a wide variety of decorative elements, most of which also are found on the region's prehistoric pottery. These may have been "remembered" by the Pamunkey from their exposure to archaeological materials on the reservation. One nonprehistoric decorative method of note was "watch-wheel rouletting," an embellishment often found on the locally made tobacco pipes of the seventeenth century. After describing the method of stone burnishing, Stern stated that culinary vessels were not polished in this manner but were simply smoothed by rubbing the dried vessel with damp fingers. Archaeological assemblages of Colono-Indian ware from colonial Anglo-American sites frequently contain both smoothed and stone-burnished examples, as noted by Noël Hume in his definition of the ware.[4] Stern (1951:43) concluded that "the earliest models to influence the Indian ware" were seventeenth-century English colonial kitchen vessels of ceramic, wood, and metal. He mentions several pertinent examples: earthenware porringers, milk pans, bowls, pie plates, jugs, pipkins, cauldrons, metal three-legged frying pans, metal flat-bottomed tripodal cauldrons, and wooden platters. When stoves became common on the reservation (ca. 1880–90), he observed, "the legs of vessels hitherto useful in setting vessels upon the hearth coals, became impediments and were no longer made" (Stern 1951:47; see also Egloff and Potter 1982:114).

Although Stern searched for evidence of non-European influences on the Pamunkey potters, he found little. He felt that African-American influence was not present. He noted some Catawba influences but posited that the Pamunkey did not have "a receptive attitude" toward Catawba forms and potting techniques. Beyond a few decorative features and some tobacco pipe-manufacturing techniques, Pamunkey pottery shared very few attributes with Catawba pottery (Stern 1951:54–55).

## The Documentary Evidence

Historical data support the archaeological observation that Indians made ceramics and traded some of these to the colonists. In 1641 Edward Bestwick's probate inventory listed "3 old Indian bowles and 2 Indian trays" and noted that a debt of "two Indian bowls" was owed from the estate of James Davis (cited in Breen and Innes 1980:54). Other Eastern Shore inventories of the mid–seventeenth century included Indian pots, bowls, and kettles. In her survey of mid-seventeenth- through mid-eighteenth-century inventories from three Virginia counties, Mary Beaudry (1980) lists the following descriptive terms for vessels: Indian baskets, bowls, trays, trenchers, piggins, and pans. While some of these containers may have been made of wood or fiber, certainly "pans" and "kettles" refer to ceramic vessels. There can be no doubt about the nature and origin of the "earthen pans" purchased for the Governor's Mansion in Williamsburg on 3 March 1769 from "the Indians" (Governor Botetourt's account books, Colonial Williamsburg microfilm 1395, D 2700 FmL 6/3/20) nor of the "Indian pots" listed in some eighteenth-century merchants' inventories. In 1719 a probate inventory was prepared for the estate of William Tapptico, Jr., the "King of the Wicocomoco Indians." The record reveals that Tapptico and his wife, Elizabeth, had become completely dependent on European-made material goods. Even so, his inventory included three "Indian milkpanns" (Northumberland County Record Book, 1718–26, fols. 79–80, cited in Potter 1977).

Inventories from the Eastern Shore, the Northern Neck, and Henrico County also include references to Indian pots and pipes (for instance, see Farrar 1905:45; Northampton County Orders 9:25, 33, 99, 11:13; Accomac County Orders, 1676–78; Henrico County Deeds and Wills, 1671–73:41, 1688–97:235, all cited in Rountree 1990:132). One individual who died in 1667 had seventy-six "Indian pipes" in his inventory. There is a 1671 reference to one Indian named "John the Bowlmaker," perhaps a craftsman who produced wares for local consumption, although we do not know if his wares were made of ceramic or other materials (Accomac County Orders, Wills, etc., 1671–73:41, cited in Rountree 1990:132). An Indian named "Potter," of unknown gender, was a servant to John Wallis of lower Norfolk County in 1673 (Nugent 1977:131).[5]

In 1686 Durand Du Dauphiné noted that the Indian women living on the Rappahannock River in the vicinity of Portobago Bay made "pots, earthen vases and smoking pipes, the Christians buying these pots or vases fill them with Indian corn, which is the price of them" (Du Dauphiné [1687] 1934:153). Du Dauphiné was visiting Ralph Wormeley's plantation holdings on both sides of the river at Nanzattico near Portobago Bay and the Camden site (Hodges and McCartney 1985). Likewise, when Francis Louis Michel visited the Huguenot settlement at Manakintown in Powhatan County in 1702, he noted that the Monacan Indians frequently visited the settlement "bringing game, rum and smaller things. . . . They often bring pot-

tery and when desired fill it with corn" (Michel [1701–2] 1916:123). Later, in Williamsburg for the celebration of the accession of Queen Anne, Michel noted that the Indians who attended the festivities at the request of the governor brought skins and "a
large number of baskets. . . . Everything they bring is bought to send it as a present
to England. They also make tobacco pipes, very beautifully cut out and formed"
(Michel [1701–2] 1916:130).

That Virginians appreciated the quality of Indian pots and pipes can be seen also
in John Clayton's writings. He noted that the Indians "smoak in short pipes of their
own making having excellent clay. . . . They also make neat pots of the same clay
which will endure the fire for any common uses" (Bushnell 1907:31–44). A year later,
he wrote that he had found "veins of clay, admirable good to make Pots, Pipes or the
like of, and whereof I suppose the Indians make their Pipes and Pots, to boil their
Meat in, which they make very handsomely and will endure the Fire better then
most crucibles."

### Is There "Colono-African" Pottery in the Chesapeake?

Historical evidence that African-American slaves were manufacturing earthenwares
in Virginia and Maryland is lacking. Seventeenth-century writers scarcely took note
of Africans, but eighteenth- and nineteenth-century travelers' accounts and diaries
describe participation in numerous crafts and trades by African-American slaves in
the colonial and antebellum Chesapeake. These activities included the making of
quilts, baskets, musical instruments, and hand tools. A thriving tradition of alka-
line-glazed pottery has been well documented (Vlach 1978:76–96). African Americans were also housebuilders, blacksmiths, coopers, and cartwrights (Vlach 1978;
Glassie 1968).

Many slaves and free blacks were dominant in these trades, not only on plantations but also in urban environments of the post-Revolution period. African-American slaves and wage laborers worked as craftspeople in the salt-glazed stoneware
pottery manufactories of nineteenth-century Richmond and other cities, but no
historical accounts of a folk tradition of hand-built, unglazed earthenware ceramics manufacture have surfaced. Folkloristic accounts and artifacts documenting
African-American crafts, culture, and lifeways in the region have been collected and
described (see, for example, Fox-Genovese 1988; McDaniel 1982; Stampp 1956; Perdue et al.). Museum collections and published works attest to the products of
African-American men and women in the Chesapeake (see, for instance, Tyler-
McGraw and Kimball 1988). However, data on African-American manufacture of
materials even vaguely similar to Colono-Indian ceramics is virtually absent from
the record. It is doubtful that this is an oversight. It is more likely that although some
African-American slaves may have made utilitarian pottery on the plantations, such
a practice was not common.

Nor is there archaeological evidence for African-American manufacture of colonoware pottery in the Chesapeake. A few colonoware vessels suggesting African-American manufacture—if the arguments presented by Ferguson and others for South Carolina are accurate—have also been informally noted by Mary Ellen Hodges in the archaeological study collections of the Colonial Williamsburg Foundation. The paste of these ceramics recovered from Williamsburg and its environs is very sandy, unlike that of Courtland and Camden ceramics. One such vessel in the Colonial Williamsburg Foundation collection is a small globular jar with a constricted neck and everted rim similar in form to ceramics attributed to African-American manufacture in South Carolina (Wheaton, Friedlander, and Garrow 1983: figs. 73, 74). Mouer (1993) has described a West Indian vessel, made in a West African potting tradition, from early seventeenth-century contexts in Virginia. Recent discoveries from some late eighteenth- and nineteenth-century sites in northern Virginia have spurred more comparative research in the attempt to identify African-American ceramics in the Chesapeake.

Leland Ferguson (1980, 1992) has been at the forefront of the research into possible African-American production of colonoware pottery. After many years of study, he has concluded that much of the Carolina low-country pottery was manufactured by African-American slaves. Ferguson and others have noted that a considerable amount of trade pottery was manufactured by southeastern Indians. This pottery is known in South Carolina as river burnished (Ferguson 1989) or Catawba ware (Garrow and Wheaton 1989). Two important sites that have contributed much to the discussion of the possible African manufacture of colonoware in South Carolina are the Yaughan and Curriboo plantations (Wheaton and Garrow 1985; Wheaton, Friedlander, and Garrow 1983; Garrow and Wheaton 1989). Even here, Amy Friedlander (1985:219) noted that listings of Indian or "mustee" (part-Indian) slaves at these plantations occur in the probate inventories. There is compelling evidence of African involvement in colonoware production in South Carolina, but given the historical fact that in the early eighteenth century fully one-third of all slaves in the low country were Indians (Nash 1974:130; Wood 1989:38, table 1, 46–47), ascribing these vessels to potters of one ethnicity or another is a dicey proposition at best, and one that requires careful study of artifacts traits and pottery-making technologies. Low-country archaeologists may be ahead of their Chesapeake colleagues in this regard.

Nonetheless, there is ample evidence that Indians made ceramic vessels and tobacco pipes in the Chesapeake and that some of these objects were manufactured for sale or trade to colonists. Archaeological and ethnographic evidence supports the view that Indians utilized Colono-Indian ceramics on their reservations. There is formal evidence that most Colono-Indian wares derived from late prehistoric Indian manufacturing technology, and that some of the attributes we associate with

Colono-Indian ceramics were developed before the founding of Jamestown and St. Mary's City. The regional variations in Colono-Indian wares mirror regional variations in the distributions of major Indian ethnic or linguistic groups, as well as variations in their well-documented protohistoric pottery technologies. Given the wide geographic and temporal range of Colono-Indian ceramics in Chesapeake historical sites, we conclude that *some* Colono-Indian-like pottery may have been manufactured by African-American slaves; however, no current evidence appears to contradict the well-established interpretation that the vast majority of colonoware in the Chesapeake is as Noël Hume first described it: the product of local Native Americans.

*Postcolonial Colonoware in the Chesapeake*

While most of the discussion concerning Colono-Indian ceramics in the Chesapeake has been focused on the colonial period, recent finds of similar ceramics in early and mid-nineteenth-century contexts have stimulated renewed discussion and investigation concerning the makers of these materials. Other than the documented nineteenth-century Pamunkey pottery and the VDHR-excavated collection of Colono-Indian ceramics from an early nineteenth-century trash pit at Pamunkey, there had been little evidence that Colono-Indian ceramics survived the explosive expansion of American redware and salt-glazed stoneware manufacture that came with independence. Recent excavations in the piedmont and northern Virginia have changed that view.

Late eighteenth-century contexts have produced a variety of "colono" ceramics from the "House for Families" site at George Washington's Mount Vernon. Surveys have turned up "colono" pottery in what appear to be early nineteenth-century contexts in the Virginia piedmont along the James River in Cumberland County (Mouer 1991e). Even more surprising is the discovery of colonoware in nineteenth-century contexts from as many as ten sites located near Manassas, Virginia. Colonoware pottery has also been recovered from the site of a house once occupied by free blacks. Nine of these post-Revolutionary-period sites have been investigated under the general direction of Stephen Potter for the National Park Service, National Capital Region. At the sites of Pohoke and Portici in Prince William County, Parker and Hernigle (1990) reported that the slave quarter contexts produced considerable quantities of colonoware ceramics (including smoking pipes) deposited during three distinct phases of plantation occupation between 1737 and 1863. Parker and Hernigle conclude that these examples may have been produced by African Americans and offer as support for this inference that "the earliest date associated with these wares is approximately 60 years after the last indigenous Native Americans resided in this area of the Virginia Piedmont" (Parker and Hernigle 1990:232). The authors refer to these materials as "African colono-ware."

Most historians and archaeologists have assumed that Indians were largely gone from both the piedmont and the adjacent Shenandoah Valley before their occupation by English and German settlers in the eighteenth century, but this is a notion that needs rethinking (Mouer 1991f). Rountree (1990) has demonstrated the previously untapped wealth of documents pertaining to the tidewater Indians of the nineteenth and twentieth centuries, and her work should chasten others into withholding judgment about areas of Indian occupation until a thorough review of written and oral historical sources can be made. Even today, there remains, in piedmont Virginia, a relict Native American community whose members identify themselves as Monacans. Until local sources have been carefully reviewed, the assertion that Indians had "disappeared" from the northern Virginia piedmont must be taken as an informed opinion, rather than a studied conclusion. Prince William County is close to sites of known nineteenth-century tidewater Indian communities—notably enclaves of Rappahannock, Mattaponi, and Pamunkey peoples. As we know little of the marketing procedures used by Indian groups to sell their pottery wares in the nineteenth century, conclusions ruling out Indian manufacture of these materials are at best premature.[6]

In an excavation sponsored by the Virginia Department of Transportation, Robin Ryder (1990) discovered colonoware vessels very similar to the Portici and Pohoke finds in slave quarter deposits at the Monroe farm site, a middling plantation near Manassas in Prince William County. The context of the materials places them in the first and second quarters of the nineteenth century. As with the other late northern Virginia examples, there appear to be different potting traditions represented at the site. These sites in northern Virginia may hold the evidence of an African pottery-making tradition, but more detailed analyses of all these assemblages is badly needed before we can make definitive conclusions.

## Chesapeake Pipes: Background and Definition

Matthew Emerson's (1988) dissertation provides the most comprehensive treatment to date of one of the most fascinating artifact groups found in the seventeenth-century Chesapeake. These are the locally produced decorated tobacco-smoking pipes, which some archaeologists refer to informally as "colono" pipes, largely because many of them resemble Colono-Indian pottery in being low-fired earthenware often finished by smoothing or burnishing, and because it has been inferred that many of these pipes were made by local Indians. Emerson has selected the less ethnically committed nomen of *Chesapeake* pipes for these objects. Chesapeake pipes are interesting primarily because they are very frequently decorated and thus provide a rare example of a coherent folk decorative arts tradition from the seventeenth-century Chesapeake. These pipes are ubiquitous in archaeological sites of Virginia and Maryland and are found in contexts as early as ca. 1608.

There is no doubt that some pipes were made on English sites in the seventeenth-century Chesapeake: pipe-making evidence has been found at St. Mary's City, Maryland (Miller 1983, 1991); at the Maine site on the Governor's Land in James City County, Virginia (Outlaw 1990); at the Hatch site in Prince George County, Virginia (L. B. Gregory, pers. comm.); at Claremont Manor in Surry County, Virginia (L. B. Gregory, pers. comm.); and at the Curles plantation site in Henrico County, Virginia (Mouer 1990a, 1990b, 1991b). Pipe-making molds were listed in occasional probate inventories and depositions (Westmoreland Co. Deeds and Patents, 1653–59:47). Historical and ethnographic evidence suggests that Indians also made pipes, which they sometimes sold or traded to English colonists. The question is, who is it that is speaking to us so eloquently through the often-exuberant and finely executed pipe decoration that has come to symbolize the seventeenth-century Chesapeake?

While Emerson's study of Chesapeake pipes is the most exhaustive, it is not the first. Papers by Harrington (1951), Henry (1979), Miller (1983), Binford (1964, 1965), Pawson (1969), Winfree (1969), Heite (1972), Mitchell (1976), and Pogue (1987), among others, have all dealt with these pipes in some detail. The problem of who made the pipes—ethnically speaking—was first articulated by J. C. "Pinky" Harrington who in his 1951 article wrote that "one of the most intriguing problems [of Jamestown archaeology] is that of the hand-molded pipes. . . . Many are obviously of Indian manufacture, but some may have been made by the settlers following Indian styles and techniques. To further complicate the problem, some of these pipes which are most Indianlike in character, have well-formed English initials incorporated in the bowl decoration. Is this a case of the Indian copying a European idea or was the maker an 'educated' Indian; or did a white man make an 'Indian' pipe and put his initials on it?" (Harrington 1951:n.p.)

Emerson studied only the decorated examples. His typology is derived from a sorting of pipe bowls from numerous sites into nine types (1988:79–99). His study focused upon decorative elements that include the patterned use of denticulate lines, stamped characters, and white-fill inlays that he suggests was derived from a generalized West African tradition (see chap. 4 in this volume). For Emerson the evidence is clear that Africans introduced this decorative style in the making of Chesapeake pipes, and he reaches this conclusion on the basis of the following observations:

1. He believes that nearly all the pipes were made in standard English molds. To Emerson, the combination of English pipe-making molds and African decoration symbolizes the nature of seventeenth-century life on the Chesapeake frontier.

2. The pipes are typically characterized by *pointillé* or "denticulate" decoration—repeated patterns of dots and dashes. Emerson asserts that this is a common African technique but not a common Indian or European technique.

3. Some pipes are also characterized by white infill or inlay within the stamped or *pointillé* decoration. That is, the impressed decorative elements are filled with white material (possibly lime or pipe clay) against the terra-cotta or brown background of the body clay. Again, this technique is purportedly common in West Africa but, according to Emerson, uncommon in Indian or European decorative arts. Likewise, Emerson states that the stamp devices used on many Chesapeake pipes are of African figures and are distinct from stamps used in English or Indian arts.

4. Many of the motifs themselves are West African in origin. Here Emerson focuses on a limited number of rouletted motifs and a few stamped ones and the "grammars" (culturally derived factors that influence how an object is made, used, or perceived) with which these are assembled. These, he concludes, are neither Indian nor English but have clear parallels in West African art.

### Mold-made or Hand-modeled?

Let's examine each of these conclusions in some detail, starting with point 1. Harrington (1951) felt that the decorated, locally made pipes were not formed in molds, as European mass-produced pipes typically were. Henry (1979) studied manufacture and decorative techniques of white and brown (or terra-cotta) hand-made and mold-made pipes from the Chesapeake through a binocular microscope. She determined that it was possible to distinguish molded from hand-built pipes, particularly by inspecting the insides of pipe bowls where makers rarely took the time and effort to remove manufacturing scars. Henry also concluded that the locally made types which are referred to as roulette or *pointillé* decorated were generally hand-modeled, not cast in molds. Her conclusion was that these pipes probably were produced by local Indian craftsmen or craftswomen. Similar conclusions were reached by Miller (1983) and Pogue (1987). Plain pipes and some pipes stamped with English motifs (e.g., Tudor roses, hearts and flowers, trefoils), and sometimes made on an "agatized" clay body made by mixing two or three clay colors, were produced in molds identical to the more commonly found imported English and Dutch white ball-clay pipes. These correspond primarily with Emerson's types 1 and 3 (1988:79, 97). On this point, Henry and Emerson are in apparent agreement: plain pipes (sometimes with simple English-style rouletted rim bands) and some mold-made pipes stamped with clearly European motifs may be the product of one or more Euro-American pipe makers living in the colonies.

Because Emerson, Harrington, Henry, Miller, and Pogue studied many of the same pipes, this contradictory finding concerning the method of manufacture suggests that more research is needed. The point, however, may be of only minor significance. Recent experiments by L. B. Gregory (pers. comm.) have reproduced

Chesapeake pipes from Virginia clays, with the simplest of homemade molds and low-temperature firing; the technology to produce pipe molds was well within the grasp of Native Americans, African Americans, and European Americans in the seventeenth century.

### Decorative Techniques: Rouletting and Small Decorative Stamp Devices

Emerson's use of the term *pointillé* or *denticulate* decoration refers to the same decorative technique as *dentate* or *rouletted* used by other archaeologists in the region. All these terms describe repeated small punctations such as might be made with a serrated rocker stamp or with a toothed wheel, such as a small watch gear or roulette. Potter has produced replicas of the rouletted decoration on pipes from the Camden site with a Miocene shark's tooth recovered from the De Shazo site directly across the Rappahannock River. The use of fossil shark's teeth to decorate Chesapeake pipes was suggested nearly four decades ago by Stewart (1954:4). Some *pointillé* decoration appears to have been made by pressing a twisted cord into the plastic clay or by individual punctations, perhaps made with a small stick or straw. It is clear that a number of different tools and techniques were used to produce the dotted effects, and future studies should attempt to distinguish among them more carefully. For the present, however, the terms *pointillé*, *rouletted*, *denticulate*, or *dentate* are used interchangeably. It is not the method of applying the decoration but the very existence of dentate, rouletted, or *pointillé* decoration itself that Emerson sees as African.[7] This is an unfortunate misapprehension. Examples of typical rouletted Chesapeake pipes are illustrated in figure 5.2.

Several early studies of rouletted pipes were conducted by prehistorians who had recovered them from Indian villages and camps. To a prehistorian, dentate stamping is not at all out of place on an Indian tobacco pipe. In fact, dentate stamping of great variety—usually applied with a carved rocker stamp—is found throughout eastern North America on pipes and pottery from at least as early as the middle Woodland period (ca. 500 B.C.–A.D. 800). Pipes with various types of rouletted or dentate decoration have been recovered from many prehistoric contexts in Virginia, North Carolina, Maryland, Pennsylvania, Delaware, New Jersey, and New York. Dentate motifs were extremely common in pottery and pipe decoration for many centuries before the arrival of Europeans. An excellent example of a Chesapeake pipe from a prehistoric context is an example from the Fout site in northwestern Virginia. It has been, for many years, on public display at the Virginia Department of Historic Resources (fig. 5.3). A number of sites of the Luray and Montgomery complexes in the Potomac piedmont and upper Shenandoah Valley have produced roulette-decorated pipes, and these reveal strong similarities not only to Chesapeake pipes from colonial tidewater sites but also to Monongahela and related Fort Ancient complex sites of the upper Ohio drainage and to Luray sites of the Potomac and Shenandoah valleys in Virginia (fig. 5.4). The Luray, Monongahela, and Fort Ancient complexes often are attributed to the protohistoric Central Algonquian peoples (e.g., Shawnee). Interactions between this large group of related cultures and the Potomac Creek peoples of the tidewater have long been acknowledged (Schmitt 1952; MacCord, Schmitt, and Slattery 1957). Such interactions apparently included trade in pottery and decorated tobacco pipes.

Margaret Blaker's (1963:27–29, pl. 10b) analysis of the aboriginal pipes from the Townsend site in Delaware lists prehistoric, protohistoric, and early contact-period Indian sites in the basins of the Susquehanna, Shenandoah, Delaware, Potomac, Rappahannock, and Pamunkey Rivers where pipes decorated with fine dentate or rouletted designs had been found as of nearly thirty years ago. Good examples can be seen in the collections from the Hughes, Winslow, Shepard, Keyser, and Potomac Creek sites, all of which are curated by the Smithsonian Institution. There is no doubt that the Hughes, Winslow, Keyser, and Shepard sites are prehistoric with no contact components (Manson, MacCord, and Griffin 1944; MacCord, Schmitt, and Slattery 1957; Slattery and Woodward, n.d.; Stearns 1940).

In describing decorated pipes from the Townsend site, Blaker observed:

> On all 6 specimens, zones are filled in with parallel lines of very fine linear dentate stamping or fine dentate rouletting.... [T]he quality of the dentated impressions varies....
>
> The question of how these impressions were made naturally comes to mind. This is not the comparatively coarse dentate stamping so well known on Middle Woodland pottery vessels and there applied with serrated bone or wooden linear stamps or roulettes.... It is conceivable that some of the more irregular work may have been done with the edge of a common clam shell.... The finer and more even impressions, however, seem to imply the use of toothed metal edges. (1963:29)

Blaker goes on to speculate that the pipes that are apparently decorated with "toothed metal edges" could be copies of mechanically rouletted European pipes. On the other hand, she notes, the European pipes may well have adopted rouletted band decoration as a simplified and mechanized form of earlier aboriginal designs. The "comparatively coarse" dentate rocker stamping to which Blaker refers is very common on Hopewellian, Point Peninsula, and Owasco-related ceramics of the Northeast and the Middle Atlantic regions. In fact, much of the dentate stamping on Chesapeake pipes from colonial sites is virtually identical to the dentate rocker-stamp technique of prehistory.

The largest single collection of Virginia Algonquian clay pipes is from the Potomac Creek site, a palisaded protohistoric- and possibly early historic-period village of the "Patawomeke" (Potomac) Indians located in Stafford County, Virginia (Potter 1989:161, 171; Schmitt 1965:14–15). The 295 specimens include examples of dentate decorative techniques, as well as smaller numbers of pipes with incision, punctation, cord-wrapping, and pinching designs. The motifs range from horizontals, bound diagonals, and infilled triangles to line designs and other geometric shapes, as well as zoomorphic and anthropomorphic figures. The decorative motifs on the pipes mimic some of the more popular motifs on prehistoric Potomac Creek pottery and are also similar to the decoration on Chesapeake pipes from colonial contexts.

The Accokeek Creek site (Stephenson, Ferguson, and Ferguson 1963) also contains examples that parallel the colonial Chesapeake pipes. Emerson argues that this is one of several sites with mixed historic and prehistoric components, from which archaeologists have mistakenly concluded that the pipes were prehistoric. Contemporary interpretation has ruled out the possibility that Accokeek is a historic site, thereby negating any possible African influence on the pipes from that site (Potter 1980:4; Dent 1984:15–16).

Kent (1984:147–51) has reported roulette-decorated pipes—including the familiar running deer and star motifs—in Pennsylvania Susquehannock sites. One rouletted pipe with a star motif was excavated at the Schultz-Funk site from a clear context of ca. 1550 or earlier (based on its association in a trash pit with well-dated Shenks Ferry materials). Kent notes that the style of pipe is more typical of the Maryland and Virginia tidewater Indians. Gardner (1986) made the same observation concerning a rouletted pipe from Cabin Run, in the northern Shenandoah Valley. This specimen comes from a context radiocarbon-dated to the fourteenth century.

The Koehler site, a prehistoric Dan River complex site in the southwestern Virginia piedmont, also produced rouletted pipes (fig. 5.5). Coleman et al. (n.d.) quote Joffre Coe (an authority on the prehistory of the Carolina piedmont) as suggesting that this and similar pipes found in the Carolina piedmont were carried along Indian trade routes from the Virginia tidewater. Upon examining the Koehler site pipe, Coe concluded that the fine rouletting must have been made with a watch wheel or other European-introduced metal object. The Koehler site dates—A.D. 1305 +/-70, A.D. 1340 +/-70, A.D. 1405 +/-55—seem to belie this notion. Rouletted pipes, some in association with human burials, were reported from a possibly related late Woodland component at the Mussel Shell Island site in the piedmont near the Virginia-North Carolina border (Wells 1971).

Perhaps the earliest example of a *pointillé*-decorated pipe in the Chesapeake is one recovered from middle Woodland II contexts (ca. A.D. 200–800) at the Great Neck site (44Vb7) in Virginia Beach (Hodges, n.d.). This fragment, illustrated in figure 5.6, exhibits simple lines of small punctations but is nonetheless reminiscent—or perhaps we should say anticipatory—of the rouletted decoration found on pipes of the late Woodland and colonial periods, including the Chesapeake pipes excavated from sites of English plantations and towns. That this style of decoration was typical in Chesapeake prehistory is also well illustrated by two beautiful bone pins excavated from similarly dated contexts at the same site (fig. 5.7).

Archaeological evidence suggests that the production and trade of such pipes was widespread centuries before the founding of Jamestown. Throughout the late Woodland period, from Delaware to North Carolina, the most common smoking pipe of coastal Algonquians and their neighbors to the west was a relatively small, clay, conical-bowled, obtuse- or right-angled elbow pipe; these are frequently decorated in dentate techniques, with motifs similar or identical to those of the colonial Chesapeake pipes.

In dealing with stamped devices, Emerson states that stamping on Chesapeake pipes differs from English or Indian stamping but is very similar to devices used to stamp West African pottery, metalwork, etc. (Emerson 1988:131). Facing the page of his dissertation on which this statement is made, and illustrating the article on Emerson's dissertation in the *New York Times* (12 July 1988), are several pipes with stamped and rouletted decoration. Yet the circular stamp devices on the pipes are virtually identical to circular punctates commonly found on prehistoric pottery and pipes in Virginia and Maryland. Prehistorians refer to this as "reed" punctation, because the stamped design appears to have been made from a small hollow reed. Small circular stamped designs are also common decorative elements on seventeenth-century English pottery and furniture. Emerson uses the example of lines of stamped punctations surmounting and underlying three rows of horizontal lines—illustrated on an Asante pot (see fig. 4.8)—as a premier example of Chesapeake-African parallelism. Very similar decorative use of punctate stamps enclosing dentate lines is extremely common on late prehistoric pottery in Virginia and Maryland.

Rouletting is also found in English decorative arts. While rouletting does not commonly appear on English pottery in Virginia and Maryland, it must be remembered that this material represents only a small subset of the rich decorative arts traditions of northern Europe. Punctate and rouletted designs can be found among the varieties of decoration not only on pottery but on metalwork, furniture, silver, leather, and other materials. Rouletting on pottery appeared in England as early as the Roman period and persisted until the nineteenth century (see Oswald et al. 1982:171, fig. 139).

Many of the types of decoration occurring on the Chesapeake pipes are also found on imported European pipes, albeit in slightly different form. Rouletted bands occur on many imported seventeenth-century (and later) European pipes, and stamped figures occur on the heels and—in the case of decorated Dutch pipes—on stems and bowls as well. One common seventeenth-century Dutch or French pipe stamped motif is the fleur-de-lis (see fig. 5.8 for a mid-seventeenth-century example). The trefoils comprised of lines and dots often stamped on the stems of Chesapeake pipes (fig. 5.9) could be viewed as attempts to copy the fleur-de-lis motif, or perhaps the ermine symbol of royalty from heraldic design (fig. 5.10). Another type of English trefoil—the club of a playing-card deck—is to this day stamped and infilled with white as a trademark on the stems of a popular brand of briar tobacco pipes. Rouletted and stamped decoration is, therefore, as much a part of the seventeenth-century European and Native American decorative arts vocabularies as it is African, and the presence of these techniques on pipes in the Chesapeake cannot be used to ascribe ethnicity to the pipe makers.

Although Emerson illustrates seventeenth-century African pipes decorated with small floral stamped motifs similar to those on Chesapeake pipes (Emerson 1988:121), identical small floral stamps occur not only on tobacco pipes but on furniture, leather, and other items of English decorative arts in the seventeenth century. Small circular stamps and punctations are common on prehistoric Indian examples; however, the floral stamps (Tudor roses and asters) appear only after European contact. The appearance of very similar stamps on seventeenth-century African pipes is suggestive, but floral motifs of various kinds appear very early on Dutch tobacco pipes. The common denominator between African and Chesapeake pipes may well be northern European stamps, a point noted by Emerson (1988:159 n.23). Still, although the floral element may be new, the use of these small devices is not substantially different from the use of circular stamps on prehistoric Indian pipes.

*White Infill (or Inlay)*

Emerson has found the white-infill technique common in West Africa on diverse forms including pottery, woodwork, and calabash decoration. He acknowledges that white inlay was used in some historic Iroquoian and seventeenth-century English contexts but argues strongly that this technique is clearly African-derived. Here is where Emerson makes his strongest argument concerning technique. However, it appears that he overstates the importance of white inlay in Chesapeake pipes. Only a small percentage of pipes exhibit this white infill, although it is possible that others once had it but have lost it. Although white infilling is not known to have been widely used in Native American decoration in this area, it does occur in some pipe decoration from prehistoric Indian village contexts. For example, one pipe in the collections of the Virginia Department of Historic Resources, from the Bowman site in Shenandoah County (MacCord 1964), contains a classic rouletted running deer motif with white infill (see fig. 5.4). This assemblage dates no later than the fifteenth or sixteenth century (based on associated ceramic types and the lack of European trade goods).

Use of white inlay in English pottery was known. Cistercian and Cistercian-like wares use stamped and applied devices in white on a dark background. English and Dutch slipwares use white clay on a dark background to make dotted lines and arches that appear very similar to the lozenge motif on the Ashanti pot illustrated by Emerson. Clifton-Taylor (1972:266) describes a seventeenth-century English tile-making industry in which red-clay floor tiles were stamped with inlays filled with white slip clay. Medieval encaustic floor tiles used white inlay at least as early as the thirteenth century (see Wheeler 1940:231–51), and similar decorative techniques were in use well into the nineteenth century, for example, in products from the Chailey Pottery in Sussex (see Brears 1974:71). Furthermore, white inlays occur commonly on pipes that Emerson accepts as the work of a Dutch or English craftsperson (Emerson 1988:138). The combination of rouletted or *pointillé* decoration and white infill is yet another characteristic of Chesapeake pipes that African, Native American, and European arts repertories all have in common.

## Decorative Motifs

In his dissertation Emerson produced a long catalog of decorative motifs and asserted the one-to-one correspondence of the grammars of their use with the decorative motifs on Chesapeake pipes. Most of the decoration is simple and basically geometric or linear in nature. Nothing in Emerson's arguments about the grammars used to assemble these lines, triangles, curves, and diamonds convinces us that the language they speak is necessarily African. Let us look at those motifs which, according to Emerson, offer the most convincing Chesapeake-West African parallels.

### HANGING TRIANGLES

Emerson is convinced of the African traditional origins of decorated Chesapeake pipes in large part because he found numerous examples of what he calls the "hanging triangles" motif in both localities (Emerson 1988:142–44). In his figure 46 (1988:146), he compares the two Chesapeake pipes illustrated to an elaborately decorated Nigerian calabash. The hanging triangles on the pipe are created of dentate lines that "hang," or point downward, from a band of linear punctations or rouletting around the rim of the pipe bowl. The calabash, too, is embellished with a variety of triangular designs, including some which appear to hang from linear elements. This motif, concludes Emerson, is clearly West African, even though he admits that "triangle designs do appear on some Late Woodland Chesapeake Indian pottery" (1988:142). There is probably no more common decorative motif on late Woodland Chesapeake Indian pottery than hanging triangles, often executed exactly as they appear on Emerson's examples. A few very typical examples are illustrated in figure 5.11. The Cabin Run site pipe described by Gardner (1986) is decorated with the hanging triangle motif and comes from a context carbon-dated to the fourteenth century.

The Quadruped Motif

One of the most common and long-recognized central decorative figures on Chesapeake pipes is known as the "running deer" motif (figs. 5.2, 5.4, 5.12). To avoid formulating premature conclusions about the identity of these zoomorphic figures, Emerson calls this the "quadruped" motif. He presents a good selection of quadrupeds from Chesapeake pipes (Emerson 1988:127, fig. 39). His figure 40 (1988:128) contains drawings of three similar quadrupeds from West African decorative arts. One of the Virginia examples has, instead of the usual short earlike forms, a long straight pair of what might be interpreted as antlers.

What do we make of these quadrupeds? Emerson agrees that the "original inspiration for quadruped pipes was probably Indian art" (Emerson 1988:144). He then ascribes this inspiration specifically to Susquehannock Indians and gives as the reason for the lack of this motif on prehistoric pipes the absence of Susquehannock in the region before the seventeenth century. How the Susquehannock came to be credited is difficult to understand, as is Emerson's assertion that the motif is absent on prehistoric pipes. The pipe from the Bowman site provides but one example to the contrary. Emerson notes the occurrence of two quadrupeds figured in shell on a garment in the Ashmolean Museum collection known as "Powhatan's mantle" and thought to be the cloak given by Powhatan to Christopher Newport in 1608 (see fig 4.5 in this volume).

In addition to artifactual evidence, several contemporary observers noted the use of animal symbols by Indians. Beverley ([1705] 1968) describes the use of "a sort of heiroglyphick, or representation of birds, beasts, or other things, shewing their different meaning by the various forms describ'd and by the different positions of the figures." Likewise, Hugh Jones ([1724] 1956:60) noted that the Indians "have certain heiroglyphical methods of characterizing things; an instance whereof I have seen upon the side of a tree where the bark was taken off. There was drawn something like a deer and a river, *with certain strokes and dashes*; the deer looking down the river." Much earlier, John Lederer ([1671] 1966:4), in describing Indians' picture writing, made special note that swiftness was denoted by the symbol of a stag. These and other remarks in the seventeenth- and eighteenth-century literature describe the "emblems" and "signs" used by the local Indians to identify themselves. The "running stag," the "standing stag," and other animal symbols are common motifs of English heraldry as well. One Englishman of the mid–seventeenth century observed the symbols on Native American shields and noted their similarities to English heraldic designs, prompting him to write a book on the universality of heraldry and its symbolism (Gibbon 1970, cited in Fischer 1989:306 n.1).

That the stylized quadruped might exist as a decorative motif in any culture that lives in proximity to quadrupeds should be self-evident. While the unusual long-horned quadrupeds depicted on a few pipes do appear to be similar not only to African animals but also to their folk art representations, others are obviously variants of the running deer motif, which is indisputably of Native Virginia origin.

## KWARDATAS AND DIAMONDS

According to Emerson the kwardata motif—a band of diamond figures formed in the negative space between groups of horizontal lines—shows "one of the most exact representations of a West African decorative motif and design that appears on Chesapeake pipes" (1988:148). Emerson compares the kwardata motif decoration found on the rim of a Nigerian beer pot to several Chesapeake pipes depicting kwardatas (see figs. 4.9 and 4.10 in this volume). He describes one pipe from the T. Gray Haddon site in King William County, Virginia (Emerson 1988:152), which includes both prehistoric and seventeenth-century Indian occupations (Winfree 1967:25). Emerson believes that the historic component at the Haddon site has been misidentified by other archaeologists as an Indian site, a mistake he feels is often made by researchers dealing with mixed components. In fact, many of the ceramic vessels and other artifacts from the site (including the large assemblage of decorated pipes) as well as its location in the heart of seventeenth-century Pamunkey-Mattaponi territory (and eighteenth-, nineteenth-, and twentieth-century Pamunkey-Mattaponi territory for that matter) convinces us that there certainly is a seventeenth-century Indian component to this site. The "few scraps of glass, less than a dozen hand-forged nails, [and] a couple of kaolin pipe fragments" described by Winfree (1967:10) could easily have been left by Native American occupants.

In Emerson's two illustrated examples of the kwardata on a Chesapeake pipe from St. Mary's City, Maryland (1988:151, fig. 49a, 153, fig. 50a), it is clear that the design has been made by impressing a twisted cord into the clay. This is among the most common decorative techniques used on middle and late Woodland prehistoric Indian pottery and pipes throughout eastern North America. Given the simplicity of such a design, we feel it cannot be considered typical of any single folk art heritage; however, the use of cord impression is clearly a Native American technique and is not included among the African decorative methods described by Emerson. These designs, on which Emerson pins his argument, are not necessarily African.

The rouletted pipe bowl depicted in figure 5.13 was recovered from the Great Neck site in Virginia Beach, where late Woodland features have been carbon-dated to A.D. 1330 +/-80 and A.D. 1510 +/-50 (Hodges, n.d.). The earlier date was obtained on a burial feature which contained in the pit fill a pipe fragment with a variation of the kwardata design. The design consists of three linear series of repeated triangles, rather than diamonds, formed in the negative space between groups of rouletted lines. This may not be a kwardata, but it is nonetheless conceptually very close to the Chesapeake pipe examples given by Emerson as typical of Nigerian decoration in Virginia.

Bands of diamonds, executed in *pointillé* technique (as well as in incising or other methods), are a common form of decoration on Indian pottery. Bands of diamonds—again, executed in *pointillé* —can be seen on the previously mentioned pair of fine bone pins recovered from middle Woodland II (ca. A.D. 200–800) contexts at the Great Neck site in Virginia Beach (Hodges, n.d.). The exuberant decoration on these pins is quite similar to much of the decoration on typical Chesapeake pipestems (see fig. 5.7). Yet another variation on the diamond shape occurs prominently in an example from the Thorogood site, a colonial occupation in Virginia, which Emerson illustrates in his figure 46b (1988:143), redrawn here as figure 5.14B. This line-filled diamond or fish shape, with lines extending beyond its vertices, is very similar to figures on both ceramic pipes and catlinite peace pipes and plates recovered from Oneota (seventeenth and eighteenth centuries) culture sites of the northern Great Plains (fig. 5.14A). There it is interpreted as a "plume" or "feather" symbol (Logan 1976:125). Could it be that such simple symbols just happen to look alike, or could a symbol on midwestern peace pipes have been adopted by Chesapeake dwellers of the seventeenth century? If the latter, who would be more likely to adopt the symbol, African slaves or Indians?

## CIPHERS, HERALDRY, AND OTHER MOTIFS

It is possible to see many of the rouletted or stamped motifs on Chesapeake pipes as local attempts to copy symbols of European heraldry. Many of the Chesapeake pipe motifs and figures could be viewed as renderings of the birth-order heraldic devices. Could Emerson's lozenge be the English crescent (second son)? Could trefoils be the sign of a sixth son or, perhaps, the ermine, symbol of royal arms? Some stamps that are very similar to heraldic roses (seventh son), molines (eighth son), and octofoils (ninth son) can be found in Emerson's excellent illustrated catalog of Chesapeake pipe motifs and figures. Some of the most complex motifs certainly represent English ships or boats, as Emerson has pointed out. Initials or ciphers, possibly copied from signets or seals, occur as well (fig. 5.15). Small floral and starlike impressions often appear along with ciphers and heraldic symbols on seventeenth-century English bottle seals, signet rings, and stamp seals. At least a percentage of the decoration on Chesapeake pipes might be interpreted as copies of armorial designs, decorations, and makers' (or owners') marks from some of the more elaborate European trade pipes, as well as seals and signets in common use during the period. We do not feel it is possible to determine from these latter designs, when they appear on Chesapeake pipes, whether they were produced by Indians, Africans, or the English.

## Do Chesapeake Pipes Speak with African Grammars?

Emerson has pointed to interesting parallels between some Chesapeake pipe art and West African decorative motifs (mostly from materials much more recent than the seventeenth century). These parallels beg for further study and, as Emerson has asserted, may represent some of the earliest African-made, or African-influenced, folk art in North America. Nonetheless, the basic form of the pipes is American Indian—what prehistorians call the elbow pipe—and its use in eastern North America is a thousand or more years old. The decorative technique of rouletting or *pointillé* occurs aboriginally in great variety and includes examples made with individual punctations, impressed cords, the serrated edges of fossil shark's teeth or shells, and carved dentate stamps. Like the pipe form itself, *pointillé* decoration was in use for at least a millennium before the founding of Jamestown. Many of the decorative motifs can be found in prehistoric Indian and contemporary English and Dutch decorative arts traditions. While some of the decorative motifs may have been African-inspired, Emerson's conclusion that the Chesapeake pipes were made primarily by Africans is one we do not share.

### Social Context of Craft Production in the Chesapeake

Deetz explains the rise of what he believes is African slave-made "colonoware" in the late seventeenth-century Chesapeake by reference to well-documented changing social relations between Africans and English at that time. Between ca. 1680 and the end of the century, racial slavery became institutionalized. The numbers of Africans in the colonies increased immensely, and various statutes began to define slaves as property and slavery as a lifetime status (see Morgan 1975; McCusker and Menard 1985; Craven 1971b). Deetz draws upon Dell Upton's (1986) premise that at the end of the seventeenth century servants were removed from the house to separate quarters, and that this reflects the cognitive and structural dimensions of changing social relations that accompanied a shift in Africans' status from indentured servitude to chattel slavery. In their separate quarters slaves now had the opportunity and perhaps the need to provide more completely for themselves. Thus, a folk pottery industry developed.[8]

Emerson looks to the very same institutionalization of slavery to explain the decline of the decorated pipe tradition at the end of the seventeenth century. In this view the slaves' removal to separate quarters (and a more distant social relationship with their masters) denied them access to English pipe molds and inhibited the development of a once-thriving craft. If the decorated pipes were not made in molds, or if simple molding technology was available to anyone who wanted to make pipes, then this explanation has little to recommend it, and the contradiction between Deetz and Emerson becomes even more baffling. How could the removal of slaves to separate quarters lead to the freedom to produce a folk pottery tradition while preventing the continuance of a folk pipe-making tradition?

In fact, separate servants' quarters are found from the very earliest period of settlement in Virginia—long before the institutionalization of slavery. In the muster of 1624–25 (Meyer and Dorman 1987), William Harwood of Martin's Hundred was listed as having six servants and three houses. In his excavation of what was probably Harwood's home compound, Noël Hume (1979) uncovered a cluster of three houses, all originally constructed to the same dimensions, but one of which was later doubled in size. Likewise, at Jordan's Journey (ca. 1622–39), Ciceley Jordan and William Farrar's household compound contained fifteen persons and five houses in 1624/25. Excavations (Mouer 1991d; Mouer and McLearen 1991) have uncovered evidence of five large houses at this site. While there were some construction and size differences between the houses, it is difficult to distinguish the housing of indentured servants from that of the compound muster and his family. There were also two small houses situated at the opposite end of this fortified compound, one with a root cellar. The West Indian pot described earlier was associated with these. Mouer (1993) has interpreted these as the earliest homes of enslaved Africans yet excavated in the Chesapeake.

While Deetz concedes that detached quarters were in common use before the influx of African-American bound labor after 1680, both he and Emerson imply that detached dwellings signal the institutionalization of slavery, and that it is this event which explains the rise of colonoware pottery and the decline of Chesapeake pipes. These conclusions are inconsistent with each other and with the historical and archaeological data.

Demographic arguments do not help the slavery model either. Deetz and Emerson both cite Robert Beverley's ([1705] 1968) estimates of Indian population in Virginia as an argument that by the turn of the eighteenth century, Native Americans had virtually disappeared from the stage of Chesapeake culture. Conversely, the rise of slavery at this time led to the well-documented influx of African slaves. To both authors the numbers speak for themselves: by the turn of the eighteenth century, there was a large population of Africans and a smaller population of Indians in Virginia. Both Colono-Indian pottery and Chesapeake decorated pipes appear on colonial sites at least as early as the 1630s, although the pottery does become more common in the late seventeenth century.

Beverley's contention that the Indians had, by the turn of the eighteenth century, ceased to occupy a significant presence in Virginia must also be critically evaluated. For over the period of a century, Virginia had developed a reputation as a deadly place: tales of disease, dangerous sea journeys, famine, and Indian massacres all served to inhibit the development of the colony (Morgan 1975). Throughout his discussion of the Indian inhabitants of Virginia, Beverley depicts them as beaten-down, childlike, simple, friendly, peaceful savages decimated by disease, alcohol, and warfare brought to them by the English. It served his purpose to depict the Indians as nonthreatening, colorful peoples, for Beverley was nothing if not a propagandist for Virginia. He was also a royalist and an apologist for former governor William Berkeley, whom his father faithfully served through Bacon's Rebellion. He promoted the notion that it was not a failed Indian policy that had caused the rebellion, as claimed by Bacon and his followers, but simply the megalomania and avarice of the Baconians that had lead to their attempted coup of 1676 (Washburn 1957; Wertenbaker 1940; Webb 1985).

Perhaps the number of Indians within the English-occupied boundaries of Virginia was small, but the colonized regions of Virginia and Maryland at the turn of the eighteenth century were also quite small. Rountree (1990:96) estimates the population of the remnant Powhatan groups alone to have been 2,900 persons in 1669, based on an English census of that year. This count does not consider the Doeg, Susquehannock, Piscataway, Delaware, Monacan, Nottoway, Meherrin, Chowan, Tuscarora, Eno, Tutelo, Saponi, Ocaneechee, Mahock, Shawnee, and numerous other Indian groups in Virginia and Maryland. By 1697 the Indian population of the Virginia coastal plain (Powhatan remnant groups, as well as Iroquoian Meherrin and Nottoway) may have shrunk to as few as 1,450 people (Rountree 1990:104). This estimate is also based on a census of tributary Indians and, by definition, does not include nontributaries, Indian servants or tenants, or other Indians living independently and beyond the reservations. Recent research suggests that the number of Native Americans in these somewhat acculturated spin-off groups was substantial (Mouer 1991a).

The late seventeenth-century and eighteenth-century historical records are replete with court cases, wills, inventories, boundary disputes, trade laws, market schedules, and other items dealing with the relationships between English and Indians. The colonial chronicles, letters, and journals of John Bannister (Ewan and Ewan 1970), Robert Beverley ([1705] 1968), Peter Fontaine (Alexander 1972), John Lawson (Harriss 1952), John Lederer ([1671] 1966), Hugh Jones ([1724] 1956), and numerous others are filled with descriptions of Indians and accounts of their interactions with the colonists. In the late seventeenth and early eighteenth centuries, a brisk trade existed between Englishmen living in Surry, Prince George, and Henrico counties and Indians living to the south and southwest of the counties, extending even to the distant Cherokee and Catawba (Briceland 1987).

To suggest that Indians were not a very significant element in the history and culture of the colonial Chesapeake would require ignoring both historical and archaeological evidence. As Gary Nash (1974:223) has written, "Our history books have largely forgotten what was patently obvious throughout [the late colonial period]—

that much of the time and energy of the [French, Spanish and English colonial] gov-
ernments . . . was spent negotiating, trading, and fighting with and against Indians
of various cultures, and filing reports, requests, and complaints to the home gov-
ernments concerning the state of Indian affairs."

In his essay on Chesapeake historiography, Thad Tate (1979) notes that historians have overlooked the role of the Indian peoples, and ethnohistorian J. Frederick
Fausz has written that "although most historians implicitly recognize that the early
English Chesapeake emerged out of the confluence of two alien worlds, recent scholarship has not yet succeeded in restoring Indians to the center stage they occupied
in the seventeenth century" (1988:48).

Indians were clearly an important factor in the colonial Chesapeake, whereas (for
instance) only three African slaves were known to be at St. Mary's City when the 127
recovered Chesapeake pipe bowls were deposited at Popes Fort ca. 1645–55. Although
estimates vary, by midcentury there were almost certainly no more than three hundred persons of African descent living throughout the Maryland and Virginia
colonies, while Indians numbered in the thousands. Of course it may not take one
person more than a few days to make 127 pipes, but this begs the question. Were
Africans in a position, in the seventeenth- and early eighteenth-century Chesapeake,
to form viable subcultural or social contexts that could produce a widespread and
consistent folk tradition of pottery and a coherent decorated tobacco pipe art form?
The premise that they were is contrary to most historical and archaeological scholarship.

In the seventeenth century the very few African-American servants and slaves
in the Chesapeake were widely dispersed among small households of white landown-
ers and among their white and Indian servants and tenants (see Morgan 1975). The
duration and consistency of Chesapeake pipe art over a long time span and broad
region indicates that the makers moved within a well-developed subculture in which
such repeated symbols would have some semiotic value. We suggest that Africans
had little opportunity to develop an identifiable, pan-Chesapeake ethnic subculture
among themselves in the seventeenth century, but that Indians clearly had such a
subculture, and revitalization efforts in the face of cultural collapse may have amplified it and spurred the emergence of a regional Indian identity (Mouer 1991c).
Aspects of this Native American culture were then available for "borrowing" by
culturally displaced European and African servants and peasants. It was almost
certainly among the lower strata of society that ethnic groups would have most
frequently interacted and would have found they had much in common, including
their mutual subjugation by the English elite (Morgan 1975).[9]

Perhaps the rise in the popularity of Colono-Indian pottery beginning in the
middle of the seventeenth century can be explained by the increased demand for

cheap earthenware brought about by a dramatically increasing colonial (including slave) population as well as decreased access to the formerly widespread Dutch, Iberian, and Italian wares that came with stricter enforcement of the Navigation Acts following the Stuart Restoration. The locally made pottery of the tributary Indians (such as the Pamunkey and Nottoway) filled a newly created market niche. The increasing prevalence of Colono-Indian ware after the drafting of the 1677 treaty may be related to the changing status of the tributary Indians to a subjugated partnership in the colony. As Binford (1967) and Hodges (1989, 1990) have noted, the tributary groups might have come to rely on pottery as an alternative means of obtaining European goods and food once local game resources were depleted. Some tributary groups were being bypassed in the fur and skin trade, and various disruptions and colonial encroachments may have made it difficult for them to provide all of their own sustenance. This appears to have been part of the impetus behind free Indian trade laws passed in 1646, 1656, 1662, 1677, and 1680. As Hodges (1989:6) notes, colonial legislation from this period provides some support for this explanation. For example, a law enacted in 1676, apparently concerned with restricting the entry of hostile Indians into the colonial settlement, prohibited all trade and commerce with the Indians. However, the act specifically stated that in regard to "our neighbor Indian friends who have occasion for corne to relieve their wives and children, it shall be lawful for any English to employ in fishing or deal with fish, canooes, bowles, matts, baskets, and to pay the said Indians for the same in Indian corne" (Hening 1809–23:2:350–51). In 1677 the Indian trade was considerably liberalized by the first of several bills establishing Indian fairs and marts and opening the trade to all colonists, with alcohol and guns continuing as prohibited trade items (Hening 1809–23:2:410–12).

## Late Colonial and Antebellum Contexts

By the mid–eighteenth century large numbers of slaves lived together, often in remote quarters, and in circumstances that permitted a large measure of interaction between slaves with minimal supervision by whites (Isaac 1982). It is noteworthy that new types of locally made earthenware and stoneware tobacco pipes are found on plantations in late eighteenth- and early nineteenth-century contexts (Heite 1970). Most of the reported locally produced pipes of the late eighteenth and nineteenth centuries are bowls of the type called modular, mogodore, or reed-stem pipes, as are the African-made pipes from seventeenth-century Ghana and Barbados illustrated by Emerson (Emerson 1988:121, 123). The making of reed-stem pipes became a significant cottage industry in nineteenth-century Virginia, particularly in the vicinity of Pamplin in Appomattox County (Heite 1971; Sudbury 1977). By the time Pamplin (and similar) pipes became commercial products widely sold throughout the United

States in the mid–nineteenth century, the bowls were often molded to resemble the faces of Indian, and some were commercially sold as "Powhatan pipes." Smoking pipes, like cigar-store wooden Indians and tobacco trademarks depicting "the Indian Queen," were a continuing reminder of the source of America's tobacco traditions.

While reed-stem pipes originated with prehistoric Native Americans (though not the Powhatan or their immediate ancestors), an argument could be made that their reintroduction into eastern North America in the late eighteenth century was by way of African or Caribbean blacks. Existing archaeological evidence suggests, however, that reed-stem pipes probably first appeared in the English colonies through introduction by German potters between 1755 and 1771 (see South 1965–66:49–50). Nonetheless, the various plantation-made pipes of the period may have been slave-made adaptations of forms that could have been familiar to a people who had seen or used them in the Caribbean or Africa.

## Creolization

As many writers (Wolf 1982; Fagan 1988; Fausz 1988; Mouer 1993) have discussed, when diverse cultures come in contact, they change each other. The process whereby cultures in contact generate new cultural forms is often called creolization. Archaeology—and particularly the archaeological remains of folk art—may offer one of the best avenues available for studying the processes by which such new ethnicities are formed.[10]

That designs, functions, and forms of Colono-Indian pottery and Chesapeake pipes share elements from Indian, English, and African origins suggests that these elements were selected from among a larger universe of designs and forms, and that it was the set of shared elements which came to characterize creole folk craft traditions in the Chesapeake. The making of pots by traditional Native American techniques in European forms reflects the creolization process at work.

The designs on Chesapeake pipes likewise attest to the existence of creolized folk culture. One pipe, in particular, seems to exemplify the process and the problems involved in its interpretation. A pipe bowl recovered from Nathaniel Bacon's Curles plantation in Henrico County, Virginia, is decorated around its rim with infilled triangles executed in rouletting (fig. 5.16). Stamped around the middle of the bowl is a repeated oval cartouche containing a stamped impression of a quadruped. This is no stick-figure deer but an impression of an English stag. The cartouche is almost certainly the imprint from an English signet ring. An excavation of burials at the Burr's Hill site, a ca. 1670 Wampanoag Indian cemetery in Rhode Island, included a group of cast brass rings, "the designs cast in intaglio" (Gibson 1980). Among the various designs were classic English heraldry motifs identified as "Horn'd Animal, Stag Running, Stag Standing," and so on. The description and measurements of one of the rings with "stag standing on oval plaque" perfectly describe the stamped motif on the Curles plantation pipe. The author of the Burr's Hill study concludes that the rings were generic signets produced for the Indian trade. William Byrd included "brass rings" among his list of items of the Virginia Indian trade in the late seventeenth and early eighteenth centuries (Briceland 1987:176).

Nathaniel Bacon was an Indian trader living on the frontier, and his probate inventory included large quantities of "Indian truck," as well as five "Negro," one "Dutch" (possibly German), one mulatto, and six Indian servants. Over forty years ago J. C. Harrington (1951) asked whether these Chesapeake pipes were made by Europeans after the Indian fashion or by Indians copying some European techniques and designs. Emerson has extended the question to include Africans, and while he feels confident in assigning a modern ethnic categorization to seventeenth-century pipe makers, we do not. Who made the Curles stag pipe? An Englishman with a signet ring? An Indian with a trade ring and a fascination with heraldry? An African who remembered from his or her youth calabashes decorated with rouletted triangles?

This question is difficult to answer and may, in fact, be the wrong question altogether. This much is clear: a creolized culture, highly influenced by Native American beliefs, values, and practices, arose in the seventeenth-century Chesapeake. At the heart of this culture was the cultivation of tobacco adopted along with the implements for its use from Native American practice by English and African societies in much the same way that Chinese porcelain tea bowls accompanied the adoption of tea drinking at a later period. While we certainly should not rule out the possibility—even the likelihood—that some of the Chesapeake pipes excavated from colonial contexts may have been made by Englishmen or Africans, these were certainly adaptations of the coveted Indian pipes "very beautifully cut out and formed." These intriguing artifacts represent the transformation of an ancient Indian tobacco pipe trade system and the transfer of Native American products and culture to colonists and slaves.

The search for African connections has been conducted by archaeologists who have sometimes underestimated the significant roles played by Native American peoples in the past. American historical archaeology has largely developed in complementary opposition to American prehistoric archaeology and, as a strange result, sometimes seems to preclude an interest in, or understanding of, Native American history and culture (Mouer 1991f). Nonetheless, it has been the intensive and dedicated interest of historical archaeologists seeking the veiled and uncelebrated history of African Americans that has spawned a dialogue reminding us that our culture is one of many roots and many branches, and that ethnicity is a contextual phenomenon rather than a monolith ascending immutably out of history.

## Notes

The authors would like to express their appreciation to Theresa Singleton, Mark Bograd, and Robin Ryder whose careful readings and criticisms of this chapter proved most helpful. The numerous suggestions and kind assistance offered by Keith T. Egloff and R. Taft Kiser are also gratefully acknowledged. All line-art figures were drawn by Anne Fletcher, whose excellent work is well appreciated. Special thanks to the staffs of Agecroft Hall Museum and the Virginia Department of Historic Resources, both in Richmond, for permission to photograph items in their collections.

1. Noël Hume's seminal article and Binford's paper on Courtland ware have both been republished in the 50th anniversary issue of the *Quarterly Bulletin of the Archaeological Society of Virginia* 45 (3) (Sept. 1990).

2. Parker and Hernigle refer to their locally made earthenware as "African Colono Ware." See the discussion on nineteenth-century "colono" wares in the Chesapeake.

3. Eastern Virginia's present Indian communities—Pamunkey, Upper and Lower Mattaponi, Rappahannock, Nansemond, and Chickahominy—are the descendants of the powerful Powhatan chiefdom encountered by the English when they arrived on these shores in 1607. Many Virginia Indians remain on their traditional lands; most of the Pamunkey and Mattaponi peoples are found today on the reservations created by treaty with the Virginia colony in 1646 and 1677 and honored as such by the state government today.

4. While Colono-Indian ware is typically smoothed or burnished, it may—albeit rarely—carry additional decoration formed by incising, punctation, cording, dentate stamping, and other techniques typical of mid-Atlantic prehistoric ceramics.

5. "Potter" was one of many Indian servants used by English settlers to claim headright lands. These Indians, therefore, were being transported to Virginia from elsewhere, presumably South Carolina or the Caribbean.

6. It is only in recent years that members of this Amherst County Indian group have come to identify themselves as "Monacan." Early twentieth-century ethnologists, who found these people living largely as squatters on small tributaries of the James River, reported their tribal name as "Issue," a name which even today is viewed by the Indians and their white neighbors as a derogatory term meaning "mixed blood." The name—especially as it would be pronounced by a country Virginian—may derive from *Issa* (or *Iswa, Esaw, Isha,* or other cognates), a Siouan term meaning "river people," which the Catawba and some of their piedmont Siouan relatives have called themselves from the sixteenth century to the present. Some of the Amherst Indians have claimed that they were driven from their home on the James River by an epidemic at the turn of this century (W. Waller, pers. comm.). The place they describe as their home is near the traditional location of a major seventeenth-century Indian settlement, the "Mahock" of John Lederer (1966 [1671]). Even today, few Virginians know of the existence of this Indian group, and yet it seems likely they have been in or near their present location since before the coming of white and black peoples to the Virginia piedmont.

7. That Emerson does not distinguish between types of rouletted or *pointillé* decoration is evident from his numerous illustrated examples, as well as from his discussion of techniques (see, for instance, Emerson 1988:52–53).

8. A view similar to that of Upton is expressed by Neiman (1978) in his study of the evolution of domestic space at the Clifts plantation.

9. Clearly there are numerous African-derived elements found in African-American culture. The argument being pursued here relates specifically to the seventeenth-century Chesapeake. The conditions and rates of interaction needed to form an African-American ethnicity did not become prevalent throughout the Chesapeake until later in the eighteenth century.

10. Perhaps the best discussion of creolization in one region of the original colonies is Joyner's (1984) wonderful ethnography and history of the Gullah speakers of South Carolina. Joyner and others posit that the term *Gullah* is derived from "Angola," a source of many African slaves. It is, perhaps, only a curious coincidence—but, in the present context worthy of note—that most of the Guale Indians who once inhabited a large section of the southeastern coast were captured and sold as slaves by Carolina traders and their Creek Indian allies in the eighteenth century.

# 6

# "The Cross Is a Magic Sign": Marks on Eighteenth-Century Bowls from South Carolina

*Leland G. Ferguson*

## Introduction

SINCE THE 1930s, archaeologists working on colonial town and plantation sites along the South Atlantic coast have been finding hand-built, unglazed pottery that is quite different from the glazed British ceramics most commonly found. Sometimes the potters had imitated European forms such as pipkins, porringers, and chamber pots; however, most of these earthenware vessels were small bowls and jars that showed no special similarity to European forms. In 1962 Ivor Noël Hume, then director of archaeology at Virginia's Colonial Williamsburg, argued that these pots were made in Indian villages and sold or traded to planters for use by their slaves. He called the pottery "Colono-Indian ware,"—that is, an Indian ware of the colonial period.

Later, during the middle 1970s, this interpretation was called into question by discoveries in South Carolina (Ferguson 1980). Several lines of evidence suggested that this class of pottery was made not only in Indian villages but also on colonial plantations by African-American slaves. To accommodate this broader notion, I proposed we simply drop the "Indian" from Noël Hume's term and call the pottery "colonoware."[1] Since that time, archaeologists have generally come to agree that this pottery was made both in Indian villages and on southern plantations. Being hand-made in the yards of colonial Americans, this ware illustrates both the pioneering craftsmanship and the domestic needs of colonial Native Americans and African Americans. In South Carolina some pieces bear marks similar to those commonly used in Central African religious expression. They appear to represent material aspects of African religion incorporated into the creolized culture of African Americans. Different from acculturation (Ferguson 1992:xli-xlv), creolizaton emphasizes the creative character of early American, including African-American, culture. In creating their American subculture, African Americans drew elements from African,

European, and Native American culture and combined these into a new and unique way of life. My argument here is that inscribing the Bakongo cosmogram on the center of clay bowls was one of those elements.

## Marked Bowls from South Carolina

Archaeologists have now examined tens of thousands of folk-made pottery sherds from colonial African-American living and working places. This hand-built pottery, colonoware, was used by enslaved plantation workers, and most of that found in South Carolina appears to have been made by them as well (Ferguson 1991; Wheaton, Friedlander, and Garrow 1983:225–50; Garrow and Wheaton 1989; Zierden et al. 1986:7.22–50). While analyzing these thousands of fragments, a few pieces—twenty-eight to be exact—have attracted attention because they have marks on them (Ferguson 1992:26). These do not appear to be the incised lines of decoration—that is, regularly placed lines designed for display; rather, they are localized incisions and scratches. They might be placed on the bottom of the vessel, out of sight of the casual user, or scratched into a finished vessel, marring its potter's smoothed or burnished surface.

When these marks were first observed, archaeologists casually called them "makers' marks" because the first to be discovered had been incised on the bottom of bowls before firing, thus bearing resemblance to the makers' marks on European and Oriental ceramic wares. However, marks were soon discovered on the interior bottom of vessels; some were found to have been inscribed after the bowl was finished (Ferguson 1992:111), or even after it had been used. The idea of owners' marks was offered, yet there was little variety to imply the individuality of owners. Most of the incisions were simple crosses or minor variants thereof.

While the marks do not satisfy some of the most basic criteria for either makers' or owners' marks, they do exhibit important similarities to generalized West African symbolism, and to cosmograms from the Bakongo culture in particular. The underwater provenience of most of the finds with such marks suggests use in African-inspired ritual.

## Kongo Symbolism in Africa and America

Although people from the entire "slaving coast" of West and Central Africa were brought to South Carolina, the majority of Carolina's slaves came from the extremities—the northwestern Windward Coast, including Senegal, Gambia, and Sierra Leone, and the Congo-Angolan region far to the southeast (Littlefield 1981:20–21, 110–14). This southeastern trading zone covered almost one thousand miles and included the coasts of modern Gabon, Congo-Brazzaville, the Democratic Republic of Congo, Cabinda, and northern Angola. During the period of heavy slave importation, from 1735 to 1740, more than two-thirds of the African peoples arriving in South Carolina were coming from this southeastern area (Wood 1974:333–41). Overall, approximately 40 percent of the slaves sold in Charleston came from the Congo-Angola region (Littlefield 1981:113).

Because slave ships trading in this territory covered such an extensive segment of the African coast, we may be sure that Carolina's colonial "Congo-Angolans" were not a single ethnic group. Nevertheless, while people from this area varied ethnically, they shared fundamental aspects of culture (MacGaffey 1986). Specifically, they shared philosophical and religious beliefs exemplified by the influential Bakongo people; the term *Kongo*—spelled with a *K* to distinguish it from the geopolitical identity—has been used to represent this generalized cultural expression. Art historian Robert Farris Thompson (1981b, 1983) has argued that Kongo traditions have informed African-American philosophy and religion from Rio de Janeiro to New York City; the "conjurers" and "root doctors" of the Carolina coast were part of this American development.

According to Kongo religion, an almighty god, *Nzambi*, emanates power that may be wielded for either good or evil by living human beings, people who make *minkisi*—sacred medicines (MacGaffey 1986:42–51, 78–82; Thompson 1983:108–31). These *minkisi* control the spirits of the Kongo cosmos, connecting the living with the powers of the dead. Kongo philosophers explain the earth, the land of the living, as a mountain over a watery barrier that separates this world from the land of the dead beneath. Each day, the sun rises over the earth and proceeds in a counterclockwise direction (as viewed from the Southern Hemisphere) across the sky to finally setting in the water. Then, during earthly nighttime, the sun illuminates the underside of the universe, the land of the dead, before rising again in the northeast. This cycle continues incessantly, representing the continuity of life: birth, death, and rebirth.

According to historian Sterling Stuckey, this circularity, especially counterclockwise circularity, pervaded West African ideology from the Congo-Angola region all the way to Gambia and Senegal on the Windward Coast. Nevertheless, agreeing with Thompson on the importance of influence from the Congo-Angolan region, Stuckey concludes that (1987:11) "the circle imported [to America] by Africans from the Congo region was so powerful in its elaboration of a religious vision that it contributed disproportionately to the centrality of the circle in slavery. . . . The use of the circle for religious purposes in slavery was so consistent and profound that one could argue that it was what gave form and meaning to black religion and art."

Beyond the circle, Stuckey argues, the watery barrier recognized in West African cosmology as separating the corporeal and spirit worlds found an important role in

American ideology. Quoting Melville Herskovits, he writes (Stuckey 1987:15) that "in all those parts of the New World where African religious beliefs have persisted . . . the river cult or, in broader terms, the cult of water spirits, holds an important place. All this testifies to the vitality of this element in African religion, and supports the conclusion . . . as to the possible influence such priests wielded even as slaves" (Herskovits 1941:106–7). Ultimately, Stuckey argues, this emphasis on water was syncretized with the Christian practice of baptism, with resulting emphasis on total immersion in natural bodies of water.

For ritual purposes, the Kongo represents the circular pathway of the sun, as well as the watery barrier and associated cosmology, by special "cosmograms"—diagrams having similarities to many ritualistic motifs of the New World, including, I propose, the marks on colonial-period bowls from the Carolina low country. According to MacGaffey (from a manuscript quoted in Thompson 1983:108), the basic form of the cosmogram is a simple cross, with one line representing the boundary between the world of the living and that of the dead and the other being "ambivalently both the path leading across the boundary, as to the cemetery; and the vertical path of power linking the 'above' with 'the below.'" Swedish missionary and ethnographer Karl Laman reported that in the late nineteenth and early twentieth centuries, Bakongo peoples also saw the cosmogram in crossroads, and that in conducting *minkisi* rituals they drew circles and crosses with chalk and yellow ocher on baskets, people, and pots (Laman 1962:149, 152, 156; Laman 1968:37).

In the cosmogram the daily course of the sun around the two halves of the cosmos is represented by a counterclockwise path or enclosure about the crossed lines. Thompson says (1983:109) that "initiates read the cosmogram correctly, respecting its allusiveness. God is imagined at the top, the dead at the bottom, and water in between. The summit of the pattern symbolizes not only noon but also maleness, north, and the peak of a person's strength on earth. Correspondingly, the bottom equals midnight, femaleness, south, the highest point of a person's other-worldly strength."

In Africa the Kongo cosmogram has a variety of ritual uses. People standing on a cross shared the harmony and power of both worlds, and any ritual focused on the "point" or "mark" brought the power of God to that very spot (e.g., Laman 1962:156). The diagram may also have been used to represent the individual's position at the center of four matrilineages. Ethnographer Wyatt MacGaffey writes (1986:123) that when he asked about a circle painted on a Kongo house, an elderly man said to him that "it suggested the bowl or pit of water formerly used by diviners to tell whether the soul of a warrior about to go into battle was complete. The bowl was divided in some way into four quadrants, corresponding to four lineages. A disturbance of the client's image in any of the quadrants would indicate that he was under witchcraft attack from that lineage and should not risk the fight."

Thompson has shown that in the Americas cosmograms have been used in this same manner to "center" initiates or to provide a "centering" location for spirits in rituals: a Kongo-Cuban priest "traced the cross-within-the-circle 'signature'" at the spot where a charm was to touch the ground, and Brazilian *macumba* ritualists use crosses to center "consecrated water and other important liquids in vessels for spirits." American usage also has focused on the notion of the pathway-and-journey aspect of the cosmogram. In the 1930s several African Americans on the Georgia coast told Works Progress Administration (WPA) interviewers (WPA 1986:5, 135, 171) that anyone who started a journey and then had to turn back should make a cross on the ground and spit on it; otherwise, bad luck would befall the person. One interpretation of this ritual, consistent with the African view of the cross, might be that if one cannot finish a journey, harmony is disrupted; to set things straight in such a case, one should make the mark of harmony and leave a part of oneself there. The local significance of the cosmogram was articulated by Ben Washington of Pine Barrens, Georgia, who told a WPA interviewer (WPA 1986:135): "If you ever see a cross mark in the road, you never walk over it. That's real magic. You have to go around it. It's put there by an enemy, and if you walk across it, the evil spell will cause you harm. The cross is a magic sign and has to do with the spirits."

Renderings of the cosmogram in the Americas also have been used as components of charms and rituals inspired by African *minkisi*—charms and rituals allowing mortals to control cosmic power (Thompson 1981b, 1983). Making an African *nkisi* (plural: *minkisi*) involves packaging a variety of spirit-embodying materials that might include cemetery earth, white clay, stones, and other items placed in *minkisi* containers. These containers are various: leaves, shells, bags, wooden images, cloth bundles, and ceramic vessels (Laman 1953, 1957, 1962, 1968). According to Thompson in Kongo mythology, "Ne Kongo himself, the progenitor of the kingdom, prepared the primordial medicines in an earthenware pot set on three stones above a fire. Clay pots have therefore always been classical containers of *minkisi*" (Thompson 1983:110, 121).

Although metal kettles have been substitutes for clay pots, Thompson has found definite evidence of New World *minkisi* and associated cosmographic marks. When Cuban priests make *Zarabanda* charms, they begin by "tracing, in white chalk, a cruciform pattern at the bottom of an iron kettle"; and when they make another charm called a *prenda* they draw "a cross, in chalk or white ashes, at the bottom of the kettle" (Thompson 1983:110, 121).

In Waycross, Georgia, not far from the rice-growing region of the coast, a twentieth-century healer described a charm that involved placing a cross within a circle on the ground, adding graveyard dirt, and then standing on the center while facing the setting sun—all components of West African ritual (Hyatt 1970, as referred to in Thompson 1981b:152).

Archaeological evidence from the South Carolina coast suggests similar ritual usage of the cross and other components of the cosmogram more than a century and a half earlier.

## Marked Pottery from South Carolina

Thus far, I have recorded twenty-eight marked vessels or vessel fragments from South Carolina collections (fig. 6.1; table 6.1). Eighteen come from underwater sites and the remaining five from sites on land. More than half of the marked vessels have come from underwater. These are from collections given to the South Carolina Institute of Archaeology and Anthropology by nonprofessional archaeological divers in the 1970s and early 1980s, before colonoware was of general interest and before the significance of marked vessels had been discussed in papers or publications. The divers who collected these pieces neither aimed at collecting representative samples nor carefully controlled for specific provenience. Of concern here is that this lack of control might have biased the samples in such a way as to seriously weaken or nullify the arguments presented in this chapter. I submit that the collecting bias does not weaken my arguments. Those arguments are based on the following patterns from the underwater collections: (1) marks are only on bowls, not jars; (2) marked bowls occur more frequently underwater than on land; (3) ring bases occur more frequently on bowls found underwater than on bowls found on land; and (4) marks are more common on bowls with ring bases than on those with flat or rounded bases.[2]

Although these specimens cannot be precisely dated, there is little doubt that the vessels were produced and used sometime between the middle of the eighteenth century and the first quarter of the nineteenth century (Ferguson 1980; Wheaton, Friedlander, and Garrow 1983; Lees and Kimery-Lees 1979). The majority of the artifacts exhibit a complex of characteristics that point toward their use in a common activity that was associated with water and required making crosses, or variations on crosses, in the center of folk-made bowls, most commonly bowls with ring bases. I have divided these twenty-eight specimens into three categories based on design consistency and similarity to Kongo cosmograms.

Category 1 contains four specimens with marks that are least like the cosmograms of the entire collection. Coming from three separate sites (Drayton Hall, 38BK48, and an unrecorded site on the Cooper River), these artifacts exhibit alphabetical marks and marks on river burnished pottery—a type of pottery believed to have been made for trade by itinerant Catawba Indians (Wheaton, Friedlander, and Garrow 1983:225–50; Garrow and Wheaton 1989; Ferguson 1989b). The most striking of these artifacts is a sherd inscribed with the initials "MHD" and found during excavations at Drayton Hall (see fig. 6.1G) (Lewis 1978:62–65). Archaeologist Lynn Lewis believes the pottery was made on the plantation; and through comparison of the artifact with documentary evidence, she has suggested the initials are those of Mary Henrietta Drayton, who grew up on the plantation, living there from the 1780s to the 1840s. The other examples in category 1 are both on fragments of river burnished type pottery (Ferguson 1989b) found at underwater sites in the Cooper River. One mark is a "J" inscribed after firing on one side of the interior base of a flat-bottomed bowl. The other is a painted design that may not be a mark at all but rather part of a larger design applied to the interior of a ring-based bowl. In this case an "X" together with two other small marks appears in black paint at the center interior base; there are small flecks of red paint on the sherd as well. The extraneous black marks and the traces of red paint suggest that this apparent mark may have been part of a larger painted design often found on river burnished pottery.

Category 2 contains only three specimens; however, the three are distinctive, stylistically consistent, and similar in their marks to the Kongo cosmogram. These three bowl fragments all came from a short section of the west branch of the Cooper River near Mepkin plantation. In each case, when the potter finished burnishing the inside of the leather-hard vessel before firing, she or he used the burnishing tool, most likely a smooth stone, to strike a large cross from rim to rim across the interior of the open bowls (fig. 6.2). Seen from above, the bowl gives the effect of a circle (formed by the vessel rim) surrounding a cross centered at the very bottom of the bowl—an image of the cosmogram similar to the one described by MacGaffey's informant for dividing a bowl into quadrants representing lineages (MacGaffey 1986:123).

The third and largest of the three categories includes marks most similar to the Kongo cosmograms. All category 3 marks incorporate straight lines and/or arcs of a circle, the same design elements used in the African cosmogram. One of the marks is simply three-quarters of a circle made with a counterclockwise incision (see fig. 6.1F); another is a straight line, perhaps a fragment of a cross. Two other designs are distinctive enough to stand out from the rest, although they have characteristics of crosses. The first of these is a simple dendritic pattern; the second (see fig. 6.1H) may be an anthropomorphic figure similar to those in Kongo ideography (MacGaffey 1986:118,125). The remaining twelve designs are clearly crosses, or variations on the cross:

1. five simple crosses without embellishment (see fig. 6.1), the basic form of the Kongo cosmogram;

2. a simple cross with a dot at the intersection (e.g., fig. 6.1). Thompson writes that "dots or small circles added to the intersecting arms of the Kongo cross indicate men or women as second suns" (1981a:43);

3. three crosses with enclosures similar to the pathway of the sun as it is rendered in cosmograms (see figs. 6.1A and 6.1C);

4. three crosses with short lines or "flags" extending counterclockwise from the ends of the cross (e.g., fig. 6.1B), similar to the pathway of the sun as depicted in cosmograms;

5. two crosses formed of parallel lines;

6. one cross formed by a straight line and an arc; in Kongo cosmography this would represent the sun crossing the boundary between the world of the living and that of the dead.

## Owners' or Makers' Marks?

Looking at all three categories, the most striking evidence is that all of the marks are on colonoware bowls. So far, archaeologists have not reported any marks on European vessels, although slaves were using them; nor have any marks been found on colonoware jars, even though jars and their fragments make up roughly one-third of colonoware collections from South Carolina.[3] The marks are clearly associated with locally manufactured bowls and no other vessel type.

This singular association with colonoware bowls, together with the fact that approximately half the marks were made after firing, negates arguments that the marks were made to designate ownership by either the makers or the owners. If the marks were inscribed by the makers to distinguish their pottery from others, we would expect marks on all pottery shapes including jars, pitchers, and other forms; but that is not the case. Moreover, six of the category 3 marks were made in the surface of finished bowls after the vessels were fired, a fact that refutes the contentions that they were used by the maker to identify vessels during the manufacturing process.

That the category 3 marks are owners' marks also seems unlikely. Colonoware vessels were handmade and are quite distinctive; variations in vessel shape, color, and firing clouds allow archaeologists to distinguish one artifact from the other, and no doubt the colonial owners would have been able to identify individual vessels without resorting to marks. We know also that slaves used European stoneware and earthenware, vessels that, because of manufacturing similarities, often looked exactly alike. Having examined thousands of sherds and vessels from slave sites, we have yet to find a single mark on one of these European vessels.[4] Thus, the notion of owners' marks is weak; again, they are not found on European vessels used by slaves, and there is little idiosyncratic design suggesting that various owners came up with their own distinctive marks. The case for these marks being associated with ritual activities is much stronger than the case for either makers' marks or owners' marks.

## The Case for Ritual Use

For the most part, historians, anthropologists, and folklorists have drawn their knowledge of African-American religion and ritual from two sources—contemporary and remembered practices stretching back into the nineteenth century and similar information from the African homeland. Overall, we know very little about religious practices of South Carolina's black pioneers in the eighteenth century and earlier. However, we may be sure that early religion was not simply Bakongo, Yoruba, or any other African belief system transferred in toto to America. Colonial religion must have been as varied as the population, which included plantation owners and overseers, African Americans born on West Indian plantations, Africans from Angola to Senegal and inland for hundreds of miles, and Native Americans from throughout the Southeast. In addition to Bakongo and other African beliefs, plantation people must have known, in varying degrees, of American Indian cosmology, Islam, and Christianity. Scholars have argued that in creating their American religions, African Americans drew elements from a variety of sources, especially those that were similar to one another, or syncretic—for example, the Christian emphasis on water baptism and the West and Central African notions of a spirit world beneath the water.

We know that the cross was an important symbol, and the cross and circle were important symbols to Native Americans (e.g., Mooney 1890; Holmes 1903; Hudson 1976). We know also that both Native Americans and African Americans made varieties of colonoware. So, circle-and-cross symbols on colonoware could be syncretic, incorporating Christian and Native American as well as African and newly created African-American meanings. Nevertheless, the constellation of these marked bowls and their associations is so consistent with aspects of Bakongo ritual and generalized West and Central African belief that in future work on African-American religion in the Carolina low country we must consider this as an archaeological manifestation that links African belief with African-American creation.

In hypothesizing a general eighteenth-century ritual pattern, we might expect many of the most fundamental and widespread practices (in more recent times in Africa and the New World) to have been present in early South Carolina. Along the coast, where Congo-Angolan peoples made up almost half the population, we would expect that among other things African-American religion would have included:

1. a notion of the cosmos similar to that of the Kongo;

2. a focus on circularity, and especially on counterclockwise circularity, common to peoples all along the West African coast (see Stuckey 1987:3–97);

3. the use of charms similar to Kongo *minkisi*;

4. an emphasis on natural bodies of water, again common along the entire coast of West Africa.

Given that African Americans in the eighteenth century had a closer tie to Africa than those living in the nineteenth and twentieth centuries, we might also expect a strong association with African-style material goods—for example, handmade earthenware pottery.

The assemblage of marked pieces of colonoware fits well with these important features of West African and African-American religion and ritual. Most importantly, these marks are only on colonoware found in areas where African Americans dominated demographically and where Congo-Angolan people made up nearly half the population. Moreover, the marks are on pieces of pottery that were definitely used by African Americans, and although we still need a better understanding of how much of this ware was produced on plantations and how much in free Indian villages, there is no question that the production of and use of low-fired, hand-built earthenware was an ancient African tradition, and that African-American slaves used similar wares. No matter who made the pottery, the general characteristics—shape, color, texture—were similar to those of traditional African pottery.

Sterling Stuckey has made a strong case for the importance of circles in African-American culture and ritual, and circles dominate this collection of marked bowls. Bowls themselves are segments of spheres, and their characteristic lines are circles. Bowls with ring bases may be seen as circles attached to circles, and bowls with ring bases make up 50 percent of the entire collection of marked vessels. In unmarked collections of colonoware, vessels with ring bases are a minority. Unfortunately, we do not have a tally of ring-based bowls versus bowls with flattened or rounded bases from archaeological sites—archaeologists simply have not reported that statistic. However, I have kept a catalog of all whole colonoware bowls from archaeological sites in South Carolina: only fifteen, or 32 percent, out of a collection of forty-seven specimens have ring bases.[5]

The association of marked and ring-based bowls with underwater sites also may be telling. While only one complete bowl with ring base has been collected from a terrestrial site, such vessels comprise 67 percent of those collected from underwater sites. Similarly, while marked vessels occur on terrestrial sites, the majority have been found by divers at underwater sites in the Cooper River, adjacent to rice plantations. Overall, it appears that both bowls with ring bases and bowls that are marked are more likely to be found underwater than on land, and that marks are more likely to be seen on bowls with ring bases than any other type of bowl.

The marks themselves have features that tie them together and tie most of them to the Kongo cosmogram. Apparently, principle dictated that a mark be applied to the very center of a circular bowl—a characteristic consistent with the emphasis on "centering" common in more recent African-American rituals. In only one case, the "J" scratched on a bowl from an unknown Cooper River site, is the mark set off center.

Most marks were composed of fundamental cosmographic features—crosses, counterclockwise circles and other enclosures, or flags extending from the ends of the longer intersecting lines. The direction of the circles can be determined by surface "dragging" of the wet clay. In other cases, by looking at the beginning and end of a line in relation to other lines, it is clear where the line started and stopped. For example, when scratching from one line to another, the artist is more likely to overshoot the second line than the first (see figs. 6.1A and 6.1C). This counterclockwise pattern shows again in the short lines or "flags" sometimes attached to the ends of crosses (see fig. 6.1B). In each of three cases in the collection, these lines go to the upper left and bottom right of a crossbar turned vertically in front of a viewer. This is opposite to the direction of the well-known Nazi swastika, and in the direction of the counterclockwise movement of the sun represented by the Kongo cosmogram. Of course since most right-handed people tend to make an enclosure counterclockwise, and since most people are right-handed, this pattern comes as no surprise and cannot be used alone to confirm that the enclosures were intended to be counterclockwise. Nevertheless, taken together with the other evidence of African-inspired ritual, the consistent counterclockwise pattern adds strength to the case.

## Summary and Conclusion

From a variety of sites, both land and underwater, archaeologists and nonarchaeologists have found vessels with marks that bear a striking resemblance to the cosmograms of the Bakongo peoples in Central Africa. These cosmograms have been used in Central Africa to represent the relationship of the living with the dead and with God and to symbolize centering or harmony with the universe, and historians have shown that similar symbols have been used in the Caribbean and the Americas.

These marks are a cross and circle or some variation thereof; and sometimes they are applied before the vessel was fired, sometimes afterwards. Although the sample of marks in categories 1, 2, and 3 is relatively small, there is a strong pattern:

1. The marks have only been found on earthenware bowls;

2. No marks have been found on imported European bowls, even though they were commonly used by African-American slaves and frequently found by archaeologists;

3. Whether on the outside or inside, inscribed before firing or after, the marks are always in the very center of the bowl;

4. Although much more colonoware has been excavated from terrestrial sites than underwater sites, more marked pieces have come from underwater than on land;

5. Marks have been found more frequently on bowls with ring bases than on rounded or flat-bottomed bowls; and in a collections of whole vessels from South

Carolina, more vessels with ring bases have been recorded from underwater than on land.

The similarity of marks to the Central African cosmogram together with several other points indicate: (1) the predominance of African Americans in the area where the vessels have been found, together with the fact that nearly half of those people came from the Bakongo region; (2) the use of the cosmogram for centering in Africa; (3) the traditional use of clay vessels for Central African charms, called *minkisi*; (4) the circularity of bowls, particularly those with ring bases, which fits with the importance of circularity in African ideology; and (5) the basic features of the cosmogram—the crossroad and an underworld beneath the water—which were commonly held ideals all along the coast of West and Central Africa and would have been potential points of syncretism for the variety of people enslaved in the low country of South Carolina.

Thus, several lines of evidence converge to suggest the marked vessels were connected to African, and particularly Central African, ritual. Yet there may well have been other connections. Both Christians and the Native Americans of the Southeast recognized the cross as an important symbol, and southeastern Indians used both the cross and circle, sometimes inscribing them in the bottom center of bowls. During the early days of the Carolina colony, relatively large numbers of Native Americans, many of them from Christian missions in Spanish Florida, were enslaved on Carolina plantations. These Native Americans became a part of African America. The result was that in creating religious ritual, African Americans of the eighteenth and nineteenth centuries had access to a wide variety of ideas. How these different patterns may have come together in the production and use of marked earthenware bowls is beyond the scope of this essay, yet the constellation of evidence and circumstances makes a compelling case for a strong African influence.

## Notes

I would like to thank Elaine Nichols for introducing me to Sterling Stuckey's work, for suggesting that the colonoware crosses might be related to African-American religion, and for her inspiring faith in archaeology as a key to learning about the African-American past. Thanks also to Wythe Dornan and an unidentified "voice from the audience" at a meeting in Williamsburg for alerting me to the similarities between the marks and the Bakongo cosmogram, and to Daonnie Barker, H. Paul Blatner, and Chris Espenshade for providing information on marked artifacts. I have appreciated the interest of many people who discussed this topic with me through the years as well as those who have alerted me to crosses on all sorts of artifacts.

At the 1989 "Digging for the African-American Past" conference, Robert Hall asked if I was using the ethnographic work of Karl Laman; I was not then, but I am now, with thanks to Dr. Hall. Sharon Pekrul, Carl Steen, and Emily Short helped with research and recording. With special appreciation I thank Aline Ferguson, Richard Affleck, Natalie Adams, Mark Groover, John Adams, Niels Taylor, and two anonymous reviewers for the University Press of Virginia for reading this chapter and providing their comments.

1. Colonoware is a broad term, like "British ceramics," used to designate a hand-built, unglazed earthenware found on colonial American sites. Within this broad category some specific archaeological pottery types and varieties have been described (e.g., Ferguson 1989b, 1994; Henry 1980; Wheaton, Friedlander, and Garrow 1983; Zierden et al. 1986). Nevertheless, we shall have to do significantly more research before we fully comprehend the complexity of this colonial craft phenomenon.

2. One appeal of underwater sites to nonprofessionals and professionals alike is that in the deep still water of the coastal plain artifacts that sank to the bottom are protected from post-depositional damage. Thus, divers find large fragments or whole artifacts in these contexts. The negative side of this underwater contexts is poor visibility. Tannin from decaying organic matter in swamps and marshes results in the so-called blackwater creeks and rivers of the low country, and this "blackwater" reduces underwater visibility in most cases to only a few inches. The result is that divers usually gather artifacts by feel rather than sight, and since large artifacts are available, they usually stuff these larger pieces into their collecting sacks. This collecting situation virtually eliminates the likelihood of divers, while underwater, selecting bowls over jars, ring bases over other types of bases, or marked vessels over unmarked vessels. Once in their boats or on shore, they might make discriminations and discard some pieces. But in this situation there is no apparent reason why they would discard jars over bowls or flat or rounded bases over vessels with ring bases. They might, on the other hand, select relatively smaller pieces that were marked over unmarked smaller pieces, and if this were the case, it would inflate the proportion of marked to unmarked vessels from underwater. However, it would not affect the proportion of marked pieces from underwater to marked pieces from sites on land. In absolute numbers, more marked pieces have been found underwater than on land even though tens of thousands more sherds of colonoware have been collected and reported from terrestrial sites by professional archaeologists. The marked pieces from underwater are all from bowls, as they are on land, and there are more from vessels with ring bases than with flat and rounded bases.

3. Small ticks and painted crosses have been found on the shoulder portion of colonoware jars. The painted crosses occur on river burnished jars within a large repertoire of decorative motifs.

4. Stanley South (1988:211, 221–22) has described postfiring incised marks on the exterior bottom of glazed Spanish majolica bowls from the sixteenth-century site of Santa Elena. However, these marks are not centered, nor are they otherwise like those found on vessels from Carolina plantations. Rather than crosses with arms of equal length, the Santa Elena marks include Roman crosses, a pentagonal star, and parallel lines. David Hurst Thomas (1988:118) has mentioned crosses incised on sherds from the late seventeenth-century Spanish mission of Santa Catalina de Guale on the Georgia coast. Presumably they are similar to those from Santa Elena.

5. This catalog includes both complete vessels and large vessel fragments that allow extrapolation of the whole vessel shape. The complete catalog includes sixty-seven vessels.

Table 6. 1. Marks on colonoware bowls

| Site/Artifact no. Plantation | Site location | Base type | Mark location | Pre- or post firing | Condition |
|---|---|---|---|---|---|
| | | | Category 1 | | |
| 38BK48-536 Mepkin | underwater | ring | interior | post | fragment |
| 38DH223/ED Drayton Hall | terrestrial | flat | exterior | pre | whole |
| Cooper River | underwater | flat | interior | post | whole |
| | | | Category 2 | | |
| 38BK48-377 Mepkin | underwater | ring | interior | pre | fragment |
| 38BK48-1-478 Mepkin | underwater | round | interior | pre | fragment |
| 38BK62-75-53 Pimilico | underwater | ? | interior | pre | fragment |
| | | | Category 3 | | |
| 38BK62-79-119 Pimlico | underwater | ring | exterior | post | whole |
| 38BK62-70-126 Pimlico | underwater | ring | exterior | pre | whole |
| 38BK48-378 Mepkin | underwater | ring | exterior | pre | whole |
| 38BK48-1-416 Mepkin | underwater | ring | exterior | post | fragment |
| 38BK48-JT-7 Mepkin | underwater | flat | exterior | post | fragment |
| 38BK48-JT-5 Mepkin | underwater | ring | interior | post | whole |
| 38BK48-1-480 Mepkin | underwater | flat | interior | pre | whole |
| 38BK38-567-2 Middleburg | terrestrial | flat | interior | pre | whole |
| 38245-1-0 Curriboo | terrestrial | flat | interior | pre | whole |

| | | | | | |
|---|---|---|---|---|---|
| 38BK38<br>Middleburg | terrestrial | flat | interior | post | fragment |
| 38BK38<br>Middleburg | terrestrial | flat | interior | post | fragment |
| 38BK38<br>Middleburg | terrestrial | flat | interior | post | fragment |
| 38BK62-70-134<br>Pimilico | underwater | ring | exterior | pre | whole |
| 38BK62-75-79<br>Pimlico | underwater | flat | exterior | pre | whole |
| 38BK-1-440<br>Mepkin | underwater | flat | exterior | post | fragment |
| 38BK48-1-446<br>Mepkin | underwater | flat | interior | pre | fragment |
| 38BU791 (V1)<br>Bonny Shore | terrestrial | ring | ext./int. | post | fragment |
| 38BU791(V5)<br>Bonny Shore | terrestrial | ring | exterior | post | fragment |
| 38BU91(V6)<br>Bonny Shore | terrestrial | ring | exterior | post | fragment |
| 38DR3-76<br>Old Dorchester | terrestrial | flat | exterior | pre | fragment |
| Privy<br>Telfair Academy<br>Savannah, Ga. | terrestrial | round | exterior | pre | whole |

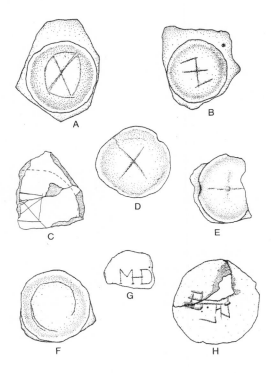

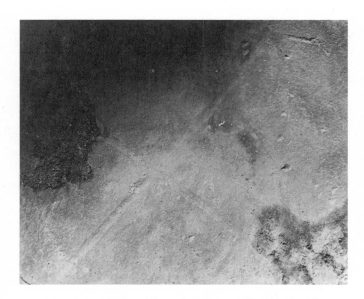

6.1. Marks on colonoware vessels from South Carolina

6.2. Cross drawn before firing when clay was "leather hard," Cooper River, Berkeley County, S.C.

# 7

# Oceans Apart: Africanist Perspectives of Diaspora Archaeology

*Christopher R. DeCorse*

ARCHAEOLOGISTS have focused increasing attention on African-American sites. While this research has been of great importance in understanding various aspects of American economic and social systems and the lifeways of enslaved Africans, many of the studies lack an appreciation of the complexity of the African cultural milieu. Regardless of avowed concerns about culture process, the research methodologies that have been employed are often ill suited to examine culture change and continuity in the populations under study. This chapter briefly examines African-American archaeology within the context of the Atlantic slave trade and archaeological research in Africa. Emphasis is placed on the interpretation of African-American societies within their cultural and historical contexts in both Africa and the Americas. The potential contribution of archaeological studies to understanding the genesis of the African-American worldview is examined.

Africa covers an area several times larger than the continental United States. Slaves destined for the Americas were not exported from all areas, but a vast portion of the continent was involved, and many different cultures and groups were affected. Some scholars have discussed unifying, Pan-African characteristics. As Jacques Maquet has noted, "To the degree to which more similarities are found between the various cultures of Africa than between African and non-African cultures, it is justifiable to place the African cultures in a separate category" (1972:11). The features that unify African cultures may provide some insight into African-American sociocultural origins, and these features are discussed below.

Despite some underlying similarities, however, the continent encompasses a tremendous range of cultural, linguistic, and ethnic diversity. Interpreting this variation archaeologically and making meaningful observations concerning African-American culture has proved difficult. A major limitation in studies of African continuities in the Americas is American researchers' lack of familiarity with African material. The tendency has been to view African cultures in generalized terms, despite the fact that very few specific phenomena can be used to characterize African cultures as a whole.

Interpretation is also constrained by the paucity of comparative data from many of the relevant parts of Africa. In some areas archaeological research is still in its preliminary descriptive stages, and succinct regional chronologies are lacking. Although African cultures may be readily defined ethnographically, they are frequently difficult to identify on the basis of archaeological data (e.g., Atherton 1983:90–96; David 1971:125–29; David and Hennig 1972; DeCorse 1989c; Hodder 1984). Culture traits ranging from pottery styles to foodways practices often crosscut ethnographically perceived cultural boundaries. Variables such as topography, climate, and environmental factors are in some cases more important in determining settlement pattern, construction methods, and other aspects of material culture than is cultural identity (Beguin 1952; DeCorse 1989c:137–39; Denyer 1978:159–68; Oliver 1971:18–24). For archaeologists interested in defining cultures or (more narrowly defined) ethnic groups on the basis of material remains, such variation poses obvious problems.

Despite interpretive difficulties, studies of material aspects of shared belief systems, or worldviews, have demonstrated that indications of cultural and ethnic differences can be perceived archaeologically. In their ethnographic study of pottery among the Mafa and Bulahay in northern Cameroon, David, Sterner, and Gavua argued that "specific decorative motifs represent cosmological and religious concepts, and similar patterns of decoration on different pot types express coherent underlying perceptions, accounting for continuities in an 'art' form in which no one is particularly interested. The interrelatedness of pottery decoration and symbolic structures quite incidentally justifies widespread use of decoration as the prime index of ethnicity preserved in the archaeological record" (1988:365). Pottery, therefore, provides a material expression of the Mafa and Bulahay worldviews. Cognitive studies of pottery in southern Africa also have demonstrated that understanding the ideographic basis of stylistic variation in ceramics is very important in defining Iron Age cultures and evaluating culture change archaeologically (Evers 1989; Huffman 1986, 1989).

In other areas different categories within the material inventory may provide expressions of cultural identity. For example, among the Limba, Yalunka, and Kuranko of northeastern Sierra Leone, material aspects of worldview and group cohesion seem to be manifested primarily in ritual structures that in many instances leave only ephemeral traces in the archaeological record (DeCorse 1989a:138). There are examples of symbols of cultural identity being transmitted by various other categories of material culture in other parts of Africa (e.g., Berns 1989, 1990; Braithwaite 1982; Cole and Aniakor 1984; David et al. 1991; Posnansky, chap. 2 in this volume).

Archaeologists examining material aspects of worldview in West Africa also have focused on artifacts within social systems and their spatial distribution. Agorsah's (1983b, 1985b, 1988) ethnoarchaeological studies of Nchumuru sites in the northern Volta Basin, Ghana, suggest that information on ethnicity is represented in spatial organization. Identification of compound, clan, and phratry relationships on the basis of the material record is particularly important in defining Nchumuru ethnicity. David's (1971) research on material aspects of Fulani settlements in Cameroon also emphasizes the importance of correctly identifying the most basic social units as a means of interpreting larger, more abstract cultural groups.

An additional dimension of African cultural dynamics which is often poorly addressed in diaspora studies is culture change in African societies during the period following European contact. The overwhelming tendency in American studies has been to view African cultures as static (Posnansky, chap. 2 in this volume). Much of the empirical data on customs, language, and material culture that have been used to characterize African societies are derived from ethnographic accounts that may or may not reflect behavioral practices and belief systems during the relevant period of the slave trade.

Documentary sources, in fact, suggest that there was a great deal of cultural continuity on the Guinea coast during the post-European-contact period. In many areas cultural practices—including rituals, cosmological perceptions, and worldview—evidence a great deal of consistency through time. Linguistic data similarly suggest there was little change in the distribution of West African populations following the Europeans' arrival (Hair 1967). This cultural continuity can be contrasted with transformations in other areas. There was, for example, tremendous change in African sociopolitical institutions during the postcontact period (e.g., Daaku 1970; Dike 1966; Inikori 1982; Kea 1982; Rodney 1970). Alliances were modified as European nations became increasingly enmeshed in local politics. There were also fundamental changes in trade and exchange as Africa was increasingly drawn into a world economic system dominated by Europe. The European trade did not destroy earlier networks, but trade was redirected toward the new frontier of opportunity provided by European outposts. The specific consequences of these developments varied in individual local settings.

A great deal of change is represented in the archaeological record. In examining archaeological sites in Ghana, several researchers have noted radical change in the material record of the post-European-contact period. Paul Ozanne (1962), surveying surface material from Accra and Shai, noted clear differences between the pottery of the "late prehistoric" and the "historic" periods. Ozanne considered the late prehistoric period to extend to the end of the sixteenth century. A similar pattern seems to be present in collections throughout the southern forest region of Ghana (Bellis 1987). In coastal communities European trade items become common. Evidence of change in settlement patterns and the material inventory are also found in other parts of West Africa (DeCorse 1991, n.d.). What remains unclear is to what degree the observed changes in the archaeological record represent culture change, as opposed to innovations in technology, modifications in economic relations, or population dislocation.

Several conclusions can be drawn with regard to archaeological studies of African cultures. The available information suggests that archaeological data can provide some indication of culturally bounded divisions. The material indicators useful in defining group expression are not uniform in all contexts, however. While ethnoarchaeological research underscores the potential importance of material culture in studies of culture, ethnicity, and culture change, it also demonstrates the complex nature of interpretation. The African data should, therefore, be carefully evaluated before generalizations are made about American continuities. The integration of the available African data with American studies is further complicated by the scope and the disruptive nature of the slave trade.

## The Atlantic Slave Trade

Approximately twelve million people were taken from Africa to the Americas, Europe, and the Atlantic islands between the fifteenth and the nineteenth centuries. The horror of the Middle Passage and the disruptive effects of slavery have been extensively treated in written accounts of the period and in other more recent studies. What have been less carefully examined are the origins of slave populations (e.g., Davidson 1980; Debien 1974; Geggus 1989:395; Higman 1984; Lovejoy 1989:373–80; Richardson 1989). Historical studies have tended to focus on the numbers involved and the areas where slaves were purchased, not on actual cultural or ethnic affiliations. An increasing amount of work is being conducted in this area, but such research is time-consuming and constrained by lack of adequate documentation. Relevant sources are scattered throughout archives in Europe, Africa, and the Americas in several different languages.

Most records describe where slaves were purchased and collected by European ships, not where they actually originated. Lovejoy has noted that "ethnicity under slavery tended to be identified with the commercial system through which the slaves passed in Africa; that is the region and/or port of export" (1989:378). The apparent prevalence of certain ethnic groups in African populations in the Americas is, at least in part, the result of historical amalgamation. Studies of plantation inventories reveal that the majority of the slaves whose cultural affiliations were recorded were generally placed within one of several major categories such as Congo, Gbe (Ewe-Fon), Yoruba, Igbo, Bambara, Akan, Mina, Angola, and Mozambique (Geggus 1989; Lovejoy 1989). At best these categories can be considered to represent broadly inclusive ethnolinguistic groups. Studies of plantation records similarly suggest that owners perceived slave populations to be ethnically homogeneous. These generalized perceptions contradict documentary accounts and African oral traditions that indicate slaves were obtained from numerous populations. As Lovejoy (1989:378) has also indicated, the slaves' perception of their own ethnic identity probably changed as people of different ethnic and cultural origins were incorporated into slave society. Unfortunately, such perceptions are largely unrecorded.

Notably, the tendency to emphasize certain groups continues in modern historical, ethnographic, and archaeological studies. Africanists have focused a great deal of attention on the Akan and Yoruba. This is partly the result of the historical importance of the regions involved, but it also reflects emphasis on areas with well-established local research institutions and infrastructures. This orientation can also be seen in North American studies of the African diaspora, as researchers have naturally drawn more heavily on those areas that have the best documentation.

The manner in which slaves reached American markets varied a great deal. For example, more European forts were established on the Gold Coast than on any other part of the continent. Despite this concentration, the area remained a poor place to obtain slaves until the late seventeenth century. The Gold Coast outposts frequently served as barracoons for slaves purchased in other parts of the coast, particularly regions to the east. Culturally, the resulting slave populations encompassed numerous groups, many quite distinct from the indigenous Gold Coast populations. The Grain or Malagueta Coast (including the area of modern Liberia), which provided many slaves to the Carolinas, had no significant European outposts. For this reason, trading was frequently done directly from ships. Slaves were captured by Europeans in some areas, particularly during the earlier years of the trade. As the trade became more entrenched in African economies, however, slaves were obtained primarily by African middlemen from deep within the hinterland and brought to the coast for trade. It is these widely scattered and ethnically diverse areas from which the slaves were obtained that need to be considered when examining African continuities in the Americas.

In the Americas the ethnically diverse slave populations experienced extensive variation in treatment, survival rates, and other local conditions. Within this context, the response of individuals also varied, as illustrated by the case studies presented by Michael Craton (1978: 191–271) in his examination of plantation life in Jamaica.

Many researchers have stressed the need to consider the disruptive nature of the slave trade when examining African societies in the Americas. Armstrong (1985:265, 1990), in his work at the Drax Hall plantation, Jamaica, posited variation in individual island and plantation systems. Other researchers have correctly stressed the need both to recognize the complexity of the historical situation and to evaluate archaeological data within their ethnohistorical context (i.e., Handler and Lange 1978; Lange and Handler 1985; Howson 1990; cf. Posnansky 1984, chap. 2 in this volume).

The difficulties involved in tracing African continuities in the Americas can be illustrated by ongoing research into connections between Curaçao, Netherlands Antilles, and Elmina, Ghana (Haviser and DeCorse 1991). Elmina was the headquarters of Dutch mercantile interests in West Africa between 1637 and 1872. Curaçao, on the other hand, emerged as a major Dutch distribution point for slaves in the Americas. At the outset it seemed that research focusing on slave origins in each area would provide a unique opportunity to examine African cultural continuities in the Americas. Documentary accounts, however, indicate that many of the slaves who reached Curaçao via Elmina actually were brought by ship from other parts of the coast, particularly the Bight of Benin, probably having been obtained in the hinterland (Manning 1979:141; cf. Van Dantzig 1978). Slaves reaching Curaçao were distributed to many other areas.

## American Studies in African Perspective

Despite the disruptive historical situation, a significant body of evidence illustrates the survival of African practices, attributes, or features in the Americas—traits Melville Herskovits referred to as "Africanisms" (1936). These range from folk traditions to scarification, carving, and language (e.g., Holloway 1990; Mintz 1974; Mintz and Price 1981; Price and Price 1980; Shapiro 1976; Vlach 1990). Studies of certain classes of African-American material culture found in archaeological contexts are of special interest, as an attempt has been made to integrate data from Africa. This research includes studies of pottery and clay tobacco pipes of supposed African-American manufacture.

The term *colonoware* has been used to describe a variety of low-fired, unglazed earthenwares of non-European origin found in the eastern United States. Similar wares also have been reported throughout the Caribbean. While similar wares are clearly associated with African slaves in plantation settings, the contribution of Native Americans has been demonstrated. There is evidence that various Native American groups continued to produce pottery for trade well into the historical period (e.g., Binford 1965; Ferguson 1989a; Hodges 1990; Brian Crane and L. Daniel Mouer 1990: pers. comm.). The term *colonoware* likely subsumes many different potting traditions representing the products of a number of different ethnic and cultural groups.

Detailed studies of colonoware have been limited by poor evidence of production techniques, variation in local traditions, and lack of appropriate comparative collections from Africa. Initial attempts to relate American finds to African potting traditions were very limited in scope and naive in interpretation. As the great cultural diversity and local variability represented in Africa would suggest, there are no general characteristics that can be readily used to distinguish "African" pottery.

In Africa, potting is generally a female occupation. In some societies, however, men as well as women may produce both pots and clay pipes. For example, in Asante, women were prohibited from making the more elaborate, figurative pipes and pots that were produced by men (Johnson 1982:212; Rattray 1959:301). Similar customs have also been reported among the Mandinka (Hill 1987). In many instances most women in a village traditionally may have known how to make pots. Yet ethnographic studies indicate that the religious and socioeconomic status of potters varies in different cultural settings, and such diversity was likely present in the past (e.g., David and Hennig 1972:4; Johnson 1982).

Specific methods of manufacture, raw materials, vessel forms, surface treatment, decorative techniques, and firing methods exhibit a great deal of variation among different African cultures and ethnic groups. A host of ethnographic descriptions may be cited to illustrate this point (e.g., Agbaje-Williams 1983; Ajayi 1985; Berns 1989; Cardew 1952, 1961; Crossland 1973; Dark 1973; David and Hennig 1972; DeCorse 1989a; Devisse 1981; Frobenius 1913; Johnson 1982; Leith-Ross 1970; Nadel 1942; Newman 1974; Nicolls 1987; Quarcoo and Johnson 1968; Rammage 1980; Rattray 1959; Rivallain 1981; Street 1980; Simmonds 1982; Willett and Connah 1969).

Reviewing the data, one is struck by the variation in form and decoration. Significant differences are present even in the ceramics of adjacent regions. Figure 7.1 illustrates some of the vessels found in archaeological contexts of fifteenth- through nineteenth-century age in Ghana. Modern Ghana is slightly larger than the states of Georgia and South Carolina combined. It encompasses between forty-five to fifty ethnolinguistic groups, plus many other divisions reflecting varying degrees of social cohesion (Kropp Dakubu 1988). The pottery forms illustrated are not meant to provide "typical" examples of African pottery of different ages or locales; rather they illustrate diversity within a relatively small portion of Africa. A very small selection of the ceramics present in Ghanaian archaeological sites is illustrated. Each of the ceramic traditions is represented by a large selection of utilitarian and ritual vessels. Similar diversity can be seen in other regions (fig. 7.2).

Temporal change in African decorative motifs and vessel forms is complex and not well understood. Despite some carefully excavated and well-described collections, the dating of many African ceramic types must be regarded as tentative. It is notable that the diversity present in archaeological collections is often not represented in ethnographic pieces. A trend in many areas (including Ghana and Sierra Leone) over the past century has been toward less decoration and the production of fewer forms. In many instances the manufacture of pottery has almost ceased. On the other hand, certain vessel shapes have diffused over wider areas in recent centuries, as in the case of Akan-style carinated pots and grinding bowls. While ethnographic and ethnoarchaeological studies of modern potters remain an important source of information, the current situation cannot automatically be equated with the past.

Although it has been suggested that certain technological attributes indicate the African-American origins of colonoware, it is the slave-associated historical context of some of the ceramics that is the salient characteristic. It would be surprising if substantial pottery technology was transported to the Americas within the context of the slave trade. Many of the best African potters were likely older women (e.g., David and Hennig 1972; Posnansky, chap. 2 in this volume), the group least represented in slave populations. It is likely that young women and men brought to the Americas as slaves did not have the opportunity to obtain extensive experience in African pottery manufacture. As Matthew Hill (1987) has pointed out, there are no striking similarities between American ceramics with purported African influence and the more elaborate decorations and vessel forms found in Africa. It is, nonetheless, difficult to generalize, and more comparative data are needed on areas from which slaves were obtained.

There are, in fact, African parallels to some American ceramic forms. The simple bowls and utilitarian jars often represented in African-American ceramic assemblages have counterparts in pottery occurring in many portions of West Africa (e.g., Ferguson 1980; Ferguson et al. 1990; Mayes 1972:102–3; Wesler 1987). Duncan Matthewson (1972) discussed Afro-Jamaican ceramics with specific reference to discoveries of eighteenth-century age from Old King's House, Spanish Town. Matthewson argued that the archaeological finds, as well as contemporary Jamaican folk pottery forms such as *yabbas*, clearly reflected African influences. While emphasizing supposed Akan characteristics of the wares, Matthewson also noted the possible contribution of Arawak and European ceramic traditions. It is significant that even those forms Matthewson noted as providing evidence of European influence also have parallels in African ceramics. For example, basal rings and flat bottoms occur in many West African ceramic assemblages. Examples of these attributes predating European contact can be seen in Matthewson's (1974) discussion of material from northern Ghana and in the McIntoshes' (1980:203–4) report on excavations at Jenne, Mali.

Leland Ferguson's (chap. 6 in this volume) study of colonoware addresses continuities between two other areas: western Central Africa and South Carolina. This work is of particular interest because the attributes considered to be evidence of African continuities are quite different from those noted in other colonoware studies. Ferguson considers marks that resemble socioreligious symbols used in Africa, particularly in the area between Gabon and Angola. During the eighteenth century many of the slaves imported to South Carolina originated in this region (Ferguson, chap. 6 in this volume; cf. Lovejoy 1989:374).

The marks noted by Ferguson are quite varied. A few are letters that simply may represent owners' marks. There are others, however, including circles, crosses, and more elaborate patterns, that bear close similarities to a number of Kongo cosmograms. That some of these marks were added by the potter while others were created after manufacture seems to indicate they are not simply makers' or owners' marks. Another set of symbols, all made during manufacture, are lines that divide the interior surface of bowls into four equal sections. The quartering of a bowl for divination is a practice that has been reported from Central Africa (Ferguson 1990, pers. comm.). The majority of the marked sherds examined by Ferguson have been recovered from slave contexts, a large portion associated with water. The position of the marks on containers, the statistical association of the vessels with rivers, and the known slave contexts of the finds are a combination of observations that suggests that the vessels functioned in a specialized context. The physical similarity of the South Carolina marks to African cosmograms may provide important insight into African religious continuities. Limited ethnohistoric information on African-American religious beliefs in the southeastern United States further suggests that such continuities existed (Ferguson, chap. 6 in this volume).

By way of caution, it is important to point out that the ideas involved—African cosmology, division between the living and the dead, and transition—are extremely complex, while the symbols involved are quite simple. Similar, but not identical, marks have been found on ceramics in other cultural and historical settings. An Iberian olive jar sherd from Santa Elena, the sixteenth-century capital of Spanish Florida, bears a simple engraved cross comparable to some of the marks noted by Ferguson (South, Skowronek, and Johnson 1988:282). Crosses also have been found on sixteenth-century Iberian ceramics from the African settlement at Elmina, Ghana (fig. 7.3). What these marks may have symbolized in these contexts is uncertain. In the case of the Kongo and South Carolina marks, it is possible that a symbol was transported but did not retain the same meaning.

Another innovative study dealing with African continuities in the Americas is Matthew Emerson's (1988, 1994, chap. 4 in this volume) examination of the syncretic nature of locally produced clay tobacco pipes from the Chesapeake Bay region of the eastern United States. Decorative elements on these pipes appear to combine European, African, and Native American features. Emerson's arguments are a potentially important means of enhancing the documentary evidence available on the African presence in the seventeenth-century Chesapeake.

Tobacco is an American cultigen that probably was introduced to Africa at the end of the sixteenth century (Philips 1983). Its inception is associated with the appearance of elbow-bend, socket-stem pipes in West Africa. These have been widely reported, and a preliminary chronological sequence, beginning ca. 1640, has been produced for southern Ghana (Ozanne 1964). There is some evidence for the smoking of other plants, as well as the use of water and earthen pipes several centuries earlier in other portions of the continent. However, none of the pipes produced in Africa before the present century closely parallel forms represented in the seventeenth-century Chesapeake assemblages. On the other hand, many of the Chesapeake bowl shapes approximate European clay pipe forms of the period (Emerson 1994). African pipes are made by hand, whereas at least some pipes from the Chesapeake were molded. African pipes, therefore, are different both in form and method of manufacture from Chesapeake examples.

Documentary records and archaeological materials provide very limited data on the manufacture of tobacco pipes in the Chesapeake (Emerson 1988:33–35; 1994). The available information indicates that pipes were produced by both Europeans and Native Americans, but these brief references do not preclude the possibility of African-American contributions (Mouer et al., chap. 5 in this volume). To examine African influence on the Chesapeake pipes, Emerson studied pipe forms and the artistic elements represented. He cites fluted bowls and certain decorative techniques—such as quadruped motifs, white fill, and *pointillé* lines—as possible evidence of African influences. The pipes, then, are argued to represent a syncretic art form combining African decorative elements with European pipe forms.

Evaluation of the potential contribution of African artistic and pipe-making traditions to American artifacts is constrained by the limitations of the African data. The best-documented African pipes come from Ghana, where socket-stem, elbow-bend pipes have been recovered in a wide range of archaeological contexts (Davies 1955; Effah-Gyamfi 1985; Ozanne 1962, 1964; Shaw 1960; Shinnie and Ozanne 1962:99–103). No pipes with fluted bowls have yet been identified in these assemblages.

Socket-stem pipes with fluting or square cross-sectioned bowls and stems have been recovered from a number of sites in Mali (Daget and Ligers 1962:19, 33, 38,42). Exactly how tobacco smoking was introduced into the western Sahara is not clear. The Malian pipes have not as yet been systematically studied, nor have chronologies been established (Philips 1983:317–19). Daget and Ligers (1962:13), in their important survey of Malian pipes, suggest the local industry may have reached its zenith in the seventeenth or early eighteenth century, possibly stimulated by trade contacts with North Africa. It is important, however, to realize that the majority of the pipes Daget and Ligers studied are from poorly dated surface collections or from the antiquities market. Pipes are still being produced in Mali (as well as in other West African countries) today. Fluting or faceting occurs on pipes examined by Daget and Ligers, but it is not characteristic of the most common bowl shapes. In fact, the pipe that provides the best example of fluting is described as unique in shape (Daget and Ligers 1962::3, fig. 2, 23). Faceted stems are more common than fluted bowls in published illustrations, but any conclusions about the frequency of these attributes need to be reexamined in light of ongoing research.

Emerson's examination of other decorative attributes of Chesapeake pipes is likewise hindered by the lack of detailed comparative material from Africa. There is no readily available corpus of material summarizing regional artistic traditions. Much of the existing work has been carried out by art historians on ethnographic pieces. While many decorative themes represented have a great antiquity in Africa, documentation of specific attributes seldom predates the nineteenth or twentieth century. How indicative these more recent attributes are of aesthetics in earlier periods is difficult to evaluate.

Given the range of artistic expression in Africa, the documentation of historical connections between the relevant areas should be a critical consideration. Emerson (1994) notes that the majority of slaves in the seventeenth-century Chesapeake may have originated in Nigeria (cf. Kulikoff 1986; Emerson 1994). The examples of African material culture he cites, however, include a number of different media widely separated in both time and space. Parallels are drawn between Chesapeake pipes and modern calabashes from the Republic of Benin; surface-collected pipes from Mali; ceramics from Nigeria, Ghana, and Mali; and a number of other categories of material culture (Emerson 1988). Emerson notes that pipes and ceramics from Mali bear the closest stylistic similarities to Chesapeake pipe art, but he identifies parallels in symbols from Nigeria, Cameroon, and Ghana. There is no question that people from all of these regions were brought as slaves to the Americas, but more historical work tracing relations with the Chesapeake is desirable.

Some of the decorative elements represented on Chesapeake pipes are clearly found in European and Native American artistic traditions as well as African ones. As Emerson (1988:124–28; 1994) illustrates with his discussion of possible antecedents for quadruped decorations, it is very difficult to trace the origins of a specific motif. Given the limited information on the historical context in which the pipes were manufactured and the mode of expression that may have served as inspiration, it is difficult to know which world area should be examined for parallels. Similarities may be found in many media, an example being the wriggle-work decoration seen on European pewter, common in the late seventeenth and early eighteenth centuries. Although different in technique from the *pointillé* decoration of Chesapeake pipes, the overall effects are quite similar (e.g., Brett 1982:41–46, 59). Naturalistic motifs, including a variety of quadrupeds, are common themes on wriggle work. On the other hand, the *pointillé*, punctate, and white-filled patterns present on Malian pipes are very similar in technique to the methods employed in the Chesapeake. However, comparable anthropomorphic or zoomorphic decorations are absent on West African pipes that have been described.

Despite these difficulties, the assemblage of decorative techniques employed on some Chesapeake pipes does bear close similarity to African decorative motifs. As Emerson (1994:14) observes, "A grammar consisting of rules for the articulation of this style would easily 'fit' examples of West African artifacts and many Chesapeake pipes."

Emerson's work is extremely important in illustrating the kind of interdisciplinary research that is needed to examine African influences in American artistic traditions. It also underscores the problems inherent in trying to trace the origin of an art form that is manifestly an amalgamation of many different traditions. It is quite likely that different manufacturers are represented, and several different cultural groups may have made contributions. With regard to the current discussion, what is most important to consider is what Chesapeake pipes may convey about African-American society and culture. They may, as Emerson suggests, provide insight into the nature of African-English interaction in the Chesapeake during the seventeenth century (cf. Deetz, chap. 3 in this volume). Even if certain African symbols were borrowed, however, we have little understanding of how they may have functioned and what meanings they may have conveyed in the Chesapeake. A symbol used on a ritual pot in Nigeria and a pipe bowl in the Chesapeake were very likely imbued with very different cultural meanings.

Various studies by anthropologists and archaeologists have focused on other "African" traits. For example, it has been suggested that blue faceted beads found on slaves sites may relate to a Moslem belief that a single blue bead wards off evil spirits (Adams 1987:204). Islam was introduced into some portions of West Africa beginning late in the first millennium A.D. The process of religious change was extremely complex and varied under different historical, geographical, and cultural conditions (Bravmann 1980, 1983; Hiskett 1984; Trimingham 1978). Many areas still maintain indigenous African (pre-Islamic) belief systems today. In other instances, current beliefs incorporate both Islamic and pre-Islamic practices. Nevertheless, it is clear that some of the slaves involved in the Atlantic slave trade were at least nominally Moslem (e.g., Lovejoy 1989:378).

Beads are extremely important in Africa, and they were produced and used by Africans before the advent of Islam. They have had many uses, and the relationship of beads to various cultures' worldviews is extremely varied (e.g., DeCorse 1989b, 1989c). In the absence of any documentary evidence of their function, the association of faceted blue beads at slave sites with Islamic practices—as opposed to any number of African belief systems—is extremely tenuous. One of the most ubiquitous uses to which beads are put in West Africa is in strands around females' waists. A child may have a single strand, whereas an adult may have multiple strands consisting of hundreds of beads. Blue faceted beads employed in this manner have been excavated at the site of Elmina, Ghana. This does not provide immediate insight into the use of blue beads on African-American sites. It does, however, offer one of many alternative interpretations (cf. Armstrong 1990:178–81; Handler and Lange 1978:144–50; Yentsch 1994:190–95).

Beads—particularly blue beads—have been consistently associated with African-American sites (Stine, Cabek, and Groover 1996), but whether this patterning is to be explained in terms of shared economic, social, or cultural characteristics is unclear. Although blue beads occur in West African contexts, assemblages frequently incorporate a diversity of colors and decorative motifs unrepresented in African-American settings (e.g., DeCorse 1989b). The simple inexpensive blue beads may speak more to the socioeconomic status of African Americans in the plantation setting than a shared system of beliefs.

Clearly no single artifact category or attribute has the potential to provide an unobfuscated material translation of African-American cultural identity or ethnicity. Rather than focus on one-to-one parallels with Africa, some American archaeologists have examined variation in artifact assemblages.

## Slave Patterns

Some North American historical archaeologists have employed methods first advocated by Stanley South (1977). On the basis of his research on eighteenth-century Anglo-American sites, South developed techniques for quantifying and examining artifact patterns. To facilitate study, artifacts were combined into groups on the basis of "functional activities related to the systemic context reflected by the archaeological record" (South 1977:93). Data systematized in this manner have been applied to questions of ethnicity, culture change, site function, socioeconomic status, and other presumably causal factors of inter- and intrasite variability. South (1977:13–17) linked this methodological approach to a nomothetic paradigm stressing the use of archaeological data to test hypotheses relating to culture processes that eventually could be used to develop generalized laws of culture dynamics. While this hypothesis-testing approach (also known as the hypothetico-deductive method) has received a great deal of criticism, South's quantitative methodology has continued in use as a means of organizing and interpreting data from historical archaeological sites.

Systematic archaeological research has been undertaken at a number of slave sites, but identification and interpretation of distinct "slave patterns" have remained unsatisfactory. Several researchers have observed patterns at the regional level (e.g.,

Singleton 1980), but the relationship of these observations to culture change within slave communities and the emergence of African-American culture or ethnicity is unclear. The research conducted has generally focused on attempts to define socio-economic status, not continuity and change within slave cultures. Overlap in the patterns produced by slave, overseer, and owner sites hinders identification of distinct "African" patterns, while local variation in construction methods, preservation, environment, and excavation techniques further confuses the picture (Joseph 1989).

One of the most insightful interpretations of change in African-American society is provided by Thomas Wheaton and Patrick Garrow (1985). In their study of plantations in the Carolina low country, they focus on specific artifact types as well as the pattern recognition techniques advocated by South. Wheaton and Garrow cite decreasing percentages of colonoware, increasing amounts of European ceramics, and a decline in the use of mud architecture during the 1740–1820 period as evidence for the assimilation of Africans into Euro-American society. These are important observations that may be indicative of changes in slave lifeways. Once again, however, it is important to evaluate what this information may convey about the cultural system. Changes in ceramic types and construction materials are changes in technology. As Joseph (1989:62–63) notes, the trends may be consequences of the Industrial Revolution. Wheaton and Garrow (1985:257) also point out that modification of housing styles may reflect the influence of the plantation owners (cf. Ferguson et al. 1990; McKee 1992). In any case, it is quite possible that the trends in ceramics and construction methods observed resulted from change in Euro-American culture, not from developments internal to slave societies.

At a conference on historical archaeology, one attendee at a session on plantation archaeology left muttering loudly: "There's no pattern! If there's a pattern, I'd like to know what it is!" That there is no single "slave" pattern should be no surprise. Given the cultural variation and the divergent historical conditions during the early years of the plantation system, there should be a great deal of local variation. Amalgamation occurred within the slave system, but some regional variation is readily discernible in modern African-American and African-Caribbean cultures. Variation in slave patterns, however, for the most part appears unrelated to elements of African ethnicity or culture in slave society.

The "pattern" in South's pattern recognition is primarily produced by variation in two of the eight artifact groups: kitchen and architecture. This may provide a useful means of distinguishing cultural variation under some conditions, but different techniques may be required in other historical and cultural settings. By stressing the identification of general patterns, historical archaeologists have diminished the information provided by artifact distributions at the intrasite level. It is in these features that the clues to continuities in African belief systems may reside. In order to better evaluate and identify distinctive aspects of slave culture, techniques should be more flexible and less constrained by rigid analytical categories. The need to employ archaeological strategies suitable to the research questions being addressed was a point made by South (1977:299) in his initial presentation of pattern recognition.

## Cognitive Approaches to African-American Culture

*Candomblé, Vodou,* and *Santería* are religious systems of the Americas that incorporate aspects of African beliefs. They are not static transplants of particularistic features brought by enslaved Africans to the Americas—they are cognitive systems that incorporate cosmological concepts, rituals, and material expressions drawn, in part, from African cultures but transformed and modified in new cultural settings. The most dynamic studies of the genesis of African-American cultures have examined origin, continuity, and change in these beliefs (e.g., Barnes 1989; Holloway 1990; Thompson 1983).

Is it possible to assess these beliefs and transformations through archaeological data? Archaeological research in Africa, as well as other world areas, suggests that worldview—encompassing cosmological and religious concepts—is expressed through material culture. Cognitive archaeology is concerned with identifying this expression. It may be defined as the study of cognitive systems of the past, that is to say, the ideals, values, and beliefs that constitute a society's worldview. Thus far, diasporan studies have only afforded limited insight into these beliefs, their origins, and their transformations. Most work has focused on the exploration of slave lifeways, the archaeological delineation of power relations, or socioeconomic aspects of culture. This is understandable as cognitive beliefs are difficult to examine using archaeological data. Nevertheless, examination of the transformations that occurred in the cultural beliefs of African populations within the context of slavery may yield rich insight into the genesis of some of the cognitive systems observable in modern societies.

Methodologically, insight into African-American beliefs systems has been constrained by approaches that focus on static models of material culture, whether individual African traits or generalized patterns. Studies such as those of colonoware are important for the information they provide on African-American contributions to American technologies and artistic traditions, as well as the role of enslaved Africans in the plantation setting. In general, however, such approaches are unlikely to provide insight into African-American cultural dynamics unless these observations are integrated with attempts to examine the cultural systems and the dynamic processes that shaped the societies involved.

The need to look beyond the artifact to the underlying cultural system has been emphasized by a number of researchers (cf. Mintz and Price 1976:27–31; Posnansky, chap. 2 in this volume). The Prices, in their study of Surinam Maroon arts, are critical of studies of African "survivals," noting that "this procedure contains fundamental methodological and conceptual weaknesses: it is based on a biased selection of examples; it infers specific historical continuities on the basis of visual similarity; it underestimates Maroon creativity; and, in focusing on form rather than process, it misconstrues the nature of cultural change" (Price and Price 1980:204). Similar criticism can be leveled at more generalized attempts to define artifact patterns.

Difficulties in delineating African-American beliefs archaeologically result from ambiguities in the way artifacts functioned in cultural systems, and how they are representative of those systems. In archaeological literature change in technology—change in the artifact inventory—has often been equated with culture change. Studies such as George Quimby's (1966) pioneering work on Native American acculturation, through South's pattern recognition studies, rely on generalized assumptions about the role of material culture in the cultural system. Unfortunately for archaeologists, it is often difficult to determine why certain technological innovations are adopted, and what this information may convey about changes in a culture's worldview. The correspondence between artifacts, culture, and culture change may be quite limited.

In sites dating within the past five hundred years, European trade items are perhaps best seen as a measure of a society's involvement in a world economic system increasingly dominated by Europe and associated changes in the European mode of production. Throughout the world European contact is marked by the proliferation of mass-produced trade items. Yet change in the artifact inventory does not necessarily reflect concomitant change in worldview.

This can be illustrated by research at the large African settlement of Elmina, Ghana. Elmina was the site of a large village when the Europeans arrived on the West African coast at the end of the fifteenth century. The settlement expanded rapidly after the founding of Castle São Jorge da Mina by the Portuguese in 1482, probably numbering over 20,000 inhabitants when it was destroyed by a British bombardment in 1873. Documentary accounts and ethnographic data indicate there was a great deal of innovation in Elmina society between the fifteenth and the twentieth centuries. Elmina changed from a settlement subservient to neighboring African polities to a small, independent state. American cultigens, including the tomato, cassava, peanut, and corn, were introduced into the region. Documentary sources also attest to extensive change in dress, house construction, and other aspects of material culture.

Between 1985 and 1990 archaeological research was conducted at the old town site of Elmina (DeCorse 1987, 1992, 1993). Over thirty stone-walled structures were identified, fifteen of which were excavated. More than 100,000 artifacts spanning the fifteenth through the nineteenth centuries were recovered. Over half of these artifacts were imported trade items, a telling indication of Elmina's external contacts. What is significant about the archaeological data from Elmina is that while there is dramatic change in the material inventory, there appears to have been a great deal of continuity in worldview and ideology among the people of Elmina. Although new construction methods were adopted, building plans and the use of space within some structures were consistent with indigenous African notions of spatial organization (fig. 7.4). Imported trade items such as Rhenish stoneware jugs and Chinese porcelain saucers were used as grave offerings, but burial without coffins beneath house floors continued. Both documentary accounts and archaeological data indicate that other ritual practices also remained unchanged in the centuries following European contact. By the nineteenth century, imported pieces make up a significant part of the ceramic inventory, but this seems to denote little change in Elmina foodways. Consistent with local eating practices, bowls account for the vast majority of the nineteenth-century ceramic assemblage, plates making up a very small percentage. Faunal remains and marine mollusks recovered also denote little deviation from pre-European contact methods of food preparation and consumption. The salient point is not that there was no change in Elminan worldview—change did occur—but rather that the transformations which did take place (and the accompanying changes in the material record) did so within an indigenous conceptual framework.

How artifacts reflect cultural beliefs is not cross-culturally universal. Culture is varied, as is the way this variation is manifested archaeologically. Archaeological indicators of worldview, ethnic identity, and culture change are different in individual cultural settings. Burial practices, foodways, cosmograms on pipes, or the ritual use of pottery may all serve as sources of information. Methods of abstracting data from a broad range of sites to examine general patterns may be appropriate for answering some research questions. However, more site-specific methods are more likely to be of greater use in other contexts. Because of the variation found in individual plantation systems, change in worldview is something that potentially may be best assessed at the intrasite level.

In order to address cultural dynamics within slave populations, archaeologists need to identify more clearly those aspects of the archaeological record which are likely to incorporate beliefs and worldview. Taken by itself, the production of colonoware by slaves provides little information about the belief systems of African Americans: economic conditions may favor the continued production of certain items long after other portions of the originating culture have disappeared. With this in mind, the most interesting aspect of Ferguson's studies concerns not the production of colonoware but the nonmaterial African-American beliefs that may be inferred from such artifacts.

As Kenneth Brown and Doreen Cooper (1990) point out, a crucial aspect of interpretation is the context with which the artifact is associated. The fact that a given number of blue beads are found at a particular plantation site conveys little about their cultural meaning. If, however, the beads were to be found in a burial in which the context suggested they had been arranged in strands around the waist of a female with various grave goods or offerings in association, and the method of interment can be contrasted with European-American burial practices, a much stronger argument for African continuities can be presented. In this burial context the beads are part of a combination of attributes that argue for a particular symbolic structure and a particular perception of the afterlife. Such an interpretation cannot be constructed on the basis of one or two artifacts or attributes. Indications of such distinctive behavioral practices have been recovered from African-American contexts (e.g., Handler and Lange 1978:125–32; La Roche 1994:8–12).

Burials are particularly important because they frequently incorporate material expressions of worldview, but other associated contexts may be equally useful in inferring cultural beliefs. An illustration is provided by Brown and Cooper's (1990) work at the Levi Jordan plantation in Brazoria County, Texas. Excavations within a structure at this site produced a collection of artifacts that the researchers refer to as a "ritual tool kit." As Brown and Cooper point out, many of the artifacts (including bullet casings, animal bones, shells, and nails) are things which could easily have been lost in the strictly quantitative methodological approaches used by some historical archaeologists.

Among the more encouraging research recently undertaken are studies that attempt to identify individual artifacts, features, and behavioral practices which inform on African-American religion and ritual. Surveying data from the American South, Orser (1994) and Wilkie (1995) draw on a diversity of artifacts to infer distinctive African-American belief systems. These are examined in terms of African antecedents, the historical context of the slave trade, and transformation in the cultural beliefs of enslaved Africans. Data such as these and the Levi Jordan ritual tool kit can be used to begin to develop an understanding of African-American beliefs which is at once both more holistic and dynamic in perspective than a generalized discussion of African "traits" or patterns.

## Unifying Themes in African-American Archaeology

Much of the preceding discussion has focused on cultural and ethnic diversity—differences between African populations that can be readily perceived by both Africans and outsiders, a condition that may have contributed to variation in African societies in the Americas. Recognition of these complexities must be an integral part of studies of the African diaspora. There is, however, also evidence of fundamental similarities linking African cultures. Despite substantial variation, certain images are conveyed when we think of European, Chinese, Islamic, Mesoamerican, or African "civilization." Aspects of this underlying unity of African cultures can be found in the writings of such diverse scholars as Horton (1868), Frobenius (1913), Du Bois (1940), Senghor (1956), Thompson (1983), Roberts (1989), and Appiah (1992). Unfortunately for the archaeologist, these common themes frequently embody the most intellectual—the most cognitive—aspects of culture, things that are by nature difficult to evaluate on the basis of material remains.

Certain sets of archaeological data from Africa and American slave sites present general similarities. One area that has received substantial attention is foodways, the suite of activities associated with food preparation and consumption (Deetz 1977:50; Yentsch 1994). Dietary practices in general tend to display a great deal of continuity within cultural groups. Certain facets of this system—including food-processing equipment, cooking implements, tableware, eating utensils, and food remains—are recovered archaeologically and provide evidence of change or continuity within one portion of the belief system.

Diet, in terms of the specific foodstuffs exploited, varies substantially in different parts of Africa. A common feature, however, is the general emphasis on soups and stews. Faunal remains from West African archaeological sites such as Elmina are characteristically shattered, probably having been butchered with cleavers and cracked for marrow extraction during consumption—a pattern observed ethnographically. Among modern African populations, vegetable foods are often cut up and pulverized using grinding stones or pottery mortars before cooking. Food is traditionally served in a bowl, and these vessel forms continue to dominate assemblages even after the advent of European ceramics. A similar pattern of consumption is suggested by the data from American slave sites, though plates are far more common than in African contexts, where they are virtually absent until the late nineteenth and early twentieth centuries (Adams 1987:243; Armstrong 1985, 1990; Fairbanks 1984:3–4; Otto 1984:68–69).

The American data suggest some continuity with West African eating practices. As a culturally transmitted set of activities, foodways convey some information about shared cultural beliefs. Taken by themselves, however, they probably provide limited evidence of cultural continuity. Given variation in local environments and the availability of resources, individuals within the same cultural group (i.e., sharing a highly integrated worldview) might exploit different foodstuffs requiring distinct food-processing equipment. Such variation would provide a skewed archaeological view of cultural differences. Within the African-American context, a number of researchers have pointed out other variables external to the slave society that may have affected the observed similarities between slave and African foodways. These include the socioeconomic constraints on diet, tableware, and food-processing technology. For example, George Miller (1980) notes that bowls were among the least expensive forms of tableware available in nineteenth-century America. This factor could have easily affected the selection of bowls more than slaves' desires to maintain certain dietary practices.

A potentially important area of study that has received more limited attention from American archaeologists is the use of space within and around slave dwellings. In his discussion of artifact patterning, South (1977:77) emphasized the importance of examining sites in their entirety, a point also raised by Joseph (1989:58). In practice, excavations of slave sites frequently have focused on the dwelling or limited portions of the yard areas (Joseph 1989:58–60).

In the African context the courtyard or compound areas convey as much information about social organization as the actual dwellings. The compound frequently reflects functional, as well as social and ideological, aspects of West African cultures (e.g., Bourdier and Minh-Ha 1985; Denyer 1978; Dmochowski 1990; Gardi 1973; Mester de Parajd 1988; Oliver 1971; Prussin 1969). Courtyards may be used for cooking, drying foods, socializing, ritual activities, or sleeping. It is useful, therefore, to conceive of an African dwelling as a series of decent-sized rooms adjacent to a large open living space, rather than as a cluster of isolated houses. Rooms within a compound often serve multiple functions. For example, in his ethnoarchaeological research among the Nchumuru of Ghana, Agorsah (1986:31) noted that the only room that had a specialized function was the shrine. An example of the pervasive importance of the courtyard in African societies is illustrated by plans of a seventeenth-century house at Elmina in coastal Ghana and a Bimoba family compound in northeastern Ghana (see fig. 7.4). The two structures are the products of different cultural groups and are formally different in many ways. In both, however, the open courtyard area is distinctive.

Open spaces may be important in defining African continuities in the Americas. Change in the material used for housing is less significant than how space was utilized within a structure. In the plantation setting, construction methods and the arrangement of slave settlements may have been influenced by the planter, but open spaces connecting areas and the use of space may be non-European. The social, utilitarian, and ritual importance of yards has been documented ethnographically in some African-American populations (Mintz 1974:231–50; Pulsipher 1994).

Studies of spatial organization have been undertaken by nonarchaeologists in the Americas (Anthony 1976a, 1976b; Jones 1985; Mintz 1974; Thompson 1993; Vlach 1990; Westmacott 1992). Archaeologists interested in the African-American past are examining the use of space in and around structures with greater frequency. Ferguson, Affleck, and Adams (1990), surveying historical and archaeological data on slave cabins in South Carolina, see parallels in African floor plans and living areas (cf. Armstong 1991; McKee 1992). At the New Seville plantation, Jamaica, Armstrong (1992) has excavated around slave dwellings specifically to determine the extent of yard areas. This research may provide indications of distinctive African (or non-European) patterns of spatial arrangement.

## Conclusion

Archaeologists are striving to apply African data to American research questions. The success of these efforts will depend on access to better comparative material from Africa. The precolonial culture histories of many areas are very poorly known, including regions that provided significant numbers of slaves. Additional and better-publicized research in Africa not only will contribute to an improved understanding of the American situation but also will better define the impact of the slave trade on African societies (DeCorse 1991). Given the complex nature of the slave trade, an integral part of all studies of the African diaspora must be the historical context in which the artifacts are found.

While it is important to identify continuity and resilience in African-American societies, it is also essential to realize the complex factors involved in their formation. Cognitive aspects of society may provide the best means of evaluating how different—or how similar—American slave societies were to contemporary African cultures. These features may be difficult to examine archaeologically; because of variation in the way artifacts function in the cultural system, the expression of beliefs and worldview is not uniform. Evidence of worldview may be conveyed in a variety of material manifestations, requiring different approaches by archaeologists. Research methods employed by many archaeologists have failed to recognize the dynamic nature of culture. Addressing these issues may be challenging, but it is the only way archaeologists can make a meaningful contribution to the study of the distinctive systems of beliefs that characterize African-American societies.

## Notes

I would like to thank Theresa Singleton, Merrick Posnansky, James Deetz, and David Whitley for commenting on earlier drafts of this chapter. I am also especially indebted to Matthew Emerson, Daniel Mouer, Mary Ellen Hodges, Brian Crane, Leland Ferguson, and Matthew Hill for sharing their research with me.

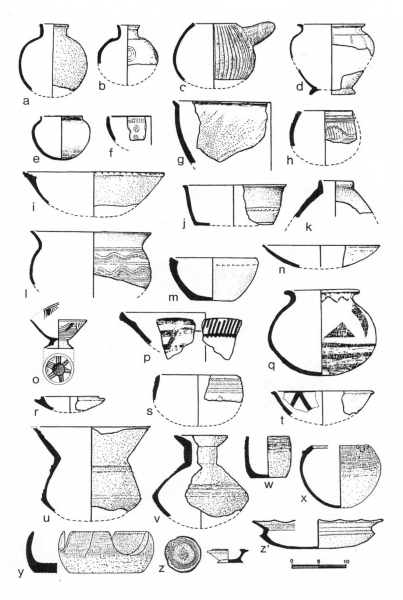

7.1. Post-European-contact-period (fifteenth- to nineteenth-century) pottery from Ghana. Plain, incised, and punctate decorated forms from Sekondi (*a-d*); Kisoto (*e*); Yendi Dabari (*f-g*); Mampongtin (*h-l*); Bono Manso (*j-n*); Biseasi (*v-w*); 1873 floor contexts at Elmina (*k-z'*). Painted pottery from Ntereso (*o*); Bima (*p*); Vume Dugame (*q*); Silima (*r-t*). (Sources: Bravmann and Mathewson 1970; Davies 1955, 1956, 1961, 1964; DeCorse 1992; Effah-Gyamfi 1985; Mathewson and Flight 1972; Shinnie and Ozanne 1962)

7.2. A Yalunka potter, northeastern Sierra Leone. Note the coils visible on the interior of the pot. The method of manufacture and the role of the potter in Yalunka culture can be used to differentiate Yalunka ceramics traditions form those of neighboring groups.

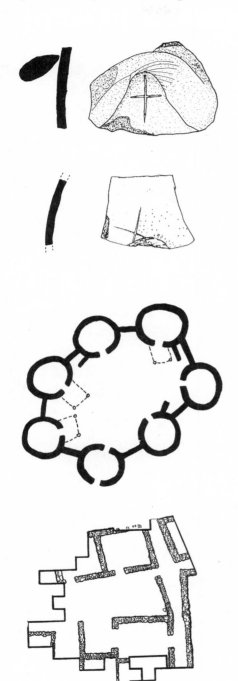

7.3. Sixteenth-century Iberian ceramics from Elmina, Ghana, with engraved marks. The position of the marks on the vessel, as well as the sherds' historical and archaeological contexts, distinguishes these artifacts from eighteenth-century marked colonoware fragments from South Carolina.

7.4. Sketch map of a modern Bimoba compound in northeastern Ghana (*top*) and an excavation plan of a seventeenth-century stone-walled dwelling at Elmina, Ghana (*bottom*). The two structures represent products of African cultural groups widely separated geographically and temporally, yet they embody certain similarities in the use of space

# Part II

# Plantation Contexts

# 8

# Constructing Difference: The Social and Spatial Order of the Chesapeake Plantation

*Terrence W. Epperson*

THE INSIGHT that race is "an ideological construct and thus, above all, a historical product" has important ramifications for the practice of plantation archaeology (Fields 1982:150; see also Fields 1990; Potter 1991). Race is not a biogenetic fact, a category of analysis, or a thing which explains patterning in the archaeological record; rather, it is a *process*, a fundamental issue which itself requires explanation (Lieberman and Reynolds 1996; Lieberman et al. 1989). As critical archaeologists, historians, and museologists working within what remains an essentially racist society, one of the most valuable lessons we can offer is the knowledge that "race" is not a universal, natural, or inevitable aspect of the human condition but is, instead, an ideology which can be apprehended historically and transcended through social practice (Chappell 1989; Fuss 1989; Gates 1986; Gilroy 1991; hooks 1990). However, analysis of the social construction race must not be reduced to a position of "vulgar anti-essentialism" which denies the material consequences and reality of being "raced" in American society (Crenshaw et al. 1995:xxxvi; see also Harrison 1995).

If race is recognized as a social, rather than biological, category, it follows that racial difference is created through processes that are discernible in the archaeological and documentary record. The first portion of this essay examines the construction—and contestation—of racial difference within law and religion as a prelude to examining analogous processes in plantation landscape and architectural space. The second portion of the essay addresses these issues within the spatial realm through the presentation of four historical and architectural vignettes addressing: the evolution of social and spatial segregation (Clifts plantation); the ambiguity of meaning in architecture, particularly the asserted concordance between spatial and social order (Shirley plantation); the question of audience in plantation architecture and the differentiation between legitimizing and disciplinary aspects of spatial control (Mount Airy); and finally, the inherent and immutable contradiction between the exclusionary and incorporative aspects of spatial domination (Gunston Hall).

I begin my discussion with a slight reorientation in our perception of colonial history. Until almost the end of the seventeenth century there were no white people in Virginia (Epperson 1990a, 1997; Allen 1994). That's right; there were significant, but decreasing, numbers of "Indians" and an increasing population of enslaved "Negroes," but no "whites." We do find people who referred to themselves as "Christians" or, less frequently, as "English," but the self-consciously racial term *white* does not appear until the end of the century. In fact, boundaries we now perceive as "racial" were quite fluid. In January 1677 the final pocket of resistance during Bacon's Rebellion was described as "eighty Negroes and twenty English which would not deliver their arms" (Grantham 1677; Breen 1980:138; Morgan 1975:269; Washburn 1972:87–89; Webb 1985:120–23). By the early eighteenth century, however, such "interracial" rebellious cooperation no longer seemed possible, although other oppositional alliances were attempted.

The first tenuous use of the term *white* in Virginia legislation did not occur until 1691, in a miscegenation law designed to prevent "that abominable mixture and spurious issue" which would supposedly arise from intermarriage between any "English or other white man or woman being free" and "any negroe, mulatto, or Indian man or woman bond or free" (Hening 1809–23:3:87). The first legislative use of *white* without the modifier *English* occurs in 1705, again in the context of miscegenation legislation. "No minister of the Church of England, or other minister . . . shall hereafter wittingly presume to marry a white man with a Negro or mulatto woman; or to marry a white woman with Negro or mulatto man" (Hening 1809–23:3:454).

Even when *white* is not utilized, we can follow the juridical construction of racial difference. For example, note the differences between two statutes, the first enacted in 1680 and the second in 1705. The first law stipulates: "If any negroe or other slave shall presume to lift up his hand in opposition against any Christian, shall for every such offence . . . have and receive thirty lashes on his bare back well laid on" (Hening 1809–23:2:481). The 1705 slave code repeated the provision, punishment, and general form of the earlier law but quietly incorporated several significant alterations: "If any Negro, mulato, or Indian, bond or free, shall at any time, lift his or her hand, in opposition against any Christian not being Negro, mulatto, or Indian, he or she so offending, shall . . . receive on his or her bare back, thirty lashes, well laid on" (Hening 1809–23:3:459).

While the 1680 act applied only to slaves, the 1705 law was explicitly racial and applied to both enslaved and nonenslaved people of color. In 1680 Christian was an unproblematic category, but the later law recognized that a "Negro, mulatto, or Indian" could be baptized; hence, they were specifically excluded from protection under this law. Significantly, the language of the act was also expanded to specifically criminalize acts of resistance committed by women of color.

One important—if unwitting—agent in the transformation from "Christian" to "white" was the Reverend Morgan Godwyn, an Anglican cleric who preached in Virginia during the 1660s and in Barbados during the 1670s (Godwyn 1680, 1681). While in Virginia, Godwyn successfully advocated passage of a 1667 law which specified that baptism of slaves did not result in their manumission (Godwyn 1681:5; Hening 1809–23:2:260). Upon his return to England in 1680, Godwyn published *The Negro's and Indian's Advocate*. While reading this book, one is led to wonder, With advocates like this, who needs enemies? Godwyn argued for baptism of slaves on both spiritual and pragmatic grounds, with a definite emphasis upon the latter: "The benefit whereof is least to the slave, tho he gain heaven thereby; whilst his master . . . doth in this world also reap the desired fruit of his servants FIDELTY. . . . For Insurrections and Revolts, nothing can be imagined a greater Security against them, than a sincere inward persuasion of the truths of Christianity" (1680:74–75, 130).

While discussing the salutary effect Christian proselytization could have in the suppression of African cultural traditions among slaves, Godwyn incidentally offered a comparison between Barbados and Virginia which is relevant to any comparative analysis of African cultural traditions in the Caribbean and the Chesapeake: "I proceed to their polygamy, their sunday labour, frequent repudiating and changing their wives [and] their idolatrous dances and revels, permitted and practiced by them with other such recreations and customs by them brought out of Africa. . . . None of which yet are heard of amongst the Virginia Negroes, tho alike Gentiles with these, and there not laid aside or forbidden, but forgotten by disuse" (1680:144).

Finally, Godwyn argued that baptism of slaves would improve planters' ability to surveil their labor force, an issue of particular importance when understanding the spatial ordering of the plantation: "Those who by their zeal for the Sabbath, do reap this great spiritual advantage of having their servants thereby always in their eye" (1680:105).

Virginia planters, however, were not easily convinced of the efficacy of baptism as a means of asserting control over enslaved laborers. The planters realized, with good cause, that Christianity could also provide a basis for resistance. Responding to a 1724 questionnaire issued by the bishop of London, the Reverend John Bagg of Essex County (himself a slave owner) provided the following response regarding "infidels" in his parish: "No Indians live in my Parish; there may be 6 free Negroes, there are many Negro slaves, and but very few baptized, nor any means used for their conversion, the owners Generally not approving thereof, being led away by the notion of their being and becoming worse slaves when Christians" (Perry 1969:315). Similarly, in a 1730 letter to the bishop of London, Commissary James Blair reported the conversion of "a very great number of Negroes" but also added, "Some allege it [baptism] makes them prouder, and infuses them with thoughts of freedom; but I take this to be rather a common prejudice than anything else" (Blair 1730).

Blair's optimism, however, was unwarranted. In the fall of 1730 Virginia's civic and religious leaders were shaken by two episodes of organized slave resistance, both of which were related—albeit in very different ways—to the practice of Christianity (Aptheker 1983:179–80; Schwarz 1988:86–87). The first insurrection was attempted by baptized slaves in early September and was reported by Lieutenant Governor William Gooch in a letter to the Council of Trade and Plantations: "There have been discovered many meetings and consultations of the negroes in several parts of the country in order to obtain their freedom; whereupon great numbers of them have been taken up and examined, but no discovery made of any formed design of their rising, only some loose discourses that [His Majesty] had sent orders for setting of them free as soon as they were Christians, and that these orders were suppressed" (Gooch 1730).

Commissary Blair was understandably concerned about the apparent role of slave baptism in the September insurrection: "It is certain that notwithstanding all the precaution we ministers took to assure them that baptism altered nothing as to their servitude, or other temporal circumstances; yet they were willing to feed themselves with a secret fancy that it did, and that the king designed that all Christians should be made free" (Blair 1731).

A second, probably related, insurrection was attempted in mid to late October by some two hundred slaves in adjacent counties south of the mouth of the James River. As reported by Gooch, this attempt resulted in the execution of four slaves: "The Negroes, in the counties of Norfolk and Princess Anne, had the boldness to assemble on a Sunday while the people were at church, and to chuse amongst themselves officers to command them in their intended insurrection, which was to have been put into execution very soon after: But this meeting being happily discovered and many of them being taken up and examined, the whole plot was detected, for which the major part of them were severely punished, and four of the ringleaders, on full evidence convicted, have been executed" (Gooch 1731).

The governor's response to the October insurrection included an order requiring militia members to bring their arms to church on Sundays and holy days, "lest they [the arms] should be seized by the slaves in their absence, if the same mutinous spirit should be revived amongst them." This measure was necessary because Sundays and holy days were the times when "the Slaves are most at liberty and have the greatest opportunity" (McIlwaine 1925:4:228).

Writing in 1680, the Reverend Morgan Godwyn was responding to perceived threats on several fronts when he advocated the baptism of slaves. Most obviously, he was expressing concern for the souls of enslaved human beings while simultaneously reassuring planters that slave conversion was in their own best interests. He was also attempting to define, control, and neutralize the meaning of slave religion in the face of Quaker missionary activity and the slaves' own demands and expectations.

Although in some senses Godwyn's work could be considered nonracist, or even antiracist, it inadvertently contributed to the elaboration of a virulently exclusionary, essentialist, and dehumanizing form of racism. By denying any linkage between spiritual equality and temporal condition and by undermining the Christian/Negro dichotomy without fundamentally challenging the social and economic institution of slavery, Godwyn unwittingly contributed to the need for a new set of oppositions in plantation slavery: white versus Negro. Although the debates regarding the profits and pitfalls of using Christianity to control slaves were unusually reflexive and forthright, the actual creation of racial difference was more an unintended consequence than a conscious conspiracy.

Like all forms of domination, colonial slavery was characterized by a fundamental contradiction: the tension between inclusion and exclusion, between the need to incorporate the oppressed people within a unified system of control and the need to create distance, difference, and otherness. Neither tendency could ever be total, and they were in constant, shifting opposition (Sider 1986, 1987). Godwyn saw baptism as a mechanism for enhancing the incorporative aspect of domination by improving surveillance, undermining African cultural traditions, inculcating purportedly shared values, and improving control through better knowledge of slaves' behavior and motivations. However, as is the case with all ideological weapons, Christianity was a double-edged sword. Although deployed as a form of control, it also became a means of challenging the denial of slave humanity, a basis for resistance which transcended African ethnic boundaries, and a mechanism for surreptitiously maintaining and asserting African spiritual values (Raboteau 1978; Stuckey 1987).

The 1730 attempted insurrections reflect the inherent limitations (from the slave owners' perspective) of both the incorporative and exclusionary impulses of domination. During the September insurrection, baptized slaves used Christianity to assert a common humanity with their masters and, on that basis, demand a common freedom. Their demands did not stem from an inability or unwillingness to apprehend the nuances of colonial law or Anglican theology. Rather, their revolt represented a sophisticated attempt to appropriate and redefine the content and significance of a body of belief, to turn the oppressors' own ideological weapons against them and assert a direct link between spiritual freedom and temporal freedom. The slaves, however, expected their freedom to come from the king, via the governor. In embracing Christianity they also may have accepted some fundamentally limiting assumptions regarding power and hierarchy that ultimately bounded their insurrectionary impulse.

Conversely, the October insurrection was facilitated by the fact that the slave owners were in church and the slaves were not. This exclusionary gesture temporarily freed the slaves from surveillance, providing an opportunity to select leaders and formulate plans. This does not negate the possibility that baptized slaves also were involved in the October attempt, but it does remind us of the Reverend Godwyn's admonition that owners of Christian slaves "do reap this great spiritual advantage of having their servants thereby always in their eye."

This examination of racial difference within the juridical and theological realms has a number of ramifications for the architectural and archaeological analysis of Chesapeake plantation society. Although we do not find discussions regarding the manipulation of plantation space that are as explicit and reflexive as the debates over the deployment of Christianity, we do find many of the same inherent contradictions and arenas of struggle. The significance, meaning, and dominative efficacy of landscape and architectural space was fiercely contested, even between various fractions of the ruling elite. Therefore, no single "correct" reading is ever possible. In the face of subaltern attempts to appropriate, redefine, and subvert spatial disciplines, we find fairly conscious attempts on the part of elites to fix meanings and control ambiguities. Since the creation and assertion of "difference" and "otherness" are, in essence, a self-projection and self-definition of the dominant group, the process can never be entirely exclusionary and is therefore much more complex than mere social and spatial segregation. In fact, it may be in the spatial realm that the fundamental tension between the exclusionary and incorporative impulses of domination may be most apparent, and it was at the nexus of this contradiction that resistance was possible.

The balance of this chapter consists of four vignettes which address social and spatial segregation, the ambiguity of architectural meaning, the question of audience in plantation architecture, and the contradiction between the exclusionary and incorporative aspects of spatial domination.

Our first vignette is introduced by the work of a French Huguenot exile who styled himself "Durand Du Dauphiné." Although he did not speak English and was in Virginia for just six months in 1686–87, Du Dauphiné was a keen observer of colonial life. During his short stay he was able to travel widely and meet two of the colony's most important planters, Ralph Wormeley of Rosegill and Colonel William Fitzhugh. Upon his return to Europe, Du Dauphiné published an account of his travels in hopes of encouraging Huguenot immigration to Virginia. Du Dauphiné's account was published seven years after both Godwyn's *Negro's and Indian's Advocate* and the first Virginia statute against "any Negro" who might presume "to lift up his hand in opposition against any Christian" and four years before the first legislative use of the term *white* in Virginia. His account contains an extremely intriguing passage regarding the spatial ordering of Chesapeake tobacco plantations: "Whatever their rank, & I know not why, they build only two rooms with some closets on the ground floor, & two rooms in the attic above; but they build several like this, according to their means. They build also a separate kitchen, a separate house for the Christian slaves, one for the Negro slaves, and several to dry the tobacco, so that when you come to the home of a person of some means, you think you are entering a fairly large village" (Chinard 1934:119–20).

Although Du Dauphiné traveled widely within Virginia, this description may have particularly reflected his visit to Rosegill, the only instance in which he described a specific plantation: "Monsieur Wormeley . . . owns twenty-six Negro slaves & twenty Christian. He holds the highest offices, & owns at least twenty houses in a lovely plain along the Rappahannock River. He has rented his most comfortable house to the Governor [Lord Howard of Effingham]. When I reached this place I thought I was entering a rather large village, but later on was told that all of it belonged to him" (Chinard 1934:142).

Even though Du Dauphiné was accompanied by a "servant" during his voyage to America, he consistently conflated indentured servitude and slavery and referred to indentured servants in Virginia as Christian slaves: "A difference exists between the slaves that are bought, to wit: a Christian twenty years old or over, cannot be a slave for more than five years, whereas Negroes & other unbelievers are slaves all their lives" (Chinard 1934:110).

Du Dauphiné's plantation descriptions reflect an extremely important transitional phase in the spatial ordering of Chesapeake plantations. The spatial separation between master and laborers and the spatial differentiation between various plantation functions were obviously well established by the late 1680s. However (allowing for the vagaries of multiple translations), it is clear that at least for Du Dauphiné, if not for his hosts, the primary dichotomy within the labor force was still between "Christians" and "Negroes and other nonbelievers." Racism, or even race consciousness, cannot be posited as a prior cause or motivation for the spatial segregation between masters and bound laborers or between "Christian" and "Negro" slaves. Indeed, the construction of racial difference is, in part, a result of processes of spatial segregation between master and servant, the origins of which can be traced to late medieval England (Carson 1976, 1978).

Several architectural and archaeological analyses have traced the processes of spatial differentiation and specialization within Virginia plantations during the last half of the seventeenth century and the first quarter of the eighteenth century (Carson et al. 1981; Hudgins 1990; Keeler 1978; Neiman 1980, 1986; Upton 1986; Wenger 1986). For example, the ca. 1670 "manner house" at the Clifts plantation on the Northern Neck initially had a cross-passage plan. This form was characterized by a narrow passage running through one end of the house, separating a service area at one end of the house from the hall and chamber at the other end. The cross passage encouraged traffic through the house and provided direct access to the hall, an undifferentiated, multipurpose space which served as the base for many plantation activities conducted by the planter, his family, and his indentured laborers. During this initial phase the private chamber was smaller and symbolically less important than the hall (Neiman 1986:308).

However, at about the time Du Dauphiné was visiting Rosegill, important transformations occurred in the architectural and landscape space at Clifts plantation. By 1690 the cross passage had been blocked, to be replaced by a more formal front lobby entrance, and many of the plantation activities had been removed from the hall. By this time the size of the chamber had been doubled, allowing it to be used as a private sitting room as well as a sleeping area. By the turn of the century, all cooking was being done in a separate building, and the hall served primarily as a formal dining and reception area. It is important to note that these spatial transformations occurred before the transition from indentured to enslaved labor at Clifts (Neiman 1980:35).

Our second vignette is introduced by archaeological excavations at Shirley plantation, constructed in ca. 1738 on the north bank of the James River by John Carter (Reinhart 1984; Reinhart and Habicht 1984). These excavations have prompted a thorough reanalysis of the plantation nucleus, revealing that the house was originally oriented toward the river and was flanked by two large "dependencies" which have long since been demolished. Reinhart and Habicht also discovered that the spatial order governing the dimensions of the buildings and the relationship between the mansion and the dependencies was defined by the ratio 3:4:5. They conclude: "These rigid and rhythmic proportions were inspired by the classical architectural principles of the Renaissance and indicate a high degree of sophistication in both the design and execution of these three buildings" (Reinhart and Habicht 1984:42). While this conclusion is accurate, it certainly does not offer a full understanding of the significance of this particular spatial order.

The archaeological (re)discovery of the "harmonic" principles governing the spatial relationship between the mansion and its dependencies raises two issues that troubled early eighteenth-century architectural practitioners: First, which was the locus or source of architectural beauty and meaning, the building itself or the eye of the beholder? Second, did universal principles govern the experience of architectural space—in other words, would a particular building or landscape have the same effect upon all observers? A consideration of these issues should help us avoid simplistic and uncritical analyses of the interrelationships between the social and the spatial.

It is within the context of the so-called Battle of the Ancients and the Moderns regarding the meaning of classical architecture and the subsequent reaction of the neo-Palladian movement in England that these issues can best be understood (Rykert 1980; Whiffen 1984; Tafuri 1980; Pérez-Gómez 1992; Wittkower 1983). While the Ancients continued to insist that meaning, beauty, and harmony were inherent in the object itself, the Moderns, particularly Claude Perrault, argued a more relativistic, empiricist position.

In a book translated into English in 1708 as *A Treatise on the Five Orders of Columns in Architecture*, Perrault rejected the classical theory of concord between musical notes and architectural elements and advocated a surprisingly relativist approach to beauty and architectural style. It must be stressed that as a Modern, Perrault did not reject classical architecture per se but rather questioned its status as a universal, innate, and immutable object (Rykert 1980:23–53).

The English counterattack was led by Lords Shaftesbury and Burlington, patrons of a self-conscious attempt to create a distinctively English Renaissance in music, art, literature, and architecture. The new style was to be based upon republican (rather than imperial) Rome because, according to Shaftesbury, after Rome lost its liberty under the Caesars, "not a Statue, not a Metal, nor a tolerable Piece of Architecture could shew itself. . . . Ignorance and darkness overspread the world, and fitted it for the Chaos and Ruin which ensued" (Wittkower 1983:180). The identity between aesthetic and political agendas intensified with the Whig ascendancy and consolidation of the liberal consensus after 1715. Apparently oblivious to the oxymoron, the advocates of this new Renaissance insisted that the new style was to be both rationalist and nationalist, that is, simultaneously embodying universal aesthetic principles and particularly British values.

One of the primary texts of the British attack against the Moderns was Robert Morris's 1724 *An Essay in Defense of Ancient Architecture*. Morris clearly saw himself as the arbiter of the classical tradition as it had been codified and conveyed by Palladio, a position which left little room for relativism. Regarding harmonic proportions and the concordance between architecture and music, he wrote: "In musick are only seven distinct notes, in architecture likewise are only seven distinct proportions which produce all the different buildings in the universe, viz the cube, the cube and half, the double cube, [and the ratios of 3:2:1, 4:3:2, 5:4:3, and 6:4:3] produce all harmonic proportions of Rooms" (Morris 1724).

Note that the dimensions and relationships between the mansion and dependencies at Shirley plantation reflect one of the seven proportions that govern the production of "all the different buildings in the universe," or at least all harmonious buildings. Similar ratios have been noted during analysis of colonial gardens in Annapolis (Leone 1988; Kryder-Reid 1994). It does not require much of a leap to move from a spatial order which asserts harmony between a plantation mansion and its dependencies to a social order which asserts harmony between a planter and his "dependencies," including slaves. Yet this assertion of innate and natural hierarchy should not be accepted as the only possible reading.

Whether they admitted it or not, eighteenth-century architects were, on some level, aware of the inherent ambiguity of the architectural project. The more Robert Morris asserted the immutable rationality of ancient architecture, the more he betrayed his nervousness about the threat of relativism and multiple readings. Furthermore, even within the ruling elite there is evidence that different class factions were reading the same architecture differently. Lord Burlington's circle interpreted neo-Palladianism as the embodiment of republican Rome and Lockean liberalism, while the colonial planters, ensconced in a slave society predicated upon the Justinian Code, interpreted the architecture as imperial and authoritarian.

Just as the Reverend Morgan Godwyn attempted—with limited success—to control the meaning of Christianity for enslaved African Americans, various practitioners attempted to define the meaning of architectural and landscape spaces. We should not, however, accept their interpretations uncritically. For example, a structuralist or symbolic attempt to read architecture in terms of purportedly universal dichotomies such as high/low, inside/outside, or dominant/subordinate recapitulates a rationalist position not necessarily held by the practitioners themselves. Although Rhys Issac (1982:354) is certainly justified in his statement that a mansion such as Sabine Hall (ca. 1740) "with its dignified centerpiece and subordinate dependencies . . . served as a template of the social hierarchy of which [the planter] was the patriarchal head," the additional assertion that "one could not argue with the basic statements embodied in the great buildings" negates the possibility that subaltern groups were creating new meanings through the "recontextualization" of items associated with or produced by the dominant class (Howson 1990; Upton 1996). Any analysis of plantation society which does not reflect this fundamental ambiguity will be inadequate, to say the least.

Our third vignette is introduced by Dell Upton's (1990) analysis of architectural and social barriers at Mount Airy plantation and addresses the question, Were slaves a part of the intended audience for elite architectural and landscape displays? Isaac, for one, seems to answer in the affirmative, while Upton, somewhat more convincingly, argues in the negative: "Few white planters imagined that slaves were susceptible to the legitimating functions of white society; they recognized that the slave's lack of standing made force the only sure legitimizer" (Upton 1985:66).

In his analysis of Mount Airy, Upton notes that a visiting white had to transcend a series of seven social and architectural barriers before being admitted to the dining table of the Tayloe family. Domestic slaves, however, had immediate side-door access, which mirrored the access routes of family members. Since slaves were excluded from the symbolic arena where displays of grandeur and status were expected to legitimate positions of power and authority, they were not subjected to the same system of architectural and social barriers that confronted a visiting lower-status white.

Ironically, this very exclusionary gesture facilitated the incorporation of domestic slaves into the most intimate social and architectural spaces of the plantation house, emphasizing once again the constant contradictory tension between incorporation and exclusion.

This is certainly not to suggest that slaves were oblivious to the power relations embedded in the landscape. In fact, Upton suggests that Virginia gentry planters and their slaves had radically disparate perceptions of the same physical landscapes. The gentry landscape was dynamic, articulated, and processual, and its meaning could only be grasped as one moved through it, forming and reforming social interactions. By contrast, the theme of the slaves' landscape was control. Some areas were subject to direct planter surveillance, while others, such as interior spaces of quarters or woodlands, were areas of relatively greater freedom. Unlike the dynamic articulated networks through which the gentry planter passed with ease, the landscapes perceived by slaves were fragmented collections of barriers and pitfalls that were not transformed or integrated by the movement of the observer (Upton 1985, 1990).

Perhaps we can force a distinction and conclude that gentry planters believed slaves were susceptible to the disciplinary aspects of the spatial order, but what Upton calls the "legitimizing" functions of landscape and architectural space were reserved primarily for peers and poorer planters. However, both aspects of spatial control ultimately contributed to the construction of racial difference.

Our final vignette focuses upon Gunston Hall, a northern Virginia plantation house constructed in 1756 by William Buckland for George Mason (Beirne and Scharff 1970). Our understanding of this plantation is enhanced by an extraordinary set of recollections written by Mason's son, General John Mason, in 1832 when he was an old man fondly recalling his pre-Revolutionary childhood on the plantation. General Mason provides detailed descriptions and interpretations of both the formal and informal landscapes surrounding the mansion. The "south front" of the mansion, oriented toward the Potomac River, adjoined a formal garden constructed on a plane created by leveling the top of a small hill. Beyond the formal garden, the landscape sloped steeply down to a "deer park, studded with trees, kept well fenced and stocked with native deer domesticated" (Rowland 1892:98).

On the "north front," or principal approach to the mansion, George Mason maintained "an extensive lawn kept closely pastured." Within this vista he commissioned an intriguing exercise in point-perspective landscape manipulation. The carriageway, described as a spacious avenue, was flanked by two footpaths. Beginning at a point about two hundred feet from the house and extending away from the house for about twelve hundred feet, the carriageway and footpaths were lined and shaded by four rows of cherry trees, with each row containing over fifty trees. According to John Mason's description, these trees were sited and trimmed in rows that radiated from the eye of an observer standing precisely in the middle of the front doorway of the mansion. From this vantage point the observer could see only the first tree in each of the four rows. However, "To the eye placed at only about two feet to the left or right of the first position, there were presented, as if by magic, four long, and apparently close walls of wood made up of the bodies of the trees, and above, as many of rich foliage constituted by their boughs stretching, as seemed to an immeasurable distance" (Rowland 1892:98–99).

In an essay on the origins of linear perspective, Cosgrove (1985) traces the history of the landscape idea as an individualist, bourgeois "way of seeing" linked to the emergence of merchant capitalism. Linear perspective utilizes the same geometry as accounting, navigation, land surveying, mapping, and artillery. Unlike earlier artistic conventions that did not assert a dichotomy between the observer and the depicted scene, representation of three-dimensional space on a two-dimensional surface through linear perspective directs the external world toward the viewer located outside of the space. The depicted space therefore becomes the visual property of detached, individual observer.

The formal landscape of Gunston Hall is thus a superb example of "aesthetic appropriation," although in this instance the process is reversed. Rather than being used to depict a three-dimensional scene on a flat surface, the principles of point perspective have been deployed to construct a landscape that exists for only one privileged viewer. The massive landscape feature consisting of over 200 large, carefully trained cherry trees could be appreciated from only one point in space (the center of the front doorway) by only one person at a time. It would be difficult to imagine a more extreme exercise in alienated, individualized perception of the landscape.

In much the same way that vanishing-point perspective in painting or the omnipotent third-person narrative voice in fiction places the viewer outside of—yet in full control over—the scene being observed, this landscape manipulation asserts that a single person, specifically the plantation owner or his privileged guest, controls the landscape visible from the front porch. Furthermore, the formal garden appears to have been constructed primarily for George Mason's private enjoyment, and his claim to mastery over nature was bolstered by the native deer kept in captivity in the deer park just beyond the formal gardens.

In his essay "Foucault's Art of Seeing," John Rajchman draws our attention to "spaces of constructed visibility," or "how spaces were designed to make things seeable, and seeable in a specific way." Yet we must also consider spaces of constructed invisibility. While trees were planted and groomed at Gunston Hall to assert symbolic (and literal) control over the formal landscape, they were also used to mask the less idyllic aspects of plantation life from view:

To the west of the main building were first the school-house, and then at a little distance, masked by a row of large English walnut trees, were the stables. To the
east was a high paled yard, adjoining the house, into which opened an outer door
from the private front, within, or connected with which yard, were the kitchen,
well, poultry houses, and other domestic arrangements; and beyond it on the same
side, were the corn house and granary, servants houses (in those days called Negro
quarters), hay yard, and cattle pens, all of which were masked by rows of large
cherry and mulberry trees. . . . The west side of the lawn or enclosed grounds was
skirted by a wood, just far enough within which to be out of sight, was a little village called Log-Town, so-called because most of the houses were built of hewn pine
logs. Here lived several families of the slaves serving about the mansion house;
among them were my father's body-servant James, a mulatto man and his family,
and those of several Negro carpenters. (Rowland 1892:99–100)

Archaeological research conducted northeast of the mansion in 1952–53 resulted
in the discovery of three eighteenth-century features: a rectangular refuse pit, a small
brick foundation, and a small rectangular pit paved with unmortared salvaged brick.
The 1953 report noted in passing that these features could be related to the "Negro
quarters" indicated by John Mason's description, but no further work was done in
this area (Fauber 1953; see also Fauber Garber, Inc. 1986 and Outlaw 1973). Subsequent archaeological investigations, particularly at Kingsmill plantations and Monticello, have found that wood- or brick-lined subfloor "root cellars" are a ubiquitous
feature of Chesapeake slave dwellings, and the features at Gunston Hall certainly
deserve reexamination in light of these recent discoveries (Kelso 1984). Although
they are not unique to African-American contexts, these features probably provided
slaves with a relatively secure place to conceal valued items.

Even when slave dwellings were screened from the gaze of the Big House, they
were usually aligned in a rigid spatial disciplinary grid (Chappell 1981, 1982; Upton
1982). Thus we can discern two conflicting impulses on the part of the plantation
owner. On one hand, he wished to assert his domination over, and difference from,
the enslaved laborers by rendering them invisible and separate. On the other hand,
he wished to maintain surveillance and incorporate the slaves and their quarters
within the rigid, formal, alienated spatial order of the plantation nucleus.

In this chapter we have examined the construction of racial difference in Virginia
within both Christian theology and plantation architectural and landscape space.
Although these are quite disparate realms of ideological discourse and social practice, we have encountered similar contradictions and arenas of struggle in each
instance. Not surprisingly, the period when Anglican religious leaders began to
aggressively advocate baptism of slaves was also marked by a shift in the self-per-
ceptions of the colonial ruling elite as evidenced by the adoption of the self-con-

sciously racial term *white* rather than *Christian* to distinguish themselves from their enslaved African-American labor force. Within the spatial realm during this period we find not only a separation of master from bound laborers but also an increased differentiation between indentured and enslaved workers.

Within both theological and architectural practice, we find deliberate attempts on the part of the elites to define and control the meaning and significance of ideologies deployed against subaltern groups. However, we also find a constant contradiction between the exclusionary and incorporative aspects of domination and a continuing effort on the part of the dominated to subvert or redefine these ideologies and disciplines. Although Christianity was deployed as a mechanism of social control, at least some slaves embraced the religion as a means of subverting their enslavement.

The tensions, ambiguities, and contested meanings embodied in plantation landscape and architectural spaces are less apparent—but no less important—than those framing religious conflicts. There are several reasons for this. While religious leaders and other members of the elite were quite forthright and reflexive in their discussions of the benefits and perils of deploying Christianity as a mechanism of social control, we do not find similar overt discussions regarding spatial control during this period. Moreover, present-day analysts have all too willingly attributed a unitary, uncontested reading to the plantation landscape (even when the architects themselves may have admitted the possibility of multiple readings) and have uncritically assumed that race is an a priori and ahistorical cause of spatial patterning.

As critical archaeologists, historians, and museologists, however, we must recognize that race is an ideological construct and remember that architecture is an important arena of ideological struggle (Cosgrove 1984, 1988; Jameson 1985). The creation, imposition, reenactment, and contestation of racial difference are processes we should be able to discern in the archaeological and architectural record. We must, however, constantly be aware that at any given time there were at least two quite different, and perhaps mutually incomprehensible, spatial conceptions of any given plantation space, and we should strive to reconstruct the subaltern as well as the dominant spatial conceptions (Anthony 1976a, 1976b; Grant 1996). Finally, we must also appreciate the contradictions between the exclusionary and incorporative aspects of spatial domination and recognize the possibilities, however limited, for resistance. While the spatial and symbolic separation of slaves from masters was an important aspect of constructing "difference," enslaved African Americans were able to use this partial isolation to nurture a vibrant culture of resistance.

# 9

# Archaeology and Ethnohistory of the Caribbean Plantation

*Douglas V. Armstrong*

## Introduction

THE HISTORICAL LANDSCAPE of the Caribbean is replete with architectural relics from now-abandoned plantations. In the eastern Caribbean windmills dot the landscape; in Jamaica massive ruins of waterwheels and sugar-boiling houses are intertwined with the roots and branches of majestic cotton trees. Planters' residences, referred to as "great houses," stand in ruins; in reconstructed form others offer the passerby a view of the past. However, missing from this visual landscape are the perishable and now-vanished houses and villages of the African slaves who lived and worked on the plantations. Similarly, the history of the region was skewed, until recently, to reflect the social and economic history of the people of European ancestry who once claimed ownership not only of the majority of the structures but also of the enslaved Africans who toiled in the plantation's fields.

Caribbean social change in the twentieth century—including labor movements in the 1920s and 1930s and the move toward nationalism and independence in the 1950s and 1960s—stimulated and supported the revision of regional histories and began to highlight the contributions of Africans and their descendants in the Caribbean (e.g., Brathwaite 1971; Dunn 1973; Hall 1959; Higman 1976, 1984; Mintz 1974; Williams 1942).[1] The growing literature on Africans in the Caribbean provides an extremely valuable tool for the understanding of the African-American experience; however, as Barry Higman points out, histories tend to be derived from sources "created and curated by the slave-owning class" (Higman 1988:85). Moreover, considerably less documentation is available on the people of slavery from the seventeenth to mid–eighteenth centuries than for their late eighteenth- and nineteenth-century descendants. Archaeological studies can provide a perspective on African-Caribbean social change and cultural transformation that is seldom found in traditional histories and difficult to address through the examination of contemporary cultures. Archaeologists have the advantage of examining the material record that has been

left by the people of slavery. Our challenge is to use these data to evaluate and interpret the social and cultural lifeways of enslaved people (Armstrong 1990a:51; Handler et al. 1989:1; Howson 1990).

The complex set of interactions between African, European, Amer-Indian, and
later Asian populations—along with localized environmental settings, economic and
power structures, and changing historical time frames—resulted in the formation
of new cultural systems in the Americas. With this complexity in mind, Sidney Mintz
and Richard Price (1976) devised a general anthropological approach for the study
of African-American cultural history. They argue that "no group, no matter how
well equipped or how free to choose, can transfer its way of life and the accompanying beliefs and values intact, from one locale to another" (Mintz and Price 1976:1).
During the era of colonization, enslaved Africans on Caribbean plantations were
of many ethnic and national origins, with differing languages and social organizations. Plantation laborers may have shared many cultural traits based upon historical relations and interactions between groups in Africa. However, they did not share
a common culture. Archaeological studies allow us to examine the processes of cultural transformation and the evolution of new societies in the Caribbean. In plantation settings these processes are controlled externally by the institution of slavery (and its inherent economic and power relationships) and internally by the
adaptive responses of the emerging African-Caribbean communities. Material and
spatial use patterns can be identified and demonstrated to reliably assess and explain
social issues such as power relationships and questions of gender, age gradation, diet
and health, and economic contexts.

## Rediscovering the African-Caribbean Past through Archaeology

Archaeological inquiry is a useful interpretive tool in at least five respects. First,
archaeological and ethnohistorical studies linking Africa with the black diaspora
allow us to examine how African heritage was transplanted, changed, or replaced in
the Americas. Second, archaeological excavations of slave settlements provide a
mechanism for examining the processes of cultural transformation associated with
the emergence of African-Caribbean communities. Third, bioanthropological studies of African-Caribbean burial and mortuary practices provide a means to understand biological and social conditions affecting the lives of Africans in the Caribbean.
Fourth, critical analyses allow us to draw upon our understanding of social structure, economics, and power relations within African-Caribbean communities and
between Africans and Europeans in the region. This evaluation process encourages
us to redefine research questions and to find new answers.

Finally, when linked with revisionist social history and critical analysis, the data
compiled from archaeological examination of African settlements on plantations

can be of tremendous value for public education. Archaeological studies provide definitive examples of houses, activity areas, and materials actually used by persons of African descent. These data can be incorporated into on-site public interpretation. The recovery of archaeological data on house design and construction, spatial organization, material use, and dietary patterns can be utilized in structuring instructional materials for local and regional schools (a process currently under way in Jamaica). The reconstruction of African-Caribbean settlements in regional heritage parks serves to counteract long-standing historical and visual-spatial voids (e.g., the absence of standing ruins) and provides details of daily life, living conditions, accommodation, and resistance. This essay draws heavily from the extensive archaeological research completed at Drax Hall (Armstrong 1985, 1990a, 1990b) and Seville plantations (fig. 9.1) (Armstrong 1989, 1990c; Armstrong and Kelly 1991). It also incorporates data from other African-American sites, both free and slave, from throughout the British Caribbean.

## The African Diaspora

In the broadest sense, elucidating the African diaspora in the Caribbean is a goal that transcends all of the research directions stated here. In practical terms, however, the aim is to examine how African heritage was transplanted, changed, or supplanted in the Americas (see also Singleton 1989). Initially, historical and anthropological studies of the African diaspora sought to identify intact African survivals in the New World (see Herskovits 1941); this view brought attention to African heritage in the Americas but was overly simplistic. Sidney Mintz's (1974) study of cultural transformations in the Caribbean provides a historically and anthropologically sound alternative to notions of whole, intact cultural survivals. Caribbean cultures are viewed as the products of adaptive strategies resulting from the synthesis of elements of African heritage, local environmental settings, and historical conditions. The maintenance of African cultural heritage was at once limited and encouraged by the institution of slavery. Whole cultures, and associated material culture, were not brought intact to the Caribbean; however, ideas, concepts, and in some cases artifacts were brought, retained, or substituted for in the Caribbean. Hence, elements of African heritage were retained and utilized in new African-Caribbean cultural settings.

A problem encountered in the study of Africanisms in the New World is a tendency to view West African cultures as monolithic. A more comprehensive knowledge of the cultural complexities of West Africa from archaeological sources is needed. This is particularly true for the fifteenth through the early nineteenth centuries, the period in which millions of Africans from a vast array of ethnic backgrounds were taken to the Americas. Although the impact of the slave trade in Africa is understood in general terms through its economic and institutional parameters, the actual impact on cultural systems, community-level social organizations, and individuals and their associated material culture has not been thoroughly examined. There is a small but growing body of archaeological information available from West African sites of this period (Posnansky 1982, 1983, 1989, and chap. 2 in this volume; Posnansky and DeCorse 1986:1; DeCorse 1989a; see also DeCorse, chap. 7 in this volume). Further investigation of the diversity of West African cultures will enhance research in the Americas.

If one were to ignore basic historical information about the location, size, and period of occupation of plantation slave settlements in the Caribbean, their initial identification would be difficult. Fortunately, an abundance of historical records and maps survive in and for the Caribbean.[2] Therefore, locating the places that were once occupied by Caribbean slaves is relatively simple, and efforts can be focused on identification and explanation of the things used by slaves: artifacts, structural remains, and dietary refuse.

The vast majority of artifacts found at these sites look no different from materials found in a variety of ethnic contexts in the seventeenth through nineteenth centuries. However, upon closer examination, elements of African continuity are clearly expressed. These include African-influenced *yabba* bowls and cooking pots and the African-inspired and internally derived boundaries and spatial arrangements of the house-yard compound that made up the slave and free settlements occupied by Africans in the Caribbean.

In Jamaica a local potting tradition, present from at least the mid–seventeenth century, derives from African practices and technology but incorporates elements of European potting technology (fig. 9.2). African-Jamaican coarse earthenware, like its colonoware counterpart recovered from North American sites, is a low-fired, hand-built pottery. The vessels are found in slave house-yards at Seville and Drax Hall plantations, as well as in urban contexts at Port Royal and the Old King's House. Similar African-Caribbean wares are reported from Montserrat (Pulsipher and Goodwin 1982), Antigua (Desmond Nicholson, pers. comm. 1989), St. Croix (Gartley 1979), Nevis, and St. Eustatius (Heath 1989). The African-Jamaican coarse earthenware is primarily represented by utilitarian cooking pot (with evidence of exterior blackening resulting from the soot of the cooking hearth) and bowl forms exhibiting few decorative elements (see fig. 9.2). These are found in house areas dating from the earliest period of slavery through the postemancipation era. Though gradually replaced by iron cooking pots and inexpensive and mass-produced ceramics, these wares increased on Drax Hall plantation in the era immediately following emancipation (Armstrong 1985). This short-term increase is seen as an adaptive strategy linked to economic stress associated with the transition to wage-labor tenancy on the plantation.

Not all of the adaptive changes found in the material record were positive. A substantial proportion of the coarse earthenware bowls recovered from Jamaican plantations have an interior lead glaze—a syncretic element borrowed from European potting traditions (see fig. 9.2). But unlike kiln-fired lead glazes (e.g., slipwares), the African-Jamaican vessels were fired at a low temperature, yielding glazes with a sugary texture that may have been a source of lead poisoning for the African-Jamaican population (Armstrong 1990a; see also Handler et al. 1986). Despite attempts to curtail their use, lead glazes are still used by modern folk potters based in Spanish Town, Jamaica.

The merger of African, European, and Amer-Indian ideas and technology can be seen in a number of items recovered from slave sites. Red- and brown-clay pipes, produced by African Jamaicans at Port Royal, have a decidedly multicultural origin. Pipe makers in Port Royal are known to have produced thousands of these red- and brown-clay pipes in the seventeenth century.[3]

The pipes are found in the ruins at Port Royal and in slave house sites of that period on the north coast of the island. The probability of their islandwide distribution is suggested by the recovery of dozens of red-clay pipestem and bowl fragments from the seventeenth-century contexts at the slave settlement at Seville plantation. Two of the stems bear the marks of Port Royal pipe makers. The presence of a local pipe-making industry suggests not only the distribution of locally made goods throughout the island, via what Mintz describes as the internal marketing system (Mintz 1974), but the interchange of ideas between cultures. Tobacco was an Amer-Indian crop which quickly spread to Europe and Africa. Tobacco probably arrived in the Upper Niger of interior West Africa via the trans-Sahara trade before its arrival on the West African coast. In the African interior local pipe-making traditions emerged that incorporate Islamic design elements (trans-Sahara trading partners) with a variety of distinctively West African forms. Among the distinctly West African artifacts found in the Caribbean is a West African-style pipe which was found in a burial at Newton Cemetery in Barbados (Handler 1983). This pipe may have been brought from Africa by a slave. A carved limestone pipe recovered from an early nineteenth-century house site at Drax Hall is similar to the African pipes in design and form, but like the ceramics it lacks additional decorative elements (Armstrong 1983:253, 257).

Much of the material culture of Afro-Caribbean populations was of perishable materials that do not survive in the archaeological record. The Caribbean calabash (*Crescentia cujete*) was used to make eating bowls, ladles, and storage vessels in much the same manner that West Africans use gourds (*Lagenaria vulgaris*) (Posnansky 1983:445). While no calabash has been recovered from terrestrial sites, Donny Hamilton recovered one from the submerged site of Port Royal, Jamaica (Armstrong 1992: cover, 2). This calabash has a design motif similar to modern examples from West

Africa (Berns and Hudson 1986). Current use and decoration of the calabash indicates that it served, and continues in use, as a functional replacement for the African gourd.

## Cultural Transformations and Community Studies

Whereas the term *acculturation* suggests a gradual adaptation of European behavior at the expense of African heritage, *cultural transformation* indicates an interactive model that presents cultural change in terms of active (rather than passive) responses to social, historical, and environmental conditions. Slaves were faced with oppressive conditions that included cultural disruption, subjugation, and isolation from their African heritage(s) and segregation from the plantocracy for which they were forced to work. Yet the people of slavery negotiated these severe conditions on internally defined terms, incorporating elements of cultural continuity within systems of culture change (Armstrong 1990a:6–7).

Archaeological studies offer us access to the materials left by slaves and the settings in which these materials were used. The artifacts recovered can be used to describe and explain both particularistic questions (such as those related to details of clothing and adornment) and complex questions involving the relationship of activities and the use of space to the internal infrastructure of the community, and in turn its relationship to the power structure of the plantation.

The data from written accounts of slave communities can be combined with the archaeological record left by the slaves to demonstrate distinctive activity area patterns. In Jamaican slave communities (and, to some extent, in modern Jamaican housing), house structures alone are not the primary residence unit. Rather, the house and surrounding yard are combined to form an inside-outside house-yard activity unit and a distinctive house-yard pattern of activities and material use. Archaeological data from Drax Hall and Seville plantations indicate hearths, cooking areas, animal pens, and cleared activity space in the yard area outside the house structure. This pattern has its origin in African traditions and is manifested in ways that are functional within the tropical Jamaican environment (Mintz 1974). The house-yard living area was also an internal, community-defined result of social interaction and can be seen as a form of resistance to imposed European spatial norms and planter authority.

Two temporally and spatially distinct African-Jamaican sites have been examined at Seville plantation. One group of houses dates from the establishment of the plantation in 1670; nearly one hundred years later, the settlement was moved to a new location. As a result, the subsurface preservation of the houses from the early settlement is remarkable: floors are intact, and soil discolorations clearly define postholes. Activity areas in the yards are clearly indicated by refuse disposal patterns, features such as hearths, and the placement of burials adjacent to houses. The houses measure 4 by 6 meters and are each divided into two rooms. The rows of houses face a central path and are tightly spaced, with only 2.5 to 5 meters separating them. All of the house foundations are constructed of unmodified limestone cobbles, with crushed marl (limestone powder) used as filler to even the floor. Postholes indicate a post-and-frame construction supporting wattle-and-daub (a woven lattice covered with mud) wall construction (fig. 9.3). While the doors opened onto the street, much of the living space utilized by the slaves was in the yard behind the house, representing an outdoor rather than an indoor living pattern. Cooking, gardening, and social gatherings all took place in the yard out of view from the planter's great house.

In the 1760s the slave settlement at Seville plantation was moved to a new location. The move appears to have occurred as an event rather than a gradual shift. A hurricane caused considerable damage to the Seville great house and probably also damaged the old village; a new settlement was built to replace it. After a century of living as slaves, community members had an opportunity to define spatial boundaries within the village on their own terms. The new village can be interpreted as an expression of the community that had evolved within the African-Jamaican settlement. While the planter controlled decisions concerning which area was occupied, there is no indication within it of the planned community organized in the previous century.

The newly constructed houses not only exhibit well-defined and expanded house-yard compound boundaries but also show considerable variation in the specifics of house design, construction, and alignment. These variations may reflect the internal social organization operative within the community; for instance, differential access to building supplies and clustered groupings of houses may reflect social relations. In contrast to the similarity in form found in the early settlement, each of the houses is oriented on a different axis and expresses a different set of building practices.

Building construction ranges from examples that are virtually identical to the earlier houses to framed wattle-and-daub houses with wood floors and, perhaps, shingled roofs (fig. 9.4). Other building types include various combinations of stone foundations and framing. Doorways tend to be oriented toward the prevailing wind and the ocean. However, houses bounding an area still referred to by people in the area as "the commons" face this open grassy site.

Yards associated with houses exhibit all of the elements found in the earlier village, including hearths and cooking areas immediately behind the house. The two major differences appear to be of scale and of distance. Cleared yard areas extend 7 to 12 meters from the house rather than the 5 to 6 meters typical in the earlier village, and most of the yards do not run directly from one to another. Instead there are marginal areas containing refuse and, presumably, vegetation. The houses of the later village are at a greater distance from the planter's and manager's residences and appear to be loosely organized around a common area. The shift in the location of the village brought it closer to the nearest provision grounds (located southwest of the village).

The study of cultural change in plantation settings should not be limited to Africans but rather should address questions related to the interaction between groups. The planter class, managers, and overseers all underwent cultural transformations even while trying to insulate themselves from island conditions and African influences. The wealth produced by the estate enabled planters to procure considerable amounts of imported foods; still, the bulk of their diet derived from the estate and included West African as well as North American cultigens. Material remains from Drax Hall indicated that while yabbas were not used within the planter household, they were present in considerable numbers in the planter's cookhouse and probably were used to prepare food for the household.

## Bioanthropological Studies

One of the richest areas for archaeological contribution to the study of the black experience in the Caribbean is in the area of bioanthropology. Mortuary practices and skeletal remains provide detailed information on nutrition and on diseases affecting the slaves, as well as insight into social life and customs (Handler et al. 1989:80). In Barbados, Jerome Handler and Frederick Lange, along with their associates, have combined archaeological and ethnohistorical interpretations of excavations at the slave cemetery at Newton plantation (Handler and Lange 1978; Handler and Corruccini 1983, 1986). Their studies provide evidence of grave goods including Indo-Pacific cowrie shells (used widely in West Africa), carnelian beads, brass bracelets, and a tobacco pipe of African origin. The presence of these materials gives empirical confirmation of a continuance of West African body ornamentation practices in the New World. Along these lines, analysis of the skeletal remains show five instances of dental mutilation or scarification of a type widely practiced in West Africa (Handler et al. 1982).

Analysis of enamel hypoplasia (arrested growth patterns on dental enamel) at Newton suggest severe environmental and nutritional stress among young children in the postweaning period. These data, indicative of the nutritional problems that affected the health and well-being of slaves, support Klein and Engerman's historical studies indicating late weaning and extended lactation among the enslaved population of the British Caribbean. The presence of high levels of lead isotopes in the skeletal remains provides further insight into possible health problems in the slave population.

African-Caribbean burials have also been recovered from the Harney slave ceme-tery (Watters 1987; Mann et al. 1987) and the burial ground at Galways plantation on Montserrat (Goodwin et al. 1990). The Harney site, associated with Bransby plan-tation, was exposed during a construction project. Skeletons of seventeen slaves were represented. Remains of adult males and females were found in equal proportions, while remains of infants were absent from the sample. Human remains in this unmarked cemetery were interred in coffins oriented in a west-headed direction; that is, facing east. Materials in the site indicate that the burial ground was used until at least the late eighteenth century. The high frequency of bone fractures, along with the evidence of anemia and enamel hypoplasia, suggests patterns of recurrent, severe malnutrition that resulted in early deaths, particularly among male slaves (Mann et al. 1987). In contrast to the Harney site, the burials at Galways plantation were marked with headstones. The skeletal remains from this site also indicate fewer pathologies, although like those found at the Harney site, they show evidence of anemia (Goodwin et al. 1990).

Adding to the growing body of bioarchaeological data, three burials have been recovered associated with house-yard compounds in the early African-Jamaican set-tlement (1670–1760) at Seville plantation (fig. 9.5). Three young adult males (ages twenty-one to twenty-five) had been interred within house-yard compounds, each within a meter of a house. The nearly identical arrangement of the three burials, all facing east, indicates a retention of West African practices of burying within house-yard compounds. This pattern has been reported by Merrick Posnansky in his research at the West African trading center at Begho in interior Ghana and by Christopher DeCorse in his study of the coastal African community of Elmina in Ghana. While the sample is small, estate records indicate nearly equal numbers of males and females on the estate; thus, the presence of three young adult males—and the absence of women, children, and the elderly—suggests a rather specific, cultur-ally defined burial practice. The burials also exhibit elements of change from con-ventional African practice: for example, all were buried in coffins, a practice not reported for African populations of West Africa before the nineteenth century. Two of the men had been interred with new kaolin tobacco pipes and one with a knife in the left hand. Pathologies include evidence of severe anemia and bone fractures (Fleischman and Armstrong 1990; Armstrong and Fleischman 1993).

Bioanthropological data from Jamaica and Montserrat and research such as Handler's more recent efforts to locate additional slave cemeteries in Barbados (Handler et al. 1989) provide additional data for comparative analysis of slave nutri-tion, health, pathology, and demography (see Handler et al. 1989:80–84). In the process archaeologists are acquiring information pertinent to a number of major questions such as why African-Caribbean populations had such high mortality rates and failed to achieve a natural increase during the period of slavery (Higman 1984:4).

## Critical Analysis

As Lewis Binford notes, "Archaeological data, unfortunately, do not carry self-evident meaning" (Binford 1983:23). Over the past twenty years, archaeologists in the Caribbean have begun to examine African-Caribbean sites, material culture, and lifeways—a fact that indicates a shift in perception. Whereas formerly, archaeologists restricted their efforts to the visible edifices of the planter's house and millworks, increasingly they focus on the African-Caribbean presence. This shift represents a democratization of archaeological inquiry, a local response to processual questions of how and why plantations operated. However, even with a perspective aimed at revisionist social history, archaeological studies are hampered by preconceived notions of material use and definitions of function and significance (Leone 1986). Critical archaeology, based on Marxist theory, emphasizes the interactive nature of culture and assumes "that people create, use, modify, and manipulate their symbolic capabilities, making and remaking the world they live in" (Leone 1986:416). Its goal is not only to critique perceptions of function in the past and to construct alternate hypotheses accounting for the artifact categories, associated belief, and ideology of the user but also to communicate the ways in which modern ideology and interpretation have tended to mask significant relations of economics, power, and dominance.

Increasingly, archaeologists are trying to understand the impact of power relations between African Americans and European Americans on the social structure of African Americans (Orser 1988a, 1989). In the Caribbean economic and power relationships are clearly demarcated in spatial relationship between parts of the plantation. Slave villages were located so as to maximize the return from slave labor and at the same time maximize the planter's control (Armstrong 1990a; Handler and Lange 1978). At Drax Hall, Seville, and nearly all other plantations on Jamaica's north coast, slave villages were located in small parcels in hilly or ruinate areas at the margins of fields, as well as in close proximity to cane fields and processing works. Planter (or managerial) housing was strategically located between sites of the key economic importance—labor, fields, and works—so as to maximize control and ensure production of a profitable cash crop. Drax Hall provides a clear example of the relationship between village location, planter-manager control, and mode of production operant at the estate (Armstrong 1990b).

During the period of slavery, settlements in Jamaica were located close to labor areas (the works and fields) and near the houses of overseers and planters. A similar pattern has been observed on Barbados (Handler and Lange 1978:30) and St. Eustatius (Delle 1990). William Beckford, an eighteenth-century planter-historian, reported that slave houses were "in general some distance from the works, but not so far removed from the sight of the overseer" (Beckford 1790:2:41). The Drax Hall data point to the importance of economic factors in determining plantation layout, with the fields and works as the primary locus or core of the estate and the planter's house centrally located between the fields-works and the slave quarters. The position of the planter's house, and its effectiveness as a center of authority over slaves, was dependent on the location of the fields and works. The works were centrally located with respect to the fields so that the sugar could be processed quickly, before it spoiled. The average distance from any field to the works is roughly one-half the distance from either the slave settlement or the planter's house to the fields. Both planter and slave lived in areas located on the perimeter of but near the fields and works, with the planter's residence located between the fields-works and the slaves. This spatial pattern not only avoided compromising valuable soils with habitation structures; it also reinforced planter control over the slave.

The power relationship at Drax Hall is driven home by changes in plantation layout over time. The earliest plans of the estate show that the planter's house was situated between the slave houses and the sugar works. The cane was ground in cattle-turned mills located west of the great house. A shift occurred by the mid–eighteenth century, indicated by the construction of first a windmill and then a waterwheel in the middle of the cane fields. Although new mills allowed more efficient mechanized processing of cane, they also shifted the center of production away from an area near the planter's house to the center of the fields, resulting in an arrangement in which the planter's house was not located between fields-works and slaves. However, soon after the production center was changed, the Drax Hall great house was replaced with a new house, again located on the perimeter of the fields and between the fields-works and slaves. The slave village itself did not move. After emancipation in 1838, the houses of the village were relocated down the hill away from the planter's house into the area formerly occupied by the old great house and closer to the main roads that provided access to areas beyond the estate. The former slaves, now laboring tenants, no longer had to pass the planter's house on the way to the fields and works. The spatial data provide an unambiguous picture of class structure and the relationship between planter and slave. Moreover, shifts in spatial patterning reflect changes in the relationship between planter and slave and in the mode of production operative at the estate.

Even though village boundaries were fixed, internal reorganization of house structures and house-yards was achievable, a form of cultural expression and an indication of informal resistance. The analysis of spatial relationships expressed in house-yard living areas and of shifts in village location allows us to look deeper into the internal infrastructure of the enslaved community, beyond the general relationship dictated by the mode of production and the institution of slavery to the actions and choices of the people bound in slavery.

The slaves created and maintained distinctive forms of behavior that were functional and effective in the tropical environment, serving at the same time to distinguish themselves from the planter class. The maintenance of this internal social system served both the slave and the planter. The planter class encouraged the slaves to maintain a degree of behavioral autonomy so that perceived differences (white/black, planter/slave) upon which the institution of slavery was based could be strengthened and retained. At the same time, the slaves devised their own internal system integrating elements of African continuity into a locally defined social context that enabled the people of slavery to act independently of the planter class. The latter view looks within the institution of slavery to the systems that were created by the slaves in spite of and in response to conditions of slavery.

## Public Interpretation

If archaeologists have access to an important set of data used for the interpretation of the African-American past, then they also have a responsibility to share their findings with today's African-American communities. Archaeologists are just beginning to recognize the importance of presenting their data through media other than scholarly journals and meetings. The basic tenets of the profession encourage dissemination of information among peers but do not demand public presentations or interaction with the local population whose ancestors are being studied. While there is certainly room for improved communication between archaeologists and local communities in the Caribbean, the majority of plantation studies have, from the outset, been geared toward both the intellectual community (archaeologists, historians, and anthropologists) and the people of the islands in which research was carried out (e.g., Armstrong 1983; Handler et al. 1989; Pulsipher and Goodwin 1982, 1988).

Several cultural heritage parks and interpretive centers are in the design phase in the Caribbean. Research at Galways plantation on Montserrat, by Lydia Pulsipher and Conrad M. Goodwin in cooperation with the Montserrat National Trust, has combined research with public interpretation examining the development of plantation society from the seventeenth century (Pulsipher and Goodwin 1982a; Goodwin 1982, 1987). A large-scale research effort aimed at establishing a historical-cultural center is currently under way at Betty's Hope plantation on Antigua. The master plan for this center includes an integrated interpretive program for the 330-year-old plantation. There are plans for integrating the reconstruction of the African-Antiguan slave settlement at the site with "living history" demonstrations. The target audience for this education initiative includes not only visitors to the island but also students from local primary and secondary schools.

Similarly, research conducted jointly by Syracuse University and the Jamaican National Heritage Trust at Seville plantation combined research and public interpretation goals. In fact, the pressing need to carry out archaeological research at Seville for interpretive purposes was underscored by a UNESCO-sponsored feasibility study for a heritage park at Seville (UNESCO 1987). The feasibility study, aimed at examining the potential of the various sites that are located within the boundaries of Seville plantation, almost totally ignored the African components at Seville while heralding the Spanish, British, and Amer-Indian (Taino) sites. In response to this neglect, research on the African-Jamaican settlements at Seville was initiated in the summer of 1987.[4] In addition to addressing specific research questions at Seville, the objective was to ensure the inclusion of the African-Jamaican slave and tenant laborer settlements in public education efforts at the Jamaican National Historic Park.

Initially the omission of the African-Jamaican settlements is startling, given Jamaica's long-standing leadership in revisionist history and cultural understanding. Upon reflection, however, the omission can be linked to Jamaica's colonial past and a tendency to disassociate plantations from African-Jamaican heritage. Seville was acquired as a historic park in the early 1960s because it contained the probable site of two of Christopher Columbus's caravels, as well as the site of Sevilla La Nueva (occupied between 1504 and 1534), and because of the survival of its great house and works dating to the eighteenth century. Archaeologists and historians were interested in the site initially because of the surviving architecture of the British-period sugar plantation, because of the Spanish settlements, and because of the presence of contact-period Amer-Indian (Taino) sites on the property. Despite the fact that for most of its postcontact history, African Jamaicans made up the majority population on the estate, this African presence was not considered in initial planning.

Disregard for Seville's African components became entrenched as architects called in to evaluate the property concentrated on the known structures, namely, the standing buildings of the sugar plantation and the excavated ruins of the Spanish sites. From the perspective of the 1990s, inclusion of the African Jamaican is essential to any interpretation at the Jamaican National Historic Park. If not for the initiation of archaeological studies of the African-Jamaican settlements, these sites would have been underrepresented in the heritage park now being designed for the site (Armstrong 1991b).[5] Plans call for the reconstruction of groups of houses representing the two slave settlements at Seville (fig. 9.6). Tours for island visitors and the public, including schoolchildren, will provide a means by which the African-Jamaican heritage of Jamaica can be explored. Research at the African-Jamaican settlements at Seville addresses oversights in past historical interpretation and calls attention to the African-Jamaican presence; in the process, history is redefined to acknowledge the contributions of all Jamaicans.

## Prospective Discussion

Archaeological studies are just beginning to illuminate the African-American experience in the Caribbean. The information gained in this region, and from comparative studies of sixteenth- through nineteenth-century Africa, will broaden our knowledge of the emergence of African-American societies. In comparison to the southern United States, where many written records were lost to war and fire, the Caribbean has excellent archival data allowing archaeologists to identify sites and the people who lived on them. Nearly everyone new to the area is amazed at the quality and consistency of information on plantation maps (see Higman 1988). Archival materials include detailed information gleaned from plantation inventories, wills, deeds, and registers of returns of slaves (triannual reports that list all slaves in the British Caribbean by estate).

Most plantations in the Caribbean were abandoned or converted to less labor-intensive production (e.g., coconut, banana, cattle) after the collapse of the sugar industry in the mid–nineteenth century. Free settlements were established adjacent to expanding towns and later incorporated with them or were situated along roadsides. In Jamaica most of the old slave villages were gradually abandoned; eventually they were overgrown by verdant tropical vegetation. Most similar settlements on Barbados have been converted to agricultural production. With the exception of severe damage to sites in expanding urban areas and on small islands with a demand for land, most of the plantation sites in the countryside are subject only to benign neglect.

While many sites in the Caribbean survive, their future is uncertain. Unlike the United States, with its extensive and enforceable historic preservation laws, the Caribbean has neither the legal nor the financial structure to support systematic attempts at preservation and archaeological investigation. Hundreds of sites containing African-American components have been excavated as part of mitigation projects in North America, but the number of sites excavated or protected in the Caribbean remains small.

Archaeological studies of Africans in the Caribbean are just beginning to branch out and address the diversity of historical settings in which Africans lived. García Arévalo has completed studies of Cimarron settlements in the Dominican Republic (García Arévalo 1986), while Kofi Agorsah has initiated Maroon settlements in Jamaica (Agorsah 1991, 1992, 1994). Candice Goucher (1993) has begun to examine the African basis of metallurgy at Reeders Pen, Jamaica. Studies of Port Royal in Jamaica have begun to isolate and examine the archaeology of urban slaves and freeholders, as well as localized industries imitated by Africans—such as the production of red-clay pipes.

Research in the region will continue to explore sugar plantations but must expand to investigate cattle pens, coffee plantations, and other activity centers in which Africans participated. Slaves on cattle pens and on small plantations may have had different experiences than their counterpart on large sugar plantations. Slaves on coffee plantations lived in high mountainous regions that were both cooler and more isolated than most sugar plantations. Coffee plantations in Jamaica expanded in both numbers and production for only a short time in the late period of slavery. These short-lived plantations occupied areas adjacent to lands traditionally held by independent Maroon communities. How did life on these plantations compare with that on sugar estates? Future research should focus on the contrast between the conditions and responses of African-Caribbean populations in the diverse island settings throughout the region and between the peoples of the Caribbean and their counterparts in North America.

Certainly all studies of the African-American experience must deal with the economic and power structures in which slaves, tenants, and free blacks lived; however, they should also elucidate and explain the internal social structures that evolved in the New World setting. Archaeology and ethnohistory combine to provide data on daily life and the process of cultural evolution within African-American communities that are not readily available from other sources. It is hoped that the initial findings from archaeological studies will provide a basis upon which fruitful comparisons can be made between the lifeways of Africans throughout the Americas. The challenge is to develop research strategies that transcend historical bias and our own limited perspectives to explore and explain the African-American experience.

## Notes

1. Armstrong (1990) and Howson (1990) discuss the importance of an integrated anthropological-historical perspective. Current archaeological scholarship draws upon the historiographic scholarship of those who have examined the development of African-Caribbean and African-American societies (e.g., in the Caribbean: Brathwaite 1971; Bush 1990; Craton 1978; Dunn 1973; Handler and Lange 1978; Higman 1976, 1987; Mintz 1974, 1985; Mintz and Price 1976; Morrissey 1989; and for the Americas: Fox-Genovese 1988; Genovese 1965; and Joyner 1984).

2. The availability of historical documentation varies from island to island. Archival data are particularly rich in Jamaica and Barbados. For example, the National Library of the Institute of Jamaica has a particularly outstanding collection of maps and plantation plans.

3. Matthew Emerson has carried out extensive research on locally made clay pipes in the Chesapeake. He is able to correlate design elements on these pipes with specific stylistic elements from Africa (Emerson, chap. 4 in this volume). In both the southeastern United States and the Caribbean, the manufacture and use of African-American clay pipes appear to taper

off soon after the beginning of the eighteenth century. Emerson correlates the cessation of local pipe making with both a historically documented shift of blacks moving out of quarters they shared with their white owners and into separate housing and the expansion of plantation slavery in Chesapeake region. In Jamaica red-clay pipe making was an established industry based in Port Royal. Its demise corresponds with a shift in the power base from a merchant-trader economy to a land-based agricultural-industrial economy founded on the production of sugar. The shift occurs at a time of increasing availability of inexpensive white kaolin clay pipes (and clay for export manufacture). While the histories of clay pipe manufacture differs for each of the two regions, expansion of the plantation system can be linked to increased populations and parallel social change in each region.

4. The African-Jamaican slave settlement project is being conducted jointly by the Jamaican National Heritage Trust and Syracuse University, assisted by grants from the National Geographic Society and the Wenner-Gren Foundation. The site will become part of the interpretive center at Seville National Historic Park and Museum.

5. The vestiges of past omissions are hard to eliminate. Even though the Jamaican National Heritage Trust (the government agency responsible for archaeology) had evaluated preliminary archaeological findings from the slave settlement and clearly defined the African settlements at Seville as essential components in any public interpretation, a contract was awarded by another government agency that used the old 1987 UNESCO report as a model. Hence, the 1991 study began with the same deficiency as the 1987 study. Fortunately, when the team of architects designated to devise a master plan for Seville arrived at the estate, they were met by the research team and representatives of the Jamaican National Heritage Trust. They were given a tour of the sites, copies of research reports, and a brief designed for public interpretation; the net result was a revision of the master plan to include, and even highlight, the African-Jamaican settlement and the contribution of Africans in Jamaica (Armstrong 1991b; Yarwood 1991).

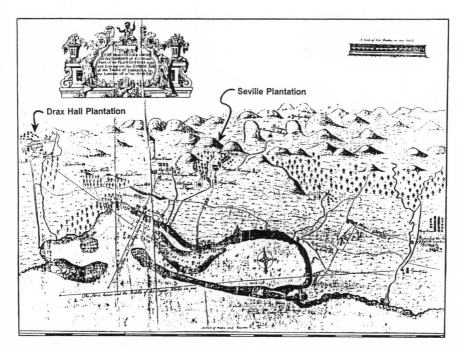

9.1. Plan view of St. Ann's Bay including Drax Hall and Seville plantations, ca. 1721

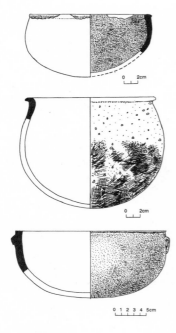

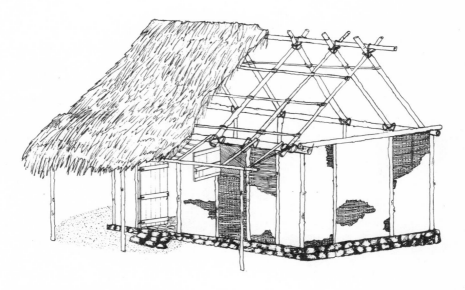

9.2. Yabba earthenware vessels, ca. 1670–1760: bowl with interior lead glaze (*top*); a cooking pot with charred bottom (*middle*); bowl with molded handles (*bottom*). (Redrawn by Marcia Bakry)

9.3. Reconstruction of early slave house at Seville, ca. 1670–1760. Note house foundation of unmodified limestone cobbles.

9.4. Reconstruction of late slave house at Seville, ca. 1760–1830. Note raised wooden floor upon stone piers.

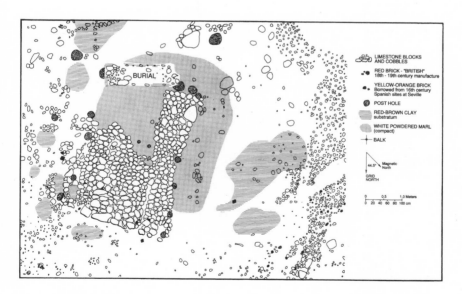

9.5. Layout of a house-yard area at the early settlement of Seville showing burial

9.6. Artist's rendering of slave settlements at Seville for a proposed re-creation for the Seville Heritage Park

# 10

# "Your Humble Servant": Free Artisans in the Monticello Community

*Barbara J. Heath*

## Introduction

O VER THE PAST TWO DECADES, historical archaeologists have studied plantation communities in the American South and the Caribbean. Much attention has focused upon defining the material manifestations of African or creole culture in the archaeological record (Deetz 1977; Handler and Lange 1978; Anthony 1979; Ferguson 1980, 1992; Armstrong 1985; Klingelhofer 1987), tracing and explaining the process of acculturation (Wheaton et al. 1983; Joseph 1989) and defining indicators of socioeconomic status differences between masters and slaves (Otto 1984; Lewis 1985; Mullins Moore 1985; Kelso 1986; Singleton 1991; Samford 1996). More recently, questions of cultural processes at work within the plantation have been posed (Sanford 1994), often in terms of the dynamics of power, manifested through economic oppression and racism (Orser 1988a; Babson 1990; Epperson 1990b).

Scholars have recognized that plantations functioned as social systems as well as economic communities made up of distinct groups with their own internal cohesion. Yet researchers have differed in their criteria for defining and interpreting these groups. In his pioneering work John Otto described Cannon's Point plantation as a community made up of planter, overseer, and slaves; a community divided by economic, racial, and legal differences in status (Otto 1984). In her introduction to *The Archaeology of Slavery and Plantation Life*, Theresa Singleton stated that "the aim of plantation archaeology today is to understand behavioral patterns within and between the three different groups of plantation residents (owners, managers and laborers)" (Singleton 1985:3). This economic rather than racial definition of internal hierarchies was upheld by Handler and Lange in an assessment of the state of plantation studies: "In much of the data gathered so far there is also a strong hint that the ethnohistorical approach needs to place less emphasis on strictly racial-ethnic divisions in plantation research. Much of the data suggests that the basic division was between the planters and their overseers and slaves, rather than a three-level separation of status and privilege. Thus, we need to revise our thinking of 'the slaves' as an ethnic-racial unit and also focus on plantation slavery at the level of socioeconomic separation" (Lange and Handler 1985:28).

This study defines the social and material worlds of two white artisans living from 1801 to 1810 at Monticello, Thomas Jefferson's piedmont Virginia plantation. Drawing on surviving documents and archaeological evidence of the physical remains of their house and its associated landscape, the study compares the economic and social standing of the free artisan on the plantation to that of skilled slaves who lived on Mulberry Row, Monticello's industrial core. This comparison serves to define the boundaries that Jefferson set for each group and to examine their acceptance or challenge of these boundaries.

Research at Monticello suggests that in the early nineteenth century, class and ethnicity were inseparably intertwined, and that perhaps an analysis of the social relations of dominance and power, as Orser and Howson have suggested (Orser 1988:739–42; Howson 1990:88), will provide the most useful path for exploring the Monticello community.

With very few exceptions, historical archaeologists have paid little attention to the free white artisans and laborers who lived and often labored alongside slaves in the antebellum South (Adams 1987; Heath 1991a, 1991b). Scholars have argued that the planters' use of slaves to perform craft work discouraged the growth of an artisan class in the white community (Calhoun in Zierdan et al. 1986:2–30); or conversely, that a lack of skilled white workers—caused on the one hand by relatively unsteady demand and on the other by the availability of land for farming—forced plantation owners to teach their slaves to master skills such as smithing, carpentry, masonry, or plastering (Russo 1988:389–91). Recent historical research has challenged this view (Russo 1988:389–432, 1992:75–78; Daniels 1993:756–60; Gillespie 1995:33–47; Rock et al. 1995), yet few studies have focused on the role of white artisans and laborers on southern plantations (Jordan 1991).

This lack of interest is, at least in part, due to the near-invisibility of many of these people in the documentary and archaeological records. Whereas many southern craftsmen turned to farming to supplement their incomes (Marzio 1972:231–32), others became roving artisans, working on plantations for a few months or a few years before moving on to the next job. The details of their working lives, often summarized in a single entry in an account book, are difficult to reconstruct. Archaeological evidence of their plantation existence can be equally scarce, as short-term occupations in impermanent dwellings left behind few traces. Nevertheless, a cursory examination of the literature has shown that white carpenters, masons, spinners, weavers, coopers, millers, sailors, bakers, and smiths lived and worked on eighteenth- and early nineteenth-century plantations throughout Virginia (Betts 1987:421–22, 456;

Brody 1989:22–23; Conway 1889; Cote 1986a:26–29; Cote 1986b:57; Jackson and Twohig 1976–79:2:275, 4:249, 5:83; Jordan 1991; Marzio 1972:231–33; Morton 1941:94–97, 117, 164, 274).[1]

Serious research is needed to determine the employment patterns of these artisans and laborers on plantations across the antebellum South. How did the planter intend free workers and their families to fit into the social and economic hierarchy of his plantation? Conversely, to what degree did their actions conform to the system he envisioned? These questions are particularly provocative at Monticello, where documentary and archaeological evidence of the material standards of living of both free white and enslaved black artisans has been gathered in a long-term research project, and where comparisons between groups within the community can now begin.

Monticello today stands as a monument to the genius of Thomas Jefferson as architect, landscape architect, gardener, statesman, and Enlightenment philosopher. Yet during his lifetime his mountaintop home served as the centerpiece of a network of working plantations, supported by a force, in his words, of both free white and enslaved black "hirelings, laborers, workmen and house servants" ("Instructions to Bacon" in Bear 1967:54). These men and women produced cash crops and goods on which Jefferson's economic survival depended, and they contributed skills necessary for the realization of Jefferson's many improvements to the property. As did other Virginia planters of the period, Thomas Jefferson created not only a built world composed of house, dependencies, and gardens but a diverse and sometimes divisive community as well.

The most powerful people in this community were, of course, the members of the Jefferson family. During her short lifetime Martha Jefferson gave birth to two daughters who survived to adulthood. Martha, the eldest, protected her father's interests during his frequent and prolonged absences from the plantation during his vice presidency and presidency. Maria, the younger daughter, died in early adulthood, but her son Francis was a frequent visitor to the property, as were various Jefferson nieces, nephews, and grandchildren.

Enslaved African Americans were also among the earliest permanent residents of the mountain. Children born into Monticello's slave families grew to maturity on the plantation and filled changing roles throughout their lives—roles that might include field hand, carter, weaver, spinner, nailboy, smith, joiner, carpenter, gardener, butler, ladies' maid, cook, and groom. While Jefferson freed a few skilled slaves (and sold others to cover debts or as punishment for repeated misbehavior), the majority of African Americans brought to or born at Monticello after 1769 remained on the property until their death or until their community was dissolved following Jefferson's death in 1826.

In contrast to these long-term plantation residents were a number of transitory free white workers, hired by Jefferson for limited periods of time because they possessed skills useful to him. Many of the men were artisans, skilled as masons, carpenters, or smiths; others were employed as overseers or laborers. For these men and their families, Monticello represented a temporary economic opportunity, a stopping point rather than the sum of their economic lives.

## The Documented World of Artisans at Monticello

In 1989 and 1990 archaeologists excavated a domestic site occupied during the first decade of the nineteenth century by William Stewart and Elisha Watkins. Surviving correspondence, finance account books, and maps indicate that Stewart, a blacksmith and whitesmith from Philadelphia, lived in the house from the summer of 1801 until sometime in late 1807 or early 1808. His three sons and two or more daughters resided with him for most of that time; his wife had lived there as well until her death in 1803. Watkins, a carpenter, occupied the dwelling for exactly one year, beginning in January 1809.

Because Jefferson, serving as president, was absent from Monticello during most of the period in which Stewart was employed, many of the details of the relationship between employer and employee were committed to paper and have survived. On the other hand, Elisha Watkins occupied the house for only a year, and this year coincided with Jefferson's return to the property. As a result, most of their interactions apparently occurred face to face instead of through the mail. While Stewart can be studied as a personality as well as a representative of his class, Watkins has largely faded into anonymity. Therefore, this discussion focuses primarily upon Stewart.

To define William Stewart's role at Monticello requires some understanding of both Jefferson's need for his services and the smith's motivations for accepting employment in Virginia. Like many plantation owners in the mid-Atlantic, Jefferson often hired white artisans who possessed specialized skills. They would both perform a required job and, ideally, teach his slaves their trades.

In the years preceding Stewart's appointment, Jefferson began work on a canal, the first step in an ambitious plan of construction that eventually resulted in the operation of a gristmill, a manufacturing mill, and a sawmill on his property. Jefferson saw these mills as a benefit to his neighbors in Albemarle County, providing the much-needed services of grinding wheat and preparing lumber, and also as a source of income for himself (Betts 1987:341–43, 353). While a master millwright would oversee construction, an experienced blacksmith was needed to create, modify, and install the metalwork each mill required to operate.

If neighborhood improvement and profit explain Jefferson's offer to hire Stewart, hard times appear, at least in part, to have motivated the smith's acceptance of the job and his subsequent move south. In the 1790s Stewart operated as both a blacksmith and a whitesmith, renting a house in southeast Philadelphia.[2] Engaged by Jefferson to "go on from Philadelphia in July" 1801 (Betts 1987:443), Stewart apparently suffered a financial loss and headed south two months early. An associate of Jefferson's reported that "the people for whom he [Stewart] wrought, have failed and he has been a loser, which soured him so much, that he would go off at once" (Betts 1987:425).

No contract between Jefferson and Stewart survives to define the financial terms of the smith's employment, yet an analysis of Stewart's debts and expenditures as recorded by Jefferson indicates that in addition to being "fixed in the house built for Powel," each year he was paid approximately $155,[3] provided with 500 pounds of pork, and probably supplied with "corn per usual." This arrangement is typical of the agreements reached between Jefferson and other white artisans and overseers (table 10.1). In exchange, Stewart was to oversee a nailery, perform the necessary forging and mending tasks of a plantation smith, and provide the expertise needed to make the mills operational. If Stewart failed in any of these assignments, Jefferson had the power to dismiss and evict the smith and his family immediately.

The financial lives of employer and employee quickly became intertwined. The memorandum books in which Jefferson recorded the details of his financial life reveal numerous small sums paid to Stewart over the years in which he lived at Monticello. Additionally, just four months after the smith's employment began, Jefferson's commission agent George Jefferson reported that Stewart had called on him "for $105—which I was obliged to let him have or I supposed suffer him to go to jail" (Betts 1987:425). On at least two other occasions, Jefferson was obliged to answer for Stewart's debts publicly.[4] Yet when Stewart had fallen behind in forging mill irons, Jefferson lacked the leverage to force him to work and even contemplated hiring another smith to complete the project on time:

> I wish you [E. Bacon, overseer] therefore to exert yourself to have the irons done immediately by Stewart, & that he never quits them till the whole are done. but if he cannot be got to do them as fast as Mr. Walker wants them, then it will be necessary to get them done elsewhere; either in some other shop, or by hiring a smith to do them in ours, as you shall find best. it is certainly more to my interest that Stewart should do them because he will do them better than any other, and they will cost me nothing but the iron, as he is heavily in my debt: but if he will not work, we must not let the mill be detained. (Thomas Jefferson to Edmund Bacon, 15 Dec. 1806, MHi)

Apparently Bacon could not persuade Stewart to comply; thirteen days later Jefferson stated, "Stuart's conduct is so intolerable that I must dismiss him" (Thomas Jefferson to James Dinsmore, 28 Dec. 1806, DLC). But dismissal did not come until nearly a year later, again tempered by the statement that if the smith would finish outstanding jobs, Jefferson would allow him to stay on and provide him with provisions (Thomas Jefferson to Edmund Bacon, 24 Nov. 1807, CSmH).

The relationship between the two men cannot be defined merely in terms of finances and failed assignments. Paternalism played a role as well. Following the death of his wife, Stewart abandoned his children and traveled to Philadelphia. Jefferson wrote to some of his agents in that city, asking them to seek the smith out and persuade him to return to his family. He also assumed Stewart's debts in his absence to head off the repossession of his belongings by angry creditors.[5] The president's motivation went beyond economic self-interest and an unwillingness to assume responsibility for a houseful of abandoned children. His daughter dismissed the crisis: "For Mrs. Stuart being dead, and Mrs. Lewis having taken charge of the girls, it appears to me of very little importance to prevent the sale of the furniture. Humanity cannot be interested in the fate of a man so well able to provide for himself. . . . so much for business, suffer me now to touch on subjects more interesting and certainly more important than any business to be transacted by or through me" (Martha Jefferson Randolph to Thomas Jefferson, 14 Jan. 1804, ViU). Yet Jefferson interceded, saving Stewart from bankruptcy and preserving the unity of his family. He continued to take an interest in members of the Stewart family long after their father had left his employ.[6]

How was authority delegated in Jefferson's absence? While relatives such as the president's son-in-law took periodic control, day-to-day management of most land and labor fell to the overseers. These men were essentially plantation managers, responsible for a variety of duties: overseeing slave and some artisan labor, both agricultural and industrial; managing land and livestock; acquiring provisions for family, slaves, and livestock; mediating between Jefferson and community members; and performing miscellaneous tasks as directed by their employer. Jefferson outlined the duties of his overseer for 1805 as being "to provide for the maintenance of a family of about 40 negroes at all times, and for my own family about 3 months in the year; to hire annually, and overlook about 10 laboring men, employed in a little farming but mainly in other works about my mills, & grounds generally; to superintend the gristmill, and a nailery of 10. to 15. hands, provide their coal, sell nails etc." (Betts 1944:302–3).

The overseers' authority regarding Stewart is ambiguous. On the one hand, Jefferson explicitly directed that "Joe works with Mr. Stewart; John Hemings and Lewis with Mr. Dinsmore; Burwell paints and takes care of the house. With these the overseer has nothing to do, except to find them [i.e., provision them]" (Betts 1987:25);

on the other, he instructed the overseer to "exert" or "direct" the smith to forge specific items (Thomas Jefferson to Edmund Bacon, 15 Dec. 1806, MHi; Jefferson to Bacon, 31 May 1807, DLC). The president also relayed instructions to Stewart through carpenters John Perry and James Dinsmore and through the millwright James Walker, suggesting that Stewart answered most often to the men who supervised the projects with which he was directly involved.

Stewart was not always on the receiving end of instructions; he acted as a manager on the property as well. Initially his duties included overseeing Jefferson's nail-making operations, a business that relied upon the efficiency of a gang of teenage slaves, or "nailboys." In less than a year Jefferson relieved the smith of his responsibilities, concluding that the nailboys "require a rigour of discipline to make them do reasonable work, to which he cannot bring himself" (Thomas Jefferson to James Dinsmore, 1 Dec. 1802, DLC). For the remainder of his employment, Stewart supervised one man, the slave smith Joe Fosset, and managed a newly constructed shop on the east side of the mansion. Joe, in turn, became the informal manager of Moses and Isabel's Davy, two other Monticello slaves, when Stewart got "into his idle frolics" ("Memo for Edmund Bacon" in Betts 1987:25).

There is no evidence that the smith ever owned slaves, yet after the death of Mary Stewart, a woman lived with him and presumably fulfilled his wife's domestic duties. The woman's legal status is unclear, but references to her by first name only, as Melinda, suggest that she was a slave. Stewart was sued by Jefferson's nephew for failure to pay him for her hire.[7]

In summary, Stewart was both managed and manager, totally answerable only to Jefferson but directed periodically by his peers. He in turn taught and structured the work schedule for some of Jefferson's slaves and became the temporary master of a local woman, who was most likely a slave.

It is not possible from documentary evidence to determine William Stewart's perception of his place in the Monticello community, for although he was a literate man, no letters in his own hand are known to survive. The smith's experiences at Monticello, like those of the majority of the free artisan and slave population, are recorded subjectively by the Jefferson family, Jefferson's business associates, and (less frequently) Stewart's coworkers. Because the Jeffersons' and their business associates' interests were primarily economic, Stewart's skill as a smith, and his productivity, provided the most frequent topics of discussion.

Both Jefferson and his overseer Edmund Bacon repeatedly praised the smith's expertise while in the same breath condemning his propensity to drink.[8] "He is the best workman in America, but the most eccentric one," Jefferson wrote, "quite manageable were I at home, but doubtful as I am not" (Betts 1987:425). From the beginning of his term of employment at Monticello until the day of his dismissal, Stewart's errant behavior and his skill hung in a precarious balance. Jefferson acknowledged his habitual "idle frolics" (Betts 1987:25), while Bacon complained, "The old man has never done on[e] or not more than one days work since you left heare. He is eternally drunk and like a mad man" (Edmund Bacon to Thomas Jefferson, 8 Nov. 1807, ViU).

Intemperance was not uncommon among workers during the early nineteenth century. In eighteenth-century England craftsmen typically celebrated St. Mondays by drinking, gambling, or engaging in other non-work-related activities, making up for these "sprees" by working longer hours later in the week (Rock 1984:295–303). Historians disagree on the persistence of this holiday in colonial and federal America (Nash 1979:12; Brody 1989:18–19) and on the overall influence of alcohol on the working schedules of artisans and laborers (Brody 1989:20–21; Rock 1984:295–303). Nevertheless, plantation owners recognized overindulgence in alcohol, to the detriment of work schedules, as a recurrent problem.

Before the arrival of Stewart at Monticello, other craftsmen, both slave and free, were known to be drinkers (Bear 1967:20; McLaughlin 1988:66–67). During his working years on the plantation, Stewart was not always alone in his bingeing. Claimed Jefferson's aggrieved carpenter, James Oldham:

> Had I, Sir, of gon into your cellars with these men and others and there of got Beastly drunk, I should of bin in there sight a clever fellow [besi'd?] geting a few bottles of wine; Had I of sind. my naim to perry's bill of lumber and also to his account of the days worke which he charg'd you with it would of still been all well, but in preference to acting dishonestly I strove to do justice to those men as also to your Honourable self. Can it be possable, Sir, that you have never lurn of Lilleys going into the cellar and getting drunk and to be oblidg'd to be carried home.... I much question if Mr. Lilley ever acquainted you how-much flower and poark he fernishd. his friends with the first year he had the supplying of us and h[...] did he supply the last year with corn. (James Oldham to Thomas Jefferson, 26 Nov. 1804, MHi)

As apparently was common among urban artisans of the time, (Rock 1984:300), craftsmen at Monticello resorted to alcohol to break away from restrictive work schedules and thus to challenge the authority of Jefferson. While unproven, Oldham's allegation of theft committed by fellow artisans suggests other ways in which free workers may have challenged the power structure. Similar thefts of time and materials by slaves have been identified by Genovese and others as acts of resistance (Genovese 1976). But whereas slaves were primarily trying to assert some level of autonomy, lessen their workload, or supplement their rations, free artisans may have used theft as a means of increasing their personal wealth and standing among their peers.

Whether or not John Perry and Gabriel Lilly drank Jefferson's wine without his knowledge will probably never be known. More importantly, Oldham's letter underlines the factionalism within the white artisan group. Hints of backbiting and out-right violence between and among white overseers and white craftsmen suggest a jockeying for position within the power structure of the plantation and attempts to break free from it. Among his other accusations, James Oldham wrote to Jefferson that the overseer Lilly and the carpenter Perry had chased him off the mountain at gunpoint; he further claimed that they, together with Stewart, were responsible for his dismissal (James Oldham to Thomas Jefferson, 26 Nov., 1804, MHi). The millwright, James Walker, attributed his failure to complete the mills on schedule to the incompetence or poor management of Bacon, Stewart, Perry, and Maddox—overseer, smith, carpenter, and mason—all free artisans (Betts 1944:327–29). Perry told Bacon that Jefferson blamed the overseer for some problem with construction of the cooper's house and stable at the mill, to which Jefferson replied, "There is not such an idea in my letter, the blame was all for himself [Perry]" (Betts 1944:341). These examples of physical force and name-calling suggest that authority and relative status were constantly renegotiated among Jefferson's hired hands.

## Archaeological Evidence

A close reading of the documents provides insights into the social and economic relationships between white artisans, on the one hand, and the Jefferson family and overseers, on the other. Archaeological data allow us to compare Stewart's and Watkins's material standard of living (and, by inference, their position within the hierarchy established by Jefferson) to that of some skilled slaves living in the Monticello community in the early nineteenth century. This discussion compares the excavated remains of slave housing to the physical evidence of the Stewart-Watkins site and considers their relative position on the Monticello landscape. Because Jefferson ultimately controlled all aspects of housing, similarities or differences observed between siting, materials, house size, and layout must necessarily be attributed to his concept of the placement of each group within the community. Comparative analyses between artifact assemblages recovered from the Stewart-Watkins house, excavated slave quarters, and the mansion should provide insights into aspects of each group's material world over which Jefferson's control was incomplete. Two levels of questioning govern comparisons drawn from the Stewart-Watkins data. First, can we determine the degree of individual choice in the assemblage of artifacts excavated from the site? Second, was the private, material standard of living the Stewart and Watkins families achieved comparable to their public standard of living, embodied in the house provided for them by Jefferson? The study concludes with an examination of the meaning of this comparability, or incomparability, relative to the hierarchy of the plantation.

*Slave and Free Worker Housing at Monticello, 1770s–1820s*

Archaeologists and historians can broadly reconstruct the Monticello landscape in the years preceding and corresponding to the occupation of the Stewart-Watkins site. During the first decade of the nineteenth century, the character of housing on the mountaintop changed as Jefferson completed work on his mansion and the attached dependency wings, which included service rooms and slave quarters.

When Stewart arrived at Monticello in 1801, slave artisans and house servants occupied single-family log dwellings on the mountaintop road known as Mulberry Row. From as early as the 1770s through the 1820s, structures such as shops, storage and food-processing areas, houses for both slaves and free workers, stables, and coops lined the thousand-foot-long road along the south side of the mountain. During the 1980s archaeologists investigated many of these structures (Kelso et al. 1984, 1985; Kelso 1986a:5–19).

Jefferson described housing for his laborers in a plan dating to the early 1770s. At this time he depicted single-family and multifamily dwellings and duplexes of stone, structures intended as residences of both enslaved and free workers (Kimball 1968:122, pls. 16 and 17). A few years later Jefferson sketched Mulberry Row, recording his plans to locate workers' houses there and to make these houses uniform in size (Kimball 1968:131–32, pls. 56 and 57). One building from these plans, measuring 17 by 34 feet and constructed of stone, was designated as "Nelson & Workmen's Hall" on the earlier drawing or "workmen's house" on the later one. It still stands along Mulberry Row. Another dwelling, believed to be a contemporary slave dwelling, was discovered archaeologically. The disturbed nature of the site, combined with a lack of good architectural remains, precluded an accurate assessment of its original dimensions. However, the location of four root cellars in relation to the "workmen's house" and the artifacts recovered within them suggest that the structure corresponds to the "Negro quarter" described in the mid-1770s plan (Sanford 1985:40–41). Remains of charred wood, stone, brick, mortar, and chinking suggest that the building was a log structure with a brick-lined hearth and wooden chimney (Sanford 1985:38–40). Although Jefferson may have envisioned dwellings of equal size and layout for free workers and slaves, it appears that when the houses were constructed, distinctions were made in building materials which resulted in more permanent and comfortable dwellings for all the white workers.

The function and placement of buildings changed over time. An insurance plat dating to 1796 described the location, size, and construction materials used for seventeen stone and log buildings standing in that year. Among the buildings identified in the insurance plat were slave quarters, or "servants houses," which Jefferson designated as buildings *r*, *s*, and *t*. Described as wooden buildings with earthen floors and wooden chimneys, each measured 12 by 14 feet (Kimball 1968:136). Building *o*, of similar construction but somewhat larger dimensions, measured 20 1/2 by 12 feet and was also described as a "servants house." Although the description does not include details of construction, other documents dating from the 1790s, in combination with archaeological evidence, indicate that the structures were log; it is probable that they were raised at different times, with building *o* preceding the others (Sanford 1985:26–27; Kelso 1986:6–10). Like other slave quarters excavated in Virginia,[9] the dwellings on Mulberry Row contained shallow wood-, brick-, and stone-lined root cellars (Kelso 1971, 1984; Kelso et al. 1985; Mouer 1991g; Singleton 1991; Samford 1996:93, 95). Archaeology has shown that buildings designated as storehouses or service buildings also functioned as dwellings during part of their life spans (Crader 1984:542–58; Kelso 1982; Kelso 1986a:11–12).

In the first decade of the nineteenth century, workers completed construction of the north and south dependency wings of Jefferson's mansion, fulfilling his long-term plan to consolidate slave housing and work spaces efficiently and aesthetically. The brick and stone dependencies were built into the sides of the mountain, so that the rooms opened along a piazza, while their back walls were largely buried. In the south wing two "servants rooms" measuring 13 by 14 feet each and a "cooks room" of 10 by 14 feet lay between the kitchen and washroom (Kimball 1968:152). Each room was floored with brick and contained a brick chimney.

While archaeological and documentary evidence suggests that some of the log houses were abandoned during the first decade of the nineteenth century, it seems clear that slaves continued to occupy others, perhaps until after Jefferson's death (Kelso et al. 1984:29–30). It is unclear how housing arrangements were determined, or what length of time an individual or family spent in a particular house. In the few surviving documents in which Jefferson directs specific slaves to move into or out of certain dwellings, it appears that close proximity to their working places was his primary consideration.[10]

Less clear is the evidence of free workers' housing after the 1780s. Artisans such as carpenters, joiners, masons, and brickmakers worked on the mountaintop throughout the late eighteenth and early nineteenth centuries. Yet with the exception of Stewart and Watkins, only Richard Richardson, a brick mason and plasterer, can be connected to a particular dwelling. He resided in at least part of the stone house designed by Jefferson in the 1770s.

## The Stewart-Watkins Site: Architectural Remains

Jefferson recorded the location of "Stewart's house" in sketches and surveys of the mountaintop executed in the first decade of the nineteenth century (Kimball 1968:168; Field Notes 1806, MHi; Betts 1944: pl. xxi) (fig. 10.1). The house sat below the south orchard, just off of one of Jefferson's roundabout roads that encircled the mountain.

Excavations revealed structural remains apparently representing a core structure and an addition. The western core, which was probably constructed in 1800, measured approximately 18 by 24 feet. Jefferson's workmen built on a steep incline, a factor which has had a strong impact upon site preservation. Although most of the foundation has been robbed or has tumbled down the slope, the relationship of the remaining stonework to the slope indicates that the south wall of the house must have begun some six feet above grade. An exterior chimney, approximately four feet square, stood along the west wall. Made primarily of slate, with some local stone, the surviving base apparently supported a brick-lined hearth. Its small size may suggest a chimney stack of wood and clay (Heath 1991b:28) or the use of a cast-iron stove.

A shallow, wood-lined cellar or half basement, measuring approximately 10 by 12 feet, lay immediately to the east of the chimney base, with a bulkhead entrance opening toward the road. The floor of Stewart's cellar lay just over two feet below subsoil. Based on measurements of the cellar's depth, the slope of the hill, and the width of the sill on which the house rested, the cellar floor was some eight feet beneath the floor of the structure (Heath 1991b:32).

Just outside of the northwest corner of the house lay a small section of stone and brick paving, believed to mark the remnants of an entrance. Survey notes dating to 1806 refer to the presence of another door on the south side of the house (Field Notes 1806, MHi; Nichols 1961:203).

Stratigraphic evidence suggests that the eastern structural remains represent a later addition to the house. It is also possible that the archaeological "footprint" which has been preserved represents an independent structure, constructed alongside the original house (Heath 1991b:38–43). In March 1803 Jefferson paid the stonemason Michael Hope "for work on Stewart's house 18D. and 2D. overpaiment on acct" (Bear and Stanton 1997) roughly equivalent to eighteen days' work.[11] It is possible that during this time Hope laid the foundations and constructed the chimney for the eastern extension of the structure.[12] The stone chimney base, located along the south wall of the addition, probably consisted of a stone stack with a brick-lined hearth. Local "greenstone" used in this chimney contrasts with the slate used to build the western base (Heath 1991b:39). At the end of its short life span, the completed house probably measured roughly 18 by 36 feet.

A surviving document supports the physical evidence of the layout and construction sequence of the house. In January 1815 Thomas Jefferson wrote a letter to William Newby, offering him a position as overseer at his Bedford County plantation, Poplar Forest. In describing the overseer's quarters, he stated: "The house is uncomfortable, being a single room [with] a loft above, but I wish to add to it to make it comfortable. Another room with a passage between can quickly be added of hewn logs as is usual in that country, plaistered, with windows, stone chimney, etc. and as this would take but a very short time, I would rather leave it to be done by yourself immediately on your arrival, that you might do it to please yourself" (Thomas Jefferson to William P. Newby, 20 Jan. 1815, DLC). The original plan of the house, the proposed modifications, the building materials used, and even the timetable for construction match the evidence available for the Stewart-Watkins house.

## The Stewart-Watkins Site: Artifacts

The individual material possessions of the Stewart and Watkins families also contribute to our understanding of their position within the plantation community. Stratigraphy on the site did not permit a distinction to be made between objects originating in the Stewart household and those owned by Watkins and his family. A thin destruction layer extending across the site contained the greatest number of artifacts, both associated with the house itself (i.e., nails, bricks, stone, mortar, window glass) and with the households (ceramics, bottle glass and stemware, bone, tools).

Ideally, we would like to be able to distinguish between the belongings of the Stewarts and those of the Watkinses, for although both families represent artisan life on the plantation, they should not be seen as identical. From the limited information available about their lives before arriving at Monticello, it appears that the Stewarts were motivated to accept their position on the plantation by failing economic prospects in Philadelphia. Several references to "old" Stewart, the death of Mary, and the existence of at least one grown child indicate that the family was established and that Stewart was more than midway through his working years when he moved to Virginia. In contrast, the absence of children, the presence of two young slaves, and the reappearance of Watkins during the decade after he left Jefferson's permanent employment all combine to suggest that Watkins was at the beginning of his career during his stay on the mountain. The artifacts on the site, representing both households, may together be indicating an economic level above that experienced by the Stewarts and below that which the Watkinses were in the process of creating.

Bearing that caution in mind, the artifacts tend to contradict the notion that white artisans enjoyed a standard of living materially superior to that of the slaves living on Mulberry Row, a position which the architectural features of the site support. With few exceptions, the discarded belongings of the Stewart and Watkins households were few, common, and in some cases worn out.

While the short occupation span of the site is itself a strong factor in the overall scarcity of artifacts, observable differences in the types of objects found on the site and their conditions, as compared to those recovered from the slave quarters, demand a fuller explanation.

A minimum of 125 ceramic vessels were recovered from the site. Pearlware and creamware predominated (48.8 percent and 29.6 percent, respectively), with lesser quantities of Chinese porcelain (12.8 percent), and small amounts of American and English stoneware, lead-glazed and slipped coarseware, and clouded earthenware (American stoneware: 4 percent; the others: less than 1 percent). The assemblage thus exhibits much less variability than that recovered from slave quarters *s* or *t*.[13] Lacking from the artisan assemblage were delft; refined earthenwares, such as engine-turned redwares and portobello; refined stonewares, such as white saltglaze, black basalt, and rosso antico; European porcelains; and bone china, all of which had been present in each of the slave quarters. Ceramic assemblages characterized by diverse vessel forms, expensive types of decorative treatments, and median production dates predating median site dates suggest that slaves living in quarters *s* and *t* received hand-me-down vessels from the Jefferson household (Gruber 1990:44–68).

A basic question raised by the differences in the slave quarter and artisan ceramic assemblages concerns how Stewart and Watkins acquired household goods.[14] The data suggest a different pattern of ceramic acquisition on the site than that postulated for the excavated slave quarters. The presence in the artisan assemblage of some outdated ceramics that do not match any patterns recovered at Monticello to date may indicate that the families brought at least a few of their own dishes with them. Decorative patterns on certain vessels that do match those recovered in both slave and Jefferson contexts suggest the possibility that some internal network of exchange existed which included the artisans, while the larger presence of contemporary vessels that do not match either slave quarter or Jefferson pieces probably indicates that the households provisioned themselves while in Charlottesville.

Tableware and food preparation vessels recovered from the site appear to have withstood heavy use. While use marks have been studied in order to define vessel function (Griffiths 1978:68–81), they may also contribute to our understanding of material standards of living. Excavated serving plates are scarred by deep and frequent knife cuts, while the glaze and slip in the center of a slipware serving dish has been worn completely off. Apparently the occupants of the site were conservative in their buying habits, perhaps out of economic necessity (fig. 10.2).

While differences in food serving and consumption vessels appear to exist between slave and white artisan sites, perhaps more dramatic is the variability in diet as reflected in the faunal assemblage. Less than five hundred bones and bone fragments were recovered from the Stewart-Watkins site. In contrast, slave quarter *r* yielded 815 bones, quarter *s* 5,776, and quarter *t* 1,289. The question of whether the shorter period of occupation at the artisans' house accounts for the discrepancy, or whether differences in status are reflected in provisioning, can be addressed through an assessment of the diversity of the faunal assemblage. Evidence of household diet preserved archaeologically points to small quantities of fresh pork, beef, squirrel, rabbit, and poultry being consumed by the Stewart-Watkins households (Crader in Heath 1991b:156).

This lack of diversity contrasts with the faunal assemblages of slave quarters *r*, *s*, and *t*. While pork constituted the most common meat in each of the slave quarters, mutton was represented in each household, as were minor quantities of bones from wild mammals (opossum, woodchuck, squirrel, rabbit, possibly deer), fish, and fowl (Crader 1989:1–10).

The reasons behind these differences are difficult to determine, yet it is possible that they reflect differences in behavior among the Jefferson family, the slaves, and the artisans. It has been suggested that house servants and slave artisans living on Mulberry Row acquired their meat through regular meat rations provided by Jefferson, supplemental hunting and fishing, the raising of poultry, gifts of leftovers from the Jefferson family, and theft (Gruber 1990:70). The absence of food remains of particular types of meat from the Stewart-Watkins household may comment on their varying food acquisition strategies. Mutton, a favorite meat of the Jefferson family, is absent from the assemblage. A different social position relative to the Jeffersons as well as physical distance from the mansion probably precluded the practice of distributing leftovers to these families.

A few objects recovered from the site contradict the notion that both families' lives were devoid of luxuries. Imported dolls were expensive in colonial and federal Virginia (Carson 1989:37–39), and the recovery of a pair of porcelain eyes attests to the presence of at least one doll on the site, undoubtedly discarded by Stewart's daughter.

Excavators uncovered a surprising quantity of artifacts related to the trades of both Stewart and Watkins, the significance of which is further explored in the Analysis section. Finds included quantities of scrap iron, brass, and lead; unfinished wrought tools, some identifiable (an axe head, a knife) and others apparently discarded in the beginning stages of manufacture; and finished tools, including a punch, an extremely worn bench chisel, a large flat file, a half-round file, and a small file for detail work. Part of a broken whetstone made of finely ground limestone completed the artisan assemblage.

While manufacturing is thus represented at the site, domestic industry also resulted in the deposition of worn, broken, or misplaced tools. Two pairs of scissors, a bone button blank, a brass thimble, a steel mattress needle, and a possible bushing for a spinning wheel may indicate two tiers of domestic work. While Mrs. Stewart and Mrs. Watkins used the sewing tools to produce clothing for their household, they may have also have sewn, upholstered, and spun for the plantation. Mrs. Watkins was paid on at least one occasion for weaving. Similarly, Jefferson paid Mrs. Goodman, the wife of his Poplar Forest overseer, for weaving in 1811.[15] A tiny brass thimble, repaired by silver soldering, indicates that the Stewart daughters were involved in the domestic economy from an early age.

*Analysis*

Analysis of architectural, stratigraphic, and artifactual remains resulted in some important insights into the nature of artisan housing and belongings on the Monticello plantation. First, the dwelling was designed with economy, and perhaps impermanence, in mind. Second, despite a short life span and the low quality of building materials, the house was consciously designed to reflect the status of its occupants relative to other inhabitants of the estate. Juxtaposed with this ascribed status was the achieved status of the artisans and their families, revealed through an assemblage of unvaried and worn ceramics, limited faunal remains indicative of a relatively monotonous meat diet, and a quantity of salvaged industrial materials and tools.

An examination of nail distributions across the site and of the building materials that remain reveals that the structures were dismantled and either moved or salvaged for parts shortly after Watkins's departure in 1810. Nails clustered in a shallow feature off of the east end of the building, suggesting the discard of salvaged wood there. Stone and brick concentrations, although high in the backfill of the cellar, were insufficient to account for the presence of a substantial stone foundation and chimney stack (Heath 1991a:13), again implying their removal.

On-site remains of the house indicate Jefferson's preference for inexpensive, readily available, or recycled materials for such constructions. These materials include bricks that were underfired, overfired, misshapen, or shaped in such a way as to reveal that they were left over from construction of the mansion. Such bricks also were recovered from service buildings excavated on Mulberry Row and from a retaining wall in the garden, suggesting that seconds were common building materials on the plantation (Kelso 1982:50, 61, 77). Similarly, poor-quality nails composed a large percentage of the nails present on the site, reflecting, perhaps, the use of nailery products unfit for sale and below the standards Jefferson set for his own house. The wood lining in the cellar, the unmortared foundation, and the unbonded pavings combine to indicate the priority of economy over workmanship (Heath 1991a:13–14).

It is also possible that workmen's houses, like many slave quarters at Monticello, were designed with impermanence in mind. In a memorandum to overseer Edmund Bacon, Jefferson stated, "There were 2 small houses to be moved or put up for Mr. Alexander about which I was either to assist, or to do the whole, I forget which. this must be done whenever he desires it" (Thomas Jefferson to Edmund Bacon, 19 Oct. 1806, CsmH). Buildings that were easily removed and reassembled enabled Jefferson to locate his workmen efficiently and economically. While the completion of the south dependency wing resolved some of Jefferson's ongoing housing needs for slaves working as servants or cooks, there was no similar need for long-term artisan housing. Perhaps Jefferson felt that craftsmen who were hired for short-term projects were best left in dwellings which matched their circumstances (Heath 1991a:14).

Although Jefferson allowed economy to guide the construction of both slave and artisan dwellings, it seems clear that he differentiated between them on several fundamental levels: size, materials used, and siting. These material differences acted to strengthen positions of servility or authority within the plantation.

All of the excavated freestanding dwellings, whether intended for black or white residents, incorporated building materials of poorer quality than those used in the mansion. However, remains indicate that the Stewart-Watkins house was superior to the slave quarters in terms of safety, convenience, and size. The use of stone, slate, and brick in one of the building's chimneys, in contrast to the wood or wood-and-clay slave quarter chimneys, reduced the likelihood of fire. The raised wooden floor of the structure, unlike the earthen floors of buildings *r*, *s*, and *t*, provided not only a more sanitary living surface but also a substantial space beneath it, which allowed walk-in access to the cellar from outside of the house. This arrangement freed floor space from the intrusions of trapdoors or boards laid over cellar openings that characterized slave dwellings. The siting of the house for the white artisans on a fairly steep slope made it necessary to raise the building's south side substantially above ground level in order to level the floor and support the walls. While no match for the grandeur of the mansion, the dwelling as seen from a nearby road must have reached an impressive height.

In terms of actual living space, the core structure at the Stewart-Watkins site alone had more than twice the floor space of slave quarters *r*, *s*, and *t*, the "cooks room," and the "servants rooms" in the south dependency wing, and it was more than half again as large as building *o*. With the addition to the east, residents enjoyed a level of privacy and comfort unknown to the enslaved inhabitants of Mulberry Row. The expanded house allowed for a more formal separation of both space and activities. This segmentation within the house stood in sharp contrast with the more communal lifestyle of the slave quarters.[16]

Analysis of artifact distributions helps to clarify the use of space within the building. SURFER distributions of industrial artifacts recovered on the site—including finished and unfinished tools, scrap iron, brass, and lead—were contrasted with those associated with domestic activities, such as sewing tools (needle, scissors, thimble, button blank, bushing), clothing items (buttons, shoe buckles), leisure objects (doll's eyes, jaw harp, writing slate and pencil, penknives) and with food storage vessels (figs. 10.3, 10.4, 10.5). When compared, the three maps reveal a concentration of industrial objects in and around the western core of the building and a concentration of domestic artifacts in and around the eastern addition.

Because at least some of the tools recovered on the site may have been used by either the smith or the carpenter, it is difficult to distinguish precisely when they were used or for what purpose. It is unlikely that actual forging was undertaken at the site, given both the building's wooden floor and the absence of forging by-products such as slag. Instead, the western room or rooms probably served primarily for storage, and possibly as work space for small-scale manufacturing in brass, lead, or wood. It appears that Stewart was stockpiling scraps of metal and unfinished tools here—perhaps for his own use at some later date or perhaps to remove wasted materials from the scrutiny of Jefferson, who was known to monitor closely the use of time and materials at the nailery. Small items made of brass or lead may have been made or repaired at home, just as woodworking may have been carried out in and around the western core, leaving little evidence beyond an occasional discarded or lost tool. Because both Stewart and Watkins were provided with work spaces away from their home, it is of interest that so much evidence of their professions can be found in a domestic setting. The line between being at work and at home appears to have been blurred for men on the early nineteenth-century plantation. For the women, of course, the terms were often synonymous.

## Conclusions

This study has demonstrated the utility of looking beyond such broadly defined categories as workers, managers, planters, blacks, and whites when exploring the social and economic structure of antebellum plantations in the American South. An examination of the experiences of two white artisans at Monticello has refined our understanding of Jefferson's ideal labor hierarchy and has initiated an exploration of the ways in which this ideal was upheld or challenged by the people upon whom it was imposed. The study not only serves to inform us about the relationship between Jefferson and his hired white workers; it also reveals the degree to which any authority or autonomy experienced by free artisans, on the one hand, and slave artisans and servants, on the other, was manifested in the material conditions of their lives.

Documents and archaeology were complementary sources of evidence used to explore the relationships of William Stewart and Elisha Watkins with Jefferson, other free artisans and overseers, and slaves living at Monticello in the late eighteenth and early nineteenth centuries. Partial reconstruction of the relationships between Stewart and his employer and coworkers is possible through an examination of surviving letters and accounts. This reconstruction suggested that while Stewart's livelihood ultimately depended upon Jefferson, on a day-to-day basis he enjoyed a substantial degree of autonomy in regulating his schedule and work habits. Whereas Jefferson hired his overseers and artisans based on his perception of their skill and willingness to work hard, these men negotiated with him and with each other for

their position within the community. They challenged Jefferson's authority and promoted their own interests through the use of alcohol, through absenteeism and theft,
and through internal friction and competition. Further study of the fate of these
men after they left Monticello is needed in order to assess the effect of these nego-
tiations on their long-term social and economic mobility.

Jefferson's ideal labor hierarchy was most readily examined through a comparison of the material remains and the siting of free artisan and slave artisan-servant
housing on the property. The data gathered during excavations of the Stewart-
Watkins site, when used comparatively, helped to contextualize data recovered from
the excavations of known slave quarters. Such a comparison began to reveal the
manner in which Jefferson categorized and distinguished his hierarchy of workers.
By providing free craftsmen and their families with living spaces that were more substantially built and more private than those designated for skilled slave artisans and
house servants, he underscored their authority.

The results of analysis of the artifacts recovered at the site add depth to the architectural data, allowing us to look beyond Jefferson's intentions and examine the lives
that artisans and their families were able to construct for themselves. Artifactual
analysis suggests that although Stewart and Watkins enjoyed accommodations superior to those of similarly skilled slaves, they furnished their home simply. Worn
plates and dishes, a limited selection of consumer goods, few luxury items, and a less
varied diet than that enjoyed by the enslaved community characterized the private
lives of these men and their families. While the architecture points to prosperity and
power, the artifacts seem to point in the opposite direction, toward scarcity and economic powerlessness. This contradiction in the material culture may reflect a real
conflict between an illusion of comfort and importance promoted by Jefferson to
maintain order within the plantation and the artisan's private reality of poverty.

The study of the Stewart-Watkins site also raises important questions for scholars studying other plantations. How typical was the situation at Monticello in the
early nineteenth century? Were all white workers equal within the community, or
was there an imposed hierarchy of position, reflected in housing, as there appears
to have been among slaves? Did the distance between slave and free artisans widen
over time or vary regionally? Investigation of these questions is needed, along with
further study of the material standards of living for slaves involved in the entire spectrum of plantation activities, in order to more fully understand the diversity of experiences and the divisions of authority across the antebellum South.

## Notes

Research for excavations at the Stewart-Watkins site was generously supported by the
Thomas Jefferson Memorial Foundation. I would like to thank the members of the Monti-

cello-UVA Archaeological Field Schools of 1989 and 1990 for their hard work at the site. I am also grateful to Mark Bograd, Mark Freeman, William M. Kelso, Theresa Singleton, and Lucia Stanton for their comments on earlier drafts of this chapter and to the Massachusetts Historical Society and the Department of Special Collections at the University of Virginia Library for permission to publish manuscript material.

1. See Curlee 1974:328–29 for a discussion of white artisan labor on a nineteenth-century plantation in Texas, and Marzio 1972:233n for a reference to itinerant carpenters in eighteenth-century South Carolina.

2. The earliest reference to William Stewart in Philadelphia that has yet been located places him at 2 Cypress Alley in 1791 (Biddle 1791:125). Over the next several years, he is listed as either a blacksmith or whitesmith living or working at 127 and 129 Spruce Street (the corner of Fifth and Spruce Streets). See Hardie 1794:147; Stafford 1797:174; Stafford 1799:133.

3. Stewart's salary is based on records of payments made by Jefferson and debts and repayments by Stewart in the period between June 1801 and June 1808. See Betts 1987:425; Bear and Stanton 1997:1052, 1060, 1070, 1092, 1095, 1101, 1106, 1112, 1113, 1124, 1126, 1131, 1134, 1136, 1142, 1149, 1158, 1160, 1167, 1179, 1182, 1188, 1204, 1207, 1213; Barnes Accounts, 19–20 Oct. 1801, 5 June 1805, CSmH; Thomas Jefferson to John Barnes, 2 June 1803, Jefferson to David Higgenbotham, 29 Sept. 1806, ViU; Jefferson to Edmund Bacon, 6 July 1807, MHi; and Bacon to Jefferson, 7 July 1808, ViU. Edmund Bacon summarized the provisioning of overseers as "an overseer's allowance of provisions for a year was . . . corn meal, all they wanted" (Bear 1967:51), and the carpenter Elisha Watkins was provided with "corn per usual" in his contract (Betts 1987:377), indicating that a standard for corn distribution existed and was understood.

4. Martha Jefferson Randolph to Thomas Jefferson, 14 Jan. 1804, ViU; Bear and Stanton 1997:1119, 1207; Thomas Jefferson to James Walker, 1 March 1807, Jefferson to Dabney Carr, 25 May 1807, MHi.

5. Thomas Jefferson to Jones & Howell, 22 Nov. 1803, Jones & Howell to Jefferson, 25 Nov. 1803, MHi; Bear and Stanton 1997:1119.

6. In 1817 Jefferson attempted to find Charles Stewart, the crippled son of William Stewart, a situation as an apprentice stocking weaver in Washington, D.C. Because of his weak constitution, Charles was unable to perform satisfactorily. The surviving correspondence between Jefferson and the managers of the weaving business confirm Jefferson's position as a benefactor to young Charles. See Thomas Jefferson to William Lee, 12 Nov. 1817, 8 Jan. 1818, J. Keller to Jefferson, 14 Dec. 1817, 15 Jan. 1818, William Lee to Jefferson, 15 Dec. 1817, 12 Jan. 1818, Jefferson to J. Keller, 24 Jan. 1818, DLC; Bear and Stanton 1997:1341.

7. See the following correspondence concerning Stewart and the woman Melinda: James Walker to Thomas Jefferson, 1 March 1807, Jefferson to Edmund Bacon, 6 July 1807, MHi; Jefferson to Dabney Carr, 25 May 1807, Carr to Jefferson, 29 May 1807, ViU.

8. On Stewart's drinking, see George Jefferson to Thomas Jefferson, 17 June, 16 Nov. 1801, Thomas Jefferson to Jones & Howell, 22 Nov. 1803, Jones & Howell to Thomas Jefferson, 25 Nov. 1803, MHi; Betts 1987:444, 25; Edmund Bacon to Thomas Jefferson, 8 Nov. 1807, ViU; Bear 1967:69–70.

9. See also Sprinkle 1991:91–93 and Yentsch 1991:3–4 for additional comments on root cellars and slaves' storage places.

10. In 1793 Jefferson directed his son-in-law to move some slaves from the stone house, which he intended for workmen: "The present inhabitants must remove into the two nearest of the new log-houses which were intended for them, Kritty [a slave] taking the nearest of the whole, as oftenest wanted about the house" (Thomas Jefferson to Thomas Mann Randolph, 19 May 1793, DLC). In 1809 he instructed his overseer to move the slave cook, Peter Hemings, out of the cook's room. "As the two cooks which are here will take the place of Peter Hemings in the kitchen, it will be necessary that one of them should have his room next the kitchen, and that it should be vacant on their arrival" (Thomas Jefferson to Edmund Bacon, 27 Feb. 1809, CSmH).

11. In 1808 Thomas Jefferson paid Stewart one dollar per day to come and do some work for him (Bear and Stanton 1997:1225).

12. In Jefferson's farm book he notes, "Davy, Lewis and Abram have done the carpenter's work of Bagwell's house in 6. days, getting the stuff & putting it together" (Betts 1987:67), while "the Outfield granary took 24. days work to get the logs, rafters & slabs & put them up completely"(ibid.). It appears, then, that utilitarian buildings could be constructed fairly rapidly.

13. Poor preservation of building *r* resulted in the recovery of relatively few ceramics.

14. Documentary evidence provides fragmentary and somewhat contradictory solutions to the question of acquisition. No direct evidence exists to suggest that Jefferson furnished either man with nonperishable items, yet a contract in 1792 between Jefferson and his new overseer, Samuel Biddle, summarizes a limited outfitting of the new overseer's house: "He is to carry his bedding. I promise to provide him half a dozen fly chairs, a table, pot etc. the carpenters to fix up little conveniences for him, to find him a horse, 5 or 600 wt. of pork, or rather mutton etc. equivalent" (Betts 1944:184). A year later Jefferson outfitted another overseer with "the same conveniences which I did to mr. Biddle. be pleased therefore to desire the latter to have made immediately a bedstead & table, and to bespeak half a dozen chairs. . . . the other small utensils which were furnished to mr. Biddle may be got from the stores"(Betts 1944:206). As both men traveled to Charlottesville from Elkton, Md., Jefferson may have been furnishing them with goods that would have been inconvenient to move. Significantly, these men received goods purchased specifically for them rather than passed down through the Jefferson family. Whether Jefferson's references to "pot etc." and "small utensils" include ceramics and glassware is unknown. On the other hand, Martha Jefferson Randolph's reference to Stewart's creditors scheduling "the sale of the furniture" during the smith's absence from Monticello suggests that he was the owner of most, if not all, of the possessions in his house.

15. It seems that an exchange of services was under way at Poplar Forest at this time. While Mrs. Goodman wove and taught Jefferson's slaves Aggy and Edy the craft, she also benefited from their labor: "As there will be no wool to spin till May, mrs. Goodman may employ the wool spinners for herself till then, if she chuses. whatever terms have been settled between mrs Bacon & mrs Randolph, shall be the same with her. (I do not know what they are) and as compensation for teaching Aggy or Edy to weave, I propose to give her the usual price for all the weaving she may do for me, the first year, considering it as her apprenticeship: and that afterwards she shall have the same proportion of her time as she is to have of the spinners" (Betts 1944:466).

16. The differences noted at the Stewart-Watkins site have also been observed for standing structures constructed during the eighteenth century. In a study of colonial architecture in Virginia, Camille Wells concluded that "the level of comfort, privacy and spatial differentiation residents of this Richmond County property might enjoy—or endure—had everything to do with their position in the plantation community and, not incidentally, the color of their skin" (Wells 1987:4238). She concludes, however, that "slave housing was never vastly inferior in terms of size and finish to buildings occupied by most of the Chesapeake's common planters and landless laborers. They were all just colonial Virginians with few material resources—they were just poor" (Wells 1987:4239).

Table 10.1. Workmen at Monticello, 1800–1823

| Name | Occupation | Dates | Salary | Provisions |
|---|---|---|---|---|
| Gabriel Lilly [1] | overseer | 1800–1805 | | beef, bacon, and oats |
| John Freeman [2] | overseer | 1805–6 | $200 | |
| Edmund Bacon [3] | carpenter | 1806–22 | $100 | 2 bar. wheat flour, cornmeal, half a beef, 600 lbs. pork |
| William Stewart [4] | blacksmith/ whitesmith | 1801–7 | $155 | 500 lbs. pork, cow |
| Elisha Watkins [5] | carpenter | 1809–10 | $150–$200 | corn "as usual." 600 lbs. pork |
| James Starke [6] | carpenter | 1810–12 | $190 | 600 lbs. pork shared with apprentice |
| Richard Durrett [7] | carpenter | 1813 | $130–$140 | a peck cornmeal per wk. 450 lbs. pork,milk cow April–November |
| Rolin Goodman [8] | carpenter | 1814–17 | $190 | 20 barrels corn |
| Edmund Meeks [9] | carpenter | 1819–23 | $150 | 600 lbs. pork |
| | superintendent of nailery [10] | ? | $150–$200 | 500 lbs. pork |

[1]  Pierson in Bear 1988:57,130–31; Betts 1987:514; Memorandum Book, Sept. 22, 1804, MHi.
[2]  Memorandum Book, Aug. 22, 1805, MHi; Betts 1987:517.
[3]  Betts 1987:519.
[4]  Pierson in Bear 1988:54; Memorandum Book, April 3, 1802, NN.
[5]  Betts 1944:377.
[6]  Memorandum Book, Feb. 26, 1810, ViU.
[7]  Pierson in Bear 1988:82).
[8]  Memorandum Book, Sept. 23, 1813, ViU.
[9]  Edmund Bacon to Thomas Jefferson, Nov. 21, 1820, ViU.
[10]  Pierson in Bear 1988:53–54.

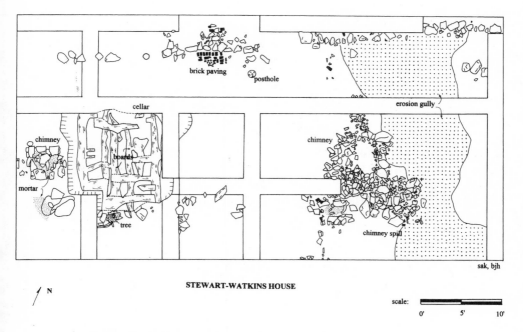

**STEWART-WATKINS HOUSE**

N

scale:

0'    5'    10'

10.1. Excavated foundations at the Stewart-Watkins house

10.2. Creamware plate fragment, uncovered from the
Stewart-Watkins house site, showing extensive wear

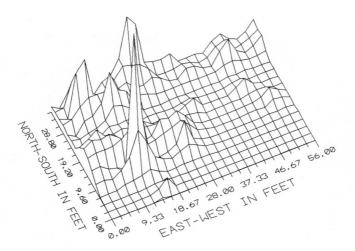

10.3. SURFER distribution map of industrial artifacts at the
Stewart-Watkins house

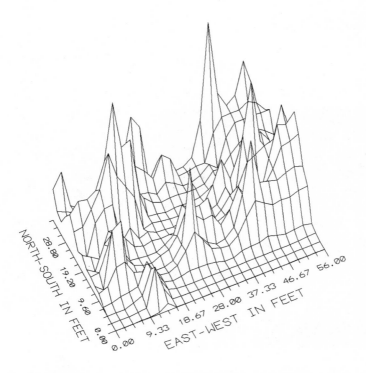

10.4. SURFER distribution map of domestic artifacts at the
Stewart-Watkins house

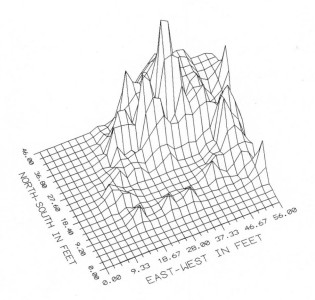

10.5. SURFER distribution map of food preparation and
storage vessels at the Stewart-Watkins house

# 11

# Food Supply and Plantation Social Order: An Archaeological Perspective

*Larry McKee*

## Introduction: Archaeology, Food, and Slavery

ARCHAEOLOGISTS search for links between artifacts and human behavior in an attempt to construct an understanding of what life was like in the past. This essay employs a discussion of animal bones found at several slave quarter sites in Virginia to draw certain conclusions about plantation food supply and the role of food in plantation social relations. Information from a variety of other sources provides a context for the studied faunal remains with the goal of developing the broadest possible understanding of what the assemblages can tell us about slave life. The broad scope of "aboveground" sources consulted—plantation management essays, the farm journals and records of several planters, the secondary literature on plantation slavery, archaeological research on other slave dwellings and other artifact assemblages, and the anthropological literature on the role of food in social relations—is necessary in order to draw the most supportable conclusions possible about what is left in the ground.

Animal bones have become a commonly analyzed category of evidence in the archaeological study of plantation life in particular and of historical archaeology in general. Bones are one class of artifacts usually abundant on archaeological sites. Considered an aspect of "technomic" (Binford 1962a:218–19) or "infrastructural" (Fairbanks 1984:1) behavior, bones are seen as a less ambiguous source of information than other classes of artifacts in archaeology. Bones equal meat, and meat equals food. But the approach taken here, again linked to established research themes in historical archaeology, is that bones should generate more than just information on the details of diet; they should provide a bridge to the exploration of the elements of human social organization enveloping diet and nutrition.

A society's dietary activities always have an intensity of involvement far beyond calorie counts and full bellies, and *hunger* is a term with as much mental as physical definition. As Mary Douglas has pointed out, "Food is not feed," and "veterinary" approaches to nutritional studies ignore much significant human behavior (Douglas 1982:123). Douglas sees a strong correlation between the ordering of social relations and the organization of foodways (Douglas 1982:85), and my analysis depends on this perspective.

Foodways, as a physically and emotionally charged category of human behavior, was an inevitable source of conflict in plantation life. An adequate diet was recognized by all as a basic "right" of the enslaved, but there was always an intense struggle over defining what was "adequate" and over attempts to add to or subtract from rations and supplements. Masters attempted to use food as an important part of their overall system of social control, and slaves in turn devised strategies to make their rations more satisfying. In working toward understanding food in plantation life, this chapter also seeks to explore broader issues of plantation social relations.

My approach to faunal analysis has been labeled as more cultural than biological (Singleton 1991b). There is no question that this study and its precursor (McKee 1988) ignore many of the finer details relating to the bones under study. I present no discussion of available meat weight, details of carcass processing, age structure of the procured populations, or evidence of seasonality. This is due to the nature of the main assemblage analyzed, from the slave cabin excavated at the site of Flowerdew Hundred (fig. 11.1), which has lost most of its potential to provide such fine-grained information. Although rigorously transformed from a "kitchen-fresh" state, the sample can still provide information on species diversity, at least at the level of presence or absence of particular animals. Emphasizing only the species represented is not a throwback to the long-rejected "laundry list" approach to faunal analysis but is employed here as the most efficient and applicable use of the bones from Flowerdew.

The principal aim of this study is to produce a model of plantation food supply developed from the perspective of the slave community. Figure 11.2 is a graphic presentation of the model, showing possible sources of food and activities by which slaves acquired it. The model's most important feature is its placement of slaves at the center of the food procurement network. The argument that slaves were active participants in defining their food supply is crucial to this study's efforts to link nutritional regimen to other, less material aspects of plantation relations. Slaves were not passive instruments completely beholden to their masters' systems of plantation order but rather had significant influence over the details of their day-to-day lives. This "active" view of slave life must be an essential element in the analysis of archaeological remains from plantation contexts and is the key to the understanding of such data in any meaningful way.

This study attempts to reconstruct the ideals, motivations, realities, decisions, and actions of both masters and slaves as a way of mapping out the range of possibilities available within the system of plantation food supply. Studying faunal assemblages within this kind of framework gives a significant boost to the analysis of such artifacts. Bones recovered from slave dwelling sites help to define the possible routes of action and serve as evidence of choices made in particular situations. The broad perspective allows us to make real progress and contributions to the archaeological study of plantation life.

## Documentary Sources on Slave Life

The artifact-document relationship might best be conceived as a core of raw archaeological data surrounded by layer upon layer of context, the whole providing a detailed and lucid image. The goal of the archaeologist is to understand the human behavior responsible for the creation of the archaeological record. It may seem that archaeological assemblages play only a small role in this approach (as in this study, first stimulated by a collection of about a thousand fragments of bone), but the excavated data remain crucial: they are the otherwise unavailable link to specific actions and behavior of the people under study.

What kinds of sources are available to those seeking information on plantation diet and food supply? Why is the question of slave foodways important, and what routes have been taken in studying the topic? What have such studies revealed about the principles that guided slaveholders in their decisions on how to feed their chattel, and how were these management ideals put into action? Are there ways to elicit more details concerning the subsistence activities directed by slaves themselves? The following discussion provides a basic outline of the answers to these questions, with emphasis on developing a context for the archaeological data at the core of this study.

## The Historian's View of Plantation Food Supply

Food has always been a topic of note in the study of American slavery, with the analysis becoming more sophisticated and multifaceted through time. Research on the question has moved from simple lists of weekly provisions culled from planters' records to detailed nutritional analyses, ecologically oriented examinations of the environmental setting of plantations, and considerations of the cultural and psychological ramifications of diet. Although many details of slave subsistence have emerged, the body of work as a whole has failed to make the crucial links between food supply, diet, and wider questions about social structure and culture.

Why the interest in what slaves ate? Mostly it is due to the interest in whether slaves were subject to ongoing physical mistreatment, or if they had an adequate— or even comfortable—way of life. Perhaps surprisingly, the consensus view is that slaves had a diet sufficient to fulfill their nutritional needs. In one of the more physiologically detailed study on the topic, Tyson Gibbs and his coauthors point out that the slaves' capacity for hard labor and their ability to maintain a high birthrate required a nutritional supply that was at least adequate (Gibbs et al. 1980:175).

What constitutes "adequate" is, however, highly debatable, and most researchers seem uneasy with concluding that the slave diets could thus be described. Most studies recognize that slave diet may have been nutritionally sufficient but still unsatisfactory to its consumers. In detailing the shortcomings of slave diet, researchers have cited its monotony, the probability of attendant nutritional imbalances (Genovese 1965:44), the seasonal hardships (Fogel and Engerman 1974:115), and the faulty knowledge of nutritional requirements used by masters in making decisions about provisioning (Stampp 1956:282). Some scholars have looked beyond biology to "intangibles" defining the unsatisfactory character of the slave's nutritional regimen. Blassingame has interpreted the problem as concerning not so much the quantity or quality of food but the lack of control by slaves over the details of their cuisine (Blassingame 1979:251–54).

Explanations of why planters would provide a sufficient diet for slaves have focused on what can be called the livestock thesis. According to Samuel Hilliard, "The slave was, in an economic sense, a domestic animal" (1972:27). Slaves were expensive pieces of property, whose physical endangerment through inadequate living conditions meant, at the least, a poor return on investments and possibly (through death) a reduction of capital assets. This interpretation has often been tempered by mention of the strong cultural value, for southern elites, in keeping an orderly operation and humanely caring for the needs of those dependent on one's beneficence and steady management. Even bearing this ideal in mind, from the master's point of view plantation rationing involved a classic economic dilemma. A good diet kept slaves at optimum health and thus at an optimum level of performance, but "feeding costs formed a burdensome part of plantation expenses" (Genovese 1965:46). Planters were interested in keeping costs down to maximize profits. A more human analysis of the situation suggests the slaves got by on a little more than, or a little less than, a bare sufficiency, depending on how their masters chose to solve the dilemma.

Studies of plantation food supply have come to some surprisingly similar views on the details of slave rations. Kiple and King note that the ration size, one to one-and-a-half pecks of cornmeal and three-and-a-half pounds of cured pork (bacon), "has been confirmed so often as to become a truism" (Kiple and King 1981:81). Others have criticized the scholarly satisfaction in leaving ration figures at a standard average amount per adult slave per week and see variation, rather than consistency, as the rule.

Sometimes writings on slavery draw a distinction between master-supplied *rations* and slave *diet*; sometimes they do not. Some conclude that diet consisted almost entirely of the weekly portion of pork and corn (Phillips 1966:312; Stampp

1956:284), although all recent work discusses the important role of supplements. Todd Savitt argues that the corn-and-pork ration was so poor in nutrition that slaves could not survive on it exclusively (Savitt 1978:93). Richard Sutch expands this point, noting that "the slave *diet* may have generally been nutritionally balanced even when the slave *ration* provided by the master was not" (Sutch 1976:281). A view of what can be called a subsistence triangle has emerged, with food regularly coming to the plantation quarter from three sources: master-distributed rations, slave-controlled gardens, and hunting and fishing done by slaves in their free time (Hilliard 1972:56).

The acknowledgment that slaves had significant influence over their diet has become a mainstay of the historical analysis of slave life over the last two decades. The works of Eugene Genovese (1974), Tyson Gibbs, K. Cargill, L. S. Lieberman, and E. Reitz (1980), Philip Morgan (1982), and Charles Joyner (1984) all have as part of their central thesis the idea that "slaves did not passively accept their lot, but actively participated in changing their diet" (Gibbs et al. 1980:177). The problem lies in trying to take this a step further and develop the links between slave subsistence and broader issues of plantation social relations. Many scholars of slavery study food in terms of quantity, calories, and vitamins, when what is of significance is control, patterns of distribution, use of food as a tool of domination, the role of food in ceremony and group communication, and the level of satisfaction for the slaves themselves. A biological approach is necessary, and there is no question that many slaves suffered and died from malnourishment. But a consideration of the social role of food provides more pertinent information on the inadequacies of slave life (see Sutch 1976 for discussion of this point).

Documentary-based scholarship has unquestionably been hampered by the lack of substantial direct evidence on life within the slave quarter. One of the main results of this is that the masters' view of plantation life remains ascendant. As Rawick (1972:xiv) noted, "The masters not only ruled the past in fact, they now rule its written history." Constructing a more culturally based analysis of plantation food supply and subsistence requires the development of a perspective based on the consumer's point of view.

## Food Supply and Plantation Management Theory

My discussion of plantation management ideals is based on letters and articles published in antebellum-period southern agricultural journals such as *DeBow's Review* and the *Southern Planter*. Most of these commentaries have been collected in *Advice among Masters*, a volume edited by James O. Breeden. The documents are an extremely valuable source on the philosophy and ideals that guided at least the most high-minded planters in managing their slaves. As both Breeden (1980:xxii) and Oakes (1982:166) have pointed out, it is difficult to assess the impact these essays had on the realities of day-to-day plantation life. Much of the work has a definite reform-minded tone, and by relating their conception of how things should be, the authors provide indirect insight into how things really were.

In discussing slave subsistence, management essays usually skip over the details such as the types and quantities of rations and deal most directly with the activities surrounding provisioning. These concerns express at least an indirect acknowledgment that food supply played an important role in broader issues of plantation social interaction and control. A master's entire conception of plantation life was reflected in how he chose to provide for his slaves. Writings from agricultural journals show that many planters saw food as the proper first concern in running an orderly plantation community: one remarked that "the most important subject to attend to in the management of negroes is to give them a sufficiency of food" ([Anonymous] 1837:32, cited in Breeden 1980:93).

A basic theme running through the writings, according to Oakes (1983:153), is the opinion that those of African descent are biologically different from and inferior to Europeans and thus require a quite different kind of nutritional regimen. As in so many situations where one ethnic group holds sway over another, southern whites rationalized their particular social system through use of biologically based arguments. Food served as a medium for both "proving" such justifications and putting related policies into play.

The main point of contention among those discussing food was where, how, and when plantation meals were to be prepared (Breeden 1980:89-90). These planter-writers usually advocated one of two diametrically opposed systems—either the central-kitchen system, in which meals for all hands were cooked together and given out at one time and place; or the allowance system, in which uncooked rations were given to families and individuals to do with as they saw fit. The concerns expressed were not so much with what those in bondage ate but with who controlled the details of preparation and consumption. This exposes a primary issue of conflict within slave management. Did a master's power over his human property extend to control over such personal choices as meal composition, scheduling, and preparation?

These essays confirm that planters considered the provisions of pork, meal, and vegetables the primary, and practically sole, constituents of their slaves' rations. But the authors also make frequent mention of the extras added by both planters and slaves themselves. The journal pieces clearly recognize the critical contribution of peripheral foodstuffs to the emotional well-being of the slave community. Masters made use of special rations, garden plots, and stock-raising privileges as ways of rewarding conformity to behavioral standards and of increasing a slave's commitment to the master's conception of orderly plantation life. The physiological benefits from such extras were of secondary interest to these writers. Christmas "bonuses" of extra rations, money, small gifts, and time off from work were recommended as ways to reward good behavior. Harvesttime and, ironically, Independence Day also served as opportunities for feasting.

Planter-essayists commented on garden plots and stock raising by their slaves not so much in terms of dietary supplementation as, in the words of one, "sources of comforts as well as profit" (Gibbes 1858, cited in Breeden 1980:274). Masters were more concerned with the problems caused by the money received by slaves from the sale of produce and handicrafts than with any issue involving diet. This frequent mention of the cash earned from these activities is interesting in light of the common perceptions of slaves as being totally separate from any economic system outside the plantation (see Morgan 1982 for a detailed discussion of the topic).

The planter journals are all but silent on the subject of hunting and foraging by slaves. Southern tradition provides frequent comment on the slaves' strong interest in and abilities with gun, trap, and rod (Genovese 1974:487–89); and archaeological evidence gives direct testimony of the constant presence of wild resources in the quarter diet. Why did owners not acknowledge this more frequently in their musing on plantation management? It may be that slave foraging was either such an accepted practice that it warranted no comment or one with such an uneasy set of accompanying implications that it was best left undiscussed.

A common theme throughout the slave management literature is the troubles planters had in controlling the minor details of their slaves' behavior, coupled with an acknowledgment that such control was necessary. That the details of foodways and provisioning were a problem to masters confirms the fact that slaves saw them as issues worth the risk of conflict as well. It is also reluctant testimony to the high level of personal autonomy held by members of the slave community and to their ability to take action and force compromise.

## Food Supply in Plantation Records

This section reviews the highlights of a study of the records of four Virginia slaveholders living in the tidewater region between Richmond and Hampton Roads (see fig. 11.1). The examined journals, receipt books, and letters date to the period between 1840 and 1862. The precursor of this essay (McKee 1988) discusses the details of each of these operations, and what is presented here is a distillation of what the documents can say about plantation food supply.

The four planters followed the same basic agricultural regimen. All planted two crops of wheat and a crop of corn through the course of the year, and all raised large numbers of hogs for meat. Many of their activities centered on producing food consumption on the plantation. In addition to the pork, flour, and meal produced on these farms, all had garden crops of fresh vegetables, all raised poultry, and all had major fishing operations. Despite this, none of these plantations achieved true self-sufficiency.

The history of the two hundred African Americans living on the five studied plantations (two owned by one man) has largely been left out of the owner's seemingly detailed records. No mention whatsoever is made about day-to-day home life in the slave quarter. The documents suggest that slave management was largely a matter of standardized, long-established routine for these four planters. It was only when the unexpected happened, or when slave and master engaged in an out-of-the-ordinary economic transaction, that it became necessary for things to be written down.

Four general topics covered in the documents provide information on slave subsistence: planter-directed food production, distribution of rations, off-time food production by slaves, and the social uses of food.

*Planter-directed Food Production*

It is not surprising that the four planters provide good coverage of plantation production in their records. Feeding their communities engaged much of these planters' time and energy, a burden made heavier by the desire for self-sufficiency.

Aside from serving as a cash product, hogs were at the center of the planters' efforts to feed their slaves. Three of the four men kept a detailed account of year-end slaughter poundage figures and closely compared the numbers from year to year (table 11.1).

Not all of this meat was intended for the use of the slaves, and not all the slaves' meat came from the home plantation. Three of the four planters sold pork at a given time of the year and then later, if necessary, bought more for their plantation community.

Each of these tidewater plantations had frontage on a river, and the planters intensively harvested the fish that returned from the sea to spawn in tributary creeks each spring. Like pork, this resource provided a high return for a relatively modest investment of labor or cash, it could be easily preserved for later consumption, and it was well tolerated by slaves.

*Rations Distribution*

The documents provide some very limited mention of slave provisioning. Perhaps feeding the hands was so routine and standardized on all these plantations that it did not require a careful accounting. It is curious that in their obsession with production measurement and cost recording, the planters did not keep a running tally of the flow of food to the quarter. It may represent a distancing in the minds of the planters of the slave community from the rest of the agricultural enterprise.

One of the planters came very close to equating provisions with wages. At one point Richard Eppes docked his slaves at the Upper Hundred plantation half of their rations for some unspecified time because of an incident of theft (Eppes, 7 July 1852). He also increased the meat allowance of his ploughmen by half a pound during the heavy fall work season.

As part of a year-end meeting with his slaves, Eppes noted he "had the provisions of the negroes given out under my own eyes" (Eppes, 29 Dec. 1852). Men received one-and-a-half pounds of meat, one quart of molasses, and one-and-a-half pecks of meal; women one pound of meat, one quart of molasses, and one peck of meal; and children a half pound of meat, one pint of molasses, and a half peck of meal. Eppes set down a similarly detailed feeding schedule for his cattle (Eppes, 29 Dec. 1852). In 1853 or 1854 in his year-end speech he offered to increase the meat allowance to three pounds for men, two-and-a-half pounds for women, and one-and-a-half pounds for children as an incentive "as soon as we can raise hogs enough." He admonished them that no such rations increase would be forthcoming "as long as we have to buy" (Nicholls 1981:73).

## Slave-directed Food Production

The documents studied provide many casual references to slaves' after-hours work for cash and extra food. Most such efforts are recorded indirectly as the result of transactions between master and slave or in notations about alterations in regular scheduling to accommodate garden work.

Tidewater slaves commonly raised chickens, and meat and eggs were frequently sold to planters. John Selden recorded at least thirteen purchases during the four years of his journal intensively studied in this research. Eppes granted the privilege of raising pork only to the quarter's elite. His foremen could have two hogs at a time, and the head ploughman a single animal (Nicholls 1981:78). The overall tone of the entries concerning the subject suggests slave-directed production was a common-place and an expected phenomenon.

Selden is the only planter of the four to note purchases of wild game from slaves. On several occasions he bought soras (*Porzana carolina*, a short-billed rail) in large enough quantities (36, 36, and 120) to suggest that these marsh-dwelling birds must have been taken by gunshot rather than in traps or by some other method (Selden, 27 Jan., 14 Oct. 1841, 25 Oct. 1858).

Spring-spawning fish frequently were involved in transactions between master and slave. William Jerdone set up a complex system whereby he would pay cash to his slaves for fish caught outside of work hours. The fish went right back to the slave community as part of their weekly rations, an arrangement that apparently satisfied both parties.

Personal gardens also supplied extra food for those in bondage. Richard Eppes again provides the most explicit discussions of how he dealt with "negro crops." In his "Code," his contractual agreement with his slaves, he notes the privileges of both "a small spot of ground for a garden" and half days off every Saturday for working these plots "except when a press then it will not be allowed you" (Nicholls 1981:78).

## Social Uses of Food

The four planters recorded both overt and subtle examples of the procurement and consumption of food as socially charged behavior, with implications far beyond the physiological well-being of their chattel.

Richard Eppes punished those who committed certain offenses (such as insolence, disobedience, and uncleanliness) by reducing their rations. Eppes apparently thought that this would serve as a strong deterrent to future transgressions, offsetting any short-term drop in productivity caused by hunger or malnourishment. He may have also counted on slaves to make up the deficit from other sources.

George Wilson went to great lengths at one point to grind a portion of his wheat crop into flour for his slaves. Wilson's reason for this was not to promote economy or self-sufficiency. His stated desire was "to give the servants a part of it as I like to give them some part of everything raised on the farm" (Wilson, 19 Oct. 1853).

Special distributions of food, cash, and time off from labor made Christmas the most important time of the year for tidewater slaves. In 1861, during Selden's last Christmas at Westover, he distributed 350 pounds of bacon and beef, along with individual apportionments of two pounds of flour, one pint of molasses, lard, "etc" (Selden, 25 Dec. 1861). Richard Eppes used the Yuletide of 1852 not only to provide a feast for his slaves but to praise, reward, and punish, then to settle accounts, and to exhort his people to be better at what they did: "Gave William White [a slave] $5 as a marriage present and $3 to Charles Lewis for good management of hogs. Paid $4 to hands who drank no whiskey in harvest and left $4 with Mr. Rogers for those not present. . . . order a good hog to be selected to be killed for negroes tomorrow & half barrel of flour to be distributed among them by foreman" (Eppes, 24 Dec. 1852).

Stealing is an important topic in the study of plantation life. Food larceny comes through in these records as a constant, largely unsolvable problem. Most tally their losses (often in the form of fattening hogs) but record little action taken to prevent its recurrence.

George Wilson altered his production strategy one year rather than have more of his pigs disappear. "I have now twenty more to kill," he wrote. "They are small . . . some of them ought to have been kept for another year: if I had done so they would have been stolen, so I must do the best I can with them" (Wilson, 5 Dec. 1854).

In 1859 William Jerdone noted the theft of eleven of sixty-nine of his "killing hogs" in the period between March 19 and July 21. He makes no mention of catching anyone involved in this activity. (Jerdone, 21 July 1859). The tone of these passages is one of resigned acceptance of pilfering as an aspect of plantation life largely out of the master's control.

It is disappointing that neither the agricultural press nor the documents from tidewater Virginia shed much light on the actual foodways of the enslaved. Both provide an important context for the topic: practical and philosophical perspectives on management, on one hand; listings of production and day-to-day routine, on the other. The written record gives the impression that the planters had little knowledge of the personal lives, including the foodways and supplementary subsistence activities, of their human property. Perhaps both master and slave preferred it that way. It remains for archaeology to provide direct glimpses into these aspects of slave life.

## Archaeological Data: Fauna from Virginia Slave Cabins

Animal bones excavated from three sites in Virginia are considered in this section. Tallies of the assemblages are presented in table 11.2. The three sites are very similar in some ways and very different in others, a condition that generates some interesting analytical pathways and clues useful in speaking about slave food supply and subsistence activities.

The bones from Flowerdew Hundred were excavated from a midden around a slave cabin built sometime during the 1830s. Flowerdew Hundred is located on the James River, well above the brackish water zone but still within the stretch affected by tidal flow. The Kingsmill bones came from a root cellar or "hidey-hole" within the foundation outline of a slave dwelling occupied during the 1780s and 1790s. The site is also located on the James, near Williamsburg, on the upper reaches of the river's brackish water zone. The Monticello collection comes from a sheet-refuse deposit which accumulated around the entrance to a building used as a slave dwelling between 1796 and about 1810. Monticello is located on a mountaintop in the foothills of Virginia's western mountain region, isolated from the riparian resources available to the occupants of the other two sites. (See Crader 1984, 1990; Kelso 1982, 1984b; McKee 1987, 1988 for extended discussions of each site.)

The bones examined for this study have been subjected to a variety of processes that affect their usefulness and accuracy as sources reflecting human behavior. Animal husbandry practices, hunting, carcass processing, ration distribution, cooking, eating, discard, burial, natural decay, excavation techniques, and even analytical methods are all actions that contribute to the formation of the archaeological data base and that affect the information-yielding potential of the record. A consideration of each site's formation processes, the label under which these actions can be grouped, is a necessary first interpretive step. (See Reitz 1987:101–5 for a fuller discussion of these factors.)

The bones from Flowerdew received the most rigorous transformation from a "kitchen-fresh" state of the three collections. Coming from a "residual primary deposit" (Schiffer 1987:63), the bones were deposited right outside the cabin, virtu-ally at their point of use. The small number of bones recovered (1,045) that could be assigned with confidence to the antebellum period of the cabin's occupation, as well as the small size of the fragments, attests to the largely destructive and subtractive processes applied to the bones after discard. What survived to be excavated and iden-tified to a precise taxonomic level are smaller, sturdier skeletal elements. The two most common elements in the sample, pig's teeth (67) and catfish pectoral spines (31), are perfect examples of bones with these attributes.

The Monticello fauna came from a depositional environment similar to that at Flowerdew. With a higher number recovered (1,477) and a shorter period of accu-mulation (approximately fifteen years versus approximately thirty), the sample can be considered less transformed by postdiscard actions than the Flowerdew material. The bone sample from Kingsmill, highest in number (2,472) of the three collections and from a filled root cellar, was clearly least affected by the negative transforma-tions going on at the open-air deposits at Flowerdew and Monticello. But because the root cellar apparently was filled quickly, the sample lacks the time depth repre-sented in the other two assemblages.

Recognition of the specifics of formation processes at the three sites under con-sideration can help guide analysis, in part by putting limits on the interpretive use of the material. The Flowerdew sample would appear to be the most flawed from this perspective, but it can still yield some important and otherwise unavailable information. The range of species present is perhaps the most noteworthy aspect of the sample, with the eighteen different kinds of animals on the list (table 11.2) pro-viding an impressive display of dietary breadth. The sample, although biased by the formation processes discussed above, gives strong evidence for heavy presence of pork and catfish in the diet of the cabin's occupants. The 120 pig bones, although accounting for almost 11 percent of the sample, still make up an extreme underrep-resentation of the amount of pork in the diet. Most of this meat would have come to the quarter boneless as bacon or salt pork and would have been distributed as rations. The eighty-one catfish bones came from at least twenty-one individual fish, as determined by the number of left-side pectoral spines. The examined plantation documents from the region make no mention of planters using this species in put-ting together slave rations. The catfish bones in the Flowerdew assemblage are most likely present as the result of individual efforts on the part of the cabin occupants to supplement their diet.

The Flowerdew bone list suggests that a very small amount of beef and mutton found its way into the slave diet. Although the site formation processes filtered out larger bones, such as those typical of cattle skeletons, cattle have an adequate num-ber of small, durable, easily identifiable elements (such as teeth, phalanges, carpals, tarsals, and articular surfaces) that would have been readily apparent in the collec-tion if present. Bones from sheep, roughly the same size as those from hogs, would have about the same probability of surviving the rigors of discard and burial. The small number of cattle and sheep bones is not a reflection of the formation of the cabin deposit but of diet composition. Chicken was apparently a more common meat source for Flowerdew slaves than beef.

The shellfish present in the assemblage perhaps reflect the extremes of the slave quarter diet. The oysters and marine clams in the sample must have been imported rather than collected, since Flowerdew is at least thirty-five miles upriver from the species' natural range. Oysters and clams may have come to slaves as dietary extras, distributed at times of feasting by the planter.

The freshwater mussels in the collection occur in great abundance in the river and creeks around Flowerdew. Nearby shell middens attest to the importance of this resource in the diet of Indian groups in the area. Mussels are a very low-quality nutritional source, with one study (Parmalee and Klippel 1974) estimating that it would take 300 to 450 mussels to provide the caloric needs of a five-member family for one day. Although a large number of mussels have been found in a trash pit at a seventeenth-century colonial site (44PG68) at Flowerdew (Taft Kiser, pers. comm., March 1987), no other recovery of *Elliptio* sp. has been reported from historic-era sites in the mid-Atlantic region. Slaves at Flowerdew may have eaten this easily collected species only as a last resort, at times during the week or year when no other food was available.

As shown by this discussion, the much-reduced assemblage of bone from Flowerdew still can generate some defendable statements about food supply. The quantity and quality of these statements are expanded through comparisons with the Monticello and Kingsmill material.

All three sites show a heavy dependence on domestic animals but with strong variation in the specific barnyard animals present. Bones identified as coming from sheep or goats (species biologically similar enough to discourage separate identifications) make up 5.7 percent of the Kingsmill sample but only .54 percent of the Monticello material and roughly 1.4 percent of the Flowerdew bones. Pig bones compose relatively the same percentage of the samples (about 11 percent) at Flowerdew and Monticello but declined to only about 2 percent of the bones recovered from Kingsmill. There are almost twice as many bird bones as pork bones at Kingsmill. Cattle representation ranges from 1.19 percent at Flowerdew, through 9.8 percent of the Monticello sample (when the large mammal category is added to the definitely identified cattle bones), to 6.35 percent at Kingsmill.

The shift from a more equitable mix of mutton, beef, and pork at Kingsmill, the earliest of the three sites, to an apparently lopsided emphasis on pork at Flowerdew might be a reflection of shifting livestock production strategies in the region (see Miller 1984 and Gray 1933:832 for further discussion on this point). But the shift in the sample percentages should not be interpreted as an automatic response by slaves to changes in production strategies put into play by their masters. Food preference and the particular mix of animals raised were clearly linked on plantations, with each influencing the other.

The Monticello assemblage reflects a narrower repertoire of wild meat sources than seen at the other two sites. The apparent greater dietary breadth at the two tide-water sites is at least in part owing to a rich and diverse environmental locale. There is unquestionably a larger set of ecological communities to draw upon in the region than on the hilltops near Monticello. More importantly, the quarter residents at Kingsmill and Flowerdew found ways to make use of this diversity. The presence of a rich resource base alone is not enough; those living in such a setting must develop the ability to exploit what is available. Monticello is located in a physical and biological landscape that is very different from that at Flowerdew or Kingsmill, and the slave community may have been in a very different social environment as well.

Bearing in mind its proximity to the James River, it is difficult to explain the low number of fish bones in the Kingsmill assemblage. It may be due to specialized activities at each site, with stock raising at Kingsmill perhaps providing enough meat to obviate the need for much augmentation from other sources. It may also be due to the nature of the Kingsmill deposit, which—as a secondary, short-term dump—may have seen activity at a time of year when little fishing took place.

It is noticeable that the most recent sample, from Flowerdew, has the smallest percentage of bones from barnyard species. Influenced by many factors, including an unrepresented but probably ample quantity of boneless salt-pork rations, this may also reflect a growing familiarity with, and "settling in" to, the local environment by the Flowerdew slave community. Armed with the knowledge accumulated over several generations, these people may have begun to "domesticate" the nearby wilderness and make use of it for an increasing portion of their dietary needs.

Most of these comments about the three samples are suggestions that cannot be substantiated. It remains unclear whether the bone counts and percentages represent actual nutritional habits or merely randomized transformations of the material. The discussion presented here requires a theoretical framework built from the data recovered from excavations at these sites and other sources in order to provide a fuller and more coherent view of food in plantation society. The focus should not be solely on what was eaten but also on why a particular culinary regimen was developed.

## A Model of Slave Procurement

The preceding examination of the secondary literature, the antebellum agricultural press, plantation records, and archaeological data guided the development of a model showing the ways slaves got their food. Figure 11.2 is a graphic presentation of this model of food procurement. The model's most important feature is that it is centered on, and presented from, the perspective of the slave consumers.

The procurement model is designed as a grid, with placement of the eight sources of food determined by two elements: whether master or slave controlled the choice of food items involved, and whether the actions engaged in obtaining the food were permitted or forbidden by the master. By thinking about food in this way, rather than in terms of quantities or nutritional quality, the connections between diet and society become much clearer. The usual rations of cornmeal and bacon no doubt provided 60 to 80 percent or more of the total diet by volume. But as in any cuisine, it is the extras, or peripheral elements, that are of the highest social significance and analytical interest. It is noteworthy that the actions by which the peripheral dietary elements were acquired are clustered in the lower right-hand area of the model, in the zone reflecting choices made by plantation hands—choices including actions that may have been mildly discouraged or completely forbidden by owners.

The "gray areas" along each axis are of particular interest as well. These reflect the points at which specific dicta issued by masters were open to interpretation and negotiation and show that "powerless" slaves may have had a certain amount of influence over decisions made by the masters. In allowing slaves to have gardens, could a planter decide what was to be grown and how the resulting produce was to be used? In purchasing extras and additions to be distributed as rations, would a master cater to particular preferences of his chattel? If slaves could take the scraps and offal from butchering, could they also appropriate leftovers from the Big House kitchen? These minor but constant questions kept the details of food supply at the center of questions about order and structure within the plantation community. The slave cabin is at the center of this model not out of a desire for graphic symmetry but because cabin occupants were figuratively perched in the gray areas of plantation society. The details of their lives, like the details of their food supply, were a matter of dynamic tension between what the master controlled and what the slave controlled, and between what was allowed and what was forbidden.

The procurement model is not intended to be an end point in the study of plantation food supply, nor is it intended to serve as a sort of "black box" in the analysis of material from archaeological sites. Bones cannot be fed in at the top to tumble neatly down into one of the labeled slots on the graph. A rib from a stolen pig looks no different from one from an animal distributed as rations. The chart does help sort out the possible food sources and actions that generated the archaeological record, and it may help the analyst begin to make connections between the kinds and parts of animals present and the activities that brought the bones to the site. But the main intention behind the construction of the model was to move the analysis to the next step—linking the details of diet to wider questions about plantation society. Specifically, the essential question here is how subsistence activities reflected and influenced plantation relations.

The model presents a view of the subsistence strategy of the black plantation community—the path of choices and decisions that slaves followed in getting their food. Although built around the "entitlements" of master-supplied pork and corn, other sources of food required an extensive amount of initiative, planning, and effort. Each action taken to supplement rations had specific risks and costs, which had to be weighed against the expected returns. Was stealing a pig worth the risk of punishment? Was tending a garden—that is, putting in even more physical labor after days of plowing, hoeing, and harvesting—worth the expected return of a bushel or two of fresh vegetables for table or trade? These were the questions slaves had to consider in deciding how to add to their food supply. Not all of the food procurement methods presented in the model were employed by all members of the plantation community. Decisions governing the selection of methods, and the success or failure these efforts met, determined the difference between hunger and contentment. A slave who had constructed a viable subsistence strategy, who could avoid hunger and eat foods of choice, had achieved a kind of independence.

The idea of satisfaction is at the heart of the important role of food in plantation social dynamics. For those, like slaves, kept on the edge of nutritional dissatisfaction, a full plate of food could provide a welcome combination of physical and emotional fulfillment. As Mary Douglas notes, "Most symbolic behavior must work through the human body" (1970:vii); thus, because of biological necessity and its associated hungers, food is a powerful category of symbolism and communication.

Sometimes planters ignored the emotional and symbolic power of food in the relationship between their human property and themselves; sometimes they sought to exploit it. Slaveholders intended their estates to be places with tight control and strong limits on social behavior. By design, slaves lived in a rarefied atmosphere, one in which their lives were programmed for constant hard work and strict adherence to rules. As a "simple race," slaves were also expected to be content with an "adequate" diet of pork and cornmeal. The shrewder planter saw the value of expanding the use of food as a way to motivate (through harvesttime supplements and holiday feasts) and subordinate (through borderline deprivation and the common little rituals of weekly rationing).

It is when slaves are included in the analysis as able and effective social actors that food's critical role becomes clearest. African Americans held in bondage were not "simple" and thus did not accept either the adequacy of their provisioning or the foreshortened symbolic statements that went with it. The ability of slaves to establish a diet that extended far beyond the planter-provided rations, and the fact that planters came to expect this ability, illustrates the slaves' effectiveness in controlling some of the details of their own lives and in influencing the policies of their owners.

The right of slaves to adequate living conditions was recognized by all involved in the plantation system. Sufficiency in housing and food was the recognized "salary" owed to plantation hands under the unwritten and unspoken but clearly understood contract between master and slave. The specifics of payment—how much food, of what quality, when to be distributed—were always subject to direct and indirect negotiation.

All slaveholders either explicitly or implicitly allowed slaves to supplement their food supply through actions outside the master's control. In allowing slaves to add to their meager rations, planters may have been trying to save some money and effort, but they also were relinquishing a certain degree of control. Slaves worked to find and exploit the resulting inconsistencies within the supposedly tight confines of plantation order. Personal production, scavenging, hunting, foraging, and theft were vital matters, precipitating slave/master clashes over autonomy, control, and power within the system of plantation order.

One way to get extras—stealing—is a particularly significant link between food and social order. Theft was the most blatantly forbidden source of food in the slave diet. The acceptance by many planters of a certain level of stealing as a fact of life indicates compromise, if not surrender, on the part of the ruling race. It is not reading too much into the record to conclude that slaves stole for emotional as well as physical satisfaction. The dual nature of food stealing, as a way of both feeding oneself and beating the system, added to its significance in the eyes of both master and slave. Eugene Genovese (1974:607–8) has noted that ultimately, theft was morally degrading to the slave community, and those who stole unfortunately gave confirmation to the negative expectations of whites. Aside from these long-term elements of the context of theft, one can still understand and believe in the justifications of the moment. Slaves usually distinguished between "stealing" and "taking," had personal experience with the sharp differences between adequate rations and a satisfying diet, and were fully cognizant of the ambiguities of their owners' moral position. Food larceny was also an emphatic statement about the ability of slaves to take effective action on their own to achieve contentment and a certain level of autonomy. If a slaveholder had trouble in keeping tabs on his fattening hogs, what else did he fail to keep under control?

This short discussion suggests that the strategy sketched out in the procurement model involved a set of actions for both feeding the body and easing the emotional burden of life as a slave. By mastering the strategy, slaves not only had a more satisfying diet but also achieved a kind of psychological independence.

A self-determined, varied, and at times abundant diet did not coincide with the ideal view of a docile, completely dependent slave population. Essentially, planters sought to establish an efficient, economical, and controlled social order by treating slaves like livestock. This attitude and approach reveal the institution's fundamental flaw. Slaves were human beings, not insensate beasts of burden, and their humanity and force of will made them able to respond to and sometimes overcome their oppression.

In the end, masters were unable to control something as "simple" as the diet of their slaves. The ideological foundations of slavery held that such control was necessary both in regulating plantation order and for taking care of the supposedly childlike, dependent folk who made up the plantation community. By defeating (or simply ignoring) these efforts to direct the intimate details of their personal and family lives, slaves helped undermine the basic rationalizations of the system that held them captive.

Slave foodways, like those of all cultures, were intimately connected to the big and small rituals of life in the quarter; to social identity; and to communication with family, other members of the slave community, and the whites who claimed ownership of these communities. Forged from African traditions, plantation deprivation, and active innovations, foodways played a major role in the way slaves took charge of the conditions of their lives. It is thus not surprising that food remains a core element of African-American cultural identity.

This study does not, because it cannot, explore the full nature of plantation subsistence. It is exciting to imagine what could be said about life in the quarter if even a single meal could be observed. The knowledge that this kind of source is lost encourages the student of the African-American experience to extend the analysis of existing sources as far as possible.

One aspect of foodways has come under particular scrutiny in this study: how food made its way to slave consumers. The nature of the main source of archaeological data considered—animal bones from slave domestic sites—actually narrows the field of view even further, to a study of the meat portion of the slave diet. I hope that the short discussion of master-slave relations presented here will encourage others to consider data from plantation sites from as wide a perspective as possible. More detailed explorations of both the archaeological data and related documents will take the analysis of plantation life ever further.

Archaeology is indispensable, but it is not sufficient in itself to provide an understanding of the past. We cannot be satisfied merely with determining from our excavations the size of buildings, the number and shape of ceramic vessels, or the amount of available meat represented by an assemblage of bones. Anthropologically oriented archaeology must focus on the details of cultural behavior behind these things. Unassailable reconstructions of the true relationships between master and slave may be beyond our grasp, but it is only in reaching for such a goal that we can begin to fulfill the potential of historical archaeology to provide us with a more complete view of the past.

Table 11.1. Pork production figures for tidewater Virginia: selected planters and years

| Planter | Year | No. of hogs slaughtered | Total poundage | Average lbs. per hog |
|---------|------|------------------------|----------------|----------------------|
| Selden | 1841 | 52 | 7,962 | 153.1 |
|  | 1844 | 58 | 9,080 | 156.6 |
|  | 1848* | 38 | 5,556 | 146.2 |
|  | 1858 | 98 | 12,682 | 129.4 |
|  | 1859 | 78 | 13,030 | 167.1 |
|  | 1860 | 94 | 13,992 | 148.9 |
|  | 1861 | 76 | 12,550 | 165.1 |
| Eppes | 1852 | 73 | 9,006 | 123.4 |
| Wilson | 1854 | 40 | 5,500 | 137.5 |
| Averages |  | 70.4 | 10,178.9 | 144.6 |

Note: William Jerdone did not record his production figures
*Data incomplete, not included in final averaging

Table 11.2. Bones identified from three slave dwelling sites in Virginia

| Species | Kingsmill | | | Monticello | | | Flowerdew | | |
|---------|----|-----|-----|----|------|-----|-----|------|-----|
|  | N | % | MNI | N | % | MNI | N | % | MNI |
| Pig (*Sus scrofa*) | 50 | 2.0 | 6 | 165 | 11.2 | 7 | 120 | 11.0 | 4 |
| Cattle (*Bos taurus*) | 157 | 6.4 | 4 | 94 | 6.4 | 3 | 13 | 1.2 | 1 |
| Horse? (cf. *Equus* sp.) | 0 | 0 | 0 | 0 | 0 | 0 | 1 | .1 | 1 |
| Sheep (*Ovis aries*) | 0 | 0 | 0 | 0 | 0 | 0 | 4 | .4 | 1 |
| Sheep/goat | 141 | 5.7 | 5 | 0 | 0 | 0 | 3 | .3 | 1 |
| Sheep/goat/deer | 0 | 0 | 0 | 0 | 0 | 0 | 8 | .7 |  |
| Deer? (cf. *Odocoileus* sp.) | 2 | 1 | 1 | 0 | 0 | 0 | 1 | .7 | 1 |
| Medium-sized mammal, unidentified | 366 | 14.8 |  | 128 | 8.7 | 0 | 147 | 13.4 |  |
| Large mammal, unidentified | 0 | 0.1 | 1 | 51 | 3.5 | 0 | 0 | 0 |  |
| Opossum (*Didelphis virginianus*) | 2 | 0.1 | 1 | 6 | 0.4 | 1 | 12 | 1.1 | 2 |

*continued on next page*

Table 11.2—*continued*

| Species | Kingsmill | | | Monticello | | | Flowerdew | | |
|---|---|---|---|---|---|---|---|---|---|
| | N | % | MNI | N | % | MNI | N | % | MNI |
| Rabbit (*Sylvilagus floridianus*) | 0 | 0 | 0 | 5 | 0.4 | 1 | 9 | 0.8 | 2 |
| Rat (*Rattus* sp.) | 0 | 0 | 0 | 0 | 0 | 0 | 1 | 0.1 | 1 |
| Squirrel (*Sciurus* sp.) | 0 | 0 | 0 | 0 | 0 | 0 | 1 | 0.1 | 1 |
| Raccoon (*Procyon loctor*) | 6 | .2 | 2 | 0 | 0 | 0 | 1 | 0.1 | 1 |
| Small carnivore, unidentified | 0 | 0 | 0 | 3 | 0.2 | 0 | 0 | | |
| Mammal, unidentified | 1528 | 61.8 | | 168 | 11.37 | | 499 | 45.6 | |
| Chicken (*Gallus gallus*) | 26 | 1.0 | 4 | 0 | 0 | 0 | 29 | 2.7 | 4 |
| Turkey (*Meleagris gallopavo*) | 6 | 0.2 | 1 | 0 | 0 | 0 | 0 | 0 | |
| Canadian goose (*Branta canadensis*) | 1 | 0.04 | 1 | 0 | 0 | 0 | 0 | 0 | 0 |
| Crow (*Corus* sp.) | 0 | 0 | 0 | 0 | 0 | 0 | 2 | 0.2 | 1 |
| Mallard/black duck (*Anas* sp.) | 0 | 0 | 0 | 0 | 0 | 0 | 1 | 0.1 | 1 |
| Bird, unidentified | 92 | 3.7 | | 35 | 2.4 | | 63 | 5.8 | |
| Catfish (*Ictalurus* sp.) | 0 | 0 | 0 | 0 | 0 | | 81 | 7.4 | 21 |
| Sturgeon (*Acipenser* sp.) | | | | | | | 42 | 3.8 | 1 |
| Striped bass? (cf. *Morone* sp.) | 0 | 0 | 0 | 0 | 0 | | 2 | 1.8 | 1 |
| Gar (*Lepisosteus* sp.) | 0 | 0 | 0 | 0 | 0 | | 1 | 0.1 | 1 |
| Fish, unidentified | 43 | 1.7 | | | | | 45 | 4.1 | |
| Snapping turtle (*Chelydra serpentina*) | 0 | 0 | 0 | 0 | 0 | | 4 | 0.4 | 1 |
| Turtle, unidentified | 41 | 1.7 | | 0 | 0 | 0 | 5 | 0.5 | |
| Blue crab (*Callinectes sapidus*) | 11 | 0.4 | | 0 | 0 | 0 | 0 | 0 | 0 |
| Nonidentifiable | 0 | 0 | | 811 | 54.9 | | 0 | 0 | 0 |
| Total | 2,472 | | | 1,477 | | | 1,095 | | |
| Oyster (*Crassostrea virginianus*) | (Shellfish counts unavailable from Kingsmill and Monticello) | | | | | | 112 | | |
| Freshwater mussel (*Elliptio* sp.) | | | | | | | 88 | | |
| Marine clam (unidentified species) | | | | | | | 12 | | |
| Shellfish, unidentified | | | | | | | 6 | | |

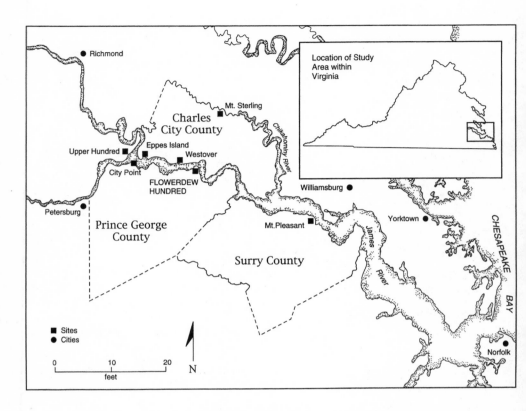

11.1. James River–tidewater region of Virginia. (Redrawn by Marcia Bakry)

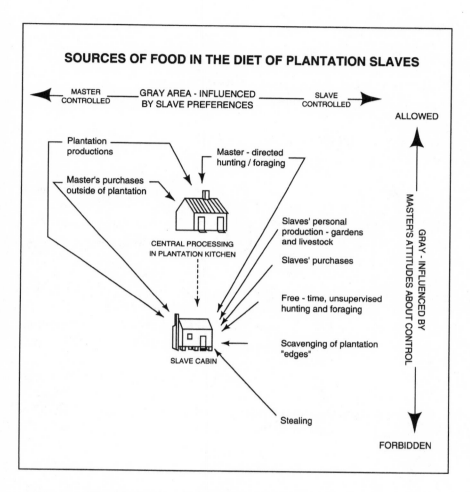

11.2. Sources of food in the diet of plantation slaves. (Redrawn by Marcia Bakry)

# 12

# Museums and American Slavery

*Edward A. Chappell*

THE SIGHT OF George McDaniel, that aficionado of black tenant-farmer life, in
his role as museum director for the grandest Georgian house in South Carolina
is one of the small miracles of the 1990s. Change is under way in American museums, as social historians, anthropologists, folklorists, and cross-disciplinary icono-
clasts have assumed policy-making roles. Even at Colonial Williamsburg, long seen
as a bastion of good taste and complacent history, rumor has it that wolves are
guarding the sheep. This changing of the guard is startling, but what is it likely to
accomplish? Can the new crowd usefully affect what academic disciplines and museums have to offer, or will they simply become sheep in wolves' clothing, rearrang-
ing the stories while failing to raise new issues? How we treat the subject of slavery
is an important case in point.

There are several reasons why American history museums should be in the business of dealing with slavery in a forthright and substantive manner. Literally millions of people visit museums each year, most of them ready to think and learn. Too
often they find the institutions functioning as little more than a refuge from the realities of modern life. Our job is not simply to amuse and divert, though entertain-
ment plays a useful role in teaching. What is more important than glitz and grace
is that we engage people in thinking about provocative issues. Race relations are an
appropriate, even essential topic, one about which we can provide some historical
background and prompt people to reconsider ideas long thought unshakable.[1] Topics like the system of slave labor, the lives of enslaved people, and the extent of the
institution's effects on both white and black Americans are highly pertinent to those
who teach about the colonial and early republican South. In short, there is a huge
audience to which museums owe some consequential ideas, and the subject of slavery is one of the chief points of entry.

It is my intention here to promote three ideas: (1) museums have an important
role to play in contributing research to the study of slavery, (2) there are dangers
inherent in that involvement, and (3) ultimately we must overcome the dangers and
the inertia of museums in order to teach a more meaningful history.

These propositions may be considered productively in the Chesapeake region because of the central role of slavery in the region's history, the extensive analysis of slavery that has taken place there, and the prominence of relevant museums in the popular perception of its culture.

## The Research Role of Museums

Museums are more than conduits for redirecting secondhand scholarship to those who do not regularly read the *William and Mary Quarterly*. Particularly in the study of Chesapeake slavery, museum professionals can play an active role in the scholarly discourse, posing questions and pursuing research methods that complement or challenge scholarship by our colleagues in the academy. In other words, we do research to learn as well as to teach.

Somewhat egotistically, I offer the reconstructed late eighteenth-century slave quarter at Carter's Grove as an example of how a museum project can identify useful problems for historians, as well as raise questions and suggest answers to the visiting public. The Colonial Williamsburg Foundation carried out a literal re-creation of the quarter, with houses, gardens, lanes, and storage and agricultural buildings, on a rural site ten miles from the old Virginia capital (fig. 12.1). Architectural historians began research in 1981, and the buildings were constructed by staff carpenters and interpreters, using eighteenth-century methods, in 1988 and 1989.

Gathering details to reconstitute a lost landscape carries a certain risk of myopia. I would be the first to admit that working for Colonial Williamsburg can make one abnormally absorbed with the physical minutiae of eighteenth-century life—how to craft a wooden hinge or assemble a riven pale fence. The point museum scholars should recognize, of course, is that these and other details reflect a complex system of economic and cultural choices, all tied to specific historical circumstances.

Aggregated in a project like the Carter's Grove quarter, such details should lead the scholar to consider what the range of living standards was, what economic and perceptual factors affected those standards, how people resisted them, and what the political implications are.

No single source of evidence tells us all we want to know about the spectrum of living conditions and typicality, or reasons for change, but together they suggest forces and processes that the historian working only with documents is likely to overlook. Given the dearth of explicit information about life in the colonial Chesapeake, one must tease out all that is possible from available sources. Our inquiry has drawn extensively on the study of extant buildings—on architectural archaeology, if you will—as well as on subterranean archaeology and documentary research.

However complete and evocative surviving buildings appear, they provide just as fragmentary a portrait of past life as do the more conventional documentary sources, though fragmentary in different and therefore useful ways. In fact, archaeological excavations probably hold the greatest promise for detailed information about the material lives of most preindustrial workers, including Chesapeake slaves. The earliest discoveries among excavated slave quarters in Virginia, Maryland, and the deeper South—much of it funded by museums in quest of information about their sites—have provided a sizable amount of data and explanation, and we have only scratched the surface.

Laboring over the late eighteenth-century quarter associated with Nathaniel Burwell's flashy gentry plantation at Carter's Grove, we came to recognize a striking difference between the material standards enforced by an eighteenth-century planter like Burwell and those followed by more calculating, managerial slaveholders of the late antebellum period. Architectural fieldwork revealed something that written records help explain, but that is only evident in the buildings themselves: slave housing of a permanent quality was seldom built before the Revolutionary War—and often not until the last decades before emancipation.

Hundreds of slave houses survive along the edges of wood lots, in the yards of larger houses, and in the fields of Virginia farms. Like those elsewhere in the South, these generally date from the half century preceding the Civil War. Only rarely can eighteenth-century exceptions be found down the hill from a piedmont plantation house or behind a great Charleston mansion. Whatever their date, the vast majority of these houses are highly threatened. Rural quarters are sometimes minimally maintained for agricultural storage, and nowadays service wings are often remodeled as guest cottages in history-conscious cities. A few are even propped up or restored by museums interested in preserving and presenting evidence of those who once lived there, but an equal number of educational institutions have knocked down the buildings or allowed them to collapse. Countless slave quarters were occupied by rural workers in the first half of this century, but these houses are rapidly disappearing from the land.

Their endangered quality makes study of the survivors all the more urgent. However idiosyncratic or conventional, they all have things to tell us about perceptions of sufficiency, in number and size of rooms, quality of construction, amount of light, degree of finish, and allowance for privacy. They reveal what features the occupants were likely to change and when they were likely to do it. We are finding that surviving quarters were among the best ever built. From ex-slave narratives and slave owners' correspondence in antebellum farm journals, it is evident that tight, well-constructed houses with wooden floors, masonry chimneys, and glazed windows were exceptional even in the nineteenth century (Herman 1984; Washington 1965:2–3). Many were much worse.

Even among surviving quarters, like the attic rooms above nineteenth-century work buildings, interior finish or heating could be absent, and total floor space could be as small as a hundred square feet. That antebellum travelers continued to employ terms like *hut*, with connotations of impermanence and poverty, reveals that many slaves continued to occupy small and flimsy houses more like those of the eighteenth century than what was prescribed for conscientious slave managers by would-be reformers (Weld 1807; Sears 1847; Randolph 1852).

What the fieldwork also reveals is that by the mid–nineteenth century, superior housing for workers had become almost formulaic (fig. 12.2). One can recognize growing concern for the appearance of better housing in the antebellum journals, often promoted by both economic and humanitarian arguments; but it is only in the field, looking at the buildings themselves rather than the prescriptive literature, that one recognizes how the diverse, often eccentric recommendations of slave owners were largely ignored in favor of a standard, predictable scheme.

More interesting are the indications that such housing was almost wholly a nineteenth-century development. It was the nineteenth-century agrarian capitalists, not the Enlightenment planters of the eighteenth century, who chose to plow a larger part of their profits back into demonstrably better housing. Improvement in workers' housing for slaves and nonslaves alike reflected new attitudes toward economic prudence as well as toward what was decent and appropriate for human beings (Chappell 1994). Antebellum farm journals signal a more systematized management of resources, be they crops, animals, or people. New and better housing reflected a fundamental change in the production system. With the profitable spread of cotton culture in the Deep South and the accompanying rise in the market value of slaves farther north, it was natural for this change to include improved housing for those valuable workers, provided by the Shelbys and Augustine St. Clares of the South if not the Simon Legrees. The extent to which slaves may or may not have profited from model housing remains to be studied in an analytical manner.

Our attempt to describe with some precision the physical character of life at a Chesapeake slave quarter before the nineteenth-century improvements in workers' housing occurred was the most demanding part of the project. By searching for evidence of how the system looked, we increasingly recognized how it was altered. The gradual change from crowding people into temporary shelters and corners of work buildings to providing securable and separate domestic environments for some slaves is one aspect of evolution from a system that threw workers at their tasks in relatively direct and uncritical ways to one that aimed at extracting maximum production by employing more complex, self-conscious strategies for managing labor resources.

Debate over the extent of white hegemony and black resistance can be usefully considered in the context of this change. Material culture scholars have conscien-

244

tiously joined documentary historians to counter what they see as too sweeping an evaluation by Kenneth M. Stampp and Stanley M. Elkins of the devastation that slavery caused to African Americans (Vlach 1978; Sobel 1987). Chesapeake archaeology has slowly delivered on the promise of evidence for non-European cultural remnants (Singleton 1991). More will be forthcoming from further excavations, yet the arguments have already become more subtle, with emphasis shifting from surviving vestiges of Old World culture to the culture created here (McKee 1987). It is now more obvious than it once seemed that both slaves and owners acted in diverse ways within a creolized world. Some owners employed popularly acclaimed methods of extracting the most capital, and others continued the old traditions of minimal investment. Slaves neither universally capitulated nor rebelled by every means available. Construction of model housing represented increased control as well as potentially improved comfort and health (McKee 1992).[2] It has been suggested that the storage pits dug below eighteenth-century slave houses provided a degree of secrecy for the houses' occupants, although the integral manner in which the features were incorporated into some contemporary owners' houses and many superior nineteenth-century kitchens argues against their being literally secret creations. Further, the relative abundance of storage pits found in seventeenth-century buildings argues against their being solely African American in origin (Kelso 1984b; Yentsch 1991; Sanford 1991a; Chambers 1992). Surviving Chesapeake slave houses reveal relatively few modifications made by occupants before the Civil War. It was in the postbellum era that the most visible change took place, in a time when rural workers resisted sharing duplexes and expected better-finished houses as well as a degree of privacy and more rooms for their families. This does not mean that resistance was slight but that it often lacked physical reflections capable of being recognized by present fieldworkers. Alice Walker reminds us that personal and ethnic identity can be strongly expressed in physical ways that leave little record (Walker 1983).

People can determine their own means of thinking and acting without necessarily constructing or changing the buildings and landscapes they inhabit (Upton 1991). Yet visualizing those environments is a means toward understanding their world. And the museum has an unique capacity to deliver this kind of learning, while the academy is often restricted to abstract presentation.

At Carter's Grove we have used the physical setting to portray a delicate negotiation between Burwell's control and the occupants' resistance (Epperson 1990b). Burwell is seen as having determined the form of the houses, their placement and orientation, and details that reflect his concern for economy in construction, as well as his sense of the occupants' community hierarchy. The buildings are all recognizably Chesapeake in technology and form, though they are more cheaply built than most surviving quarters.

Two generations of structures portray a move toward separate households for family groups, though even at the date of this late colonial portrait, most rooms are not occupied solely by family members. In form, all three of the dwellings resemble Anglo-American single-room houses (Glassie 1975; Herman 1984), two of them doubled to form pairs of independent rooms for multiple households—a form that marked much housing for workers into the third quarter of the nineteenth century (see fig. 12.1). As depicted by the reconstruction, the only group not sharing a house with others is the foreman's family, which occupies a single-room house with a sleeping loft. One of the duplexes also has a loft, but this is intended for the storage of fodder rather than as extended space for workers to occupy. The foreman's house is superior in several other details such as the construction of shuttered windows and a wooden chimney, but its superiority in Burwell's eye is most clearly expressed in its site, slightly elevated over the rest of the quarter and standing between the houses of slaves and owner. The foreman's modest access to money and goods is also illustrated by the greater number and variety of household objects in his house, though all the spaces are furnished with what seems disturbingly little to twentieth-century visitors. Few tables and chairs are in sight, though there is evidence of some amusement (a fiddle) and power (powder and gunshot) (fig. 12.3). Oddly, the building for storing corn is slightly better built than the houses. The careful observer can find a few overtly African articles (for example, a mortar used as a drum), but the overall appearance is of a creolized Chesapeake community.

It is not an entirely owner-dominated community. While the occupants have left the structures much as they (and their forebears) were directed to build them, some visually subtle but socially significant changes are apparent. All three houses were built with the same orientation, facing the James River, using the site as almost any eighteenth-century Anglo-Virginian would do. As a result, the front of the old duplex faces the back of the newer one, providing a degree of separation among the people occupying the various rooms. But an occupant of one of the houses has cut a doorway in its back wall, creating direct access to shared outside space (fig. 12.4). Without radically altering the buildings, the residents have reordered the environment to form a more physically integrated community. The character of the ground and accumulation of detritus, as well as the presence of staff and museum visitors, demonstrate that the area between the two houses is where much activity takes place. What Burwell intended as a yard for the second house is left vacant.

Tending gardens and fowl are among the best-documented independent activities in which Chesapeake slaves participated. At the Carter's Grove quarter, we employed a fragmentary posthole pattern to develop several round, fenced areas that enclose chicken yards and gardens, while—less overtly—forming limits for the common area between the houses. In addition to giving a sense of enclosure to the yard without closing it off, the fences to a degree shield activities there from the outside world, including the foreman and owner (fig. 12.5).

The fences are more demonstrably African-American than the houses—one scholar from Elmina has suggested that they represent a fusion of central and southern Ghanaian traditional fences—but there is reason to believe that some poor Anglo-Virginians also constructed cheap, round enclosures with wattled vines and riven pales. Still, the image of little impermanent Anglo-American houses doubled in order to economize on labor, bracketed by fenced garden plots and chicken yards that could as easily be in West Africa, suggests a web of competing authorities as well as the influence of different cultures.

Although also a slave, the foreman has a complex role to perform in balancing his personal interests against those of his owner and fellow workers. Some of that tension is suggested by the landscape of his house. Already removed from the residential center of the quarter he oversees, he has chosen to create further distance by using a fence to enclose a European-style yard around his house. The construction of the fence is not significantly different from those of his neighbors, but its function is markedly so. Still, the foreman's household is proximately and materially close to those of other slaves, and worlds apart from that of the Burwells.

Modern museum research is not carried out in an intellectual vacuum. Historians Gloria Main and Alan Kulikoff have analyzed in detail living conditions and family relations under slavery, and architectural historian Dell Upton has offered a probing interpretation of the differing ways blacks and whites used the landscape in their negotiation of racial politics (Main 1982; Kulikoff 1986; Upton 1985 and 1990). Much of the discussion that African-American archaeology has generated has addressed issues of cultural conflict and power relations (e.g., Orser 1988a, 1988b). Bringing such interpretive perspectives together with new data, museum presentations can help historians and anthropologists penetrate further into precisely what the changing spectrum of living conditions was, what aspects of those conditions slaves and owners controlled in different times and places, and why particular choices were made. While one need not be a museum scholar to explore certain issues, the special needs of the museum sometimes can usefully direct inquiry. By offering a re-creation of something as elusive as an eighteenth-century Virginia quarter—assuming the re-creation is based on good research and lively debate—the museum creates a literal image against which both scholars and the public can test their ideas and sharpen their perceptions. The limited nature of the eighteenth-century evidence makes the product all the more provocative. The hypothetical quality of this re-created scene does not diminish its value as a means of advancing scholarly dialogue while making it accessible to a much broader audience; rather, it helps form useful questions.[3]

For example, how were patterns of cooking and eating affected by the apparent proliferation of separate dwellings concomitant with the development of African-

American families? One of the few articles regularly provided to slaves by eighteenth- and nineteenth-century owners was a cooking pot for each household. Were the pots used individually or communally? Was the eating directed by slaves individualized or divided among groups? How did the social elements of cooking and eating change over time and place, and what attitudes or external factors affected the change? Such questions address the nature of life at the quarter and the degree to which slaves rejected European-American standards and constructed their own community in opposition to white hegemony. People might occupy Anglo-looking houses in a very non-Anglo manner.

Given the remote and mysterious quality of eighteenth-century Chesapeake slavery—and the fact that the Carter's Grove site had no surviving buildings, very fragmentary archaeological remains, and relatively poor documentation—the project is also useful as a demonstration of how much a museum can do with a historically elusive topic. It has been possible to portray particular circumstances at Carter's Grove and focus somewhat on the specific people who lived there, while creating a broader portrait of domestic circumstances and political relations. Consider how much easier museums could teach about slavery in the late antebellum era, a period rich in surviving buildings and records. For researchers with access to extensive documentation of family relationships and who occupied which house, a site like Somerset plantation in Washington County, North Carolina, offers the opportunity to tell a much more detailed and compelling story (Redford 1988).

## The Dangers of Involving Museums

There are substantial dangers inherent in allowing museums to frame our perceptions of the past. Museums are notoriously conservative in what they are willing to present because of fears that frank, dismal portrayals will frighten away a clientele in search of fine furniture and pretty gardens. Their boards are often unbalanced in favor of financial rather than intellectual weight, and museum bureaucracy often produces its own programmatic inertia.

History museums in the South have a particularly bad name for cultivating a romantic view of slavery and a benign view of racism. Passive "mammy" figures have disappeared from most open-hearth kitchen displays, and much of the related prose has been excised from museum guidebooks. Nevertheless, the pervasiveness of museum racism remains evident in ahistorical products like "darkie" spoon holders and "Mulberry Row Bearnaise Mix," both still available in museum shops. The first is overtly racist; the second is irresponsibly romantic. Nostalgia has become a safe haven for racist caricatures of slave life, and many museums continue to promote this sort of ignorance.[4]

Ironically, the well-intentioned caution of enlightened staff, those same thought-ful people who support the presentation of controversial subjects, can also be inju-rious. It is not difficult to see why a full-size, three-dimensional portrayal interpreted by live teachers on an original slave quarter site could be a more frightening prospect than written analysis. The charmingly subversive historian Rhys Isaac suggests guer-rilla warfare as a metaphor for Chesapeake slavery, and he argues that such horrific relations cannot be plausibly "re-created" in the museum (Isaac 1985, 1990). Even when the museum deals with indirect forms of labor control such as housing and food provisions rather than corporal punishment, there is a very strong tendency toward caution, toward a little less full and frank exposition than was actually the case in the lives of ordinary people. The motive is not necessarily a desire to white-wash an abusive system like Chesapeake slavery: if this were the only problem, it would be relatively easy to identify and counter. In fact, a much more common impediment is staff concern that in showing the unvarnished realities of ordinary life in the preindustrial past, we will seem to condemn those people least empow-ered to affect their own material circumstances. Dirty rooms and the absence of specialized furniture, for example, can send unintended and false messages about ordinary people's abilities and desire to overcome their circumstance (Chappell 1989b). Motivated by concern that museum visitors, like antebellum slaveholders, will blame slaves for "the condition of their houses, and the manner in which they live" (Draughon 1850:66), even some of the most tough-minded members of the Carter's Grove interpretive staff have lobbied for keeping the houses and landscape at the quarter cleaner and trimmer than archaeology suggests was usual. For all the apparent radicalism of the new buildings' designs, the site exhibits little evidence of the refuse, disorder, and smells suggested by the artifact-filled strata at the Kingsmill, Monticello, and other excavated quarters. Increasingly I notice the weeds are trimmed back and the debris left from construction is discreetly carried away. In 1988 and 1989 we built the wooden chimneys and log walls with clay infill, a choice that resulted in the same deterioration and need for seasonal maintenance common to the eighteenth century. Modern hard mortars have since been added, destroying the unevenness and mutability that previously characterized the buildings.

Indeed, precisely how well to maintain the scene has been debated among those staffing and administering the site since before it opened to the public. While some of the urge to cleanse our portrait of eighteenth-century life is understandably linked to concern for safety and conservation, a stronger force seems to be the fear that twentieth-century visitors can be taken only so far, and that preindustrial squalor will divert attention from more essential issues of race relations and per-sonal survival. Similarly, there exists the worry that limited visibility of physical resistance to forced labor may lead visitors to conclude that slaves supinely acquiesced and the concern that suggestions of self-determination within the community are too subtle to be taken in by many observers. Levels of maintenance and the means of handling trash are significant characteristics of peoples' lives, ones that have changed dramatically in the last 250 years. For archaeologists, trash disposal constitutes one of the most important patterns available for analysis. Reproducing refuse at a site like the Carter's Grove quarter may, then, represent more than a fetish for authentic detail. But could interpreters be right in arguing that these are details too minor to be of primary importance in engaging people to think about slaves yet so unsettling as to divert people from that effort? Further, why should exhibitions of African Americans' experiences focus on the messiness of life in the past, when sites illustrating the ways of European Americans are commonly kept much more manicured than they were originally? Almost all museum presentations cleanse the scenes they purport to reproduce accurately. Costumed black interpreters at sites like Carter's Grove already face tremendous emotional and intellectual demands in telling a difficult story to a predominately white and sometimes unsympathetic audience (Ellis 1992). Why stack the deck against them?

The fear that unpleasant historical reality will encourage museum visitors to blame the victims is not confined to the treatment of slavery. I heard the same concerns expressed in a discussion of how nineteenth- and twentieth-century immigrants would be portrayed at the Lower East Side Tenement Museum in New York City. Staff members shared worries that squalid surroundings might be equated with innate inferiority of the tenants. There, planners feel compelled to present a vision of tenement life in which, despite adversity, people maintained their domestic environments with a degree of neatness acceptable to modern middle-class observers. It is well known from photographs and fiction that sweatshops and boardinghouses could be packed with people who had little opportunity to create seemly domestic environments. Such scenes may be slow to appear in museums, even one with the laudable aims of the Tenement Museum. But selective presentation is a problem that is especially pertinent to the subject of slavery. It is a problem we need to wrestle with thoughtfully, finding ways to tell the simple truths while helping our audiences understand the more complex realities of which they were a part. Otherwise, the history that museums present will indeed be sweet but insubstantial fare, less thought-provoking and less truthful than that found in the literature.

## Overcoming the Dangers and Inertia of Museums

The difficulties inherent in presenting accurate museum portraits need to be surmounted because the lives of enslaved and free African Americans are essential subjects for museums dealing with the early South. These are not optional or supporting stories; they are central to what we teach. Different museums should deal with race relations in different ways. I would not suggest that all southern open-air history museums reconstruct a quarter like that at Carter's Grove, which is intended to represent a specific kind of community at a specific date. Further, it is not the right choice financially or intellectually for every restored town or plantation in the Chesapeake. Churches, great houses shared by blacks and whites, and workers' housing of recent vintage can contribute to the understanding of diverse lifeways. Winston-Salem's derelict St. Philip's Church—built by an African-American congregation in 1861—can more graphically portray the changing relationship between slaves and the Moravian white community than could a re-created scene of domestic life at Old Salem. Likewise, the postemancipation tenant houses surviving on farms across the South offer generous opportunities to deal with the change and continuity in an oppressive economic structure.

Traditional museum media like exhibit cases and texts also can deliver consequential lessons. One of the most remarkable developments in the museum presentation of slavery was the show "Before Freedom Came: African-American Life in the Antebellum South" mounted by—of all places—the Museum of the Confederacy in Richmond. The idea caused some initial fear that the subject would be manipulated by an institution hardly known for its liberal social agenda. However, the exhibition—illustrated by a rich collection of objects and images, most of which had not been widely seen before (Campbell and Rice 1991)—provided sober analysis of the system and its toll on the lives of slaves.

Smaller fragments of the slaves' story are increasingly evident at museums that have traditionally ignored or romanticized their lives. The exhibition at the Monticello visitors' center featuring a normal week's ration for Thomas Jefferson's slaves offers a simple but very powerful message about the relative amounts of food that both masters supplied and slaves acquired for themselves. Original artifacts, whether vast landscapes or small personal articles, can convey past realities more effectively than can the statistical abstractions of tenured cliometricians.[5] When considered in light of other objects found on Chesapeake slave sites, a single cowrie shell, for example—possibly brought from Africa and discovered by the archaeologists working on Mulberry Row at Monticello—provides an eloquent suggestion of the continued vitality of some African cultural affectations on Jefferson's mountaintop (Kelso 1986b). The same seems to be true of what may be Mancala gaming pieces found at Poplar Forest, the other Virginia house of Jefferson and his slaves (Patten 1992a, 1992b).

Despite the ability of such small items to transport the imagination, the re-creation of whole historical environments remains one of the most effective means we have of teaching a history that has now become almost incomprehensible.

Although it is evident how much thoughtful research has been done on slavery at Monticello, we should recognize that in employing the great house and its landscape to present Thomas Jefferson while using only a few museum cases and a brochure to deal with his slaves, the museum is denying its most potent medium to black Americans.

If a museum chooses to use reconstructions to represent, for example, Jefferson's garden house because it is pretty and safe, or the oculus over his dome room because it is technologically interesting, but not those threatening or less attractive environments occupied by slaves, then we must question the intentions behind these exhibits. Perhaps reconstruction of the chronologically relevant parts of Mulberry Row should wait until we know more about the workforce from excavations at outlying quarters, although archaeological and documentary evidence for what these buildings were like is already plentiful, and more Mulberry Row archaeology does not seem imminent at Monticello. There are, however, very easy and useful steps the Thomas Jefferson Memorial Foundation can take in the meantime. Surviving in Monticello's south range are workers' dwellings for which relatively detailed records of occupancy exist, and there are at least two workers' rooms in the main cellar, all directly accessible from exhibition areas. For the museum to continue using these intact spaces for redundant toilets, break rooms, and storage is, frankly, outrageous. As much as the Monticello excavations have contributed to the scholarship on the material world of Chesapeake slavery, one wonders why the organization has expended so much money and effort on research if it will resist employing what the archaeology and documentary analysis offer.[6]

The candid discussion of slavery seems particularly pertinent in Jefferson's case because of all he represents in terms of republicanism, revolutionary thought, and racism. Jefferson's ambiguous feelings toward black people and slavery make the subject essential to the portrayal of life and thought at Monticello. Equally relevant is consideration of Jefferson's choices about workers' housing, including log cabins with wooden chimneys located just beyond the genteel compound, a stone temple-fronted quarter, and rooms visually suppressed and made part of grand symmetrical schemes for ordering the master's world (Gruber 1991; Shumate 1991). The choices reveal a role that is both exceptional and representative of his milieu. Jefferson was at once an eighteenth-century Chesapeake gentry plantation owner and a nineteenth-century agrarian manager (Sanford 1991b).[7] While pursuing efficiency and maximization of profit with energetic planning and record keeping, Jefferson moved his slaves through diverse kinds of housing. Despite his preference for incorporating the Monticello quarters into a visually coherent and rational design, he never built model housing of the familiar nineteenth-century variety. Rather, he most closely approximated the practices of his fellow slaveholders when he built cheap log houses on Mulberry Row. Jefferson's decisions about slave housing, like those about his own housing, were at once idiosyncratic and representative of a changing norm (Wenger 1991).

The Carter's Grove story finds added dimensions at Monticello, where the black community experienced the new managerial system of slaveholding, and where a more provocative intellect was present. The benefits of grappling with the issues likewise seem greater at Monticello.

On a more emotional level, it is harder to break free from the feeling that Monticello is about only one individual, to admit that Jefferson and his family constituted a racial minority on their property.[8] I concede that it may be easier to share Nathaniel Burwell's landscape with those who built it than Jefferson's. But the problem of whether or not to confront slavery, or even substantially acknowledge racial diversity, is not confined to Monticello. Recently I talked with a bright young curator at a well-financed gentry house museum in eastern Virginia. She explained to me, with much pride, how she had just rearranged her furnishings to reflect the eighteenth-century social uses of rooms suggested by a surviving inventory. She was in one case able to remove a long-admired but inappropriate piece of furniture because, happily, it would not fit through the door to its intended room. I accepted this as correct curatorial behavior and asked—naively, not censoriously—about a small first-floor room that the inventory suggested was occupied by a domestic worker, presumably a slave. The ground quickly shifted. This intelligent, educated professional looked me squarely in the eye and responded that neither she nor her director was likely ever to furnish that room in the spartan manner the inventory suggested. She explained, further, that while the principal rooms would follow the inventory, the house was actually a decorative arts museum, not a museum about the family that once lived there.

Obviously, there is a substantial flaw in the logic of this argument. More to the point, the argument reflects an attitude that is profoundly political, in that it persists in excluding people as well as things that do not meet certain effete criteria. I use the example because for all its apparent irrationality, it is actually much more representative of the norm among American museums than is Monticello, where at least one can see evidence of much thought and hard work. By consistently presenting scenes made possible by an extremely unequal class structure while omitting everything except the genteel activities of those most benefiting from the structure, such museums are what their harshest critics say: less educational institutions than stones in the hegemonic walls of elite culture.

Finally, I should not let my own employer off the hook. While the re-created slave quarter at Carter's Grove may break new ground and raise some challenges, it does not entirely fulfill the need for more realistic historical environments and more demanding programs in Williamsburg. Despite the presence of the quarter, the eighteenth-century insane asylum, and the beginnings of an industrial site, Williamsburg still has far to go before we have the settings necessary to teach a broadly representative history. Why do we show only poor blacks, for example, and no whites below the level of affluent craftsmen and taverners? Where among our depictions is unskilled labor, debt, or even the degree of environmental disorder familiar in Hogarth's prints, not to mention the garbage commonly uncovered by Chesapeake archaeology? Richly appointed parlors still vastly outnumber rude domestic spaces of the kind occupied by most people, white and black, in early Virginia. We increasingly recognize that many of the eighteenth-century townspeople were tenants, renting all or parts of houses, but this has not affected the choice of houses open to the public. The score remains: affluent homeowners 6, tenants 0. Landscape design and maintenance policies reinforce the impression that every white occupant of the town was comfortably in control of his or her piece of the suburb. Still, the physical expression of racial and economic relations within the community is the most elusive subject for a museum like Williamsburg. The presence of free blacks is dealt with only indirectly, and the role of Native Americans in the capital is virtually ignored.

One of the subjects discussed in classes with the staff at the Carter's Grove quarter was the similarity in quality between much housing for Chesapeake whites and that of the re-created slave houses.[9] Interpreter Felix Simmons uses this point effectively on the job. When a group of white Virginians arrives at the site, he asks how many are descended from Carters, Lees, Randolphs, or other exalted gentry families. Seldom do more than a handful step forward. To the others, he dramatically announces "Welcome home!" and proceeds to describe the living conditions of ordinary whites in the same era. This offers an unexpected revelation for most museum goers, without diluting his principal observations on slavery. On the other hand, Simmons's imaginative technique is as limited as Monticello's Plexiglas-case treatment of slave life. It is a well-articulated point, but to be fully appreciated and believed it needs to be illustrated on the land. Because visitors' impressions of life at Williamsburg and Monticello are so strongly affected by the environments they see there, the alternative perspectives offered by a single written or spoken text seem overwhelmed by the appearance of unassailable reality. While the consensus text embedded in the principal restored and re-created environments need not eclipse what Simmons and his colleagues have to say, those scenes keep the interpretation at the Carter's Grove quarter literally a minority story.

The African-American program at Colonial Williamsburg is strong and active, and some of its offerings are sufficiently shocking to require warning labels about parental discretion (Ellis 1990). A dramatic presentation called "The Runaway" at the Benjamin Powell property directly confronts the impact of racism on the lives of eighteenth-century blacks and whites. The result comes close to Isaac's chilling metaphor of guerrilla warfare, and both actors and museum goers say that it is extremely successful. Miscegenation has become a common topic on the street, and other aspects of life in Williamsburg's slave community are presented on the properties owned by tavern keeper Henry Wetherburn and Mayor Thomas Everard. Yet the kind of physical settings that would bring the most attention and convey a sense of veracity to such programs remain largely undeveloped, and substantial treatment of slavery remains absent from most exhibition sites.

Despite historian Cary Carson's claim of victory for everyday things and people at the American museum, there remains limited use of artifacts to plumb even white social relations in the streets of Williamsburg or elsewhere (Carson 1990, 1991). Certainly there is reason for satisfaction in the increased use of material culture to present social relations among affluent Americans. This is insufficient, though, both as museum education and as the kind of research we know museums can pursue. Taken in its modern museum context, the Carter's Grove quarter seems exceptional, with little planning under way to make it part of a broader scene.

I have great affection for Williamsburg as well as for Monticello, but affection should not be confused with thoughtless devotion. Perhaps the more affection we have for our museums, the more we need to confront their shortcomings. My intention is not to bemoan our limitations but to point out the need for consequential progress. I am relatively optimistic about change but impatient with how long it takes in coming.

Chesapeake history and material culture scholarship, more than the New England community studies of a previous generation, has grown up around museums. Increasingly such institutions fund research in order to enliven their public programs. Part of our responsibility as museum employees is to help the institutions find means of implementing that research, ensuring that it is not left asleep on the shelf.

The special blindness of museums toward race relations is a pervasive problem that scholars and museum administrators need to address. It is time to deal with the essential issues of social structure in the past, as difficult and unpleasant as they may often seem. It is time to examine our own motives for working in museums and to help our visitors confront the effects those past structures still have on them today. In the end, the history we write and display will be vastly improved. We have nothing to lose but our complacency.

## Notes

A briefer version of this chapter was read at the conference "Re-creating the World of the Virginia Plantation, 1750–1820," sponsored by the University of Virginia and the Thomas Jefferson Memorial Foundation, Charlottesville, 2 June 1990. For thoughtful discussion and help with editing, I am indebted to Cary Carson, Willie Graham, Vanessa Patrick, Drake Patten, Susan Williams, and especially Mark R. Wenger.

1. Remember, for example, how C. Vann Woodward's *The Strange Career of Jim Crow* (1955)

helped Kennedy-era Americans recognize that segregation was not necessarily an immutable institution.

2. Material culture scholars who utilize Gramscian interpretation of buildings as part of a system intended to control labor are supported by the arguments of farm journal correspondents, who suggest using everything from improved housing to music as means of motivating and disciplining slaves. Among the management techniques offered to journal readers by a Georgia physician in 1860 is that Fourth of July farm festivals "may be made a powerful controlling power in the management of negroes, by having it understood that the dinner is a mere gratuity to be given or withheld according to merit or demerit." Clarifying his point, the doctor continued, "With the prospect of the 'big dinner' ahead, they will be greatly animated and encouraged in their labors; and the fear of losing it will often be more effective in keeping such childish and sensual creatures 'straight' than the terrors of the rod itself" (Wilson 1860:367).

3. I have discussed the degree to which the portrait is hypothetical in Chappell, "Re-creation of the Carter's Grove Quarter and the Archaeology of American Slavery" (1990). What is demonstrably evident from analysis of the site and what is constructed beyond that evidence is freely admitted at the site, without apologies. The same should be done at older reconstructions, particularly those built on assumptions that have come to be accepted as fact.

4. In 1989 an exceptional show called "Jim Crow: Racism and Reaction in the New South—Richmond, 1865–1940" at the Valentine Museum in the old capital of the Confederacy began with a section that employed similar commercial objects to help the observer develop a definition for racism (Chappell 1989a). Alas, more such material remains for sale in shops than in exhibits about racial stereotyping.

5. W. B. Yeats: "We taste and feel and see the truth. We do not reason ourselves into it."

6. Monticello recently has developed a special Plantation Community Tour that includes the vacant sites of Mulberry Row slave quarters was implemented in 1995. Despite this effort, most visitors who tour the house and grounds at Monticello confront very little information on slavery.

7. The duc de La Rochefoucauld-Liancourt's 1796 description of slave management at Monticello is relevant here: "His negroes are nourished, clothed, and treated as well as white servants could be. As he cannot expect any assistance from the two small neighboring towns, every article is made on his farm; his negroes are cabinetmakers, carpenters, masons, bricklayers, smiths, &c. The children he employs in a nail-manufactory, which yields already a considerable profit. The young and old negresses spin for the clothing of the rest. He animates them by rewards and distinctions; in fine, his superior mind directs the management of his domestic concerns with the same abilities, activity, and regularity, which he evinced in the conduct of public affairs, and which he is calculated to display in every situation of life" (La Rochefoucauld-Liancourt 1799:2:80).

8. The public is generally allowed to overlook the fact that Jefferson was no modest slaveholder. He owned upwards of two hundred slaves through much of his adult life; he bought slaves and sold others to pay debts and rid himself of troublesome workers (Miller 1977).

9. The poor quality of much white as well as black housing has been a favorite topic for students of the Chesapeake's vernacular architecture. See Dell Upton (1978, 1980); Wells (1987); Chappell (1994).

12.1. Re-created Carter's Grove slave quarter. (Courtesy of the Colonial Williamsburg Foundation, photograph by Thomas E. Green)

12.2. Mid-nineteenth-century slave houses at Ben Venue, Rappahannock County, Va. (Courtesy of the Colonial Williamsburg Foundation, photograph by Edward A. Chappell)

12.3. A room at re-created Carter's Grove quarter shown as occupied by a slave named Old Paris who had use of a gun. (Courtesy of the Colonial Williamsburg Foundation, photograph by Dave Doody)

12.4. Rear of a house at re-created Carter's Grove quarter, shown with a door cut by one of its occupants. (Courtesy of the Colonial Williamsburg Foundation, photograph by Vanessa E. Patrick)

12.5. Fences around chicken yards and gardens, shielding the shared space at Carter's Grove quarter. (Courtesy of the Colonial Williamsburg Foundation, photograph by Edward A. Chappell).

# Part III

# Beyond the Plantation

# 13

# Fort Mosé: Earliest Free African-American Town in the United States

## *Kathleen A. Deagan and Jane Landers*

Fort Mosé—or Gracia Real de Santa Teresa de Mosé—was established near St. Augustine, Florida, in 1738 and is generally held to be the first legally sanctioned free black town in the United States. Since 1986 it has been the focus of a multidisciplinary historical archaeology research program carried out by the Florida Museum of Natural History and funded by the State of Florida. Our discussion describes the inception and chronological development of the Mosé project, summarizes the most pertinent documentary and archaeological information, and concludes with some of the insights gained through the Fort Mosé project.

### Context and Development of the Fort Mosé Project

Research at Fort Mosé has been erratic and frequently plagued by misunderstanding and bias. The ruined fort site was still in evidence as late as 1860, when the U.S. Geological Survey (USGS) coastal survey by Orr noted the ruins on a map of that year. In the early part of this century, the St. Augustine Historical Society placed a commemorative marker at the correct location and purchased the site, but by 1965 it was decided that this was, in fact, not the site of Mosé (see Arana 1973).

The property was purchased in 1968 by F. E. Williams III, a resident of St. Augustine and avocational military historian, who believed that the location of the historical society marker (in spite of the society's disclaimer) was in fact the correct site of Mosé. In 1971 Williams contacted the late Professor Charles Fairbanks of the University of Florida about the site, and Fairbanks brought the University of Florida archaeological field school to Mosé for a two-day test project. The work verified that mid-eighteenth-century remains were deposited at the southernmost portion of Williams's property, and Fairbanks concluded that this was the probable location of Fort Mosé (Spencer 1972).

A more extensive survey was carried out in 1976 by the Florida State University archaeological field school under the direction of Kathleen Deagan, who had been a first-year graduate student at Fairbank's field school. The 1976 work confirmed Fairbank's original suggestions. It also eliminated from consideration several other areas of the property that yielded no remains from more than a hundred subsurface tests.

It was not until 1985 that ongoing efforts to secure funding for the extensive excavation of Mosé were successful. In that year Florida state representative Bill Clark of Fort Lauderdale visited the site and was both moved and impressed by its importance to African-American history. After discussions with Florida Museum staff, Clark introduced a bill in the Florida legislature that provided funds for the historical and scientific study of Fort Mosé. That work began in 1986, with Deagan serving as principal investigator.

The first six months of the project were devoted to historical research by Jane Landers (1987, 1988) and were followed by two field and lab seasons (1987–88) under the direction of Deagan and the supervision of John Marron of the University of Florida (Marron 1988, 1989).

It is noteworthy that the original impetus for interest in the site—for landowner Williams as well as for nearly all previous owners and researchers—was the Anglo-American military significance of Mosé, rather than the fact that it was the first legally sanctioned free African-American community in the country. We comment upon this because it has been a significant factor in the social and political context of our research at Mosé and has affected the way that research has been conducted.

Two historical events provided the focus for most public interest in the Mosé site before the current project. We might even speculate that the data leading to the location and identification of the site might not have been available or preserved had it not been for these other events in Mosé's history. The first occurred in 1740, during Oglethorpe's raid on St. Augustine. Mosé was captured and occupied by Colonel John Palmer of Oglethorpe's force. A short time later the Spaniards and their Indian and African-American allies captured and destroyed the fort. This battle was a turning point in the raid, ending in Oglethorpe's retreat.

Some seventy-two years later, during the territorial period in Florida, Mosé was again used as a base camp for Anglo-Americans hoping to capture Florida. This time it was the "Florida Patriots," a group of Americans who, during the war of 1812, unsuccessfully tried to capture Florida for the United States (Patrick 1949). It is interesting to note that on this occasion African-American militias operating as guerrillas were Spain's most effective force on the frontier (Landers 1988).

Both of these events have loomed large in local interest in Mosé. Although the presence of a black community was acknowledged, it did not figure importantly in the research at Mosé until the 1970s. St. Augustine has had a troubled history of race relations over the past century (Colburn 1987), and negative reaction to the presence of a very important site in African-American history continues to the present. Both Deagan and Landers have been accused publicly of fabricating spurious research in order to revise history, as well as of placing artifacts in a nonexistent site (letter of William Walton, *St. Augustine Record*, 1 Jan. 1989; "Woman Challenges Archaeologist's Findings on Fort Mosé," ibid., 12 Dec. 1987; "Ms. Houston Contends Her Property Was Site of Historic Fort Mosé," ibid., 1 Nov. 1989).

We must in fairness point out that these attitudes reflect the positions of a small, vocal group of residents, and that there has also been considerable support for and interest in the project, particularly among the historical organizations and the African-American community in St. Augustine. It is evident, however, that the idea that free African Americans made important contributions to the defense and culture of St. Augustine is an unfamiliar and difficult concept for many residents, for whom slavery remains the dominant (if not exclusive) paradigm for black history.

The current stage of the project is intended to begin correcting this situation, on both the local and the national level. Funds were secured from the legislature in 1987 to prepare a large traveling exhibit on Fort Mosé and African-American colonial history in Florida. The exhibit opened in February 1991 at the Florida Museum of Natural History, and after touring nationally—accompanied by curriculum materials for primary schools, brochures, tabletop exhibits, and a video—it will take its place among the permanent exhibits there. Since the opening of the exhibition, a monograph (Deagan and MacMahon 1995) geared toward a general audience has been published which nicely complements the exhibition. Those working on the Fort Mosé project share the strong mandate and commitment of our many colleagues working in African-American history and archaeology to translate and disseminate—without delay and in popular and accessible formats—the results of scholarly research.

### Research at Mosé

The focus of research at Mosé has been the African-Spanish occupation of 1738–63, although both documentary and archaeological evidence for the many previous and subsequent occupations, spanning the period of ca. 1500 B.C. to A.D. 1850, has been recovered and recorded. The investigation of Mosé has been a continuous exchange and interplay between historical and scientific inquiry, with each data category informing the other at different stages. It was, for example, the specific needs of the archaeological program that provided the impetus and resources for the historical research on Mosé. This research, furthermore, emphasized certain spatial and environmental elements that might not typically have been part of a historical research project—land alteration activities, postoccupation impacts, and a strong focus on physical and environmental data, for example.

The documentary research in the Archivo General de Indias, in Seville, the Archivo Nacional in Madrid, and the Archivo General de Simancas, all in Spain, and in the superb microfilm collections of Spanish documents at the P. K. Yonge Library of Florida History at the University of Florida was carried out before the archaeological work and provided the basis from which the archaeological field research program was designed. Hypotheses regarding the site's location, configuration, and postabandonment alteration were developed from the historical data; and appropriate recovery strategies were designed to locate the kinds of ephemeral architectural and material remains documented in the historical research.

This interplay has continued in subsequent stages of the project. Once the site was located and uncovered, for example, the documentary information about the fort itself was sufficiently detailed to allow direct comparison with the archaeological remains, and this permitted the site to be verified beyond doubt or disclaimer as Mosé. Archaeological information obtained from remote sensing and used in combination with historic maps allowed us to more specifically identify the excavated site as the second Fort Mosé and to locate the first Fort Mosé—facts unappreciated before the project began. And the archeological remains have, predictably, provided a means of assessing and verifying the reliability of a series of maps on which Mosé and the St. Augustine landscape were depicted over the years.

The archaeological remains—when considered in the context of the historical data—have also informed our understanding of ecology and environment at the site and of the dramatic but largely undocumented ecological changes that have occurred there since Mosé was occupied. Analysis and reanalysis of documentary maps and accounts have verified that Mosé was surrounded by farmland during the period of occupation by blacks. Today the second fort is surrounded by inundated marshlands, and the first fort is underwater. These findings have important implications for the overall study of sea-level rise in Florida and its potential impact on human settlement in the state.

The archaeological research at Mosé, however, has contributed far less than has the documentary information to what we know specifically about the lifeways and community at the black town. To date, the most important contributions of the research project at Fort Mosé have been the identification and verification of the site, the reconstruction of its physical setting, the recovery of a somewhat limited array of material remains from the black occupation, and the sponsorship of the archival research that has given us most of the substantive details of life at Mosé that we now know.

Both the historical research and archaeological verification were costly and time-consuming; however, they were essential, we contend, because of the community context within which we conducted research into Mosé. Local reluctance to identify and commemorate Mosé as an African-American town made it critically important to establish beyond doubt that this site was the Gracia Real de Santa Teresa de Mosé known to historians, and a greater-than-usual proportion of project resources was devoted to this objective.

## Archival Background

Relatively little archival research into Florida's African-American colonial community had taken place before Landers's doctoral research and subsequent work as historian on the Fort Mosé project (we acknowledge here the pioneering work of Irene Wright [1939], John TePaske [1975], and Luis Arana [1973]). Florida's "borderland" location between Anglo North America and the Spanish Empire to the south and west as well as its misleading but long-lived reputation as a stagnant backwater has meant that few scholars of either North American or Latin American colonial history have thought it worthy of study. Research on colonial Florida is at an added disadvantage in that most of the primary materials are in seventeenth- and eighteenth-century Spanish, and many are in Spain. Moreover, because of the biases and interests of royal officials who generated the historical record, documentary evidence for the underclass is difficult to "unearth," often being scattered throughout a wide variety of archival record groups. Nevertheless, the variety of historical documentation available for Mosé—including a census; maps; treasury accounts; militia lists; baptism, marriage, and death registers; petitions to the governor and the king; and other civil and judicial records—is in stark contrast to that available for Africans in many other European colonies. The Spanish colonial records represent an important patrimony for a people too long considered "voiceless" or pathologically affected by the slave experience. They are an affirmation of African presence—as tangible as the artifacts uncovered at Mosé.

## Mosé's History

Mosé was born of the initiative and determination of Africans who, at great risk, manipulated the extended Anglo-Spanish conflict over the "debatable lands" between St. Augustine and Charleston to their own advantage. The community was composed of former slaves who escaped from British plantations and made their way south to Spanish Florida, where eventually they secured their freedom. That they became free was not unusual, for Spanish law and custom allowed many routes out of bondage, and free Africans had played active roles in Spain long before the voyages of Columbus. Africans were also critical to the exploration and settlement of the so-called New World, especially in the inhospitable coastal areas of the circum-Caribbean.

From the founding of Charleston in 1670 onward, African Americans were embroiled in European struggles to control the Southeast. Following Caribbean precedents, Spain employed free Africans in Florida to further imperial objectives, that is, to populate and hold territory threatened by foreign encroachment. Africans, both free and slave, were also regularly employed in military operations, and a black militia was established in St. Augustine by 1683 (Second Lieutenant Domingo Masias, Roster of the Free *Pardo* and *Moreno* Militia of St. Augustine, Santo Domingo 226, Archivo General de Indias, Seville, Spain).

In 1686 a Spanish force, which included Africans and Indians, raided English plantations at Port Royal and Edisto and captured thirteen Africans, two of whom escaped back to Carolina; the next year a group of fugitives—including eight men, two women, and a small child—arrived by canoe in St. Augustine, where they were given sanctuary and protection from extradition on the basis of their religious conversion to Catholicism (Landers 1987, 1988, 1990a). By 1693 the Spanish Crown had decreed that all such escaped fugitives would be given sanctuary and, eventually, freedom in Spanish Florida, "so that by their example and by my liberality, others will do the same" (royal edict, 7 Nov 1693, John B. Stetson Collection, P. K. Yonge Library of Florida History). African slaves in the English colonies took immediate advantage of this opportunity, and increasing numbers successfully made the dangerous and difficult journey to Florida through the late seventeenth and early eighteenth centuries. Although the Carolinians set up patrol systems and placed scout boats on water routes, slaves still escaped to St. Augustine in a variety of watercraft, by horseback and on foot, and they were often assisted and accompanied by Indians.

The sanctuary policy dealt an economic and psychological blow to the English, and it enhanced the economic and defensive resources of the Spanish colony. Africans proved to be fierce and effective fighters. It is possible some had acquired these skills in Africa. Others had fought for years alongside the Yamassee in their war against Carolinian settlers, and on more than one occasion Florida's black militias served bravely in the defense of the Spanish colony against the English (Landers 1987, 1988, 1990a, 1990b).

By 1738 more than a hundred African refugees had arrived in St. Augustine, and in that year Governor Montiano of Florida formally established the town of Gracia Real de Santa Teresa de Mosé, about two miles north of the Castillo de San Marcos.

Mosé was strategically located to block land and water access to St. Augustine from the north and served as an outpost against anticipated British attacks. The freedmen understood this and vowed to be "the most cruel enemies of the English" and to spill their "last drop of blood in defense of the Great Crown of Spain and the Holy Faith" (Memorial of the Fugitive Slaves, 10 June 1738, Santo Domingo 844, on microfilm reel 15, P. K. Yonge Library of Florida History). While Mosé served obvious political and defensive functions for the Spaniards, it also served the interests of the new homesteaders who had the most to lose should the British take the colony. In Spanish Florida they gained free status, an autonomy at least equivalent to that of Spain's Indian allies, and a town of their own. They built their own shelters and a walled fort described in British reports as constructed of stone "four square with a flanker at each corner, banked with earth, having a ditch without on all sides lined round with prickly royal" (South Carolina Archives 1954:25). These documents also state that a well, a house, and a lookout were built inside the walls (ibid.). Thirty-eight men, most of them married, lived at Mosé and were expected to farm their new lands as well as man their fort. They planted fields and harvested the shellfish and fish that were said to be plentiful in the saltwater creek that ran nearby.

Mosé was considered a village of "new converts" and treated administratively in much the same way as the Indian mission towns located on St. Augustine's periphery during the eighteenth century. Both African and Indian towns were served by Franciscan priests and were provided with similar supplies from government stores. Both Africans and Indians established militia units to defend their homesteads and the Spanish city of St. Augustine, and they served many of the same peacetime functions on the frontier—scouting; tracking escaped prisoners; serving as interpreters; hunting, fishing, and trapping; herding cattle; and rounding up wild horses. They also worked on government construction projects—on fortifications and public buildings.

The initial settlement at Mosé lasted less than two years. In 1740 the forces of General James Oglethorpe laid siege to St. Augustine and occupied Fort Mosé. The settlement's inhabitants were evacuated to St. Augustine but later joined in the successful recapture of the fort. They also conducted dangerous reconnaissance missions for the Spaniards within the walls, as did members of the Indian militia. In the course of the occupation and battle, the fort at Mosé was so badly damaged that its former residents thereafter lived in St. Augustine, where they probably led lives similar to those of free blacks in other Spanish port cities. Men from the Mosé militia took part in a Spanish counteroffensive against Georgia in 1742 and also transferred their military skills to the sea, accepting corsairing commissions that took them throughout the Atlantic (Landers 1990a).

In 1752 the new governor, Fulgencio García de Solís, reestablished the fort and settlement of Mosé, but he faced resistance from the former inhabitants. They had blended into the city life of St. Augustine, and many of the men had formed unions with slave women living there. The freedmen and women were also reluctant to return to a dangerous frontier still under periodic attack by Indians. Governor García punished the protesters and enforced the resettlement. The people of Mosé built a second fort very close to the location of the first, but larger and of a different configuration. The governor provided cannon and an armed guard to assist in the town's defense (Landers 1987, 1988). In 1762 the men of Mosé added an earthwork and moat extending from the fort to the San Sebastian River some two miles distant. They also rebuilt their homes of palm thatch huts, which were described as "like those of the Indians," the buildings within the fort, including a large parish church of wood and thatch (Solana 1759).

A Spanish census of 1759 lists twenty-two households and sixty-seven residents at Mosé, including thirty-seven men, fifteen women, and fifteen children. By this time Mosé's population surpassed the combined total of the allied Indian villages. As might be expected of a frontier outpost, males predominated by more than two to one, but surprisingly, children under the age of fifteen represented almost a quarter of the population. Thirteen of the twenty-two households were composed of nuclear or nuclear-extended families, and almost 75 percent of the total population lived with immediate members of their families (Landers 1988, 1990a).

The leader of the community was a Mandingo who took the name Francisco Menéndez at his baptism. He was literate and signed with a flourish several petitions to the king. Menéndez was appointed captain of the black militia in 1726, a role he held until at least 1763, and he was commended for bravery in the battle to retake Mosé in 1740. He was acknowledged by the Spaniards as the "casique" of Mosé, and in his correspondence the governor referred to the townspeople as the "subjects" of Menéndez.

The Mosé community represented a diverse ethnolinguistic group. At least one man was married to an Indian woman with whom he had fled from Carolina, and others married Indian women who maintained residence in their own villages. In addition to Mandingas, other Africans at Mosé included Congos, Carabalís, Minas, Gambas, Lucumís, Sambas, Gangas, Araras, and Guineans. Many of the newcomers were *bozales*—unacculturated Africans who had escaped from Charleston and Savannah. The governor complained of their "bad customs"; the priests noted their religious "backwardness" and despaired over those who continued to pray in their native language. Many of the residents had previously lived among the English and Yamassee, and Mosé was a remarkably polyglot community incorporating a wide variety of cultural traditions.

During their urban interlude some male residents of Mosé married female slaves in St. Augustine while others married women from the nearby Indian villages. Meanwhile, the core group of Carolina fugitives formed intricate ties among themselves—marrying within the group for at least two generations, serving as witnesses at each other's weddings and as godparents for each other's children. As new Africans filtered in from Carolina and Georgia, they were also incorporated into the settlement at Mosé. Although the settlers shared in the general misery and deprivation of the colony in the postwar years, the freed men and women of Mosé managed to shape a viable community under extremely dangerous conditions.

Mosé was occupied until 1763, when, by the Treaty of Paris, Florida became a British colony. The thirty-four families then at Mosé—eighty-seven individuals in all—joined the Spanish evacuation and left for Cuba with the rest of the Florida colonists. There they became homesteaders on another rough frontier in Matanzas (Landers 1990a). Mosé was partially dismantled by the English, but it was still described as a "stronghouse" by Spanish officials in the late eighteenth century. Although engineers recommended refurbishing the fort and defense works, this was never done, and private citizens instead used Mosé's remaining structures to house slaves near their fields.

## The Archaeological Program

The physical setting of Mosé today, apart from the site of the second fort itself, is almost completely inundated and increasingly crosscut by tidal creeks (fig. 13.1). The fort, located on the site of a long-occupied Indian shell midden, has escaped such inundation.

The location indicated in figure 13.1 is the second Fort Mosé. This identification was originally determined by scaling contemporary aerial photographs and historic maps showing Mosé (figs. 13.2, 13.3) and producing an overlay that placed the fort in the location shown in figure 13.1. Subsequent topographic mapping activities further verified this, in that the original earthen walls of the fort are still topographically evident, except for the southwest corner, which has been eroded by tidal water activity.

The earthwork walls were about 8 feet tall, faced on the outer side with marsh clay and planted along the top with prickly-pear cactus. The moat was 2 meters wide and about 2 1/2 feet deep. Although it has long since been filled in, its configuration is clearly evident in profile, as is the layer of clay along its inner slope.

Contemporary maps have provided considerable information about the configuration of the second fort and have indicated that it contained several buildings (see fig. 13.3). Archaeological evidence has not modified these data. None of the buildings is identified on the maps, nor has the village itself ever been indicated. It is likely, given the convergence of documentary and archaeological evidence as well as the prevailing frontier conventions of the era, that the people of Mosé lived inside the confines of the fort. This area today encompasses about 2 1/2 acres.

Excavations in the fort have revealed construction details of the structure itself, including the moat (located in three places), part of the earthwork curtain, and the posts from large and small interior wood-post structures (see fig. 13.1). The structures include what was probably a watchtower with posts some 45 centimeters in diameter, as well as a smaller oval or circular wood and thatch structure, roughly 12 feet in diameter, which may have been residential.

Archaeological evidence for the Mosé occupation is extremely ephemeral, and subsequent construction activity at the fort during the British (1764–84), Second Spanish (1784–1821), and American Territorial (1821–45) periods had severe impact upon Mosé deposits. The site was excavated and water-screened in 5-centimeter levels, to be certain of isolating the approximately 15 to 20 centimeters of deposit and feature initiation that represented Mosé (fig. 13.4). Some 112 discrete deposits dating to the Mosé occupation have been recovered, including sheet-deposit levels, post molds, the moat fill, pits, and other features (Marron 1989).

The area surrounding the fort itself has been of equal interest, in that it was initially a candidate for the location of the village and fields. Traditional archaeological methods for a ground-search survey are inappropriate here, because the earth was submerged during most of the field investigations. In an attempt to recover more information about the area and possible human-deposited soils, the project arranged to acquire multispectral imagery data on the region through NASA's National Space Center Institute for Technology Development obtained through the use of a aircraft-mounted Daedalus Multispectral Scanner. The scanner produced a series of images measuring various light spectra, as well as thermal holding properties of the earth. The thermal data were the most useful: they indicated the approximate location of the original 1738–40 fort, a colonial road, and probable agricultural fields. However, no evidence for a midden or shell-bearing deposit that might reflect village occupation outside of the fort was indicated.

The area around the fort also has been cored as extensively as inundation has permitted, but thus far this activity has yielded no evidence of human occupation in any of the areas targeted in the thermal imagery. Given the negative results of the ground reconnaissance and remote sensing activities, the striking contrast in the extent of remains from inside and outside of the fort, and the specific statements of at least two contemporary observers that the village was within the walls of the fort (Solana 1759; Puente 1763), we are left with the deposits from inside the fort itself as the primary archaeological evidence for human activity during the Mosé occupation.

Research by architectural historian Albert C. Manucy (retired, National Park Service) and historian Luis Arana (Castillo de San Marcos National Monument) has suggested a settlement configuration with residential structures interspersed with those having military and religious functions. The partial oval structure noted previously dated to the Mosé era (Marron 1989) and is believed to have been residential. This was a post structure with a roughly oval shape, measuring approximately 4 meters (12 feet) in diameter. The absence of large quantities of nails, plaster, or clay daub suggests that it was constructed of thatch.

## Material Remains

The interpretation of material patterns based on the artifact assemblage from Fort Mosé is difficult and tentative at best, owing in large part to archaeological considerations. The village occupation of Mosé was brief (eleven years) and resulted in very few deposited artifacts. It is possible that much of the household refuse was discarded in the adjacent creeks and thus did not survive in the archaeological record of the site. Out of 3,190 artifacts recovered from the site as a whole, only 110 artifacts were recovered from undisturbed proveniences that could be assigned confidently to the Mosé occupation (table 13.1).

The Mosé-era proveniences at the site account for about 17 percent of both excavated soil (volumetrically) and recovered faunal remains (by weight). Some 10 percent of the shell at the site came from Mosé proveniences, but only about 4 percent of the total site artifacts. Given that the archaeological recovery techniques were identical for all site deposits, this statistical profile may reflect either disposal practices or a material assemblage with very few durable remains. The latter proposition is more supportable from the archaeological record, since it seems unlikely that durable artifacts would have been separated for disposal in the creek while faunal and shell refuse was deposited in the ground. Elizabeth Reitz's analysis of faunal remains from the site (Reitz 1990, 1994) revealed an abundance of faunal remains in the Mosé proveniences as compared to other contemporary sites—indicating that much faunal refuse was not discarded in the creek—and supports the notion of an artifact-poor material assemblage.

The small number of artifacts also exacerbates the difficulty of interpretation, particularly comparisons between the Mosé assemblages and those from contemporary sites in St. Augustine (table 13.2). The sample size of the Mosé assemblage is in no way comparable to that from even the smallest assemblage from the town (although the faunal sample is), and this factor, along with the potential for differential deposit processes in the two areas, requires that any interpretation of these data be considered with extreme caution.

The solidly dated Mosé assemblage comprises ceramics, lead shot, bottle glass, pipestems, nails, and a very few beads and buttons. Some 56 percent of the material consists of non-European and aboriginal ceramics. This overall proportion of ceramics in the assemblage is dramatically lower than that found in any of the contemporary Spanish St. Augustine sites.

This circumstance obviously affects the statistical profile of the Mosé assemblage, in that categories of nonceramic wares make up a greater proportion of the artifact assemblage. Architectural remains (nails), for example, although few in number (twelve), were proportionately more frequent at Mosé (11 percent of the assemblage), owing at least in part to the relatively small percentage of ceramics present and to the small size of the sample. However, this statistic may also reflect the fact that wooden architecture (as opposed to the masonry of the town) prevailed at Mosé.

Another material category in which Mosé shows a sharp contrast to the sites of Spanish St. Augustine is that of military-related items. The two military-related items from Mosé contexts make up 1.7 percent of the assemblage, more than twice the proportion of similar items found in St. Augustine. This is not unexpected at a military outpost, although the sample-size factors noted above must also be considered.

In both proportion and composition, the ceramic assemblage is also quite distinct from that found on contemporary Spanish sites. The Mosé-era proveniences, for example, yielded only forty-one non-European sherds, or some 35 percent of the assemblage. This is dramatically lower than the proportion of aboriginal wares at even the highest-status sites in St. Augustine (see table 13.2). In eighteenth-century St. Augustine, furthermore, the Guale Indian-affiliated San Marcos series dominates the Spanish household assemblages (see Deagan 1983), while at Mosé we find primarily the Timucua-affiliated St. Johns ceramics.

It is likely, however, that the presence of these Timucua ceramics is at least partly a result of redeposition of earlier remains into the Mosé deposits at the site, because the Timucua were largely extinct by the time the second Fort Mosé was established (see Deagan 1978:115). It is worthy of note, however, that the last Timucua Indian lived at "Mosa" with a remnant group of Apalachee Indians in 1729, some years before Mosé was established (ibid.; Valdez 1729).

Material interaction between the Mosé community and the Guale immigrants from Georgia is suggested in the assemblage, which contains only a single sherd of San Marcos (Guale-affiliated) pottery. This single San Marcos sherd stands in sharp contrast to the St. Augustine sites, where the great majority of the material assemblage is comprised of Guale ceramics.

Previously undescribed sand-tempered plain and incised wares compose 13 percent of the assemblage. No sherds of this group have been large enough to permit either formal analysis or design analysis; thus, the cultural origin of these wares is impossible to determine until more samples are available.

It is also perhaps noteworthy that in the very small assemblage of European ceramics at the site, British-made wares overwhelmingly dominate the assemblage. Forty percent of the European wares are of English origin (delftware, white salt-glazed stoneware, North Devon gravel-tempered wares, etc.), 40 percent are of undetermined origin (coarse unglazed wares), and 20 percent are of Spanish origin. This tends to support the suggestion made earlier by Deagan (1983:240) that the locally available British ceramics, although often cheaper and superior in quality to Spanish wares, were not preferred by Spanish residents in St. Augustine. They are more abundant at Mosé than elsewhere in the town, and British ceramics may have been part of the supply pattern for outlying dependencies.

No materials suggesting African influence have yet been recovered from the excavation. However, a small handmade pewter religious medallion was found in the creek adjacent to the fort site. The medallion depicts St. Christopher on one side and on the other bears a design reminiscent of the mariner's compass rose. The only other items of possible religious affiliation are glass beads, which could have been used either in a rosary or as adornment. Rosary chain links, possibly dating to the Mosé occupation, have been found in later contexts at the site.

Elizabeth Reitz's analyses of the dietary remains from the Fort Mosé occupation reveal a diet dominated by locally available estuarine fish and shellfish, although domestic mammals were occasionally consumed. The size of the fish suggest that they were caught by line rather than in nets, and that they were not acquired by commercial purchase.

Overall, there is a heavy dependence on wild, locally available foods; Reitz suggests a dietary pattern sharing some traits with patterns documented among the local Amerindian groups and some traits with dietary patterns of the St. Augustine residents. The Mosé dietary pattern, however, like the material assemblage, is quite distinct from those of both groups. While maintaining a cautious assessment of the nature of the assemblage, we might suggest that the residents of Mosé shaped and sustained a distinctive material identity, even in the absence of familiar African elements. Although they had available to them essentially the same range of local resources as did the other white and Indian colonists, the people of Mosé made certain "grammatical" choices in combining these resources into a distinctive pattern.

## Discussion

The archaeological study of Fort Mosé is essentially in a preliminary stage. A considerably larger sample of Mosé-era materials must be recovered before assertions about Mosé or reconstructions of life there can be made with confidence. It is clear, however, that the material assemblage recovered so far is dramatically different from contemporary assemblages in St. Augustine. A much lower proportion of aborigi-nal interaction is indicated materially in the Mosé assemblage, and a much higher proportion of non-Spanish European wares is present at Mosé than at Spanish sites in St. Augustine.

This emerging pattern may be affected by cultural circumstances in the past, such as poverty and isolation from the town center, trash disposal in the adjacent creeks, the use of perishable materials (wood, basketry) at the expense of durable materi-als, or rejection of both European and Amer-Indian templates by the people of Mosé. We must also note that the patterns suggested in the assemblage have almost certainly been affected to some extent by the size of the sample, which is extremely small by archaeological standards for sites in St. Augustine.

Nevertheless, the maintenance of an arguably distinct material identity at Mosé—if supported by future work—may hold lessons about social identity for us as his-torians and archaeologists. It suggests that colonial African Americans not only maintained an identity apart from that of other colonial American groups but also made material choices that helped define and reflect this distinction. The concept of more or less passive adjustment to the restrictions imposed by a dominant (white) group does not adequately explain the assemblage from Mosé, where utilitarian wares of neither Spanish nor Indian origin were used. Unlike Amerindian groups, the people of Mosé apparently used European tablewares, but these were predom-inantly non-Spanish in origin. A preference for wood, leather, and basketry as con-tainers may have operated at Mosé.

Methodologically, the situation at Mosé underscores the essential linkages in the historical-archaeological research process among the archaeological, documentary, and biological data sets. None of these data sets alone could have provided a basis for these preliminary interpretations, but taken together, they provide important convergent evidence upon which to generate a hypothetical explanation that can be tested further.

Perhaps the most important contributions of the historical-archeological pro-gram at Mosé, however, have been to stimulate innovative historical research, to heighten local national consciousness of the free African presence in the past, and to focus attention on the physical site. As a tangible symbol of African-American history, self-determination, and participation in colonial American life, Mosé has generated a kind of public fascination and governmental commitment that is rarely achieved when a story is told with words alone.

Table 13.1. Artifact remains from first Spanish-period Fort Mosé

| Group/Item | No. | % |
|---|---|---|
| *Ceramics* | | |
| Spanish majolica | | |
|   B/W: UID | 1 | |
|   POLY: UID | 1 | |
|     Total | 2 | .010 |
| European utilitarian ceramics | | |
|   Black lead-glazed coarse earthenware | 1 | |
|   Lead-glazed coarse earthenware | 1 | |
|   North Devon gravel-tempered | 2 | |
|   Green-glazed olive jar | 1 | |
|   Unglazed, UID coarse earthenware | 10 | |
|     Total | 15 | .130 |
| European tablewares | | |
|   Creamware | 1 | |
|   Delftware | 1 | |
|   Jackfield ware | 1 | |
|   Refined earthenware, UID | 1 | |
|   Rhenish stoneware | 1 | |
|   White salt-glazed stoneware | 1 | |
|   Tin-enameled, UID | 2 | |
|     Total | 8 | .070 |
| Aboriginal ceramics | | |
|   Grit-and-shell-tempered plain | 2 | |
|   Grit-tempered stamped | 5 | |
|   Sand-tempered plain | 6 | |
|   Sand-tempered decorated | 1 | |
|   Sand-tempered incised | 1 | |
|   St. Johns plain | 7 | |
|   St. Johns stamped | 18 | |
|   San Marcos stamped | 1 | |
|     Total | 41 | .370 |
| Total ceramics | 66 | .600 |

*continued on next page*

Table 13.1.—*continued*

| Group/Item | No. | % |
|---|---|---|
| *Food preparation items—nonceramic* | | |
| Glass fr. | 1 | |
| Green glass | 5 | |
| Dark green glass | 1 | |
| Clear glass | 2 | |
| Total | 9 | .080 |
| *Architectural items* | | |
| Iron nails | 12 | |
| Iron tacks | 2 | |
| Total | 14 | .12 |
| *Military items* | | |
| Lead shot | 2 | .010 |
| *Personal items* | | |
| Shell bead | 1 | |
| Pipestems | 3 | |
| Total | 4 | .030 |
| *Activities* | | |
| Projectile point | 1 | |
| Wire | 2 | |
| Chert debitage | 2 | |
| Total | 5 | .040 |
| Total artifacts | 110 | |

*continued on next page*

Table 13.1.—*continued*

| Group/Item | No. | % |
|---|---|---|
| *Weighed substances* (in grams) | | |
| Metal fragments | | |
| Brass | .06 | |
| Iron | 129.46 | |
| Lead | 7.8 | |
| UID | 8.3 | |
| Construction materials | | |
| Brick | 205.2 | |
| Mortar | 38.4 | |
| Coquina rock | 441.4 | |
| Mortared coquina | 31.2 | |
| Plaster | 15.1 | |
| Other substances | | |
| Faunal bone | 1,257 | |
| Charcoal | 108 | |
| Sand concretion | 509 | |
| Rock | 14 | |
| Shell | 522,947.2 | |

Table 13.2. Comparison of Fort Mosé assemblage with first Spanish-period sites in St. Augustine

| Group | Mosé No. | Mosé % | SA16-23 No. | SA16-23 % | SA7-4 No. | SA7-4 % | SA7-5 No. | SA7-5 % | SA36-4 No. | SA36-4 % |
|---|---|---|---|---|---|---|---|---|---|---|
| Spanish majolica | 2 | .010 | 237 | .025 | 670 | .106 | 284 | .136 | 698 | .123 |
| European utilitarian ceramics | 15 | .130 | 153 | .016 | 844 | .133 | 234 | .112 | 916 | .162 |
| European tablewares | 8 | .070 | 103 | .011 | 393 | .062 | 72 | .035 | 293 | .052 |
| Aboriginal ceramics | 41 | .370 | 8,363 | .883 | 3,520 | .555 | 805 | .386 | 2,791 | .493 |
| Total ceramics | 66 | .600 | 8,856 | .936 | 5,427 | .856 | 1,395 | .669 | 4,698 | .830 |
| Food preparation nonceramic items | 9 | .080 | 138 | .015 | 293 | .046 | 269 | .129 | 608 | .107 |
| Architectural items | 14 | .12 | 421 | .044 | 589 | .099 | 383 | .183 | 307 | .054 |
| Military items | 2 | .010 | 11 | .001 | 3 | .0005 | 19 | .009 | 20 | .004 |
| Personal items | 4 | .03 | 9 | .0009 | 24 | .037 | 5 | .002 | 11 | .020 |
| Activities | 5 | .04 | 31 | .003 | 3. | .0005 | 10 | .004 | 8 | .014 |
| Furniture | 0 | | 0 | | 1 | .001 | 5 | .002 | 5 | .009 |
| Total artifacts | 110 | | 9,466 | | 6,340 | | 2,086 | | 5,657 | |

*SA16-23*: 18th-century low-income mestizo site (Deagan 1983, chap. 6). Occupied by María de la Cruz (Guale Indian) and Mexican soldier Joseph Gallardo. Income: 91 pesos. (*Mestizo*: mixed Indian and Spanish ancestry)

*SA7-4*: 18th-century low-income *criollo* site (Shephard 1983 in Deagan 1983, chap. 5). Occupied by Geronimo de Hita, *criollo* infantry soldier who served as the daytime commandant of Mosé, and *criolla* Juana de Avero. Income: 264 pesos. (*Criollo*: Of Spanish ancestry, born in the Americas)

*SA7-5*: 18th-century high-income *criollo-peninsulare* site (Deagan 1976). Occupied by the royal storehouse official, *peninsulare* Joaquin Blanco, and *criolla* Antonia de Avero. Income 590+ pesos (*Peninsulare*: Spaniard from Spain)

*SA36-4*: 18th-century upper-income *criollo* site (Deagan 1983, chap. 10; Poe 1978). Occupied by Francisco Ponce de León, the sergeant major of the presidio. Income: 480 pesos.

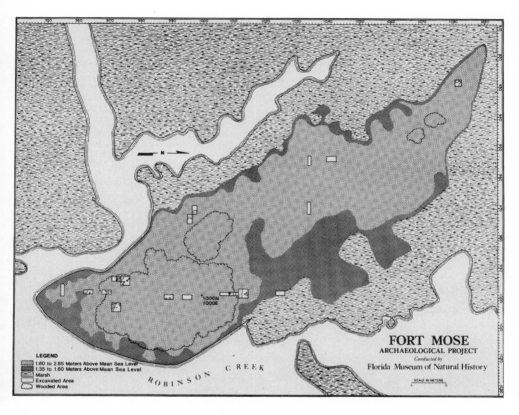

13.1. Archaeological base map, Fort Mosé site. (Florida Museum of Natural History)

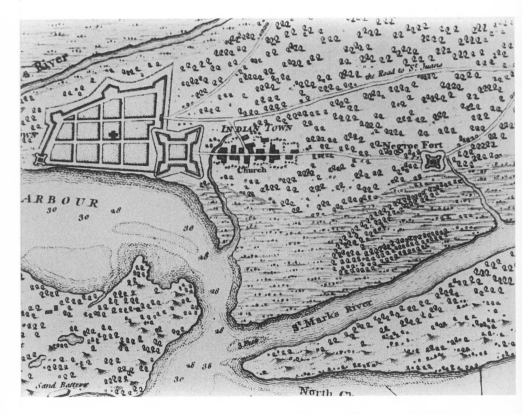

13.2. *St. Augustine: capital of East Florida*. Map by Thomas Jeffries, 1769. (Collections of the St. Augustine Historical Society)

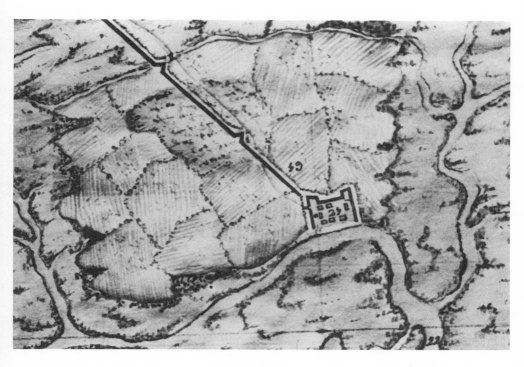

13.3. Enlarged detailed of Fort Mosé from the Pablo Castello map of 1756. (Collections of the St. Augustine Historical Society)

13.4. Representative soil profile at the Fort Mosé site, showing the level of the black community's occupation

# 14

## Elmwood: The Archaeology of Twentieth-Century African-American Pioneers in the Great North Woods

*Beverly E. Bastian*

THE ELMWOOD archaeological site (20IO58) was an early twentieth-century logging camp in the Upper Peninsula of Michigan, not far from the Wisconsin border (fig. 14.1). The camp was south of the town of Elmwood in Iron County and was separated from it by the south branch of the Paint River. Though its origins are obscure, Elmwood apparently grew up around one of the fueling and watering stops of the Chicago and Northwestern Railroad during the 1890s. In its heyday during the white pine logging days of the nineties, the town had three boardinghouses, two hotels, two streets, and a dozen or more houses. A passenger train made two stops daily. Two large lumber companies had warehouses in the vicinity of Elmwood and shipped their logs via the Chicago and Northwestern (Brozonowski 1986; Hill 1955:35–36; Bernhardt 1981:84; Lindahl 1896; Larsen 1963:318; Vanderpool 1986).

White pine logging in the area ended around the turn of the century. Although documentary sources have not disclosed exactly when the Elmwood logging camp was built, county records revealed that in August 1919 all of its equipment, livestock, and buildings were sold to a local bank (Iron County Miscellaneous Records, book 16, 393). If the history of the camp had ended there, it would be just another of the hundreds of abandoned logging camps in the northern Great Lakes states, having no special significance, let alone the National Register eligibility that has since been accorded it.

But under some very unusual circumstances, this camp was reoccupied in the late 1920s. In the spring of 1926, several African-American families from Chicago came to Elmwood to homestead and to farm the cutover timber tracts. They were able to occupy the Elmwood camp because—contrary to the common logging company practice of dismantling and moving camp buildings to a new location—it had been left standing and abandoned. These settlers apparently had been recruited by an unscrupulous land agent, one perhaps in the employ of a large lumber company owning vast tracts of nearly worthless denuded lands in Iron County. Unaware that the land was worthless, the black settlers had been enticed by the opportunity to buy twenty acres of potential farmland with the money they could earn cutting pulp-wood from the very acres they would thus clear for farming. Fraudulent schemes of this sort had been perpetrated at various times during the 1920s on gullible urban dwellers in Michigan and other Great Lakes states. Warnings to the public about such bogus "opportunities" appeared in regional newspapers during this period (*Diamond Drill*, 16 Jan. 1925).

What the African-American pioneers could not know was that cutting pulpwood (the last, low-grade timber remaining after logging) was not lucrative enough even to provide them a living let alone to enable them to buy land. Neither were they aware that the land they desired (and would have to laboriously clear and prepare for farming) was not suitable for agriculture, or that they would be facing a cold and hostile reception from both Mother Nature and the white community in Iron County. The strains imposed by all of these obstacles took their toll on the African Americans. By 1930 they left Elmwood. After they left, the county game warden burned the camp buildings so that poachers and squatters could not use them. The site was never reoccupied.

More than fifty years later, cultural resources managers recognized that Elmwood was unique and intriguing. Its peculiar history qualified the site for listing on the National Register of Historic Places, as well as for thorough documentary and archaeological study when the Michigan Department of Transportation and U.S. Forest Service plan to straighten Federal Forest Highway 16 necessitated running a new right-of-way through the site. Preliminary reconnaissance at the site identi-fied three embanked outlines of structures, several large depressions, and several peripheral trash dumps—the typical remains of Upper Peninsula logging camps (Hakari 1983). Subsequent surface collection indicated excellent physical integrity for the site; a documentary records check revealed good local newspaper coverage of some aspects of the African-American settlement (Keene and Karamanski 1984). Further historical background research and archaeological excavation being war-ranted, mitigation work on the site began in November 1985.

A three-pronged approach was devised. First, historical research would be pur-sued, concentrating on a variety of county and state records, newspapers, and pub-lished histories and memoirs. Second, oral history interviews would be conducted with both elderly, longtime white residents in the Iron River–Elmwood area and with any surviving African-American Elmwood pioneers or their relatives who could be located in the Chicago area. Third, archaeological excavation and recordation of the site itself would be undertaken, to be guided by the findings from the docu-mentary and oral historical research.

The study was conceived initially as an opportunity to investigate possible early twentieth-century expressions of ethnicity in the archaeological record. To exploit this opportunity, it would be necessary to differentiate the (later) African-American component at the site from the (earlier) white logging crew component. This would be possible because of the probable ten-to-thirty-year time interval between the two occupations and the resultant artifact date differentials. Also of importance in identifying ethnicity in the archaeological record would be any information that the black settlers themselves, if located and interviewed, could provide as to how they used and adapted the logging camp to their purposes.

When documentary, oral history, and archaeological research was completed and the resulting data were analyzed and interpreted, an opportunity arose to reconcile the conflicting stories that emerged from three lines of evidence. What really happened at Elmwood in the late 1920s? What finally forced the African-American pioneers to abandon their version of the American dream? The lack of money? The poor soil? The harsh climate? Racism? Addressing these questions became a major concern of the study and the focus of this chapter.

The documentary and oral historical research in the Upper Peninsula was fairly productive.[1] The most detailed information came from contemporary newspaper accounts, which provided the names of many of the African-American settlers. The eight elderly local residents who were interviewed contributed useful information on life in early twentieth-century logging camps, and three of them provided some particulars on the African-American settlement. Iron County deed and tax records contained some information on logging companies that had owned or leased the land where the Elmwood logging camp was located, but it could not be established from these sources who had built the camp and when, nor could it be deduced who, in the words the newspapers attributed to one of the African-American settlers, "boncoed" the would-be pioneers.[2]

Of all the documentary sources, contemporary newspapers proved to have the richest accounts, although they generally provided a biased and sometimes lurid picture of the African-American settlement at Elmwood. The local whites were alarmed at rumors that a "colonization company in Chicago" was sending African-American farmers to Iron County, expressing fear that the settlers would become "county charges." When the settlers first arrived, the sheriff visited them at the logging camp and reported to the press that they had money, were satisfied with their land purchase, and resented the interference of the authorities (*Iron River Reporter*, 4 May 1926; *Diamond Drill*, 7 May 1926). The next winter, however, the sheriff and the Poor Commissioner returned to investigate the request of one of the settler families for county assistance. The settlers had not been paid for the pulpwood they had cut and shipped in the summer and fall, and in discouragement one family sought help in returning to Chicago.

The newspaper descriptions were laden with judgmental phrases: "flimsy shack," "gaunt and undernourished children," "team of horses starving to death tied in the barn," "[colony] members . . . too lazy to cut wood to heat their homes," "men shiftless and lazy." One reporter, stating that the county officials were sending the family back to Chicago, expressed the opinion that "whether they will be bettered any there is questionable but they will be among their own people and among those who understand them"(*Iron River Reporter*, 21 Jan. 1927; *Diamond Drill*, 21 Jan. 1927). The newspapers also noted that although the sheriff had been informed that the African Americans were making moonshine, no evidence of this was found.

A year later, however, the newspaper headlines read, "Negro Caught in Holiday Raid; Sheriff's Forces Made a Cleanup on West Side of County; Twenty Niggers Taken" (*Diamond Drill*, 6 Jan. 1928). The story that followed recounted the arrest of all of the adults of the Elmwood settlement on charges of trafficking in illicit liquor. All but two were later released on bond, and fifteen accepted a deal whereby charges were dropped in exchange for their using the one-way train tickets to Chicago that the county provided them.

Apparently this harassment did not sufficiently discourage the settlers, because approximately one year later the remaining African Americans were arrested again. One newspaper story about the incident began, "Darkness fell on the Iron County Jail Saturday afternoon when Sheriff James A. Dickey brought in seven negroes who had been arrested at their homes in the Elmwood district on various violations of the liquor laws." The article stated that the African Americans were unaccustomed to farming and unprepared for the severe winter weather and so "had turned to less difficult means of making a living . . . supporting themselves on the revenue they have received from their moonshine and wine sales" (*Diamond Drill*, 7 Dec. 1928). Again, all but three of the arrestees were offered dropped charges and train tickets. One newspaper crowed that the "colony" was "virtually extinct due to the efforts of Superintendent of the Poor, Carl Sholander and Sheriff James A. Dickey" (*Diamond Drill*, 25 Jan. 1929). The reporter went on to predict that the settlers remaining in the county jail would be tried, convicted, paroled, and sent back to Chicago at county expense. The county was said to have paid the train fare of thirty-two African Americans over the previous three years. Contemporary newspaper coverage of this attempt by African Americans to pioneer in the Great North Woods ended at this point.

While rather sparse, the particulars gleaned from Upper Peninsula documentary sources provided a starting point for documentary and oral history research in Chicago.[3] The city's black newspapers, school records, telephone books, and city directories of the period—as well as contemporary periodicals listing African-American business persons—were located and searched, but no further concrete evidence of the land scam or any other unambiguous trace of the African-American settlers was found. The managing editor of Chicago's current African-American newspaper, the *Daily Defender*, was then contacted. The paper was sufficiently interested in this research to run an article about the Elmwood research project in the one Sunday edition in March 1986. The closing lines of the article invited anyone who had any information about these events to contact the newspaper.

Within a few days an elderly black man and his sister came to the newspaper office wanting to talk to the historians about Elmwood. An interview was arranged, and seventy-six-year-old Josephus Keeble and his younger sister, Ethel, related the experiences of their family at Elmwood and graciously answered questions about the physical character and day-to-day life at the camp. Josephus had been a teenager and Ethel a child when their family had moved from southeastern Missouri to Chicago and then, shortly thereafter, from Chicago to Elmwood as part of a three-car caravan.

Their father, a minister and a farmer, had been persuaded to pioneer in northern Michigan by his boyhood friend John Williams, a successful Chicago restaurateur. The Keebles did not know what the arrangement between their father and Williams had been, but they knew that their father had been very bitter about the outcome and refused to talk about it or to communicate further with John Williams after the settlers returned to Chicago. At Elmwood the elder Keeble had farmed, cut pulpwood, cut and sold Christmas trees, and occasionally held services at the store in the camp.

The Keeble family had not lived in the camp but instead had lived in a cabin in the town itself. Josephus had worked at the store in the camp, which was operated by John Williams, and had lived in a room in the rear of the store, so he was quite familiar with the camp and the other settlers, most of whom were also John Williams's friends. All of the African-American families had vegetable gardens as well as farmland. Mrs. Keeble canned food from her garden. Some families raised rabbits, and some raised chickens; one family had a milk cow. Horses were used to load pulpwood on flatcars. Cats and dogs were kept as pets. Deer were hunted for food, and many of the settlers fished the Paint River. The Keebles had known snowy winters in Missouri and did not mind the cold in Michigan. They had warm clothing, and their cabin was always warmed by the firewood their father cut.

Josephus asserted that the African-American settlers did not make moonshine, although some did use it, obtaining it from whites. He and his father were arrested in late 1928, Josephus on the charge of acting as John Williams's bartender. Two months later, when he was released from jail, his family had moved back to Chicago. He caught the train and joined them, settling there. The Keeble siblings did not know what happened to the other Elmwood settlers (Keeble 1986; Rogers 1986).

Besides recalling these and other details of their days at Elmwood, the Keebles were able to assist in the drawing of a sketch map of the logging camp site as they remembered it.

The dramatic contrast between the Keebles' account of a normal family life at Elmwood and the contemporary newspaper depictions of the desperate circumstances of the African-American settlers is keen. Could the archaeological investigation resolve the conflict?

Surface-collecting and mapping the entire site clearing and its wooded periphery added two new structures to the site inventory, for a total of five (fig. 14.2). One of them was found only because of the Keebles' map showing its location. Excavation of features and structures consisted of bisecting or quadrisecting trenches, with additional square units placed within structures to follow up on features. Areas around structures were surveyed using a metal detector, with recordation and recovery of artifacts signaled by this device. Shovel testing was also carried out across the rest of the clearing. All removed soils were screened through 1/4-inch mesh. The young age of the site and its lack of disturbance were readily evidenced by its relative shallowness. Artifacts came from the surface, the root zone, or the upper part of the topsoil, with the only stratigraphy on the site restricted to features.

Excavation sampled the four structures in the highway impact area, a root cellar, a privy, a well, several borrow areas near structures, and a number of peripheral trash dumps. Excavations of the floor and berm outlines of what were identified as the original camp cookhouse (structure A), bunkhouse (structure B), and blacksmith shed (structure C) indicated that these were log buildings. They lacked foundations but had sawed joist and plank floors on prepared pads of earth and rocks. Structure C, the blacksmith shed, had a rock-paved floor over its western half and may have had only a dirt floor in the rest of the area. All of the buildings, in the usual fashion for log cabins in the North Woods, had been insulated partway up their outside walls by packed earth, except for their entrances. Cast-iron stove parts were found in structures A and B. All structures gave ample evidence of having been burned, and all contained both domestic and work-related artifacts. This evidence and the Keebles' information suggest that the African-American settlers used all of these structures as residences, whatever their original logging camp use had been.

Structure D (one of the two unidentified structures) was rather small. It was isolated from the core of the camp but had the same high berms as structures A, B, and C. Originally it may have been the office of the camp. In the area between structure D and the core of the camp, both the Keebles and a local informant indicated that there had been a barn, but no physical evidence of this building was found.

Behind structure A was a root cellar, supporting the identification of structure A as the original cookhouse from the logging occupation. There was probably a dingle (an open-sided, roofed storage area) between structure A and the root cellar, which was a shallow dugout, with a sand floor and mounded-up dirt walls, partially shored by horizontal log cribbing. It probably had a log roof with a dirt covering. Few artifacts were found in the slumped walls or on the floor of the cellar. The doorway faced the rear door of the cookhouse.

Structure E, the house identified by the Keebles as that of Bessie Carter (who according to contemporary newspaper accounts ran a speakeasy there) was located quite close to the highway. Its low-relief berms appear to be oriented to the road. Rotted sills in the berms indicated that this building was made of sawed lumber, and there is evidence of interior partitioning, as well as an add-on room. Many pieces of a cast-iron stove were recovered. Artifacts from this structure were predominantly domestic, but some work-related items were also present. Both oral history and archaeological evidence suggest that this building was constructed by the black settlers and occupied solely by them. Oral history indicates that the original logging camp had only four structures and a barn, and notable differences in physical remains distinguish structure E from the other camp structures.

Several important features contributed information on camp life. A well—consisting of square, notched log cribbing lining a 1.5-meter-deep shaft—was located near structures A and B but produced few noteworthy artifacts. Another necessary convenience, a large privy pit, had been dug on the wooded southern periphery of the clearing. No evidence of a superstructure or of the seating arrangements was found. A few incidental and quite varied artifacts were recovered from the privy, including neatly torn denim and burlap rags in small square and oblong shapes, possibly used as toilet paper or as women's sanitary supplies. The privy also yielded a single human coprolite, the analysis of which indicated a nutritious and varied diet, with some utilization of the wild fruits available in the Upper Peninsula during the summer months (Van Ness 1987). While the well and the privy probably were used by both the earlier loggers and the later African-American families, loggers only occupied logging camps during the winter, so the nutritious diet indicated by the coprolite analysis can be attributed to the African-American occupants.

Both loggers and African-American families produced trash that they disposed of in somewhat different ways. Late-dating artifacts, gender-specific artifacts such as women's shoes, and technologically advanced artifacts such as automotive parts distinguished African-American trash disposal patterns from logger trash disposal patterns. Both used surface dumps, and some surface dumps evidence use by both loggers and settlers. However, all holes that appeared to have been dug deliberately for trash disposal and all holes incidentally utilized as trash pits contained trash discarded by the black settlers.

One unique feature, feature 12, was found in the southeast quad of structure C, in the dirt-floored area. A basin-shaped fire pit, with much ash and charcoal from sawed lumber, was found to contain a large graniteware double boiler. Local lumberjack lore identifies such vessels as equipment for home distillation of liquor, although they had common kitchen uses as well. But other equipment for distilling liquor—pieces of copper tubing—were also found south of structure C. Further evidence of possible moonshining activity on the site was feature 9, a large cache of refillable 1920s-era beverage bottles in structure A, located in a place that was only accessible through the floorboards of the building.

Artifact analysis revealed no distinctively African-American artifacts, with one possible exception. A single artifact was recovered that could evidence a practice existing among some African-American people, especially urbanites, in this period. It was Carrel Cowan-Ricks's suggestion that African-American hair-care products and devices are an artifact type which would identify the distinctive presence of African-American people on an archaeological site of the early twentieth century, and that such items were available at the time of the African-American occupation at the Elmwood site, as were products and devices for straightening African-American hair so that it could be worn in the styles affected by whites. While no combs, chemicals, or devices for hair straightening were found by the excavators at Elmwood, a McBrady's Hair Pomade jar lid found in structure A led Cowan-Ricks to suggest that this product may have been purchased and used by an African-American woman who desired the kind of flowing, wavy hair shown on the white woman whose likeness embellishes the pomade lid.

It is fortunate for the success of the research on Elmwood that the brief period (less than ten years) intervening between the logging occupation and the black pioneer occupation of the Elmwood logging camp occurred at a time when World War I technological advancements and 1920s prosperity-driven market expansion greatly changed the variety and kinds of goods available to Americans, making it fairly easy to distinguish the artifact deposits of the two occupations. It is also very fortunate that most of the black pioneers were relatively sophisticated urban dwellers, who brought to Elmwood their modern possessions, including automobiles and electrical appliances (even though they could not use the latter there).

However, while temporal differences in the artifacts made distinguishing the two components possible, and functional differences could also be observed and described, all differences were primarily related to the nature of the contrasting occupations, rather than to the groups' ethnicity. Regardless of their ethnic origins, the archaeological remains of a large group of men devoting most of their time to one specialized and seasonal activity, logging, is bound to contrast with the archaeological remains of several year-round families involved in a variety of activities. In contrast to the remains of the logger occupation, the black settlement relics included women's and children's possessions, as well as items relating to a more technologically advanced and sophisticated urban life, such as automobile parts and devices requiring electricity. There was also evidence of opportunistic efforts to adapt to a new and difficult natural and social environment, exemplified by the distillation and bottling equipment. In this particular circumstance it is ironic that their more sophisticated and diverse material culture distinguishes the black settlers from their white predecessors and probably, one can speculate, from their white contemporary neighbors as well.

However, no distinctively African-American artifacts were found (with the pomade lid as the one possible exception), and no particular material culture pattern was discovered that can be specifically attributed to early twentieth-century African-American families and generalized to other sites. The ready availability of a diverse range of goods to all Americans in the late 1920s, but especially to urban dwellers, largely obscures differences between blacks and whites in the ownership and use of material things. Distinguishing black from white domestic remains of this period is thus all but impossible in the absence of other data.

In the matter of how well the African-American settlers adapted to the harsh Michigan winters and to what extent their tenure at Elmwood was a difficult, frontier-type experience, not all data point to the same conclusion. The contemporary local newspapers assert that the black pioneers could not adapt to the extreme cold and that their winters at Elmwood were a great trial for them. The elderly local informants generally echo this opinion. But it was not the black settlers' response to the hardship of winter that was the subject of most of the newspaper stories, it was their repeated arrests by local authorities for alleged liquor law violations. The newspaper accounts document one family leaving Elmwood because of their inability to cope with the climate. All of the others left under threat of imprisonment, and despite that threat, some even returned.

The Keebles, in contrast to the contemporary newspapers' and the informants' accounts, have relatively pleasant memories of wintertime in Elmwood. Their experience does not necessarily represent that of all of the black families at Elmwood, however, and it is certainly possible that some families fared badly. Nonetheless, it is difficult to believe that any family could be in quite the desperate circumstances reported by the local newspapers and not have more fortunate settlers—such as the Keebles—assisting them. After all, these were people who had known each other in the same neighborhood in Chicago, and they must have had at least a moderate sense of community due to their physical and social isolation in Elmwood.

The archaeological evidence indicates neither that African-American settlers had a Spartan frontier lifestyle nor that they made a poor adaptation to the area. Artifact deposits dated to the time of the African-American occupation contained material goods that were far from being strictly utilitarian, multipurpose, and limited in variety. On the contrary, they were richly diverse, occasionally ornamental and frivolous in nature, evidencing activities beyond simple subsistence, and possibly even exceeded in their technological development the possessions of the Elmwood whites.

The dietary evidence provided by the faunal remains (Martin 1987) and the coprolite specimen suggest utilization of wild food sources, implying that the settlers were sufficiently adapted to the local environment to exploit it successfully for some kinds of foods. Furthermore, the archaeological evidence suggests that the settlers erected an additional building in the camp during their sojourn there. This implies expenditure of time, the possession of means and materials, and a commitment to staying there, which is not the profile of destitute, desperate people living in the marginal way contemporary newspapers described.

So, what really happened at Elmwood? Were the contemporary newspapers sensationalizing the plight of the African-American homesteaders, and if so, why? Have Josephus Keeble and his sister come to see their family's stay at Elmwood bathed in the rosy glow of nostalgia, disregarding hardships that are, perhaps, too painful to remember? Were the African Americans really making moonshine at the Elmwood camp, or was evidence planted to make it seem so, as one local informant confided? If they were making moonshine, were they the only ones in the area engaged in the practice, or were whites doing so as well? Was there "discretionary" (i.e., discriminatory) enforcement of the prohibition laws?

The evidence does not exist that will answer these questions with complete certainty. It is only possible to consider the conflicting evidence in the light of broad cultural patterns and to suggest what probably happened. From the fact that racism was widespread in America in the 1920s—it was at this time that an especially virulent Ku Klux Klan was reborn in the Midwest—racism can be assumed to have been the dominant factor in the fate of the African-American settlers at Elmwood.

It is likely that sparsely populated, all-white Iron County did not want African Americans as neighbors, in their schools, in their churches, or in their polling places. Comforting themselves at first with the idea that the hard winter would force the Elmwood settlers out, Iron County whites turned to active measures when the black pioneers endured. Distillation equipment may have been planted at the camp in a conspiracy to implicate the black settlers, or illicit manufacture of liquor may have been going on there independently (this was an era when many people knew how to make "bathtub gin"); either way the result was that Iron County authorities had the tool they needed to rid the county of these unwanted residents. It is very likely that there were white moonshiners in Iron County, and doubtless some of them were arrested and tried for their crimes. It is, however, unlikely that any of them were arrested, charged, and then given the choice of jail or a one-way train ticket to Chicago. This form of justice was reserved for African Americans. Compared to the way other American communities at this time handled unwelcome blacks, Iron County's methods were relatively benign, but the conclusion that the Prohibition laws were applied in a discriminatory fashion—and were used to force African Americans to leave the Upper Peninsula—is inescapable.

All in all, it seems likely that the contemporary newspaper accounts and the treasured memories of the old white informants greatly exaggerated both the plight and the legal offenses of the black settlers. To the local whites this exaggeration served to justify the county officials' discriminatory expulsion of the black Elmwood settlers from the county and to reinforce the regional lore that only whites could tame the Great North Woods.

## Notes

The research summarized in this chapter was funded by the Michigan Department of Transportation and the Bureau of History of the Michigan Department of State, with technical oversight provided by the USDA, Forest Service, Ottawa National Forest. Permission from the Michigan Department of Transportation to use data from this research is gratefully acknowledged. The opinions, findings, and conclusions expressed in this publication are those of the author and not necessarily those of the Michigan Department of State or Bureaus thereof, or the Michigan Department of Transportation, or the Michigan State Transportation Commission and the United States Department of Transportation or agencies thereof.

1. This part of the Elmwood research was carried out by William E. Rutter, now of the Michigan Bureau of History. Rutter also acted as a field director for the archaeological phase of the project and coauthored the final report (Bastian and Rutter 1987).

2. *Bonco* is an outdated slang term for a kind of fraud. The approximate equivalent is a *scam*.

3. This research was carried out by the late Ms. Carrel Cowan-Ricks of Wayne State University, whose contributions to this project are gratefully acknowledged.

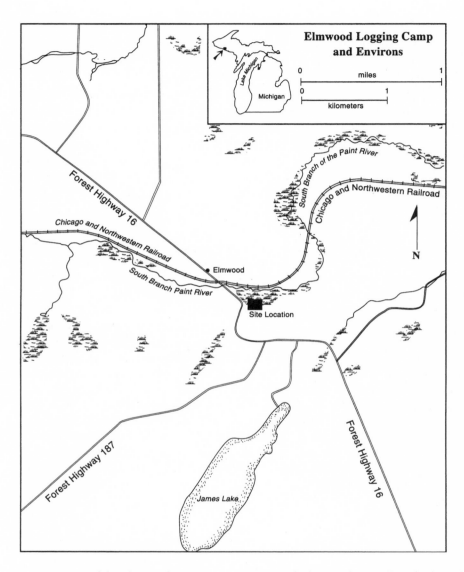

14.1. Location of the Elmwood site in Iron County, Mich. (Drawn by Marcia Bakry)

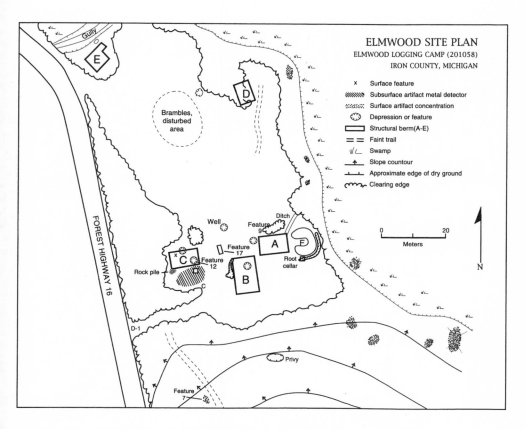

14.2. Extent of excavations at the Elmwood site. (Redrawn by Marcia Bakry)

# Part IV

# Epilogue

# 15

# Artifacts, Ethnicity, and the Archaeology of African Americans

*Warren Perry and Robert Paynter*

T HIS VOLUME is a collection of articles by scholars concerned with African-American history—specifically, the historical archaeology of the African diaspora in the Americas. Using a variety of theoretical and methodological approaches, these provocative and stimulating articles discuss the latest research in the historical archaeology of African Americans. The inclusion of contributions by archaeologists specializing in African historical archaeology makes this volume essential for a scientific and critical understanding of the history of the African diaspora.

The editor, in assembling these essays, has developed a number of themes that guide research on the archaeology of the African diaspora. Issues of method and theory, the relations between the material world of Africa and that of the Americas, life both within and outside the context of plantations order the major strands of research, and the chapters fairly represent and often advance our understanding of each of these areas.

Many of these articles emerged from a highly productive conference on "Digging the Afro-American Past: Archaeology and the Black Experience," which neither of us was able to attend. Clearly, this volume and the conference from which it resulted, along with other publications (e.g., Orser 1990; Ferguson 1992) and the establishment of a newsletter on African-American archaeology, all point to the growing maturity of the field. We would like to add a few comments—inspired by the articles in the volume but not directed at specific contributions—to this stimulating field of research. These fall into the areas of method and authority and history and perspective.

## Method and Authority

"The problem of the twentieth century is the problem of the color-line," wrote W. E. B. Du Bois in *The Souls of Black Folk*, "the relation of the darker to the lighter races of men in Asia and Africa, in America and the islands of the sea" (Du Bois

[1903] 1969:54). A major line of research in African-American archaeology is the
search for material items of African origin, items presumed to mark the color line.
The reasons for seeking such objects vary: some are useful and admirable research
objectives, while others are hobbled by inadequate notions of sociology and cultural
theory. Depending upon the goals, the methods chosen to identify and study
African-American material culture should vary.

Establishing an African presence through the identification of Africanisms is
hardly necessary. A post-Columbian African demographic presence in the Western
Hemisphere is, on the archaeological timescale, inseparable from the European
demographic presence. Indeed, one might suggest that given the necessity of coerced
African labor in the European colonial enterprise, a cultural presence of Africa is
even more widespread than the demographic distribution of its people.

Sometimes, however, it seems that our methods trap us into addressing this non-
problem. The problem of establishing presence with objects alone is a significant
one. Considerable methodological thinking has gone into interpreting population
movements, various kinds of intercultural interaction, and independent invention
(e.g., Adams et al. 1978; Rouse 1986:1–18, 157–82) from material traces. Though in the
abstract the standards for establishing presence are sensible enough, in particular
applications they can lead to considerable contention and argumentation (e.g., van
Sertima 1985; Davies 1979:125–65).

Historical archaeologists, however, search for Africanisms for different reasons.
We search for Africanisms to study the distinctive character of the African presence,
the level and domains of cultural autonomy and creativity, the degree of suppression and censorship, the forgotten or unacknowledged sources of the colonial life.
The study of Africanisms in historical archaeology is fundamentally associated not
with the establishment of an African presence but with the study of the character of
that presence, especially as this concerns the effect of African captivity and the Middle Passage on the place of Africa and African Americans in American culture. Did
the Middle Passage and slavery strip Africans of their cultural heritage, or is the
African cultural heritage one of the persistent strands of American identity? Did
African Americans survive this horror to become culture creators in the Western
Hemisphere, or did they only bear the culture given them by captors?

These debates are as old as the Atlantic slave trade itself. For instance, European
observations on African culture: (1) justified slavery to European Americans by identifying purportedly uncivilized practices, (2) led European Americans to enslave and
purchase people who were known to have particularly desirable cultural practices,
and (3) buttressed antislavery arguments by providing evidence of the unity of
humankind (e.g., Abrahams and Szwed 1983:10-22; Du Bois 1939; Holloway 1990b;
Jordan 1968). After emancipation in the United States, the purported lack of evi-

dence of Africanisms was used again to demonstrate the insufficiencies of African culture (opinions cataloged and refuted, for instance, in Herskovits 1941:1–32) as well as to emphasize the effects of captivity and the Middle Passage (e.g., Holloway 1990a; Mintz 1970:7–8, 12–13). Even into our time, political policies find their justification in historical understandings of the effect, or lack thereof, of African culture on people's relations today (Abrahams and Szwed 1983:1–9; Valentine 1968).

This is not the place to untangle the many and intricate ways that Africanisms have figured in American ideology. Rather, we draw attention to these issues to make two points. First, throughout the history of the debates, it has been the issue of the character of African-American culture, not the presence of people of African descent, that has been at stake. Thus, the methodologies used to establish presence with artifacts alone—methodologies involving the study of attribute, artifact, architectural, and site continuities and discontinuities—seem a bit beside the point when applied to the material culture of colonial North America. Second, any discussion of Africanisms, even by historical archaeologists, will (intentionally or unintentionally) reverberate with various aspects of the long debate over the character of African Americans and of African culture. Debates in historical archaeology would benefit from a recognition of their significance for and embeddedness in this long discourse. Deep matters of theory, history, and politics are all present whenever African culture is on the table, matters deserving as much care as do provenance, context, and form if we are to advance an understanding of the character of the African presence in the Western Hemisphere.

Along with recognizing that our observations fit within strands of an older discourse, we need to develop methods—i.e., lines of argument—that do justice to the intricacies of cultural construction under conditions of economic and political domination. An important starting point for such methodologies is the issue of agency for the various social players. It is the denial or repression of agency that is at the heart of characterizations of African and African-American cultures as "savage" or "uncivilized," lacking in the resilience necessary for Africanisms to survive captivity. By starting with an assumption of agency, as happens in the historical archaeology of African Americans, archaeology engages these debates. Simply finding evidence of African agency—cowrie shells, African cosmograms on colonoware pots, African-Jamaican ceramic traditions, gaming pieces, kwardata motifs on pipes, or magician-curer's kits—constitutes a significant component in a historical construction that emphasizes the creativity and significance of African Americans. In this way archaeological evidence contributes to the theme of vindicationist arguments (Drake 1980). Such arguments seek to contradict stereotypical and racist characterizations of African Americans.

But agency involves more than identifying action informed by particular cultural positions. Vindicationist arguments alone always have the problem of playing by the rules of white racism, which measure legitimate African-American agency against a standard made up of the practices of European Americans. Moving beyond vindicationist arguments admits to agency and cultural construction for a variety of players—especially in colonial contexts. An exploration of these agencies and their unique and diverse cultural positions can begin with artifacts. The agency of European Americans in enslaving and thereby brutalizing Africans and their descendants is critical in understanding the colonial and postcolonial worlds and has received voluminous attention by scholars. The chapters in this volume argue for investigating the range of African-American positions. As Mouer and his coauthors remind us in chapter 5, the unique position of Native Americans in the social relations of colonialism also needs to be considered. The result would be a broader field of social agency, which, especially in the seventeenth century, was made up of subjectivities that would not recognize twentieth-century racial divisions of Red, White, and Black.

Assuming that agency extends beyond Europeans and their descendants, it would be possible to observe the transformation of these agencies as their positions are contested on the colonial landscape with words, actions, and objects. Indeed, from this perspective what seems most striking about the pipes and pots of the Chesapeake is our ready identification of these objects with people of color, rather than with Europeans. Thus, does the history of production, use, and discard of these items track the early form of Du Bois's color line, when white racism was in its infancy, and provide a very rare window into the formative dynamics of this most powerful consciousness and the resistances to it?

When we consider the variety of social agents and wonder about their alliances, differences, and divisions, we see that the social and cultural field of the African diaspora is quite complex. When viewed simultaneously as the means of production, objects of production, and the bases for social identification and struggle, colonial artifacts can no longer be associated with a single social group or assigned a single unique meaning. Plumbing this complexity requires methods and insights that appreciate processes of appropriation and renewal tied to social relations of domination and resistance.

Take the case of the appropriation of Africanisms into European national culture, with European Americans and African Americans concomitantly forgetting their origins. African captives held diverse occupations and tasks and incorporated their ideas on form and style in the production of objects for use in the Americas, especially before the Industrial Revolution. Several scholars, for example, have noted the African roots of much southern folk agricultural knowledge and practice, and especially of coastal rice farming (Wood 1974:35–62). Philips (1990) gives an even longer list of African-influenced practices and objects, including elements of music, language, etiquette, foodways, and religion, many of which would not be recognized as Africanisms (see also Herskovits 1941). Thus, the roles of objects in reproducing a sense of identity become disengaged from the historical agents responsible for their initial construction in the Western Hemisphere.

This reminds us that African Americans and European Americans used a similar range of objects, though (as a number of authors in this volume point out) in quite different ways (see also Howson 1990; Paynter 1992; Sobel 1987; Upton 1985). We refer to this condition as multivalency (see also Tilley 1989). Multivalency exists when an object or set of objects takes on strikingly different meanings for different social groups, with dominating groups often totally ignorant of the meaning system of subordinated groups.

For example, Du Bois attributes great significance to the iron fire tongs of his great-grandfather, associating them with his African ancestry (Paynter 1992:282). These objects, although not unique to African-American sites nor exemplifying discernible African stylistic characteristics, possess special meanings for African Americans beyond reminiscence. Such things were and are used to create African-American culture, rooting people in a shared African past; as a result, they were and are fundamental to the sanity of African Americans.

The problem with multivalent objects is not that historical archaeologists have no idea how to interpret them. It is not that multivalent objects are somehow obscure and exotic items that appear in our miscellaneous categories. It is rather that all too often they are given the interpretation used by the dominant culture. Fire tongs are functional items; agricultural practices are "just common knowledge"; rice cultivation landscapes are "just the lay of the land." The problem in method is to capture these meanings and their social relations *and* to discover alternative understandings and practices associated with them.

How are these multivalencies to be identified and investigated? One good method, again abundantly demonstrated in this volume, is to study the relations between items, attributes, assemblages, and so on, noting how differences in patterning provide clues to differences in use and significance. But where will we get the content of these differences in significance? Again, as reported in this volume, ethnographic studies of and by Africans and African Americans are an important source of insight. We would remind the reader that there is also a rich scholarship in anthropology itself by Africans and African Americans that rarely makes its way into our studies (e.g., Blakey 1990; Cole 1980a, 1980b; Drake 1980, 1987, 1990; Harrison 1991, 1992, 1995; Page 1988; Willis 1972 for examples and bibliography). This scholarship not only provides insight into particular objects but more importantly provides models of how to work with these insights to make anthropological sense.

Searching for objects of African origin quickly leads to the complex field of colonial relations in which objects rarely take on simple one-to-one relations with social groups. Most categories of material culture were used by European, African, and Native Americans, though quite often in strikingly different ways. It is these multivalencies that, as much as Africanisms, Europeanisms, or Nativisms, mark the color line. Our challenge is to understand these multivalent objects. As Lippard (1990:9) reminds art historians, "Among the pitfalls of writing about art made by those with different cultural backgrounds is the temptation to fix our gaze solely on the familiarities and the unfamiliarities, on the neutral and the exotic, rather than on the area in between—that fertile, liminal ground where new meanings germinate and where common experiences in different contexts can provoke new bonds."

The daunting challenge in surveying this ground is to hear the varied voices that engaged one another in this colonial field. The challenge can be met by bringing new authoritative voices to the interpretation of these objects—the voices of African and Native Americans. We wonder if the methodological problem of developing rich and divergent interpretations of African material culture might seem less daunting if the color line did not run so deeply through the academy, including historical archaeology. Understanding multivalencies will require incorporating more African-centered thinking, so that both sides of the color line may be illuminated.

## History and Perspective

"The Negro," wrote W. E. B. Du Bois, "is a sort of seventh son, born with a veil, and gifted with second-sight in this American world. . . . It is a peculiar sensation, this double-consciousness, this sense of always looking at one's self through the eyes of others, of measuring one's soul by the tape of a world that looks on in amused contempt and pity" (Du Bois [1903] 1969:45). Du Bois's veil falls between many of the understandings that make up the discourses of the hegemonic American consciousness and that of subordinated groups. Historical archaeology, as many of the essays in this volume note, is a discipline that offers to lift part of the veil by tracking the history of people documented in only the most biased of manners. The veil is the ideological effect of the operation of the totalizing system of white racial hegemony (Omi and Winant 1986). But because historical archaeology is itself enmeshed in the very discourses that arise from this racist social formation, we cannot hope to lift the veil by ignoring it. We can hope to accomplish this goal only if we study the veil and keep in mind the distorted visions it imposes.

An important task is to come to grips with the history of white racism. As chapters in this volume remind us, racism is not a universal feature of human culture but a historically specific ideology associated with historically specific economic and power-laden practices. It was and is a malleable construct of specific historical circumstances (Allen 1994; Fredrickson 1981; Gregory and Sanjek 1994; Hall 1992; Harrison 1995; Roediger 1991, 1994; Schrire 1994; Shackel 1996; Smedley 1993). It would be worth knowing its dimensions. What were its intellectual and material roots in Anglo culture? How did its "naturalness" get implanted in European-American psyches? What were its effects on the people marked as members of racial groups? Under what conditions was its hegemonic grip loosened?

The process through which plantations melded together practices and ideology so that Euro-Americans willingly participated in the enslavement of other humans is becoming better understood. The chapters by Deetz, Epperson, and Heath (chaps. 3, 8, and 10 in this volume; see also Deetz 1993; Epperson 1990) and work by Leone (1984), Singleton (1985, 1988, 1995), Upton (1985), and Orser (Orser and Nekola 1985; Orser 1988b), among others, show how plantations and grand houses were built to give white supremacy ideological foundations in the landscape. The effect was to naturalize the social order of white domination.

Much less clear is how the landscapes were constructed outside of plantations and manors to support white racial hegemonies. Appropriately, the studies in this volume of African-American life outside plantations focus on African-American lifeways, and less so on the construction of white racism. It is worth noting that the sites discussed in this volume that were not part of plantation contexts—Fort Mosé and Elmwood—were locales of cultural conflict. Fort Mosé's location and significance were misremembered by local European Americans; Elmwood was misrepresented by local European Americans. In a similar vein, when the site of W. E. B. Du Bois's boyhood home was dedicated as a national landmark in 1969, the local paper ran an editorial condoning local townspeople's hostility to Du Bois and to the dedication ceremony, a sentiment the same editorialist reversed ten years later (Paynter 1990:58). Ideological processes of forgetting, selective memory, and outright contestation seem associated with landscapes suffering from "benign" neglect at these African-American sites outside plantations (e.g., Cowan-Ricks 1991). Careful analyses of these cases and others should further disclose how landscapes are manipulated in settings other than plantations to maintain white supremacy (Fitts 1996; Garman 1994; La Roche and Blakey, 1997).

Close studies of life both on and off plantations also will reveal the interweaving of the lives of European Americans and African Americans, too often according to the strictures of white racism. In comparing cases, not only the material culture but also the forms of social relations and ideologies will appear distinct. For instance, the benign neglect or paternal concern/contempt of the citizens of Berkshire County, Massachusetts, toward the Du Bois site will be different from the panoptic gaze of the planter, the give-and-take of the Monticello craftsman, and the hostility of North Woods lumbermen. In short, white racism is not monolithic: its diversity needs to be studied as a way to understand the forces that caused variations in the veil over time and space.

How then to conceptualize the relations between African and European Americans in ways that acknowledge the power of the constructions of white racism and yet also acknowledge the mutability of the concepts and practices? For despite the intellectual recognition that "race" is an ideological construct and a historical product (e.g., Fields 1990) which itself requires explanation (e.g., Howson 1990; Epperson 1990b, and chap. 8 in this volume; Drake 1987, 1990), on the ground racial, patriarchal capitalism as a form of domination creates variations and distances that matter. Ethnicity has been offered in many recent accounts as a way to acknowledge simultaneously that "races" are historical constructs, not biological realities, and yet do make a difference.

The strength of the notion of ethnicity lies in its disarticulation of culture and biology. There are also pitfalls inherent in the concept. Ethnicity tends to be approached in two ways: as a primordial notion in which some cultural or inheritable essence lies at the root of social identity and as a relational notion in which social identities form and dissolve in the context of interactions with others. The primordial notion of ethnic most closely matches the lay use of the word and is likely to be how we will use the word in an undertheorized manner (Williams 1989:402).

The attraction of the primordial notion of ethnicity is that it matches the emics (insider perspectives) of the groups under study, promising to divide the social field into discrete, internally homogenous units, whose collective fate describes the course of social history. Additionally, these models can attach to a considerable amount of social theory that works with the idea that social dynamics require the definition of discrete social essences—social processes that Wolf describes in terms of billiard balls moving about a world-scale billiard table (Wolf 1982:6–7). Wolf (1982) also points to the problems that such metaphors create for studying real historical trajectories. Internal relations are rarely homogenous; boundaries are rarely unambiguous; identities are rarely stable over extended periods of time. Even the notion of creolization, when underwritten with primordial notions of ethnic groups, falls prey to these pitfalls (Singleton 1995:133). Creolization can become, with a primordial notion of ethnicity, a process in which—to extend the metaphor—two or more billiard balls merge to become a new one. Clearly, this does not help explain why a particular set of balls were found adjacent to one another, or why the new ball takes on a specific color and number. In short, primordial notions of ethnicity substitute a social physics for social process.

Relational approaches seek to capture the dynamism of ethnic identity by situating identity in a field of social interactions. Considerable debate ensues about which relations are more important for understanding the crystallization and dissolution of particular identities. Williams (1989:439) reviews a wide range of this theory and concludes that especially when trying to understand notions of race, "ethnicity labels the visibility of that aspect of the identity formation process that is produced by and subordinated to nationalist programs and plans—plans intent on creating putative homogeneity out of heterogeneity through the appropriative processes of a transformist hegemony. . . . In short, ethnicity labels the politics of cultural struggle in the nexus of territorial and cultural nationalism that characterizes all putatively homogeneous nation-states. . . . it identifies those who are at the borders of the empire." As Jordan (1968:315–41) points out, the hegemonic nation-state program for Anglo-Americans consisted in defining American nationalism as that of a modified English person, a plan that leaves no room for modified Africans as anything other than "Other."

Recent work critiques the collapsing of race into the category of ethnicity (Gregory and Sanjek 1994; Harrison 1995:47–48; Smedley 1993:29–33; Wolf 1994:7). For instance, Sanjek (1994) is dismayed at how the topic of race dropped out of the anthropological debates in the 1970s in favor of the analysis of ethnic relations. He and Gregory (1994; Gregory and Sanjek 1994) tie this to changes in the world political economy and argue for the necessity of renewing the interest of anthropologists in its study. From this critical perspective race refers to the historical positioning of people within the global processes of capitalist accumulation (Sanjek 1994). Harrison (1995:50) captures this position by noting that "racism is characterized by an international hierarchy . . . in which wealth, power, and advanced development are associated largely with whiteness or 'honorary whiteness.'" Ethnicity, as noted by Williams (see also Wallerstein 1991:82–84) refers to more local ramifications of worldwide accumulation. In light of these critiques, historical archaeologists need to be wary of collapsing "race" into "ethnicity."

The transformation of cultural forms in the Americas happened in the setting of severe and persistent economic and power inequalities. The retention, elimination, appropriation, amplification, and modification of forms were part of cultural struggles in a context of extreme exploitation. Groups were identified, their identities transformed, assimilated, co-opted, and finally eliminated as struggles on economic, political, and cultural fronts took shape. The veil finds its construction within these processes. But rather than seeing this construction solely as the result of practices of European domination, previous pleas for African agency must be kept in mind.

Two related but distinct processes were, and continue to be, in operation. One of these, as Williams notes, is the formation of racial identities as part of the actions by dominant groups to define a hegemonic "self" in opposition to marginal "others." But equally important are the independent processes of identification indigenous to the groups undergoing marginalization. Gailey and Patterson (1987:9) make use of the notion of ethnogenesis. Ethnogenesis is "the creation of authentic culture ... [which] may involve forging a national identity in opposition to the state-sponsored ideologies.... Ethnogenesis may occur in a particular group designated by the state as an ethnicity. It may also involve people in a range of such state-identified groups, where the basis for identity is their shared position in the state-sponsored or imposed division of labor. Peoples who had not had a firmly focused ethnic identity ... may come to recognize their commonality." The notion of ethnogenesis calls attention to: (1) the fact that social identity formation occurs in a social field of power inequalities, (2) the fact that despite the differentials in social power, an ability to control cultural expression of identity continues to lie with the less powerful, and (3) the fact that this autonomous identity process may work with a variety of identities and mechanisms for their reformulation, which historically precede this specific round of identity formation.

Indeed, as many of the essays in this volume remind us, numerous social identities, some forged within African state formations and some forged outside the context of state politics, were the basis of African-American identities. We would add that in addition to attempting to better understand these diverse African identities, we should also seek to understand the processes used to transcend social difference in pre-Atlantic slave trade Africa, for these undoubtedly played a role in bringing an autonomous order to the African communities of the Western Hemisphere.

Understanding the autonomous and diverse lives of African-American communities is what the veil obscures from hegemonic culture. The veil obscures the creativity and purpose, the agency, of African Americans, by editing the official histories and/or by reducing people to a few monolithic categories, such as "slaves," or "sharecroppers," or "farmers." To recall the complex presence and effects of what were/are a significant proportion of this hemisphere's inhabitants, it is necessary to forge a non-Eurocentric (Amin 1989) view of the African-American world, to examine "the Great Enslavement" (Asante 1990) through African-American eyes. As many of the chapters in this volume give evidence, historical archaeology is well equipped to meet this challenge, especially when objects, documents, perspectives, and words are brought together to see life on the African-American side of the veil (Singleton 1995).

Not surprisingly, what these studies find is the rich diversity of experiences that made up African-American lives: curers and healers, scholars and farmers, urbanites and rural people. These stories represent serious and ongoing challenges to the structures of white racism that seek to confine African-Americans to a few rural and urban ghettos on the historical landscape and to a few aspects of social life. Developing these views of the diversity, vitality, autonomy, and exploitation of African-American lives has been, and as amplified herein continues to be, one of the major research projects of African-American archaeology (Singleton 1985, 1990).

Grasping the power and malleability of white hegemonic racial domination and discovering the resiliency and power of African-American resistance are tasks necessary to counteract the effects of the veil on the practice of historical archaeology. And, in taking on these issues, historical archaeology addresses the issue raised in the title of this book, *"I, Too, Am America."* The fate of the nation-state known as America is inseparable from the struggles of African-American ethnogenesis. These struggles have sought to make the hegemonic culture acknowledge the sources of its wealth and live up to the promises of its own political idealism. With this recognition comes the realization that African-American archaeology is not a specialty ethnic study; it is an inquiry into the nature of the course of cultural history in the Western Hemisphere. When the veil is lifted, Langston Hughes's appraisal in the poem "I Too" will be acknowledged.

## Conclusion

It is the color line of our world that gives an imperative to the study of African-American archaeology; and in studying the historical archaeology of the color line, we discover its malleability. Objects, social relations, even bodies take on different meanings and participate in different structures, depending on one's temporal, spatial, and social position in the societal formation of the Western Hemisphere. An awareness of this contextual multivalency is a necessary tool for countering the stultifying effects of the veil of racism. Goals for historical archaeology include the elucidation of the role that the material world of commodities, architecture, and landscapes played in the creation and perpetuation of race-class-ethnic-gender lines as they shifted to contribute to the accumulation of wealth and power for the few. Furthermore, we must comprehend how place, tradition, identity, and objects of domestic labor were configured and reconfigured to transform and resist this regime of accumulation. The African diaspora has many historical landscapes, formed in contradiction and tension, that offer vantage points from which to observe the global political economy and the local relations of resistance, rebellion, and revolution. The studies in this volume show us how to stand in these places, study and lift the veil of racism, and as a result more fully bring to light the African-American experience.

## Notes

Thanks to Theresa Singleton and Mark Bograd for asking us to comment on these chapters and for their insights on African-American archaeology. Perry must thank all of his courageous African ancestors whose struggles have privileged him with the opportunity to interpret the material aspects of their captivity and resistance. Perry also especially thanks Jim Moore, Carol Kramer, Eric Wolf, Paul Welch, Greg Johnson, the Working Class Anthropology Project, and Martin Hall's inspiring writing for helping him formulate links between racism and archaeology. Paynter especially thanks Helan Page, Nancy Muller, Susan Hautaniemi, Irma McClaurin, Maki Mandela, G. L. Wallace, Kamela Heyward, Paul Mullins, Jim Delle, Jim Garman, Rita Reinke, Rick Gumaer, Ellen Savulis, Sheila Brennan, Beth Bower, Byron Rushing, John Bracey, and Bill Strickland for their thoughts and conversations on African-American identity and power. And we both thank Ruth Mathis and Tom Patterson for joining us on this journey.

# References

Abrahams, Gabbebah. 1984. "The Development of Historical Archaeology at the Cape, South Africa." *Bulletin of the South African Cultural History Museum* 5:20–32.

Abrahams, Roger D., and John F. Szwed. 1976. "Introduction" to special thematic issue on Discovery Afro-America. *Journal of Asian and African Studies* 9 (3–4): 135–38.

——. 1983. *After Africa*. New Haven: Yale Univ. Press.

Adams, W. Y., D. P. Van Gerven, and R. S. Levy. 1978. "Retreat from Migrationism." *Annual Review of Anthropology* 7:483–532.

Adams, William, ed. 1987. Historical Archaeology of Plantations at Kings Bay, Camden County, Georgia. Reports of Investigations 5. Department of Anthropology, University of Florida, Gainesville.

Agbaje-Williams, Babatkunde. 1983. A Contribution to the Archaeology of Old Oyo. Ph.D. diss., Department of Archaeology, University of Ibadan, Ibadan, Nigeria.

Agorsah, Emmanuel K. 1983a. An Ethnoarchaeological Study of Settlement and Behavior Patterns of a West African Traditional Society. Ph.D. diss., University of California, Los Angeles.

——. 1983b. "Social Behavior and Spatial Context." *African Study Monographs* 4:119–28.

——. 1985a. "Archaeological Implications of Traditional House Construction among the Nchumuru of Northern Ghana." *Current Anthropology* 26:103–15.

——. 1985b. "The Internal Spatial Organization of Traditional Houses in the Northern Volta Basin of Ghana." *Research Review* 2 (2): 104–34.

——. 1986. "House Forms in the Northern Volta Basin: Evolution, Internal Spatial Organization, and the Social Relationships Depicted." *West African Journal of Archaeology* 16:25–51.

——. 1988. "Evaluating Spatial Behavior Patterns of Prehistoric Societies." *Journal of Anthropological Archaeology* 7:231–47.

——. 1990. "Ethnoarchaeology: The Search for a Self-corrective Approach to the Study of Past Behavior." *African Archaeological Review* 8:189–208.

——. 1991. "Archaeological Expedition to Nanny Town." *Archaeology Jamaica*, n.s., 1 (3): 8–11.

——. 1992. "Archaeology and the Maroon Heritage in Jamaica." *Jamaica Journal* 24 (2): 2–9.

Agorsah, Kofi E., ed. 1994. *Maroon Heritage: Archaeological, Ethnographic, and Historical Perspectives*. Kingston, Jamaica: Canoe Press, Univ. of the West Indies.

Ajayi, Babfemi Ayodele. 1985. An Evaluation of Ceramic Development Potentials in Ondo State. Ph.D. diss., Department of Fine and Applied Arts, University of Nigeria, Nsukka.

Alexander, Edward P., ed. 1972. *The Journal of John Fontaine: An Irish Huguenot Son in Spain and Virginia, 1710–1719.* Williamsburg: Colonial Williamsburg Foundation.

Allen, Theodore W. 1994. *The Invention of the White Race,* vol. 1, *Racial Oppression and Social Control.* London: Verso.

Amin, S. 1989. *Eurocentrism.* New York: Monthly Review Press.

Anonymous. [1649] 1836–46. *A Perfect Description of Virginia . . .,* London, reprinted in *Tracts and Other Papers Relating Principally to the Origin, Settlement, and Progress of the Colonies in North America, From the Discovery of the Country to the Year 1776.* Vol. 2, ed. P. Force. Washington, D.C.: Peter Force.

Anonymous. 1799. *Robinson's Philadelphia Register and City Directory for 1799.* Philadelphia: John Bioren.

Anonymous. 1837. "Management of Slaves, &c." *Farmers' Register* 5:32–33.

Anthony, Carl. 1976a. "The Big House and the Slave Quarters, Part I: Prelude to New World Architecture." *Landscape* 20 (3): 8–19.

———. 1976b. "The Big House and the Slave Quarters, Part II: African Contribution to the New World." *Landscape* 21 (1): 9–15.

Anthony, Ronald. 1979. "Descriptive Analysis and Replication of Historic Earthenware: Colono Wares from the Spier's Landing Site, Berkeley County, South Carolina." *Conference on Historic Site Archaeology Papers* 13:253–68.

Antwi, Ibraham Kwabena, comp. 1976. The Historical and Cultural Significance of Ashanti Artefacts: An Annotated Bibliography. Paper presented for the graduate diploma in Library Studies, University of Ghana, Legon.

Appiah, Kwame A. 1992. *In My Father's House: Africa in the Philosophy of Culture.* New York: Oxford Univ. Press.

Aptheker, Herbert. 1983. *American Negro Slave Revolts* (40th Anniversary Edition). New York: International Publishers.

Arana, Luis. 1973. "The Mosé Site." *El Escribano* 10:50–62. St. Augustine Historical Society.

Armstrong, Douglas V. 1983. The Old Village at Drax Hall Plantation: An Archaeological Examination of an Afro-Jamaican Settlement. Ph.D. diss., Anthropology, University of California, Los Angeles. Ann Arbor, Mich.: University Microfilms.

———. 1985. "An Afro-Jamaican Slave Settlement: Archaeological investigations at Drax Hall." In *The Archaeology of Slavery and Plantation Life,* ed. T. A. Singleton, 261–85. Orlando, Fla.: Academic Press.

———. 1990a. *The Old Village and the Great House: An Archaeological and Historical Examination of Drax Hall Plantation, Jamaica.* Urbana: Univ. of Illinois Press.

———. 1990b. "Research at Seville Plantation: A Progress Report." *Archaeology Jamaica,* n.s., 1 (2): 7–8.

———. 1991a. "The Afro-Jamaican House-yard: An Archaeological and Ethnohistorical Perspective." *Florida Journal of Anthropology,* Special Publication 7:51–63.

———. 1991b. "Seville African Jamaican Settlement Concept Design Brief." In *Master Plan for Seville Heritage Park,* ed. J. Yarwood. Kingston, Jamaica: Report to the Jamaican Urban Development Corporation.

———, ed. 1992. Conference Program. Society for Historical Archaeology 25th Annual C Conference. Kingston, Jamaica.

Armstrong, Douglas V., and Kenneth Kelly. 1991. Processes of Change and Patterns of Meaning in a Jamaican Slave Village. Paper presented at the 56th annual meeting of the Society of American Archaeology, New Orleans.

Armstrong, Douglas V., and Mark Fleischman. 1993. *Seville African Jamaican Project. Summary Report: Analysis of Four House Area Burials from the African Jamaican Settlement of Seville.* Report to Jamaica Heritage Trust. Syracuse University Archaeological Reports 6. Syracuse: Department of Anthropology, Syracuse University.

Armstrong, Patricia. 1991. Late Eighteenth and Early Nineteenth Century Nails: An Analysis of the William Stewart Site. Thomas Jefferson Memorial Foundation, Monticello, Charlottesville, Va. Manuscript.

Arneberg, Halfdan. 1951. *Norwegian Peasant Art: Men's Handicrafts.* Oslo: Fabritus and Sonner Publishers.

Asante, M. K. 1990. *Afrocentricity.* Trenton, N.J.: African World Press.

Ascher, Robert. 1974. "Tin*Can Archaeology." *Historical Archaeology* 8:7–16.

Ascher, Robert, and Charles H. Fairbanks. 1971. "Excavation of a Slave Cabin: Georgia, U.S.A." *Historical Archaeology* 5:3–17.

Askins, William. 1988. Sandy Ground: Historical Archaeology of Class and Ethnicity in a Nineteenth-Century Community on Staten Island. Ph.D. diss., Department of Anthropology, City University of New York, New York. Ann Arbor, Mich.: University Microfilms.

Atherton, John Harvey. 1983. "Ethnoarchaeology in Africa." *African Archaeological Review* 1:75–104.

Ayensu, Edward. 1978. *Medicinal Plants of West Africa.* Algonac, N.Y.: Reference Publications.

———. 1981. *Medicinal Plants of the West Indies.* Algonac, N.Y.: Reference Publications.

Babson, David. 1990. "The Archaeology of Racism and Ethnicity on Southern Plantations." *Historical Archaeology* 24 (4): 20–28.

Baker, Stephen G. 1972. *Colono-Indian Pottery from Cambridge, South Carolina, with Comments on the Historic Catawba Pottery Trade.* Notebook 4. Columbia: South Carolina Institute of Archaeology and Anthropology, University of South Carolina.

Barka, Norman F. 1973. "The Kiln and Ceramics of the Poor Potter of Yorktown: A Preliminary Report." In *Ceramics in America*, ed. I. M. Quimby, 291–318. Charlottesville: Univ. Press of Virginia.

Barnes Accounts. The Papers of Thomas Jefferson, Manuscript Division, Special Collections Department, University of Virginia Library (ViU). Charlottesville, Va.

———. Henry E. Huntington Library and Art Gallery (CsmH). San Marino, Calif.

Barnes, Sandra T. 1989. *Africa's Ogun: Old World and New.* Bloomington: Indiana Univ. Press.

Barse, William P. 1985. A Preliminary Archaeological Reconnaissance Survey of the Naval Ordnance Station, Indian Head, Maryland. Draft manuscript on file, Maryland Historical Trust, Annapolis.

Bastian, Beverly E., and William E. Rutter. 1987. *Documentary, Oral Historical, and Phase III Archeological Investigations at Elmwood Logging Camp (20IO58), Iron County, Michigan.* Jackson, Mich.: Gilbert/Commonwealth, Inc.

Bear, James A., Jr., ed. 1967. *Jefferson at Monticello.* Charlottesville: Univ. Press of Virginia.

Bear, James A., Jr., and Lucia Stanton, eds. 1997. *Jefferson's Memorandum Books: Accounts, with Legal Records and Miscellany, 1767–1826*. 2 vols. The Papers of Thomas Jefferson, 2d Series. Princeton, N.J.: Princeton Univ. Press.

Beaudry, Mary C. 1980. "Or What Else You Please to Call It": Folk Semantic Domains in Early Virginia Probate Inventories. Ph.D. diss., Department of Anthropology, Brown University.

Beckford, William. 1790. *A Descriptive Account of the Island of Jamaica*. Vols. 1 and 2. London: T. and J. Egerton.

Beguin, Jean-Pierre. 1952. *L'Habitat au Cameroon*. Paris: Office de la Recherche Scientifique Outre-Mer.

Beirne, Rosamond R., and John Henry Scharff. 1970. *William Buckland, 1734–1774: Architect of Virginia and Maryland*. Alexandria, Va. and Annapolis, Md.: Gunston Hall Board of Regents and Hammond-Harwood Association.

Bellis, James o. 1987. "A Late Archaeological Horizon in Ghana: Proto-Akan or Pre-Akan?" In *The Golden Stool: Studies of the Asante Center and Periphery*, ed. E. Schildkrout, 36–50. *Anthropological Papers of the American Museum of Natural History* 65 (1). New York: American Museum of Natural History.

Bernhardt, Marcia, ed. 1981. *Frames for the Future: Iron River Centennial History*. Iron, Mich.: Iron County Historical and Museum Society.

Berns, Marla. 1986. Art and History in the Lower Gongola Basin, Northeastern Nigeria. Ph.D. diss., University of California at Los Angeles.

———. 1989. "Ceramic Arts in Africa." *African Arts* 22 (2): 32–36.

———. 1990. "Pots as People: Yungur Ancestral Portraits." *African Arts* 23 (3): 50–60.

Berns, Marla, and Barbara R. Hudson. 1986. *The Essential Gourd*. Los Angeles: Museum of Cultural History, UCLA.

Betts, Edwin Morris, ed. 1944. *Thomas Jefferson's Garden Book, 1766–1824*. Philadelphia: American Philosophical Society.

———. 1976. *Thomas Jefferson's Farm Book*. 1953. Rept., Charlottesville: Univ. Press of Virginia.

Beverley, Robert. [1705] 1968. *The History and Present State of Virginia*. Ed. and with an introduction by L. B. Wright. Charlottesville: Univ. Press of Virginia.

Biddle, Clement. 1791. *The Philadelphia Directory*. Philadelphia: James and Johnson.

Biedermann, Galerii. 1981. *Nupe Kakanda Basa-Nge*. Munich, Ger.: Fred Jahn Publisher.

Billings, Warren M. R. 1975. *The Old Dominion in the Seventeenth Century: A Documentary History of Virginia, 1606–1689*. Chapel Hill: Univ. of North Carolina.

Binford, Lewis R. 1962a. "Archaeology as Anthropology." *American Antiquity* 28:217–25.

———. 1962b. "A New Method of Calculating Dates from Kaolin Pipe Stem Fragments." *Southeastern Archaeological Conference Newsletter*, A Special Issue of Papers presented at the 1st and 2nd Conferences on Historical Site Archaeology, ed. S. South (June): 19–21.

———. 1964. Archaeological and Ethnohistorical Investigation of Cultural Diversity and Progressive Development among Aboriginal Cultures of Coastal North Carolina and Virginia. Ph.D. diss., Department of Anthropology, University of Michigan.

———. 1965. "Colonial Period Ceramics of the Nottoway and Weanock Indians of Southeastern Virginia." *Archaeological Society of Virginia, Quarterly Bulletin* 19 (4): 78–87.

———. 1967. "An Ethnohistory of the Nottoway, Meherrin, and Weanock Indians of Southeastern Virginia." *Ethnohistory* 14 (3–4): 103–218.

———. 1983. *In Pursuit of the Past: Decoding the Archaeological Record*. London: Thames and Hudson.

Blair, James. 1730. Blair to the Bishop of London, 20 July. Fulham Palace Papers 13:131. Reproduced in the Virginia Colonial Records Project. Richmond: Virginia State Library.

———. 1731. Blair to the Bishop of London, May. Fulham Palace Papers 15:110. Reproduced in the Virginia Colonial Records Project. Richmond: Virginia State Library.

Blaker, Margaret. 1963. "Aboriginal Ceramics: The Townsend Site near Lewes, Delaware." *Archaeolog* 15 (1): 14–39.

Blakey, Michael L. 1990. "American Nationality and Ethnicity in the Depicted Past." In *The Politics of the Past*, ed. P. Gathercole and D. Lowenthal, 38–48. London: Unwin Hyman.

Blassingame, John. 1979. *The Slave Community: Plantation Life in the Antebellum South*. 2d ed. New York: Oxford Univ.

Blier, Suzanne Preston. 1987. *The Anatomy of Architecture: Ontology and Metaphor in Batammaliba Architectural Expression*. London: Cambridge Univ. Press.

Blomberg, Belinda. 1989. *The Formation of Free Black Communities in Nineteenth Century Alexandria, Virginia*. Alexandria Archaeology Publications no. 2. City of Alexandria, Va.: Alexandria Archaeology, Office of Historic Alexandria.

Bograd, Mark D., and Theresa A. Singleton. 1997. "The Interpretation of Slavery: Mount Vernon, Monticello, and Colonial Williamsburg." In *Presenting Archaeology to the Public*, ed. J. H. Jameson, Jr., 193–204. Walnut Creek, Calif.: Altamira.

Bohannon, Paul. 1956. "Beauty and Scarification amongst the Tiv." *Man* 129:117–21.

Bourdier, Jean-Paul, and Trinh T. Minh-Ha. 1985. *African Spaces: Designs for Living in Upper Volta*. New York: Africana Publishing Company.

Bower, Beth A. 1991. "Material Culture in Boston: The Black Experience." In *The Archaeology of Inequality*, ed. R. H. McGuire and R. Paynter, 55–63. New York: Basil Blackwell.

Bower, Beth Anne, and Byron Rushing. 1980. "The African Meeting House: The Center for the 19th Century Afro-American Community in Boston." In *Archaeological Perspectives on Ethnicity in America*, ed. R. L. Schuyler, 69–75. Farmingdale, N.Y.: Baywood Publishing.

Bowdich, Edward T. 1819. *Mission from Cape Coast to Ashantee*. 3d ed., ed. with notes and introduction by W. E. F. Ward. London: Frank Cass & Co.

Boyce, Hettie, and Lori A. Frye. 1986. *Radiocarbon Dating of Archaeological Samples from Maryland*. Maryland Geological Society Archeological Studies no. 4. Baltimore.

Brathwaite, Edward. 1971. *The Development of Creole Society in Jamaica, 1770–1820*. Oxford: Clarendon Press.

Braithwaite, Mary. 1982. "Decoration as Ritual Symbol: A Theoretical Proposal and an

Ethnographic Study in Southern Sudan." In *Symbolic and Structural Archaeology*, ed. I. Hodder, 80–88. Cambridge: Cambridge Univ. Press.

Bravmann, René A. 1974. *Islam and Tribal Art in West Africa*. London: Cambridge Univ. Press.

———. 1983. *African Islam*. Washington, D.C.: Smithsonian Institution Press.

Bravmann, R. A., and R. D. Mathewson. 1970. "A Note on the History and Archaeology of 'Old Bima.'" *African Historical Studies* 3 (1): 133–49.

Brears, Peter D. 1974. *The Collector's Book of English Country Pottery*. London: David and Charles.

Breeden, James O., ed. 1980. *Advice among Masters: The Ideal in Slave Management in the Old South*. Westport, Conn.: Greenwood.

Breen, T. H. 1973. "A Changing Labor Force and Race Relations in Virginia, 1660–1710." *Journal of Social History* 8:3–25.

———. 1980. "A Changing Labor Force and Race Relations in Virginia, 1660–1710." In *Puritans and Adventurers: Change and Persistence in Early America*, 127–47. 1973. Rept., Oxford: Oxford Univ. Press.

Breen, T. H., and Stephen Innes. 1980. *Myne Owne Ground: Race and Freedom on Virginia's Eastern Shore, 1640–1676*. New York: Oxford Univ. Press.

Brett, Vanessa. 1982. *Phaidon Guide to Pewter*. Englewood Cliffs, N.J.: Prentice-Hall.

Brewer, James H. 1955. "Negro Property Holders in Seventeenth-Century Virginia." *William and Mary Quarterly*, 3d ser., 12:575–80.

Briceland, Alan Vance. 1987. *Westward from Virginia: The Exploration of the Virginia-Carolina Frontier, 1650–1710*. Charlottesville: Univ. Press of Virginia.

Bridges, Sarah T., and Bert Salwen. 1980. "Weeksville: The Archaeology of a Black Urban Community." In *Archaeological Perspectives on Ethnicity in America: Afro-American and Asian American Culture History*, ed. R. L. Schuyler, 38–49. Farmingdale, N.Y.: Baywood Publishing Company.

Brody, David. 1989. "Time and Work during Early American Industrialism." *Labor History* 30 (1): 5–46.

Brooke-Little, J. P. 1970. *Boutell's Heraldry, Revised by J. P. Brooke-Little, Richmond Herald of Arms*. London: Frederick Warme and Co.

Brown, Kenneth L., and Doreen C. Cooper. 1990. "Structural Continuity in an African American Slave and Tenant Community." *Historical Archaeology* 24 (4): 7–19.

Brozonowski, Simon. Telephone interview by William E. Rutter. 11 Feb. 1986.

Bruce, Philip Alexander. 1935. *Economic History of Virginia in the Seventeenth Century*. 2 vols. New York: Macmillan.

Bush, Barbara. 1990. *Slave Women in Caribbean Society, 1650–1838*. Bloomington: Indiana Univ. Press.

Butler, Mary. 1939. *Three Archaeological Sites in Somerset County, Pennsylvania*. Bulletin of the Pennsylvania Historical Commission no. 753. Harrisburg, Pa.

Calhoun, Jean. 1986. "Historical Overview for the Charleston Vicinity." In Home Upriver: Rural Life on Daniel's Island, Berkeley County, South Carolina. Ed. Martha Zierdan, L. Drucker, and J. Calhoun, 2–13–33. Report (Contract No. FA1-526-41[63]) pprepared by Carolina Archaeological Services and the Charleston Museum. Submitted to South Carolina Department of Transportation, Federal Highway Administration, Columbia.

Campbell, Edward D. C., Jr., and Kym S. Rice, eds. 1991. *Before Freedom Came: African-American Life in the Antebellum South*. Richmond: Museum of the Confederacy, and Charlottesville: Univ. Press of Virginia.

Cardew, Michael. 1952. "Nigerian Traditional Pottery." *Nigeria* 39:188–201.

Carney, Judith. 1993. "From Hands to Tutors: African Expertise in the South Carolina Rice Economy." *Agricultural History* 67:1–30.

——. 1996. "Landscapes of Technology Transfer: Rice Cultivation and African Continuities." *Technology and Culture* 37 (1): 5–35.

Carr, Lois G., Phillip D. Morgan, and Jean B. Russo, eds. 1988. *Colonial Chesapeake Society*. Chapel Hill: Univ. of North Carolina Press.

Carson, Cary. 1976. "Segregation in Vernacular Buildings." *Vernacular Architecture* 7:24–29.

——. 1978. "Doing History with Material Culture." In *Material Culture and the Study of American Life*, ed. I. M. G. Quimby, 41–64. New York: Norton.

——. 1990. Recent Trends in History Museums. Paper, Conference on Re-creating the World of the Virginia Plantation, 1750–1820, University of Virginia and Monticello.

——. 1991. "Front and Center: Local History Comes of Age." In *Local History, National Heritage: Reflections on the History of the American Association for State and Local History*, 67–108. Nashville: AASLH.

Carson, Cary, Norman F. Barka, William M. Kelso, Garry W. Stone, and Dell Upton. 1981. "Impermanent Architecture in the Southern American Colonies." *Winterthur Portfolio* 16 (2/3): 135–96.

Carson, Jane. 1965. *Colonial Virginians at Play*. Williamsburg: Colonial Williamsburg Press.

Catts, Wade P., and McCall Davy. 1991. "A Report of the Archaeological Investigations at the House of Thomas Cuff, a Free Black Laborer, 108 Cannon Street, Chestertown, Kent County, Maryland." *North American Archaeologist* 12 (2): 155–81.

Caywood, Louis R. 1955. *Excavations at Green Spring Plantation*. Colonial National Historical Park. Yorktown, Va.: National Park Service.

——. 1957. "Green Spring Plantation." *Virginia Magazine of History and Biography* 65:67–84.

Cerroni-Long, E. L. 1987. "Benign Neglect? Anthropology and the Study of Blacks in the United States." *Journal of Black Studies* 17 (4): 438–59.

Chambers, Douglas B. 1992. "Afro-Virginian Root Cellars and African Roots? A Comment on the Need for a Moderate Afrocentric Approach." *African American Archaeology* 6:7–10.

Chappell, Edward. 1981. "Williamsburg Architecture as Social Space." *Fresh Advices*. November. Williamsburg, Va.: Colonial Williamsburg Foundation.

——. 1982. "Slave Housing." *Fresh Advices*. November. Williamsburg, Va.: Colonial Williamsburg Foundation.

——. 1989a. " Museums." *Nation* 249:102–4.

——. 1989b. "Social Responsibility and the American History Museum." *Winterthur Portfolio* 24:247–65.

——. 1990. Re-creation of the Carter's Grove Quarter and the Archaeology of American Slavery. Paper, Jamestown Archaeological Conference, Popes Creek, Va.

——. 1994. "Housing a Nation: Transformation of Living Standards in Early America." In *Of Consuming Interests: The Style of Life in the Eighteenth Century*, ed. C. Carson, R. Hoffman, and P. J. Albert, 167–232. Charlottesville: Univ. Press of Virginia.

Chinard, Gilbert, ed. and trans. 1934. *A Huguenot Exile in Virginia; Or, Voyages of a Frenchman Exiled for His Religion, with a Description of Virginia and Maryland*. 1687. Rept. New York: Press of the Pioneers.

Clifton-Taylor, Alec. 1972. *The Pattern of English Building*. London: Faber and Faber.

Colburn, David. 1985. *Racial Change and Community Crisis: St. Augustine, Florida, 1877–1980*. New York: Columbia Univ. Press.

Cole, Herbert M., and Chike C. Aniakor. 1984. *Igbo Arts: Community and Cosmos*. Los Angeles: Museum of Culture History, University of California.

Cole, Herbert M., and Doran H. Ross. 1977. *The Arts of Ghana*. Los Angeles: Museum of Cultural History, UCLA .

Cole, Johnetta B. 1980a. "Race toward Equality: The Impact of the Cuban Revolution on Racism." *Black Scholar* 11:2–29.

——. 1980b. "Women in Cuba: The Revolution within the Revolution." In *Comparative Perspectives on Third World Women*, ed. B. Lindsey, 162–78. New York: Praeger.

Coleman, Garry N., Richard P. Gravelly, Jr., Keith T. Egloff, Suzi Kirby, and Douglas Belcher. N.d. Archaeological Investigations at the Koehler Site, 44Hr6. Virginia Department of Historic Resources Special Publication, Richmond. In press.

Conway, Moncure Daniel, ed. 1889. "George Washington and Mount Vernon: A Collection of Washington's Unpublished Agricultural and Personal Letters." *Memoirs of the Long Island Historical Society*, 4. Brooklyn, N.Y.: Published by the Society.

Copes Tobacco Plant Office. 1895. *The Pipes of Asia and Africa*. Smoke Room Booklets, 11. Liverpool: Privately printed.

Cosgrove, Denis E. 1984. *Social Formation and Symbolic Landscape*. Totowa, N.J.: Barnes and Noble.

——. 1985. "Prospect, Perspective, and the Evolution of the Landscape Idea." *Transactions, Institute of British Geographers*, n.s., 10:45–62.

——. 1988. "Introduction: Iconography and Landscape." In *The Iconography of Landscape: Essays on the Symbolic Representation, Design, and Use of Past Environments*, ed. D. Cosgrove and S. Daniels, 1–10. Cambridge: Cambridge Univ. Press.

Cote, Richard. 1986a. "Jefferson's Workmen and the Virginia Landmarks Register." *Notes on Virginia* 28:26–29.

——. 1986b. The Architectural Workmen of Thomas Jefferson in Virginia. Ph.D. diss., Boston University, Boston.

Cotter, John L. 1958. *Archaeological Excavations at Jamestown, Virginia*. Archaeological Search, no. 4, National Park, Washington, D.C.

Cowan-Ricks, Carrel. 1991. African American Cemeteries: Historical Symbols. Paper presented at the annual meeting of the American Anthropological Association, Chicago.

Crader, Diana C. 1984. "The Zooarchaeology of the Storehouse and the Dry Well at Monticello." *American Antiquity* 49:542–58.

——. 1989. Faunal Remains from Slave Quarter Site at Monticello. Thomas Jefferson Memorial Foundation, Charlottesville, Va.

——. 1990. "Slave Diet at Monticello." *American Antiquity* 55:690–717.

———. 1991. The Faunal Remains from the Stewart-Watkins House Site at Monticello. Appendix 4 in A Report on the Archaeological Excavations at Monticello, Charlottesville, Va.: The Stewart/Watkins House, 1989–1990, by Barbara Heath, 154–62. Thomas Jefferson Memorial Foundation, Charlottesville, Va. Manuscript.

Crahan, Margaret E., and Franklin W. Knight, eds. 1979. *Africa and the Caribbean: The Legacies of a Link*. Baltimore: John Hopkins Univ. Press.

Crass, David Colin. 1981. A Formal Analysis of the Clay Pipes from Green Spring. M.A. Thesis, Department of Anthropology, College of William and Mary, Williamsburg, Va.

Craton, Michael. 1978. *Searching for the Invisible Man: Slaves and Plantation Life in Jamaica*. Cambridge: Harvard Univ. Press.

Craven, Wesley Frank. 1971a. "Twenty Negroes to Jamestown in 1619?" *Virginia Quarterly Review* 47:416–20.

———. 1971b. *White, Red, and Black: The Seventeenth-Century Virginian*. Charlottesville: Univ. Press of Virginia.

Crenshaw, Kimberlé, Neil Gotanda, Gary Peller, and Kendall Thomas. 1995. "Introduction." In *Critical Race Theory: The Key Writings That Formed the Movement*, ed. K. Crenshaw, N. Gotanda, G. Peller, and K. Thomas, xiii–xxxii. New York: New Press.

Cressey, Pamela. 1985. *The Archaeology of Free Blacks in Alexandria, Virginia*. Alexandria Archaeology Publications no. 19. City of Alexandria, Va.

Crossland, Leonard B. 1973. A Study of Begho Pottery in the Light of Excavations Conducted at the Begho-B2 Site. M.A. Thesis, Department of Archaeology, University of Ghana, Legon.

Curlee, Abigail. 1974. "The History of a Texas Slave Plantation, 1831–63." In *Plantation, Town, and County: Essays on the Local History of American Slave Society*, ed. E. Miller and E. Genovese, 303–34. Urbana: Univ. of Illinois Press.

Curtin, Philip D. 1969. *The Atlantic Slave Trade: A Census*. Madison, Wis.: Univ. of Wisconsin Press.

Daaku, Kwame. 1970. *Trade and Politics on the Gold Coast: A Study of the African Reaction to European Trade*. Oxford: Clarendon Press.

Daget, J., and Z. Ligers. 1962. "Une ancienne industrie Malienne: Les pipes en terre." *Bulletin de l'Institut Français d'Afrique Noire*, ser. B, 24 (1–2): 12–53.

Daniels, Christine. 1993. "'Wanted: A Blacksmith Who Understands Plantation Work': Artisans in Maryland, 1700–1810." *William and Mary Quarterly*, 3d ser., 50 (4): 743–67.

Dark, Philip J. C. 1973. *An Introduction to Benin Art and Technology*. Oxford: Clarendon Press.

David, Nicholas. 1971. "The Fulani Compound and the Archaeologist." *World Archaeology* 3 (2): 11–131.

David, Nicholas, and Hilke Hennig. 1972. "The Ethnography of Pottery: A Fulani Case Seen in Archaeological Perspective." *Addison-Wesley Modular Publications, Module* 21:1–29.

David, Nicholas, Judy Sterner, and Kodzo Gavua. 1988. "Why Pots Are Decorated." *Current Anthropology* 29:365–89.

David, Nicholas, Kodzo Gavua, A. Scott MacEachern, and Judy Sterner. 1991. "Ethnicity and Material Culture in North Cameroon." *Canadian Journal of Archaeology* 15:171–77.

Davidson, Basil. 1980. *The African Slave Trade*. Boston: Little, Brown and Company.

Davies, N. 1979. *Voyagers to the New World*. Albuquerque: Univ. of New Mexico Press.

Davies, Oliver. 1955. Excavation at Mampongtin, 1955: A Corpus of Eighteenth-Century Ashanti Pottery. Department of Archaeology, University of Ghana, Legon. Manuscript.

———. 1956. Excavations at Sekondi, Ghana, in 1954 and 1956. Department of Archaeology, University of Ghana, Legon. Manuscript.

———. 1961. *Archaeology in Ghana*. London: Thomas Nelson and Sons.

———. 1964. "Gonja Painted Pottery." *Transactions of the Historical Society of Ghana* 7:4–11.

Deagan, Kathleen. 1976. *The Archaeology of the National Greek Orthodox Shrine, St. Augustine, Florida*. Gainesville: Univ. of Florida Presses.

———. 1978. "Cultures in Transition: Assimilation and Fusion among the Eastern Timucua." In *Tacachale*, ed. J. T. Milanich and S. Proctor, 89–119. Gainesville: Univ. Presses of Florida.

———. 1983. *Spanish St. Augustine: The Archaeology of a Colonial Creole Community*. New York: Academic Press.

Deagan, Kathleen A., and Darcie MacMahon. 1995. *Fort Mosé: Colonial America's Black Fortress of Freedom*. Gainesville: Univ. of Florida Press.

De Barros, Philip. 1990. "Changing Paradigms, Goals, and Methods in the Archaeology of Francophone West Africa." In *A History of African Archaeology*, ed. P. Robertshaw, 155–72. London: James Curry.

Debien, Gabriel. 1974. *Les Esclaves aux Antilles françaises (XVIIe-XVIIIe siècles)*. Base Terre: Société d'histoire de la Guadeloupe.

DeCorse, Christopher R. 1987. "Historical Archaeological Research in Ghana, 1986–1987." *Nyame Akuma* 29:27–31.

———. 1989a. An Archaeological Study of Elmina, Ghana: Trade and Culture Change on the Gold Coast between the 15th and 19th Century. Ph.D. diss., Archaeology Program, University of California, Los Angeles.

———. 1989b. Beads as Chronological Indicators in West African Archaeology: A Reexamination. *Beads: Journal of the Society of Bead Researchers* 1:41–53.

———. 1989c. "Material Aspects of Limba, Yalunka, and Kuranko Ethnicity: Archaeological Research in Northeastern Sierra Leone." In *Archaeological Approaches to Cultural Identity*, ed. S. J. Shennan, 126–40. London: Unwin Hyman.

———. 1989d. "Review of *Beads from West Africa Trade*, Vols. 1–4, by John Picard and Ruth Picard." *Beads: Journal of the Society of Bead Researchers* 1:96–98.

———. 1991. "West African Archaeology and the Atlantic Slave Trade." *Slavery and Abolition* 12 (2): 92–96.

———. 1992. "Culture Contact, Continuity, and Change on the Gold Coast, A.D. 1400–1900." *African Archaeological Review* 10:163–96.

———. 1993. "The Danes on the Gold Coast: Culture Change and the European Presence." *African Archaeological Review* 11:149–74.

———, ed. N.d. *Historical Archaeology in West Africa: Culture Contact, Continuity, and Change*. Washington, D.C.: Smithsonian Institution Press. Forthcoming.

Deetz, James. 1977. *In Small Things Forgotten*. New York: Anchor Books.

———. 1985. "Harrington Histograms versus Binford Mean Dates as a Technique for Establishing the Occupational Sequence of Sites at Flowerdew Hundred, Virginia." *American Archaeology* 5:3.

———. 1988. "American Historical Archaeology: Methods and Results." *Science* 239:362–67.

———. 1993. *Flowerdew Hundred: The Archaeology of a Virginia Plantation, 1619–1864.* Charlottesville: Univ. of Virginia.

Delle, James. 1990. The Sugar Plantation as a Frontier Mode of Production. Paper presented at the 23d meeting of the Society for Historical Archaeology, Tucson.

Dent, Richard J. 1984. "Archaeological Research at the Accokeek Creek Site." In *The Accokeek Creek Complex and the Emerging Maryland Colony.* Accokeek, Md: Alice Ferguson Foundation.

Denyer, Susan. 1978. *African Traditional Architecture.* New York: Africana Publishing Company.

Devisse, Jean. 1981. "Pour une histoire globale de la céramique africaine." In *Le Sol, la parole, et l'écrit: Mélanges en hommage à Raymond Mauny,* 1:119–203. Paris: Société Français d'Histoire d'Outre-Mer.

*Diamond Drill.* 1925–29. Crystal Falls, Mich.

Dike, Kenneth O. 1956. *Trade and Politics in the Niger Delta.* Oxford: Clarendon Press.

Dmochowski, Z. R. 1990. *An Introduction to Nigerian Traditional Architecture.* 3 vols. London: Ethnographica.

Donnan, Elizabeth. 1969. *Documents Illustrative of the History of Slave Trade to America.* Vols. 1–4. New York: Octagon Books.

Douglas, Mary. 1970. *Natural Symbols.* New York: Pantheon Books.

———. 1982. "Food Is Not Feed." In *The Active Voice,* ed. M. Douglas. London: Routledge and Kegan Paul.

Drake, St. Clair. 1980. "Anthropology and the Black Experience." *Black Scholar,* Sept.-Oct.: 2–31.

———. 1987. *Black Folk Here and There: An Essay in History and Anthropology.* Vol. 1. Los Angeles: University of California, Center for Afro-American Studies.

———. 1990. *Black Folk Here and There.* Vol. 2. Los Angeles: University of California, Center for Afro-American Studies.

Draughon, Robert J. 1850. "Houses of Negroes: Habits, Modes of Living." *Southern Cultivator* 8:66.

Du Bois, W. E. B. 1939. *Black Folk, Then and Now: An Essay in the History and Sociology of the Negro Race.* New York: Henry Holt.

———. 1940. *Dusk of Dawn: An Essay toward an Autobiography of a Race Concept.* New York: Harcourt Brace and Company.

———. [1903] 1969. *The Souls of Black Folk.* With Introductions by Dr. Nathan Hare and Alvin F. Poussaint, M.D. New York: New American Library.

Du Dauphiné, Durand. [1687] 1934. *A Huguenot Exile in Virginia; Or, Voyages of a Frenchman Exiled for His Religion, with a Description of Virginia and Maryland.* Trans. and ed. G. Chinard. New York: Press of the Pioneer.

Dunn, Richard S. 1973. *Sugar and Slaves: The Rise of the Planter Class in the English West Indies, 1624-1713.* New York: W. W. Norton and Company.

Edwards, R., and L. G. G. Ramsey, eds. 1956. *The Tudor Period, 1500–1603*. London: Connoisseur Period Guides.

Effah-Gyamfi, Kwaku. 1985. *Bono Manso: An Archaeological Investigation into Early Akan Urbanism*. African Occasional Papers, no. 2. Calgary: Univ. of Calgary Press.

Egloff, Keith T., and Stephen R. Potter. 1982. "Indian Ceramics from Coastal Plain Virginia." *Archaeology of Eastern North America* 10:95–117.

Ellis, Rex. 1990. "A Decade of Change: Black History at Colonial Williamsburg." *Colonial Williamsburg* 12:14–23.

———. 1992. "We've Got a Visitor: Living and Teaching Black History in Mainstream Museums." *Broken Chains* 1 (2): 4–6.

Emerson, Matthew C. 1979. Afro-American Archaeology: Identifying Black Mortuary Customs in the American South. Honors thesis, Brown University, Providence.

———. 1987. Excavations at the Barker-Lucy Site at Flowerdew Hundred: A Preliminary Report. Manuscript on file at Flowerdew Hundred Foundation, Hopewell, Va.

———. 1988. Decorated Clay Tobacco Pipes from the Chesapeake. Ph.D. diss., University of California, Berkeley.

———. 1989. African Inspirations in a New World Art and Artifact: Clay Tobacco Pipes from the Chesapeake. Paper presented at the conference "Digging the Afro-American Past," 17–20 May, University of Mississippi, Oxford.

———. 1994. "African Inspirations in a New World Art and Artifact." In *The Historic Chesapeake: Archaeological Contributions*, ed. P. A. Shackel and B. J. Little, 34–49. Washington, D.C.: Smithsonian Institution.

Epperson, Terrence W. 1990a. "To Fix a Perpetual Brand": The Social Construction of Race in Virginia, 1675–1750. Ph.D. diss., Department of Anthropology, Temple University.

———. 1990b. "Race and the Disciplines of the Plantation." *Historical Archaeology* 24:29–36.

———. 1997. "The Institution of Whiteness in Early Virginia." *Race Traitor* 7:9–20.

Eppes, Richard. Plantation Diary, 1851–62. Eppes Family Muniments, Virginia Historical Society, Richmond.

Evers, T. Michael. 1989. The Recognition of Groups in the Iron Age of Southern Africa. Ph.D. diss., University of Witwatersrand, Johannesburg.

Eyo, Ekpo. 1979. *Nigeria and the Evolution of Money*. Lagos: Central Bank of Nigeria and Federal Department of Antiquities.

Ewan, Joseph, and Nesta Ewan. 1970. *John Bannister and His Natural History of Virginia, 1678–1692*. Urbana: Univ. of Illinois Press.

Fagan, Brian M. 1984. *Clash of Cultures*. New York: Freeman and Company.

Fairbanks, Charles. 1962. "A Colono-Indian Ware Milk Pitcher." *Florida Anthropologist* 15 (4): 103–6.

———. 1974. "The Kingsley Slave Cabins in Duval County, Florida, 1968." *Conference for Historic Site Archaeology Papers, 1971* 7:62–93.

———. 1984. "The Plantation Archaeology of the Southeastern Coast." *Historical Archaeology* 18:1–14.

Fauber, J. Everette, Jr. 1953. Archaeological Survey—Gunston Hall. Report on file, Gunston Hall library, Lorton, Va.

Fauber Garber, Inc. 1986. Consolidation of All Archaeological Research concerning the Dependencies around the Mansion "Gunston Hall." Report on file, Gunston Hall library, Lorton, Va.

Fausz, J. Frederick. 1988. "Merging and Emerging Worlds: Anglo-Indian Interest Groups and the Development of the Seventeenth-Century Chesapeake." In *Colonial Chesapeake Society*, ed. L. G. Carr, P. D. Morgan, and J. B. Russo, 47–91. Chapel Hill: Univ. of North Carolina Press.

Feest, Christian F. 1978. "Virginia Algonquians." In *Northeast*, ed. Bruce G. Trigger, 253–70. *Handbook of North American Indians*, ed. William Sturtevant, vol. 15. Washington, D.C.: Smithsonian Institution Press.

Ferguson, Leland. 1980. "Looking for the 'Afro' in Colono-Indian Pottery." In *Archaeological Perspectives on Ethnicity in America*, ed. R. Schuyler, 14–28. Farmingdale, N.J.: Baywood Publishing Co.

———. 1989a. "The Cross Is a Magic Sign": Marks on 18th Century Bowls from South Carolina. Paper presented at the conference "Digging the Afro-American Past," 17–20 May 1989, University of Mississippi, oxford.

———. 1989b. "Low Country Plantations, the Catawba Nation, and River-Burnished Pottery." In *Studies in South Carolina Archaeology: Essays in Honor of R. S. Stephenson*, Anthropological Studies 9, ed. A. C. Goodyear III and G. T. Hanson, 185–91. Occasional Papers of the South Carolina Institute of Archaeology and Anthropology. Columbia: University of South Carolina.

———. 1991. "Struggling with Pots in Colonial America." In *The Archaeology of Inequality*, ed. R. H. McGuire and R. Paynter, 28–39. New York: Basil Blackwell.

———. 1992. *Uncommon Ground: Archaeology and Early African America, 1650–1800*. Washington, D.C.: Smithsonian Institution Press.

———. 1994. "MESDA's Colono Ware Bowl." *Luminary* 15 (1): 5. Winston-Salem, N.C.: Museum of Early Southern Decorative Arts.

Ferguson, Leland, Richard Affleck, and Natalie Adams. 1990. An 18th-Century African-American Community in a South Carolina Rice-Growing District. Paper presented to the 83d annual meeting of the organization of American Historians, Washington, D.C.

Fields, Barbara Jean. 1982. "Ideology and Race in American History." In *Region, Race, and Reconstruction: Essays in Honor of C. Vann Woodward*, ed. J. M. Kousser and J. M. McPherson, 143–78. New York: Oxford Univ. Press.

———. 1990. "Slavery, Race, and Ideology in the United States of America." *New Left Review* 181:95–118.

Fischer, David Hackett. 1989. *Albion's Seed: Four British Folkways in America*. New York: Oxford Univ. Press.

Fitts, Robert K. 1996. "The Landscapes of Northern Bondage." *Historical Archaeology* 30 (2): 54–73.

Fleet, Beverley. 1942. *Virginia Colonial Abstracts*, vol. 13, *Charles City County Court Orders, 1664–1665, Fragments, 1650–1696*. Richmond: Beverley Fleet.

Fleischman, Mark, and Douglas V. Armstrong. 1990. *Preliminary Report: Analysis of Burial SAJ-B1 Recovered from House-Area 16, Seville Afro-Jamaican Settlement*. Report to the Jamaica National Heritage Trust. Syracuse University Archaeological Reports no. 6. Syracuse: Department of Anthropology, Syracuse University.

Fogel, Robert W., and Stanley L. Engerman. 1974. *Time on the Cross*. Boston: Little, Brown and Co.

Fox-Genovese, Elizabeth. 1988. *Within the Plantation Household: Black and White Women of the Old South*. Chapel Hill: Univ. of North Carolina Press.

Franklin, John H. 1980. *From Slavery to Freedom: The History of the Negro Americans*. 3d ed. New York: Alfred Knopf.

Frederickson, George M. 1981. *White Supremacy: A Comparative Study in American and South African History*. New York: Oxford Univ. Press.

Friedlander, Amy. 1985. "Establishing Historical Probabilities for Archaeological Interpretations: Slave Demography of Two Plantations in the South Carolina Lowcountry, 1740–1820." In *The Archaeology of Slavery and Plantation Life*, ed. T. A. Singleton, 215–38. Orlando, Fla.: Academic Press.

Frobenius, Leo. 1913. *The Voice of Africa*. Vol. 1. London: Hutchinson and Company.

Fuss, Diana. 1989. *Essentially Speaking: Feminism, Nature, and Difference*. New York: Routledge.

Gailey, C. W., and T. Patterson. 1987. "Power Relations and State Formation." In *Power Relations and State Formation*, ed. T. Patterson and C. Gailey, 1–26. Washington, D.C.: American Anthropological Association.

Galenson, David W. 1981. *White Servitude in Colonial America: An Economic Analysis*. New York: Cambridge Univ. Press.

García Arévalo, Manuel A. 1986. "El Maniel de José Leta: Evidencias arqueológicas de un posible asentamiento cimarrón en la región sudoriental de la Isla de Santo Domingo." In *Cimarrón*, by J. J. Arrom and M. A. García Arévalo. Monografica no. 18. Santo Domingo, República Dominicana: Fundación García-Arévalo.

Gardi, René. 1973. *Indigenous African Architecture*. New York: Van Nordstrand Reinhold Company.

Gardner, William J. 1986. *Lost Arrowheads and Broken Pottery: Traces of Indians in the Shenandoah Valley*. Front Royal, Va.: Thunderbird Museum.

Garman, James C. 1994. "Viewing the Color Line through the Material Culture of Death." *Historical Archaeology* 28 (3): 74–93.

Garrard, Timothy F. 1973. "Studies in Akan Goldweights (IV): The Dating of Akan Goldweights." *Transactions of the Historical Society of Ghana* 14 (2): 149–68.

———. 1983. "Akan Pseudo-Weights of European Origin." In *Akan Transformations Problems in Ghanaian Art History*, ed. D. H. Ross and T. F. Garrard, 70–81. Museum of Cultural History, UCLA, Monograph Series, no. 24. Los Angeles.

Garrow, Patrick, and Thomas Wheaton. 1989. "Colonoware Ceramics: The Evidence from Yaughan and Curriboo Plantations." In *Studies in South Carolina Archaeology: Essays in Honor of Robert L. Stephenson*, Anthropological Studies 9, ed. A. C. Goodyear III and G. T. Hanson, 175–84. Occasional Papers of the South Carolina Institute of Archaeology and Anthropology. Columbia: University of South Carolina.

Gartley, John. 1979. "Afro-Cruzan Pottery: A New Style of Colonial Earthenware from St. Croix." *Journal of the Virgin Islands Archaeological Society* 8:47–61.

Gates, Henry Louis, Jr. 1986. "Introduction: Writing 'Race' and the Difference It Makes." In *"Race," Writing, and Difference*, ed. H. L. Gates, 1–20. Chicago: Univ. of Chicago Press.

Gebauer, Paul. 1979. *Art of Cameroon*. Portland, Ore.: Portland Art Museum Association.

Geggus, D. 1989. "Sex Ratio, Age, and Ethnicity in the Atlantic Slave Trade: Data from French Shipping and Plantation Records." *Journal of African History* 30 (1): 23–44.

Genovese, Eugene D. 1965. *The Political Economy of Slavery*. New York: Pantheon.

———. 1974. *Roll, Jordan, Roll: The World the Slaves Made*. New York: Vintage Books.

———. [1972] 1976. *Roll, Jordan, Roll: The World the Slaves Made*. Rept., New York: Random House, Vintage Books.

Gibbes, R. W. 1858. "Southern Slave Life." *DeBow's Review* 24:321–24.

Gibbs, Tyson, K. Cargill, L. S. Lieberman, and E. Reitz. 1980. "Nutrition in a Slave Population: An Anthropological Examination." *Medical Anthropology* 4:175–262.

Gibson, Susan G., ed. 1980. *Burr's Hill: A 17th Century Wampanoag Burial Ground in Warren, Rhode Island*. The Haffenreffer Museum of Anthropology Studies in Anthropology and Material Culture, 2. Providence: Brown University.

Gillespie, Michele K. 1995. "Planters in the Making: Artisanal Opportunities in Georgia, 1790–1830." In *American Artisans: Crafting Social Identity, 1750–1850*, ed. H. B. Rock, P. A. Gilje, and R. Asher, 33–47. Baltimore: Johns Hopkins Univ. Press.

Gilroy, Paul. 1991. *"There Ain't No Black in the Union Jack": The Cultural Politics of Race and Nation*. Chicago: Univ. of Chicago Press.

Glassie, Henry. 1968. *Pattern in the Material Folk Culture of the Eastern United States*. Philadelphia: Univ. of Pennsylvania Press.

———. 1975. *Folk Housing in Middle Virginia*. Knoxville: Univ. of Tennessee Press.

Godwyn, Morgan. 1680. *The Negro's & Indians Advocate, Suing for Their Admission into the Church: or A Persuasive to the Instructing and Baptizing of the Negro's and Indians in our Plantations, . . . To Which Is Added, A Brief Account of Religion in Virginia*. London.

———. 1681. *A Supplement to the Negro's and Indian's Advocate: or Some Further Considerations and Proposals for the Effectual and Speedy Carrying out of the Negro's Christianity in Our Plantations (Notwithstanding the Late Pretended Impossibilities) without Any Prejudice to Their Owners*. London.

Gooch, William. 1730. Lt. Governor Gooch to the Board of Trade, 14 Sept. 1730. C.O. 5/1322:158. Reproduced in the Virginia Colonial Records Project. Richmond: Virginia State Library.

———. 1731. Lt. Governor Gooch to the Board of Trade, 12 Feb. 1731. C.O. 5/1322:160–63. Reproduced in the Virginia Colonial Records Project. Richmond: Virginia State Library.

Goodwin, Conrad M. 1982. "Archaeology of Galways Plantation." *Florida Anthropologist*. 34 (4): 251–58.

———. 1987. Sugar, Time, and Englishmen: A Study of Management Strategies on Caribbean Plantations. Ph.D. diss., Department of Anthropology, Boston University.

Goodwin, Conrad M., Lydia M. Pulsipher, Donald C. Jones, and William Bass. 1990. The Tschuh-Chahd Burying Ground at Galways Plantation, Montserrat, West Indies. Manuscript.

Goody, John Rankine. 1962. *Death, Property, and the Ancestors: A Study of the Mortuary Customs of the LoDagaa of West Africa*. Stanford: Univ. of Stanford Press.

Goucher, Candice L. 1993. "African Metallurgy in the Atlantic World." *African Archaeological Review* 11:197–215.

Goucher, Candice, Eugenia Herbert, and Carol Saltman. 1986. *The Blooms of Banjeli: Technology and Gender in African Ironmaking*. Somerville, Mass.: Saltman Productions. Filmstrip.

Grant, Bradford C. 1996. "Accommodation and Resistance: The Built Environment and the African American Experience." In *Reconstructing Architecture: Critical Discourses and Social Practices*, ed. Thomas A. Dutton and Lian Hurst Mann, 202–33. Minneapolis: Univ. of Minnesota Press.

Grantham, Thomas. 1677. Captain Thomas Grantham to Secretary of State Henry Coventry. Coventry MSS. 77:301. Reproduced in the Virginia Colonial Records Project. Richmond: Virginia State Library .

Graves-Brown, P., S. Jones, and C. S. Gamble. 1996. *Culture Identity and the Archaeology: The Construction of European Communities*. London: Routledge.

Gray, Lewis Cecil. 1933. *History of Agriculture in the Southern United States to 1860*. Washington, D.C.: Carnegie Institution of Washington.

Gregory, Steven. 1994. "We've Been Down This Road Already." In *Race*, ed. S. Gregory and R. Sanjek, 18–38. New Brunswick, N.J.: Rutgers Univ. Press.

Gregory, Steven, and Roger Sanjek, eds. 1994. *Race*. New Brunswick, N.J.: Rutgers Univ. Press.

Griaule, Marcel. 1965. *Conversations with Gotemmêli: An Introduction to Dogon Religious Ideas*. London: International African Institute and Oxford Univ. Press.

Griaule, Marcel, and Germaine Dieterlen. 1935. "Calabasses Dahomeennes." *Journal de la Société des Africanistes* 5:203–7.

Griffiths, Dorothy. 1978. "Use Marks on Historic Ceramics: A Preliminary Study." *Historical Archaeology* 12:68–81.

Grimé, William E. 1979. *Ethno-Botany of the Black Americans*. Algonac, N.Y.: Reference Publications.

Groover, Mark. 1990. The *Yowa* Cross as Sacred Center and Mandala: An Analysis of African and African-American Religion. Department of Anthropology, University of South Carolina. Photocopy on file.

Gruber, Anna. 1990. The Archaeology of Mr. Jefferson's Slaves. M.A. thesis, Winterthur Program, University of Delaware, Wilmington.

——. 1991. "The Archaeology of Slave Life at Thomas Jefferson's Monticello: Mulberry Row Slave Quarters "r", "s", "t." *Quarterly Bulletin of the Archeological Society of Virginia* 46:2–9.

Gutherie, Patricia. 1996. *Catching Sense: African American Communities on a South Carolina Sea Island*. Westport, Conn.: Bergin & Garvey.

Hair, Paul E. H. 1967. Ethnolinguistic Continuity on the Guinea Coast. *Journal of African History* 8:247–68.

Hakari, Roger C. 1983. "F.F.H. 16 Reconstruction, University Road to Elmwood." USDA Forest Service, Cultural Resource Reconnaissance Report 09-07-03-20. Ironwood, Mich.: Ottawa National Forest.

Hall, Douglas. 1959. *Free Jamaica*. New Haven: Yale Univ. Press.

Hall, Martin. 1992. "'Small Things and the Mobile': Conflictual Fusion of Power, Fear, and Desire." In *The Art and Mystery of Historical Archaeology*, ed. A. E. Yentsch and M. C. Beaudry, 373–99. Boca Raton, Fla.: CRC Press.

Handler, Jerome S. 1982. "A Ghanaian Pipe from a Slave Cemetery in Barbados, West Indies." *West African Journal of Archaeology* 11:93–99.

———. 1983. "An African Pipe from a Slave Cemetery in Barbados, West Indies." In *The Archaeology of the Clay Tobacco Pipe: America*, ed. P. Davey, 245–54. British Archaeological Reports, International Series 175. Oxford: Oxford Univ. Press.

Handler, Jerome S., and Frederick Lange. 1978. *Plantation Slavery in Barbados: An Archaeological and Historical Investigation*. Cambridge: Harvard Univ. Press.

Handler, Jerome S., and R. S. Corrucini. 1983. "Plantation Slave Life in Barbados: A Physical Anthropological Analysis." *Journal of Interdisciplinary History* 14: 65–90.

———. 1986. "Weaning and Lactation in West Indian Slaves: Historical and Bioanthropological Evidence from Barbados." *William and Mary Quarterly*, 3d ser., 11:111–17.

Handler, Jerome S., Arthur Aufderheide, Robert S. Corruccini, Elizabeth M. Brandon, and Lorentz E. Wittmers. 1986. "Lead Content and Poisoning in Barbados Slaves: Historical, Chemical, and Bioanthropological Evidence." *Social Science History* 10:399–425.

Handler, Jerome S., Michael D. Conner, and Keith P. Jacobi. 1989. *Searching for a Slave Cemetery in Barbados, West Indies: A Bioarchaeological and Ethnohistorical Investigation*. Research Paper no. 59. Center for Archaeological Investigations. Carbondale: Southern Illinois University.

Handler, Jerome S., Robert S. Corruccini, and Robert Mutaw. 1982. "Tooth Mutilation in the Caribbean: Evidence from a Slave Burial Population in Barbados." *Journal of Human Evolution* 11:297–313.

Hardie, James. 1794. *Philadelphia Directory and Register*. Philadelphia: T. Dobson.

Harrington, J. C. 1951. Tobacco Pipes from Jamestown. *Archaeological Society of Virginia Quarterly Bulletin* 5 (4): 2–3.

———. 1954. "Dating Stem Fragments of Seventeenth- and Eighteenth-Century Clay Tobacco Pipes." *Quarterly Bulletin, Archaeological Society of Virginia*, Sept.: n.p.

Harrington, M. R. 1908. "Catawba Potters and Their Work." *American Anthropologist*, n.s., no. 10: 399–407.

———, ed. [1714] 1972. *Lawson's History of North Carolina*. Richmond: Garrett and Massie.

Harrison, Faye V. 1992. "The Du Boisian Legacy in Anthropology." *Critique of Anthropology* 12 (3): 239–60.

———. 1995. "The Persistent Power of 'Race' in the Cultural and Political Economy of Racism." *Annual Review of Anthropology* 24:47–74.

———, ed. 1991. *Decolonizing Anthropology*. Washington, D.C.: American Anthropological Association.

Harriss, Francis L., ed. [1714] 1972. *Lawson's History of North Carolina*. Richmond: Garrett and Massie.

Haviser, Jay, and Christopher R. DeCorse. 1991. "African-Caribbean Interaction: A Research Plan for Curaçao Creole Culture." Proceedings of the Thirteenth International Congress for Caribbean Archaeology, Curaçao, Netherlands Antilles, *Reports of the Archaeological-Anthropological Institute of the Netherlands Antilles*, no. 9: 326–37.

Heath, Barbara. 1989. Afro-Caribbean Pottery from St. Eustatius, Netherlands Antilles. Paper presented at the 22d annual meeting of the Society for Historical Archaeology, Baltimore.

———. 1990. Excavations at Monticello: The William Stewart Site. Paper presented at the 23d Annual Society for Historical Archaeology Conference, Tucson.

———. 1991a. "Artisan Housing at Monticello: The Stewart/Watkins Site." *Quarterly Bulletin of the Archaeological Society of Virginia* 46 (1): 10–16.

———. 1991b. A Report on the Archaeological Excavations at Monticello, Charlottesville, Va., The Stewart/Watkins House, 1989–1990. Thomas Jefferson Memorial Foundation, Charlottesville, Va. Manuscript.

Heite, Edward F. 1970. "An Eighteenth-Century Reed-Stem Pipe from Lancaster County." *Quarterly Bulletin of the Archaeological Society of Virginia* 24 (4): 226.

———. 1971. "Pipes from the Pamplin Factory in Appomattox County." *Quarterly Bulletin of the Archaeological Society of Virginia* 25 (3): 195–96.

———. 1972. "American-Made Pipes from the Camden Site." *Quarterly Bulletin of the Archaeological Society of Virginia* 27 (2): 94–99.

Hening, William Waller, ed. 1809–23. *The Statutes at Large: Being a Collection of All the Laws of Virginia from the First Session of the Legislature in the Year 1619.* 13 vols. Philadelphia: Thomas Desilver; Richmond: Samuel Pleasants.

Henry, Susan L. 1976. Preliminary Investigation into the Phenomenon of the Terra-Cotta Clay Pipe. Report on file at Virginia Research Center for Archaeology, Richmond. Manuscript.

Henry, Susan. 1979. "Terra-cotta Tobacco Pipes in 17th-Century Maryland and Virginia: A Preliminary Study." *Historical Archaeology* 13:14–37.

———. 1980. Physical, Spatial, and Temporal Dimensions of Colono Ware in the Chesapeake, 1600–1800. M.A. Thesis, Department of Anthropology, Catholic University of America, Washington, D.C.

Herman, Bernard L. 1984. "Slave Quarters in Virginia: The Persona behind Historic Artifacts." In *The Scope of Historical Archaeology: Essays in Honor of John L. Cotter*, ed. D. G. Orr and D. G. Crozier, 253–83. Philadelphia: Temple Univ. Press.

———. 1988. "Settler Houses." In *A Land and Life Remembered: Americo-Liberian Folk Architecture*, ed. M. Belcher, S. E. Holsoe, and B. L. Herman, 95–150. Athens: Univ. of Georgia Press.

Herskovits, Melville J. 1936. "The Significance of West Africa for Negro Research." *Journal of Negro History* 21 (1): 15–30.

Herskovits, Melville. 1941. *Myth of the Negro Past.* Boston: Beacon Press.

Higman, Barry. 1976. *Slave Population and Economy in Jamaica, 1807–1834.* Cambridge: Cambridge Univ. Press.

———. 1984. *Slave Population in the British Caribbean, 1807–1834.* Baltimore: Johns Hopkins Univ. Press.

———. 1987. "The Spatial Economy of Jamaican Sugar Plantations: Cartographic Evidence from the Eighteenth and Nineteenth Centuries." *Journal of Historical Geography* 13 (1): 17–19.

———. 1988. "The Archaeology of Slavery." *Slavery and Abolition* 9 (1): 85–92. London: Frank Cass.

Hill, Jack. 1955. *A History of Iron County, Michigan.* Iron River, Mich.: Reporter Publishing Company.

Hill, Matthew H. 1987. "Ethnicity Lost? Ethnicity Gained? Information Functions of 'African Ceramics' in West Africa and North America." In *Ethnicity and Culture: Proceedings of the Eighteenth Annual Chacmool Conference,* ed. R. Auger, M. F. Glass, S. MacEachern, and P. McCartney, 135–39. Calgary: Archaeological Association, University of Calgary.

———. 1989. Personal communication, Department of Anthropology, University of Waterloo, Ontario, Canada, 30 Nov.

Hilliard, Samuel B. 1972. *Hogmeat and Hoecake.* Carbondale: Southern Illinois Univ. Press.

Hiskett, Mervyn. 1984. *The Development of Islam in West Africa.* New York: Longman.

Hodder, Ian. 1984. *Symbols in Action.* Cambridge: Cambridge Univ. Press.

———. 1987. "The Contextual Analysis of Symbolic Meanings." In *The Archaeology of Contextual Meanings,* ed I. Hodder, 1–10. Cambridge: Cambridge Univ. Press.

Hodges, Mary Ellen N. 1986. "Camden: Another Look Seventeen Years after Registration." *Notes on Virginia* 29:11–15.

———. 1989. Colonoware in Virginia. Paper presented at the Jamestown Archaeology Conference, 18 May, Fredericksburg, Va.

———. 1990. Multi-Dimensional Assessment of Colono Ware Ceramics in Virginia. Paper presented at the Jamestown Conference, George Washington's Birthplace, Pope Creek, Va.

———. N.d. Native American Settlement at Great Neck: Report on the Virginia Department of Historic Resources Excavations of Woodland Components at Site 44 Vb7, Virginia Beach, Va. Draft manuscript on file, Virginia Department of Historic Resources, Richmond.

Hodges, Mary Ellen N., and Martha W. McCartney. 1985. Camden. Addendum to the 1969 National Register of Historic Places Inventory—Nomination Form. On file at the Virginia Department of Historic Resources, Richmond.

Hogan, Edmund. 1795. *The Prospect of Philadelphia and Check on the Next Directory, Part 1.* Philadelphia.

Holloway, Joseph E. 1990a. "Introduction." In *Africanisms in American Culture,* ed. J. E. Holloway, pp. ix–xxi. Bloomington: Indiana Univ. Press.

———. 1990b. "The Origins of African-American Culture." In *Africanisms in American Culture,* ed. J. E. Holloway, 1–18. Bloomington: Indiana Univ. Press.

———, ed. 1990. *Africanisms in American Culture.* Bloomington: Indiana Univ. Press.

Holme, Randle. [1627–99] 1972. *A Reprint of Part III of the Academy of Armory: Concerning Art of Printing and Typefounding.* Menston, Eng.: Scholar Press.

Holmes, William H. 1903. "Aboriginal Pottery of the Eastern United States." *Twentieth Annual Report of the Bureau of American Ethnology,* 1–201. Washington, D.C.: Smithsonian Institution Press.

hooks, bell. 1990. *Yearning: Race, Gender, and Cultural Politics.* Boston: South End Press.

Howson, Jean. 1990. "Social Relations and Material Culture: A Critique of the Archaeology of Plantation Slavery." In special issue on Historical Archaeology of Southern
Plantations and Farms, ed. Charles E. Orser, Jr. *Historical Archaeology* 24 (4): 78–91.

Hudgins, Carter L. 1990. "Robert 'King' Carter and the Landscape of Tidewater Virginia
in the Eighteenth Century." In *Earth Patterns: Essays in Landscape Archaeology,* ed. W.
M. Kelso and R. Most, 59–70. Charlottesville: Univ. Press of Virginia.

Hudson, Charles. 1976. *The Southeastern Indians.* Knoxville: Univ. of Tennessee Press.

Hudson, Charles M., ed. 1971. *Red, White, and Black: Symposium on Indians in the Old
South.* Southern Anthropological Society, Proceedings 5. Athens: Univ. of Georgia
Press.

Hudson, J. Paul. 1975. "Pottery-Making in Seventeenth Century Virginia." *Quarterly Bulletin of the Archaeological Society of Virginia* 30 (1): 41–52.

Huffman, Thomas N. 1986. "Cognitive Studies of the Iron Age in Southern Africa." *World
Archaeology* 18 (1): 85–95.

———. 1989. Ceramics, Settlements, and Late Iron Age Migrations. *African Archaeological Review* 7:155–82.

Inikori, J. E., ed. 1982. *Forced Migration: The Impact of the Export Slave Trade on African
Societies.* New York: Africana Publishing Company.

Iobson, Richard. 1968. *The Gold Trade,* no. 56, *The English Experience.* New York: Da Capo
Press.

Iron County Deeds. 1874–1949. Various books. Crystal Falls, Mich.: County Clerk's Office.

Iron County Land Entries. N.d. Single volume. Crystal Falls, Mich.: County Clerk's
Office.

Iron County Miscellaneous Records. 1877–1947. Various books. Crystal Falls, Mich.:
County Clerk's Office.

Iron County Tax Records. 1886–1940. Annual Ledgers. Crystal Falls, Mich.: County
Clerk's Office.

*Iron River Reporter (Stambaugh-Caspian Reporter).* 1926–29. Iron River, Mich.

Irvine, Frederick R. 1961. *Woody Plants of Ghana, with Special Reference to Their Uses.*
London: Oxford Univ. Press.

Isaac, Rhys. 1982. *The Transformation of Virginia, 1740–1790.* Chapel Hill: Univ. of North
Carolina Press.

———. 1985. Communication and Control: Authority Metaphors and Power Contests on
Colonel Landon Carter's Virginia Plantation, 1752–1778. In *Rites of Power: Symbolism,
Ritual, and Politics since the Middle Ages,* ed. R. Sean Wilentz, 275–302. Philadelphia:
Univ. of Pennsylvania Press.

———. 1990. The Enlightenment and the Problems of Systematizing the Plantation. Paper
presented at Conference on Re-creating the World of the Virginia Plantation,
1750–1820, University of Virginia and Monticello.

Jackson, Donald, and Dorothy Twohig, eds. 1976–79. *The Diaries of George Washington.*
6 vols. Charlottesville: Univ. Press of Virginia.

Jameson, Fredric. 1985. "Architecture and the Critique of Ideology." In *Architecture, Criticism, Ideology,* ed. J. Ockman, 51–87. Princeton, N.J.: Princeton Architectural Press.

Jefferson, Louise E. 1973. *The Decorative Art of Africa.* New York: Viking Press.

Jefferson, Thomas. [1787] 1982. *Notes on the State of Virginia, by Thomas Jefferson.* Ed. William Peden. New York: W. W. Norton.

———. Papers of Thomas Jefferson. Manuscript Division, Special Collections Department, University of Virginia Library, Charlottesville (ViU).

Jefferson Papers. Huntington Library, San Marino, Calif. (CSmH).

———. Library of Congress, Washington, D.C. (DLC).

———. Massachusetts Historical Society, Boston (MHi).

Jerdone, William M. Plantation Diary, 1855–62. Jerdone Family Papers, Swem Library Special Collections, College of William and Mary, Williamsburg, Va.

Johnson, Marion. 1982."Two Pottery Traditions in Southern Ghana." In *Earthenware in Africa and Asia*, ed. J. Picton, 208–17. University of London, Colloquies on Art and Archaeology in Asia.

Jones, Hugh. [1724] 1956 . *The Present State of Virginia.* Ed. R. L. Morton. Chapel Hill: Univ. of North Carolina Press.

Jones, Sian. 1997. *The Archaeology of Ethnicity.* London: Routledge.

Jones, Steven L. 1985. "The African American Tradition in Vernacular Architecture." In *The Archaeology of Slavery and Plantation Life*, ed. T. A. Singleton, 195–213. Orlando, Fla.: Academic Press.

Jordan, Elliott J. T. 1991. The Role of White Labor in Piedmont Virginia Plantations, 1790–1820. Corporation for Jefferson's Poplar Forest, Forest, Va. Manuscript.

Jordan, Winthrop. 1968. *White over Black: American Attitudes toward the Negro, 1550–1812.* Baltimore: Penguin Books.

Joseph, Joe. 1989. "Pattern and Process in the Plantation Archaeology of the Lowcountry of Georgia and South Carolina." *Historical Archaeology* 23 (1): 55–68.

Joyner, Charles W. 1984. *Down by the Riverside: A South Carolina Slave Community.* Urbana: Univ. of Illinois Press.

———. 1986. "Introduction." In *Drums and Shadows: Survival Studies among the Georgia Coastal Negroes.* Athens: Univ. of Georgia Press.

Kea, Ray A. 1982. *Settlements, Trade, and Polities in the Seventeenth-Century Gold Coast.* Baltimore: Johns Hopkins Univ. Press.

Keeble, Josephus. 1986. Taped interview by Carrel Cowan-Ricks. Chicago, 2–3 April.

Keeler, Robert W. 1977. *An Earthy Look at Life on a 17th-Century Farm.* Paper presented at the Annual Meeting of the Society for Historical Archaeology, Ottawa.

———. 1978. The Homelot on the Seventeenth-Century Chesapeake Tidewater Frontier. Ph.D. diss, University of Oregon.

Keene, David, and Theodore Karamanski. 1984. *Cultural Resources Evaluation of Site 09-07-03-115, Ottawa National Forest, Michigan.* Chicago: Mid-American Research Center of Loyola University.

Kelly, Kenneth G. 1995. Transformation and Continuity in Savi, a West African Trade Town: An Archaeological Investigation of Culture Contact on the Coast of Benin during the 17th and 18th Centuries. Ph.D. diss. University of California at Los Angeles.

Kelso, William. 1971. A Report on Exploratory Excavations at Carter's Grove Plantation, James City County, Va. (June 1970–Sept. 1971). Colonial Williamsburg Foundation, Williamsburg, Va. Manuscript.

———. 1982. A Report on the Archaeological Excavations at Monticello, Charlottesville,

Va., 1979–1981. Thomas Jefferson Memorial Foundation, Monticello, Charlottesville, Va. Manuscript.

——. 1984a. Archaeological Excavation of the Levy Tomb/Stonehouse Site. Thomas Jefferson Memorial Foundation, Monticello, Charlottesville, Va. Manuscript.

Kelso, William M. 1984b. *Kingsmill Plantations, 1619–1800: Archaeology of Country Life in Colonial Virginia*. Orlando, Fla.: Academic Press.

——. 1986a. "The Archaeology of Slave Life at Thomas Jefferson's Monticello: 'A Wolf by the Ears.'" *Journal of New World Archaeology* 6 (4): 5–21.

——. 1986b. "Mulberry Row: Slave Life at Thomas Jefferson's Monticello." *Archaeology* 39:28–35.

Kelso, William, and Edward A. Chappell. 1974. "Excavations of a Seventeenth-Century Pottery Kiln at Glebe Harbor, Westmoreland County, Virginia." *Historical Archaeology* 8:53–63.

Kelso, William, Douglas Sanford, Anna Gruber, Dinah C. Johnson, and Ann M. Smart. 1985. Monticello Black History/Craft Life Archaeological Project, 1984–85 Progress Report. Thomas Jefferson Memorial Foundation, Monticello, Charlottesville, Va. Manuscript.

Kelso, William, Douglas Sanford, Dinah Crader Johnson, Sondy Sanford, and Anna Gruber. 1984. A Report on the Archaeological Excavations at Monticello, Charlottesville, Va., 1982–1983. Thomas Jefferson Memorial Foundation, Monticello, Charlottesville, Va. Manuscript.

Kense, François. 1990. "Archaeology in Anglophone West Africa." In *A History of African Archaeology*, ed. P. Robertshaw, 135–54. London: James Currey.

Kent, Barry G. 1984. *Susquehanna's Indians*. Anthropological Series No. 6. Harrisburg: Pennsylvania Historical and Museums Commission.

Kimball, Fiske. 1968. *Thomas Jefferson, Architect*. Rept., Orlando, Fla.: Da Capo Press.

Kiple, Kenneth F. 1984. *The Caribbean Slave: A Biological History*. Cambridge: Cambridge Univ. Press.

Kiple, Kenneth F., and Virginia Himmelsteib King. 1981. *Another Dimension to the Black Diaspora: Diet, Disease, and Racism*. Cambridge: Cambridge Univ. Press.

Klingelhofer, Eric. 1987. "Aspects of Early Afro-American Material Culture: Artifacts from the Slave Quarters at Garrison Plantation, Maryland." *Historical Archaeology* 21 (2): 112–19.

Kropp Dakubu, Mary E. 1988. *The Languages of Ghana*. London: Kegan Paul International.

Kryder-Reid, Elizabeth. 1994. "The Archaeology of Vision in Eighteenth-Century Chesapeake Gardens." *Journal of Garden History* 14:42–54.

Kulikoff, Alan. 1986. *Tobacco and Slaves: The Development of Southern Cultures in the Chesapeake, 1680–1800*. Chapel Hill: Univ. of North Carolina Press.

Laman, K. E. 1953. *The Kongo I*. Studia Ethnographica Upsaliensia 4. Uppsalla: Almqvist and Wiksells.

——. 1957. *The Kongo II*. Studia Ethnographica Upsaliensia 4. Uppsalla: Almqvist and Wiksells.

——. 1962. *The Kongo III*. Studia Ethnographica Upsaliensia 4. Upsalla: Almqvist and Wiksells.

———. 1968. *The Kongo IV*. Studia Ethnographica Upsaliensia 4. Uppsalla: Almqvist and Wiksells.

Landers, Jane. 1987. Historical Report on Gracia Real de Santa Teresa de Mosé. Part 1. Prepared for the Ft. Mosé Archaeological Project on file, Florida Museum of Natural History, Gainesville. Manuscript.

———. 1988. Historical report on Gracia Real de Santa Teresa de Mosé. Part 2. Prepared for the Fort Mosé Archaeological Project on file, Florida Museum of Natural History, Gainesville. Manuscript.

———. 1990a. Gracia Real de Santa Teresa de Mosé: A Free Black Town in Spanish Colonial Florida. *American Historical Review* 95 (1): 9–30.

———. 1990b. "African Presence in Early Spanish Colonization of the Caribbean and the Southeastern Borderlands." In *Columbian Consequences*, vol. 2, *Archaeological and Historical Perspectives on the Spanish Borderlands East*, ed. D. H. Thomas, 315–27. Washington, D.C.: Smithsonian Institution Press.

Lange, Frederick W., and Jerome S. Handler. 1985. "The Ethnohistorical Approach to Slavery." In *The Archaeology of Slavery and Plantation Life*, ed. T. A. Singleton, 15–32. Orlando, Fla.: Academic Press.

Larsen, Herbert F., Sr. 1963. *BE-WA-BIC Country*. New York: Carlton Press.

La Roche, Cheryl. 1994. "Beads from the African Burial Ground, New York City: A Preliminary Assessment." *Beads: Journal of the Society of Bead Researchers* 6:3–20.

La Roche, Cheryl J., and Michael L. Blakey. 1997. "Seizing Intellectual Power: The Dialogue at the New York African Burial Ground." *Historical Archaeology* 31 (3): 84–106.

La Rochefoucauld-Liancort, F. A. F. 1799. *Travels through the United States of America*. 2 vols. London: R. Phillips.

Lederer, John. 1966 [1671]. *The Discoveries of John Lederer*. Readex Microprint.

Lees, William B., and Kathryn Kimery-Lees. 1979. "The Function of Colono-Indian Ceramics: Insights from Limerick Plantation, South Carolina." *Historical Archaeology* 13:1–13.

Leith-Ross, Sylvia. 1970. *Nigerian Pottery: A Catalogue*. Ibadan, Nigeria: Ibadan Univ. Press.

Leone, Mark P. 1984. "Interpreting Ideology in Historical Archeology: The William Paca Garden in Annapolis, Maryland." In *Ideology, Power, and Prehistory*, ed. D. Miller and C. Tilley, 25–35. Cambridge: Cambridge Univ. Press.

———. 1986. "Symbolic, Structural, and Critical Archaeology." In *American Archaeology Past and Future: A Celebration of the Society for American Archaeology, 1935–1985*, ed. D. L. Meltzer, D. D. Fowler, and J. Sabloff, 415–38. Washington, D.C.: Smithsonian Institution Press.

———. 1988. "The Georgian Order as the Order of Merchant Capitalism in Annapolis, Maryland." In *Recovering Meaning: Historical Archaeology in the Eastern United States*, ed. M. P. Leone and P. Potter, 235–61. Washington, D.C.: Smithsonian Institution Press.

Leslie, Vernon. 1970. "The Pointillé Pipe in the Upper Delaware Valley: Contribution to Tocks Island Reservoir Area Archaeology." *The Chesopiean* 8 (3): 57–66.

Lewis, Lynne. 1978. *Drayton Hall: Preliminary Archaeological Investigations at a Low Country Plantation*. National Trust for Historic Preservation. Charlottesville: Univ. Press of Virginia.

———. 1985. "The Planter Class: The Archaeological Record at Drayton Hall." In *The Archaeology of Slavery and Plantation Life*, ed. T. A. Singleton, 121–40. New York: Academic Press.

Lieberman, Leonard, and Larry T. Reynolds. 1996. "Race: The Deconstruction of a Scientific Concept." In *Race and Other Misadventures: Essays in Honor of Ashley Montagu*, ed. L. T. Reynolds and L. Lieberman. Dix Hills, N.Y.: General Hall Press.

Lieberman, Leonard, Blaine W. Stevenson, and Larry T. Reynolds. 1989. "Race and Anthropology: A Core Concept without Consensus." *Anthropology and Education Quarterly* 20 (2): 7–73.

Lightfoot, Kent G. 1995. "Culture Contact Studies: Redefining the Relationship between Prehistoric and Historical Archaeology." *American Antiquity* 60 (2): 199–217.

Lindahl, Art. 1986. Interview by William E. Rutter, Iron River, Mich., 15 and 18 May.

Lippard, L. R. 1990. *Mixed Blessings: New Art in a Multicultural America*. New York: Pantheon.

Littlefield, Daniel C. 1981. *Rice and Slaves: Ethnicity and the Slave Trade in Colonial South Carolina*. Baton Rouge: Louisiana State Univ. Press.

Lovejoy, Paul E. 1989. "The Impact of the Atlantic Slave Trade on Africa: A Review of the Literature." *Journal of African History* 30 (3): 365–94.

McCarthy, Michael R., and Catherine M. Brooks. 1988. *Medieval Pottery in Britain, A.D. 900–1600*. Leicester: Leicester Univ. Press.

McCartney, Martha W., and Mary Ellen N. Hodges. 1980. Pamunkey Indian Reservation Archaeological District. National Register of Historic Places Inventory—Nomination Form. On file at the Virginia Department of Historic Resources, Richmond.

MacCord, Howard A., Sr. 1964. The Bowman Site, Shenandoah County, Virginia. *Quarterly Bulletin of the Archaeological Society of Virginia* 19 (2): 43–49.

———. 1969. "Camden: A Postcontact Indian Site in Caroline County." *Quarterly Bulletin, Archaeological Society of Virginia* 24 (1): 1–55.

MacCord, H. A., Sr., Karl Schmitt, and Richard Slattery. 1957. "Shepard Site Study." *Archaeological Society of Maryland Bulletin*, no. 1.

McCusker, John J., and Russell R. Menard. 1985. *The Economy of British America, 1607–1789*. Chapel Hill: Univ. of North Carolina Press.

McDaniel, George W. 1982. *Hearth and Home: Preserving a People's Culture*. Philadelphia: Temple Univ. Press.

MacGaffey, Wyatt. 1986. *Religion and Society in Central Africa: The Bakongo of Lower Zaire*. Chicago: Univ. of Chicago Press.

McIlwaine, H. R., ed. 1925. *Executive Journals of the Council of Colonial Virginia*. 6 vols. Richmond: Virginia State Library.

McIntosh, Roderick J. 1974. "Archaeology and Mud Wall Decay in a West African Village." *World Archaeology* 6:154–71.

———. 1976. "Finding Lost Walls on Archaeological Sites: The Hani Model." *Sankofa* 2:45–53.

McIntosh, Susan K., and Roderick J. McIntosh. 1980. *Prehistoric Investigations in the Region of Jenne, Mali: A Study in the Development of Urbanism*. Cambridge Monographs in African Archaeology 2, British Archaeological Reports, International, Series 89 (ii). Oxford.

———. 1984. "Current Directions in West African Prehistory." *Annual Review of Anthropology* 12:215–58.

McLaughlin, Jack. 1988. *Jefferson and Monticello: The Biography of a Builder.* New York: Henry Holt and Co.

McLearen, Douglas C., and L. Daniel Mouer. 1989. Middle Woodland II Typology and Chronology in the Lower James River Valley of Virginia. Paper presented to the Middle Atlantic Archaeology Conference, Rehobeth Beach, Del.

McKee, Larry. 1987. "Delineating Ethnicity from the Garbage of Early Virginians: Faunal Remains from the Kingsmill Plantation Slave Quarter." *American Archaeology* 6:31–39.

———. 1988. Plantation Food Supply in Nineteenth-Century Tidewater Virginia. Ph.D. diss., Department of Anthropology, University of California, Berkeley.

———. 1992. "The Ideals and Realities behind the Design and Use of 19th Century Virginia Slave Cabins." In *The Art and Mystery of Historical Archaeology: Essays in Honor of James Deetz,* ed. A. E. Yentsch and M. C. Beaudry, 195–214. Boca Raton, Fla.: CRC Press.

Main, Gloria L. 1982. *Tobacco Colony.* Princeton, N.J.: Princeton Univ. Press.

Mann, R. W., L. Meadows, W. M. Bass, and D. R. Watters. 1987. Description of Skeletal Remains from a Black Slave Cemetery from Montserrat, West Indies. *Annals of Carnegie Museum* 56 (19): 319–36.

Manning, Patrick. 1979. "The Slave Trade in the Bight of Benin, 1640–1890." In *The Uncommon Market: Essays in the Economic History of the Slave Trade,* ed. H. A. Gemery and J. S. Hogendorn. New York: Academic Press.

Manson, Carl, H. A. McCord, Sr., and James B. Griffin. 1944. "The Culture of the Keyser Farm Site." *Papers of the Michigan Academy of Science, Arts, and Letters* 29: 375–418.

Maquet, Jacques. 1972. *Civilizations of Black Africa.* London: Oxford Univ. Press.

Marron, John V. 1988. Archaeological Excavations at Fort Mosé, Florida, Spring 1988. Preliminary field report on file, Florida Museum of Natural History, Gainesville. Manuscript.

———. 1989. Archaeological Excavations at Fort Mosé, Florida, 1989. Preliminary field report on file, Florida Museum of Natural History, Gainesville. Manuscript.

Martin, Terrance J. 1987. Personal communication. Letter report on faunal material recovered from 20IO58.

Marzio, Peter C. 1972. "Carpentry in the Southern Colonies during the Eighteenth Century with Emphasis on Maryland and Virginia." *Winterthur Portfolio 7,* ed. I. Quimby, 229–50. Charlottesville: Univ. Press of Virginia.

Mason, Otis T. 1877. "Anthropological News." *American Naturalist* 11 (10): 624–27.

Mathewson, Duncan. 1972. "Jamaican Ceramics: An Introduction to 18th Century Folk Pottery in West African Tradition." *Jamaica Journal* 7 (1–2): 25–29.

———. 1973. "Archaeological Analysis of Material Culture as a Reflection of Sub-cultural Differentiation in 18th Century Jamaica." *Jamaica Journal* 7 (1–2): 25–29. Kingston.

———. 1974. "Pottery from the Chuluwasi and Jimasangi River Sites, Northern Ghana." *West African Journal of Archaeology* 4:149–60.

Mathewson, R. Duncan, and Colin Flight. 1972. "Kisoto Bowls: A Fifteenth- and Sixteenth-Century Pottery Type in Northern Ghana." *West African Journal of Archaeology* 2:81–92.

Mayes, Philip. 1972. *Port Royal, Jamaica: Excavations, 1969–70.* Kingston: Jamaica National Trust.

Menard, Russell R. 1977. "From Servants to Slaves: The Transformation of the Chesapeake Labor System." *Southern Studies* 26:355–90.

Mester de Parajd, Corinne. 1988. "Regards sur l'habitat traditional au Niger." *Cahiers de Construction Traditionelle,* no. 11. Nonette: Editions Creer.

Meyer, Virginia M., and John Frederick Dorman, eds. 1987. *Adventurers of Purse and Person: Virginia, 1607–1624/5.* 3d ed. Richmond: Dietz Press.

Michel, François Louis. [1701–2] 1916. "Report of the Journey of a François Louis Michel from Berne, Switzerland, to Virginia, October 2, 1701–December 1, 1702." Trans. W. J. Hinke. *Virginia Magazine of History and Biography* 24 (1): 1–43, (2): 113–41, (3): 275–303.

Miles, William, comp. 1975. *Michigan Atlases and Plat Books: A Checklist, 1872–-1973.* Lansing: Michigan Department of Education, State Library Services.

Miller, Daniel, Michael Rowlands, and Christopher Tilley. 1989. *Domination and Resistance.* London: Unwin Hyman.

Miller, Elinor, and Eugene Genovese. 1974. *Plantation, Town, and County: Essays on the Local History of American Slave Society.* Urbana: Univ. of Illinois Press.

Miller, George L. 1980. Classification and Scaling in 19th Century Ceramics. *Historical Archaeology* 14:1–40.

Miller, Henry. 1983. *A Search for the "Citty of Saint Maries."* St. Maries City Archaeology Series no. 1. St. Mary's City Commission, Maryland.

———. 1984. Colonization and Subsistence Change on the Seventeenth-Century Chesapeake Frontier. Ph.D. diss., Department of Anthropology, Michigan State University.

———. 1991. "Tobacco Pipes from Pope's Fort, St. Mary's City, Maryland: An English Civil War Site on the American Frontier." In *The Archaeology of the Clay Tobacco Pipe,* vol. 12, *Chesapeake Bay,* ed. P. Davy and D. J. Pogue. BAR International Series 566. Oxford.

Miller, J. C. 1977. *The Wolf by the Ears: Thomas Jefferson and Slavery.* New York: Free Press.

Minchinton, Walter, Celia King, and Peter Waite. 1984. *Virginia Slave-Trade Statistics, 1698–1775.* Richmond: Virginia State Library.

Mintz, Sidney W. 1974. *Caribbean Transformations.* Baltimore: Johns Hopkins Univ. Press.

Mintz, Sidney. 1976. "Foreword." In *Afro-American Anthropology,* ed. N. E. Whitten and J. F. Szwed, 1–16. New York: Free Press.

———. 1985. *Sugar and Power.* Baltimore: Johns Hopkins Univ. Press.

Mintz, Sidney W., and Richard Price. 1976. *An Anthropological Approach to the Afro-American Past: A Caribbean Perspective.* Occasional Papers No. 2. Philadelphia: Institute for the Study of Human Issues.

———. 1992. *The Birth of African-American Culture: An Anthropological Perspective.* Rept., Boston: Beacon Press.

Mitchell, Vivienne. 1976. "Decorated Brown Clay Pipebowls from Nomini Plantation: A Progress Report." *Quarterly Bulletin of the Archaeological Society of Virginia* 31 (2): 83–92.

———. 1983. "The History of Nominy Plantation with Emphasis on the Clay Tobacco

Pipes." In *Historic Clay Tobacco Pipe Studies*, vol. 2, ed. B. Sudbury, 1–38. Ponca City, Okla.: B. Sudbury.

Mooney, James. 1890. "Cherokee Theory and Practice of Medicine." *Journal of American Folklore* 3:44–50.

Moore, Mullins Sue. 1985. "Social and Economic Status on the Coastal Plantation: An Archaeological Perspective." In *The Archaeology of Slavery and Plantation Life*, ed. T. A. Singleton, 141–60. Orlando, Fla.: Academic Press.

Morgan, Edmund S. 1975. *American Slavery, American Freedom: The Ordeal of Colonial Virginia*. New York: W. W. Norton.

Morgan, Philip D. 1982. "Work and Culture: The Task System and the World of Low-country Blacks, 1700–1880." *William and Mary Quarterly*, 3d ser., 39:563–99.

———. 1988. "Slave Life in Piedmont Virginia, 1720–1800." In *Colonial Chesapeake Society*, ed. L. G. Carr, P. D. Morgan, and J. B. Russo, 433–84. Chapel Hill: Univ. of North Carolina Press.

Morris, Robert. 1724. *An Essay in Defense of Ancient Architecture*. London.

Morrissey, Marietta. 1989. *Slave Women in the New World: Gender Stratification in the Caribbean*. Lawrence: Univ. of Kansas Press.

Morton, Louis. 1941. *Robert Carter of Nomini Hall: A Virginia Planter of the Eighteenth Century*. Williamsburg, Va.: Colonial Williamsburg Inc.

Mouer, L. Daniel. 1978. Up Stony Creek without a Cord-wrapped Paddle: Ceramic Variation in the James River Piedmont and Coastal Plain. Paper presented at the annual meeting of the Archaeological Society of Virginia, Arlington.

———. 1987. Farming, Foraging, and Feasting: Powhatan Foodways and Their Influences on English Virginia. Paper presented to the Foodways Research Planning Conference, April, Colonial Williamsburg Foundation.

———. 1988. Nathaniel Bacon's Brick House and Associated Structures, Curles Plantation, Henrico County, Va. Paper presented in the symposium "Varieties of the Virginia House: New Archaeological Perspectives on Domestic Architecture in Late 17th-Century Chesapeake." Annual Meeting of the Archaeological Society of Virginia, Hampton.

———. 1989. The Rebel and the Renaissance: Nathaniel Bacon at Curles Plantation. Paper presented at the Middle Atlantic Archaeology Conference, Rehobeth Beach, Del.

———. 1990a. "An Ancient Seat Called Curles": The Archaeology of a James River Plantation, 1984–1989. Paper presented to the Conference on Historical and Underwater Archaeology, Tucson.

———. 1990b. Chesapeake Pipes: Another Perspective. Paper presented to the Jamestown Archaeology Conference.

———. 1991a. Chesapeake Creoles: Approaches to Colonial Folk Culture. Paper presented to the Council of Virginia Archaeologists Virginia Archaeology Symposium V: The 17th Century, Williamsburg.

———. 1991b. "Digging a Rebel's Homestead." *Archaeology* 44 (4): 54–57.

———. 1991c. "My Father Told Me, I Tell My Son": Indians, Education, and Identity in Virginia, Past and Present. Colloquium presented in the conference "To Lead and to Serve", sponsored by Jamestown Settlement and the Virginia Foundation for the Humanities, May, Williamsburg.

——. 1991d. "New Discoveries at Jordan's Point." In *Notes on Virginia* July/August.

——. 1991e. Phase 1 Cultural Resource Survey for a Proposed Electric Power Generating Facility in Cumberland County, Virginia. 2 vol. Report prepared for Virginia Power, Inc., by Virginia Commonwealth University Archaeological Research Center.

——. 1991f. Rebecca's Children: A Critique of Old and New Myths concerning Indians in Virginia's History and Archaeology. Paper presented at the 1991 Conference on Historical and Underwater Archaeology, Richmond.

——. 1991g. "'Root Cellar' Revisited." *African American Archaeology* 5:5–6.

——. 1993. "Chesapeake Creoles: The Creation of Folk Culture in Colonial Virginia." In *The Archaeology of Seventeenth-Century Virginia*, ed. T. Reinhart and D. J. Pogue, 105–66. Special Publication no. 30. Richmond: Archaeological Society of Virginia.

Mouer, L. Daniel, and Douglas C. McLearen. 1991. "Jordan's Journey": An Interim Report on the Excavation of a Protohistoric Indian and Early 17th Century Colonial Occupation in Prince George County, Virginia. Report presented to the Virginia Department of Historic Resources.

Muller, Nancy L. 1994. "The House of the Black Burghardts: An Investigation of Race, Gender, and Class at the W. E. B. Du Bois Boyhood Homesite." In *Those of Little Note: Gender, Race, and Class in Historical Archaeology*, ed. E. M. Scott, 81–94. Tucson: Univ. of Arizona Press.

Mullings, Leith. 1978. "Ethnicity and Stratification in the Urban United States." Papers in Anthropology and Linguistics. *Annals of the New York Academy of Sciences* 318:10–22.

Murdock, George P. 1959. *Africa: Its People and Their Culture History*. New York: McGraw Hill.

Nadel, Siegfried Frederick. 1942. *A Black Byzantium: The Kingdom of Nupe in Nigeria*. London: Oxford Univ. Press.

Nash, Gary. 1974. *Red, White, and Black: The Peoples of Early America*. Englewood Cliffs, N.J.: Prentice-Hall.

——. 1979. *The Urban Crucible: Social Change, Political Consciousness, and the Origins of the American Revolution*. Cambridge, Mass.: Harvard Univ. Press.

Neiman, Fraser D. 1978. "Domestic Architecture at The Clifts Plantation: The Social Context of Early Virginia Building." *Northern Neck Historical Magazine*, vol. 28.

——. 1980. *The "Manner House" Before Stratford (Discovering the Clifts Plantation)*. Stratford, Va.: Robert E. Lee Memorial Association.

——. 1986. Domestic Architecture at the Clifts Plantation: The Social Context of Early Virginia Building. In *Common Places: Readings in American Vernacular Architecture*, ed. Dell Upton and John Michael Vlach, 292–314. Athens: Univ. of Georgia Press.

Newman, Thelma R. 1974. *Contemporary African Arts and Crafts*. New York: Crown Publishers.

Nicholls, Michael L. 1981. "'In the Light of Human Beings': Richard Eppes and the Island Plantation Code of Laws." *Virginia Magazine of History and Biography* 90:67–78.

Nichols, Frederick Doveton. 1961. *Thomas Jefferson's Architectural Drawings, Compiled and with Commentary and a Check list*. Boston: Massachusetts Historical Society.

Nicolls, Andrea. 1987. Igbo Pottery Traditions in Light of Historical Antecedents and Present-Day Realities. Ph.D. diss., Department of Fine Arts, Indiana University, Bloomington.

Nketia, J. H. Kwabena. 1977. Lecture at the African-Caribbean Summer School, Kingston, Jamaica.

——. 1979. "African Roots of Music in the Americas: An African View." *Jamaica Journal* 43:12–17.

Noël Hume, Ivor. 1962. "An Indian Ware of the Colonial Period." *Quarterly Bulletin of the Archaeological Society of Virginia* 17 (1): 2–12.

——. 1963. "A Late Seventeenth-Century Pottery Kiln near Jamestown." *Antiques Magazine* 83 (5).

——. 1966. *Excavations at Tutter's Neck in James City County, Virginia, 1960–1961.* United States Museum, Bulletin 249. Contributions from the Museum of History and Technology, Paper 53. Washington, D.C.: Smithsonian Institution Press.

——. 1975. *Historical Archaeology.* New York: W. W. Norton.

——. 1979. *Martin's Hundred.* New York: Alfred Knopf.

Nugent, Nell Marion. 1977. *Cavaliers and Pioneers: Abstracts to Virginia Land Patents*, vol. 2, *1666–1695.* Richmond: Virginia State Library.

Oakes, James. 1982. *The Ruling Race.* New York: Alfred A. Knopf.

Oliver, Paul. 1971. *Shelter in Africa.* New York: Praeger Publishers.

Omi, M., and H. Winant. 1986. *Racial Formation in the United States.* New York: Routledge and Kegan Paul.

Orser, Charles E., Jr. 1988a. "The Archaeological Analysis of Plantation Society: Replacing Status and Caste with Economics and Power." *American Antiquity* 53:735–51.

——. 1988b. "Toward a Theory of Power for Historical Archaeology: Plantations and Space." In *The Recovery of Meaning: Historical Archaeology in the Eastern United States*, ed. M. P. Leone and P. B. Potter, 314–43. Washington: Smithsonian Institution Press.

——. 1989. "On Plantations and Patterns." *Historical Archaeology* 23 (2): 28–40.

——. 1992. "Beneath the Material Surface of Things: Commodities, Artifacts, and Slave Plantations." *Historical Archaeology* 26 (3): 95–104.

——. 1994a. "The Archaeology of African-American Slave Religion in the Antebellum South." *Cambridge Archaeological Journal* 4 (1): 33–44.

——. 1994b. "Toward a Global Historical Archaeology: An Example from Brazil." *Historical Archaeology* 28 (1): 5–22.

——. 1996. *A Historical Archaeology of the Modern World.* New York: Plenum.

——, ed. 1990. Historical Archaeology on Southern Plantations and Farms, special issue of *Historical Archaeology* 24 (4).

Orser, Charles E., Jr., and A. M. Nekola. 1985. "Plantation Settlement from Slavery to Tenancy: An Example from a Piedmont Plantation in South Carolina." In *The Archaeology of Slavery and Plantation Life*, ed. T. A. Singleton, 67–94. Orlando, Fla.: Academic Press.

Oswald, Adrian, et al. 1982. *English Brown Stoneware, 1670–1900.* London: Faber and Faber.

Otto, John. 1975. Status Differences and the Archaeological Record: A Comparison of

Planter, Overseer, and Slave Sites from Canon's Point Plantation (1794–1861), St. Simons Island, Georgia. Ph.D. diss., Department of Anthropology, University of Florida.

——. 1984. *Cannon's Point Plantation, 1794–1850: Living Conditions and Status Pattern in the Old South*. New York: Academic Press.

Outlaw, Alain C. 1973. Archaeological Excavations at Gunston Hall. Report on file, Gunston Hall library, Lorton, Va.

——. 1990. *Governor's Land: Archaeology of Early Seventeenth-Century Virginia Settlements*. Charlottesville: Univ. Press of Virginia.

Outlaw, Merry. 1985. Personal communication, Sept. 1985, Virginia Research Center for Archaeology, Yorktown.

Ozanne, Paul. 1962. "Notes on the Early Historic Archaeology of Accra." *Transactions of the Historical Society of Ghana* 6:51–70.

——. 1964. Tobacco Pipes of Accra and Shai. Institute of African Studies: Legon, Ghana. University of Ghana.

Pagan, John R. 1982. "Dutch Maritime and Commercial Activity in Mid-Seventeenth-Century Virginia." *Virginia Magazine of History and Biography* 90 (4): 485–501.

Page, Helena. 1988. "Dialogic Principles of Interactive Learning in the Ethnographic Relationship." *Journal of Anthropological Research* 44 (2): 163–81.

Parker, Kathleen A., and Jacqueline L. Hernigle. 1990. Portici: Portrait of a Middling Plantation in Piedmont Virginia. Occasional Report no. 3, Regional Archaeology Program, National Capital Region, National Park Service, Washington, D.C.

Parmalee, Paul W., and Walter E. Klippel. 1974. "Freshwater Mussels as a Prehistoric Food Resource." *American Antiquity* 39:421–34.

Parrinder, Geoffrey. 1982. *African Mythology*. New York: Peter Bedrick Books.

Patrick, Rembert, ed. 1949. Letters of the Invaders of East Florida, 1812. *Florida Historical Quarterly* 28 (July): 53–69.

Patten, Drake. 1992a. The Archaeology of Playtime: Artifacts of African-American Games in the Plantation South. Paper, Society for Historical Archaeology Annual Conference, Kingston, Jamaica.

——. 1992b. "Mankala and Minkisi: Possible Evidence of African-American Folk Beliefs and Practices." *African American Archaeology* 6:5–7.

Pawson, Michael. 1969. "Clay Tobacco Pipes in the Knowles Collection." *Quarterly Bulletin of the Archaeological Society of Virginia* 23 (3): 115–47.

Paynter, Robert. 1990. "Afro-Americans in the Massachusetts Historical Landscape." In *The Politics of the Past*, ed. P. Gathercole and D. Lowenthal, 49–62. London: Unwin Hyman.

——. 1992. "W. E. B. Du Bois and the Material World of African-Americans in Great Barrington, Massachusetts." *Critique of Anthropology* 12 (3): 277–91.

Perdue, Charles L., Jr., Thomas E. Barden, and Robert K. Phillips, eds. 1976. *Weevils in the Wheat: Interviews with Virginia Ex-Slaves*. Charlottesville: Univ. Press of Virginia.

Pérez-Gómez, Alberto. 1983. *Architecture and the Crisis of Modern Science*. Cambridge, Mass.: MIT Press.

Perry, William S., ed. 1969. *Historical Collections Relating to the American Colonial Church*, vol. 1, *Virginia*. New York: AMD Press.

Philips, J. E. 1990. "The African Heritage of White America." In *Africanisms in American Culture*, ed. J. E. Holloway, 225–39. Bloomington: Indiana Univ. Press.

Philips, John E. 1983. "African Smoking and Pipes." *Journal of African History* 24 (3): 303–19.

Phillips, Ulrich Bonnell. [1918] 1966. *American Negro Slavery*. Baton Rouge: Louisiana State Univ. Press.

Picton, John. 1992. "Tradition, Technology, and Lurex: Some Comments on Textile History and Design in West Africa." In *History, Design, and Craft in West African Strip-Woven Cloth*, 13–52. Washington, D.C.: National Museum of African Art.

Poe, Charles B. 1978. Status Variability in Eighteenth-Century Criollo Culture: Archaeological Investigations at the Francisco Ponce de León Site, St. Augustine. Project report on file, Historic St. Augustine Preservation Board, St. Augustine, Fla. Manuscript.

Pogue, Dennis J. 1987. "Seventeenth-Century Proprietary Rule and Rebellion: Archaeology at Charles Calvert's Mattapany-Sewall." *Maryland Archeology* 23 (1): 1–37.

Pollard, John Garland. 1894. *The Pamunkey Indians of Virginia*. Bureau of American Ethnology 17. Washington, D.C.: Smithsonian Institution.

Posnansky, Merrick. 1982. "African Archaeology Comes of Age." *World Archaeology* 13:345–58.

——. 1983. "Towards the Archaeology of the Black Diaspora." In *Proceedings of the Ninth International Congress for Caribbean Archaeology* (Santo Domingo), 443–50. Montreal: Centre de Recherches Caraives, Université de Montreal.

——. 1984a. "Towards an Archaeology of the Black Diaspora." *Journal of Black Studies* 15:195–205.

——. 1984b. "Early Agricultural Societies in Ghana." In *From Hunters to Farmers : The Causes and Consequences of Food Production in Africa*, ed. D. Clark and S. A. Brandt, 147–53. Berkeley: Univ. of California Press.

——. 1984c. "The Ethnoarchaeology of Farm Shelters at Hani, Ghana." *Anthroquest* 30:11–13.

——. 1986. "The Anatomy of a Continent." In *The Africans: A Reader*, ed. Ali A. Mazrui and T. K. Levine, 31–60. New York: Praeger.

——. 1989. West African Reflections on African-American Archaeology. Paper presented at the conference "Digging the Afro-American Past," 17–20 May, University of Mississippi, Oxford.

Posnansky, Merrick, and Christopher DeCorse. 1986. "Historical Archaeology in Sub-Saharan Africa: A Review." *Historical Archaeology* 20 (1): 1–14.

Potter, Parker B., Jr. 1991. "What Is the Use of Plantation Archaeology?" *Historical Archaeology* 25 (3): 94–107.

Potter, Stephen R. 1977. "Ethnohistory and the Owings Site: A Re-analysis." *Quarterly Bulletin of the Archaeological Society of Virginia* 31 (4)–32 (1): 169–75.

——. 1980. A Review of Archaeological Resources in Piscataway Park, Maryland. National Park Service, National Capital Region, Washington.

——. 1989. "Early English Effects on Virginia Algonquian Exchange and Tribute in the Tidewater Potomac." In *Powhatan's Mantle: Indians in the Colonial Southeast*, ed. P. Wood, G. Waselkov, and M. T. Hatley, 151–72. Lincoln: Univ. of Nebraska Press.

Price, Sally, and Richard Price. 1980. *Afro-American Arts of the Suriname Rain Forest*. Los Angeles: Museum of Cultural History, UCLA.

Prussin, Labelle. 1969. *Architecture in Northern Ghana: A Study of Forms and Functions*. Berkeley: Univ. of California Press.

Puente, Elixio de la. 1764. Plano de la Real Fuerza, Baluarte y Linea de la Plaza de St. Augustin de la Florida. Map. Photostat on file, St. Augustine Historical Society.

Pulsipher, Lydia Mihelic. 1994. The Landscapes and Ideational Roles of Caribbean Slave Gardens. In *The Archaeology of Garden and Field*, ed. N. F. Miller and K. L. Gleason, 202–21. Philadelphia: Univ. of Pennsylvania Press.

Pulsipher, Lydia M., and Conrad M. Goodwin. 1982. Galways: A Caribbean Sugar Plantation. Report on the 1981 Field Season. Knoxville: Department of Geography, University of Tennessee.

———. 1988. Betty's Hope Estate, Antigua, West Indies: Conservation Project. Pilot Study Report. Knoxville: Department of Geography, University of Tennessee.

Quarcoo, A. K., and Marion Johnson. 1968. "Shai Pots: The Pottery of the Shai People of Southern Ghana." *Baessler-Archiv*, Neue Folge 16:47–87.

Quimby, George I. 1966. *Indian Culture and European Trade Goods*. Madison: Univ. of Wisconsin Press.

Quimby, Ian, ed. 1972. *Winterthur Portfolio 7*. Charlottesville: Univ. Press of Virginia.

Raboteau, Albert J. 1978. *Slave Religion: The "Invisible Institution" in the Antebellum South*. Oxford: Oxford Univ. Press.

Rajchman, John. 1988. "Foucault's Art of Seeing." *October* 14:89–119.

Rammage, Alix. 1980. *Ashanti and Hausa Pottery*. Birmingham, Eng.: School of Art Education, Birmingham Polytechnic.

Randolph, J. Thornton. 1852. *The Cabin and Parlor; or Slaves and Masters*. Philadelphia: T. B. Peterson.

Rattray, R. S. 1959. *Religion and Art in Ashanti*. London: Oxford Univ. Press.

Rawick, George P. 1972. *From Sundown to Sunup*. Westport, Conn.: Greenwood Press.

Redford, Dorothy S., with M. d'Orso. 1988. *Somerset Homecoming: Recovering a Lost Heritage*. New York: Doubleday.

Reinhart, Theodore R., ed. 1984. *The Archaeology of Shirley Plantation*. Charlottesville: Univ. Press of Virginia.

Reinhart, Theodore R., and Judith A. Habicht. 1984. "Shirley Plantation in the Eighteenth Century: A Historical, Architectural, and Archaeological Study." *Virginia Magazine of History and Biography* 92:29–49.

Reitz, Elizabeth J. 1987. Vertebrate Fauna and Socioeconomic Status. In *Consumer Choice in Historical Archaeology*, ed. Suzanne M. Spencer-Wood, 101–19. New York: Plenum.

———. 1990. Zooarchaeological Analyses of African-American Foodways: Gracia Real de Santa Teresa de Mosé. Report on file, Florida Museum of Natural History, Gainesville. Manuscript.

———. 1994. "Zooarchaeological Analysis of a Free African Community: Gracia Real de Santa Teresa de Mosé." *Historical Archaeology* 28 (1): 23–40.

Richardson, David. 1989. "Slave Exports from West and Central Africa, 1700–1810." *Journal of African History* 30 (1): 1–22.

*Richmond Enquirer*. 18 Jan. 1823.

Rivallain, Josette. 1981. "Un Artisanat ancien: La Poterie dans le sud du Bénin." *In Le Sol, la parole, et l'écrit: Mélanges en hommage à Raymond Mauny*, 1:247–63. Paris: Société Française d'Histoire d'Outre-Mer.

Roberts, John W. 1989. *From Trickster to Badman: The Black Folk Hero in Slavery and Freedom*. Philadelphia: Univ. of Pennsylvania Press.

Robertshaw, Peter, ed. 1990. *A History of African Archaeology*. London: James Currey.

Rock, Howard. 1984. *The Artisans of the New Republic: The Tradesmen of New York City in the Age of Jefferson*. New York: New York Univ. Press.

Rock, Howard, Paul A. Gilje, and Robert Asher, eds. 1995. *American Artisans: Crafting Social Identity, 1750–1850*. Baltimore: Johns Hopkins Univ. Press.

Rodney, Walter. 1970. *A History of the Upper Guinea Coast*. New York: Monthly Review Press.

Roediger, David. 1991. *The Wages of Whiteness: Race and the Making of the American Working Class*. New York: Verso.

———. 1994. *Towards the Abolition of Whiteness*. New York: Verso.

Rogers, Ethel. 1986. Taped interview by Carrel Cowan-Ricks. Chicago, 2–3 April.

Rountree, Helen C. 1990. *Pocahontas's People: The Powhatan Indians of Virginia through Four Generations*. Norman: Univ. of Oklahoma Press.

Rouse, Irving. 1986. *Migrations in Prehistory*. New Haven: Yale Univ. Press.

Rowland, Kate Mason. 1892. *The Life of George Mason, 1725–1792*. New York: G. P. Putnam's Sons. [Manuscript and typed transcript on file, Gunston Hall library, Lorton, Va.]

Royce, Anya P. 1982. *Ethnic Identity: Strategies of Diversity*. Bloomington: Univ. of Indiana Press.

Russo, Jean. 1988. Self-Sufficiency and Local Exchange: Free Craftsmen in the Rural Chesapeake Economy. In *Colonial Chesapeake Society*, ed. L. Carr, P. Morgan, and J. Russo, 389–432. Chapel Hill: Univ. of North Carolina Press.

———. 1992. A Model Planter: Edward Lloyd IV of Maryland, 1770–1796. *William and Mary Quarterly*, 3d ser., 49 (1): 62–88.

Rutsch, Edward S. 1973. *Smoking Technology of the Aborigines of the Iroquois Area of New York State*. Cranbury, N.J.: Associated Univ. Presses.

Ryder, Robin L. 1990. Phase 2 Archaeological Evaluations of the Monroe House Site (44Pw80). Report prepared for the Virginia Department of Transportation, Virginia Commonwealth University Archaeological Research Center, Richmond.

Rykert, Joseph. 1980. *The First Moderns: The Architects of the Eighteenth Century*. Cambridge, Mass.: MIT Press.

Samford, Patricia. 1996. "The Archaeology of African-American Slavery and Material Culture." *William and Mary Quarterly*, 3d ser., 53 (1): 87–114.

Sanford, Douglas W. 1985. A Report on the Archaeological Excavations of Servant's Houses "r," "s," and "t" and the Related Landscape. In Monticello Black History/Craft Life Archaeological Project, 1984–85 Progress Report, by William Kelso, Douglas Sanford, Anna Gruber, Dinah C. Johnson, and Ann M. Smart. Thomas Jefferson Memorial Foundation, Monticello, Charlottesville, Va. Manuscript.

———. 1991a. "A Response to Anne Yentsch's Research Note on Below-Ground 'Storage Cellars' among the Ibo." *African-American Archaeology* 5:4–5.

———. 1991b. "Middle Range Theory and Plantation Archaeology: An Analysis of Domestic Slavery at Monticello, Albemarle County, Virginia, ca. 1770–1830." *Quarterly Bulletin of the Archeological Society of Virginia* 46:20–30.

———. 1994. "The Archaeology of Plantation Slavery in Piedmont Virginia: Context and Process." In *Historical Archaeology of the Chesapeake*, ed. P. A. Shackel and B. J. Little, 115–30. Washington, D.C.: Smithsonian Institution Press.

Sanjek, Roger. 1994. "The Enduring Inequalities of Race." In *Race*, ed. Steven Gregory and Roger Sanjek, 18–38. New Brunswick, N.J.: Rutgers Univ. Press.

Savitt, Todd L. 1978. *Medicine and Slavery*. Urbana: Univ. of Illinois Press.

Schiffer, Michael B. 1987. *Formation Processes of the Archaeological Record*. Albuquerque: Univ. of New Mexico Press.

Schmitt, Karl. 1952. "Archaeological Chronology of the Middle Atlantic States." In *The Archaeology of the Eastern United States*, ed. J. B. Griffin, 59–82. Chicago: Univ. of Chicago Press.

———. 1965. "Patawomke: An Historic Algonkian Site." *Quarterly Bulletin, Archaeological Society of Virginia* 20 (1): 1–36.

Schrire, Carmel. 1994. *Digging through Darkness: Chronicles of an Archaeologist*. Charlottesville: Univ. Press of Virginia.

Schwarz, Philip J. 1988. *Twice Condemned: Slaves and the Criminal Laws of Virginia, 1705–1865*. Baton Rouge: Louisiana State Univ. Press.

Schuyler, Robert, ed. 1980. *Archaeological Perspectives on Ethnicity in America: Afro-American and Asian American Culture History*. Farmingdale, N.Y.: Baywood Publishing,

Scott, Elizabeth M., ed. 1994. *Those of Little Note: Gender, Race, and Class in Historical Archaeology*. Tucson: Univ. of Arizona Press.

Scurry, James D., and Helen Haskell. 1979. "Appendix E: Preliminary Analysis of Colono-Ware Ceramics from Hampton Plantation." In *Hampton: Initial Archaeological Investigations at an Eighteenth-Century Rice Plantation in the Santee Delta, South Carolina*, ed. K. E. Lewis, 108–24. Research Manuscript 151, Institute for Archaeology and Anthropology, University of South Carolina, Columbia.

Sears, R., ed. 1847. "Description of the State of Virginia." In *New Pictorial Family Magazine* 4.

Selden, John A. Plantation Diary, 1841–1848. Swem Library Special Collections, College of William and Mary, Williamsburg, Va.

Senghor, Leopold S. 1956. L'Esthetique Negro-Africaine. *Diogene* 16:43–61.

Shackel, Paul A. 1996. *Culture Change and the New Technology*. New York: Plenum.

Shapiro, Linn, ed. 1976. *Black People and Their Culture: Selected Writing from the African Diaspora*. Washington, D.C.: Smithsonian Institution Press.

Shaw, Thurstan. 1960. "Early Smoking Pipes: In Africa, Europe, and America." *Journal of the Royal Anthropological Institute of Great Britain and Ireland* 90 (2): 272–305.

Shennan, Stephen. 1994. "Introduction: Archaeological Approaches to Cultural Identity." In *Archaeological Approaches to Cultural Identity*, ed. S. J. Shennan, 1–32. London: Rutledge.

Shephard, Steven. 1983. "The Spanish Criollo Majority in Colonial St. Augustine." In *Spanish St. Augustine*, ed. K. Deagan, 65–98. New York: Academic Press.

Shinnie, P. L., and Paul Ozanne. 1962. "Excavations at Yendi Dabari." *Transactions of the Historical Society of Ghana* 6:87–118.

Shumate, M. Scott. 1991. "The Architecture of Jefferson's Mulberry Row: Changes in Form, 1770–1826." *Quarterly Bulletin of the Archeological Society of Virginia* 46:31–41.

Sider, Gerald. 1986. *Culture and Class in Anthropology and History: A Newfoundland Example.* Cambridge: Cambridge Univ. Press.

——. 1987 "When Parrots Learn to Talk, and Why They Can't: Domination, Deception, and Self-Deception in Indian-White Relations." *Comparative Studies in Society and History* 29:3–23.

Simmonds, Doig. 1982. "Pottery in Nigeria." In *Earthenware in Africa and Asia*, ed. J. Picton, 54–91. Colloquies on Art and Archaeology in Asia 12. London: Univ. of London.

Singleton, Theresa. 1980. The Archaeology of Afro-American Slavery in Coastal Georgia: A Regional Perception of Slave Household and Community Patterns. Ann Arbor: University Microfilms International.

——. 1988. "An Archaeological Framework for Slavery and Emancipation, 1740–1880." In the *Recovery of Meaning: Historical Archaeology in the Eastern United States*, ed. Mark P. Leone and Parker Potter, Jr., 345–370. Washington, D.C.: Smithsonian Institution Press.

——. 1989. African-American Archaeology within the Southern United States. Paper presented at the conference "Digging the African American Past," 17–20 May, University of Mississippi, Oxford.

——. 1990. "The Archaeology of the Plantation South: A Review of Approaches and Goals." *Historical Archaeology* 24 (4): 70–77.

——. 1991. "The Archaeology of Slave Life." In *Before Freedom Came: African-American Life in the Antebellum South*, ed. E. D. C. Campbell, Jr., and K. S. Rice, 155–75. Richmond: Museum of the Confederacy.

——. 1991. Comparisons of Slave Archaeology from the Tidewater and Lowcountry. Paper presented at the symposium "Plantation Archaeology of the Virginia and Maryland Tidewater Region and the Lowcountry of Georgia and South Carolina: A Synthesis and Comparison," annual meeting of the Society for Historical Archaeology, Richmond, Va.

——. 1995. "The Archaeology of Slavery in North America." *Annual Reviews of Anthropology* 24: 119–40.

——, ed. *The Archaeology of Slavery and Plantation Life*. Orlando, Fla.: Academic Press.

Singleton, Theresa, and Mark D. Bograd. 1995. *The Archaeology of the African Diaspora in the Americas.* Guides to the Archaeological Literature of the Immigrant Experience in America, no. 2, the Society for Historical Archaeology, Tucson, Arizona.

Slattery, Richard G., and Douglas R. Woodward. N.d. The Montgomery Focus. Draft manuscript on file, Maryland Historical Trust, Annapolis.

Smedley, Audrey. 1993. *Race in North America.* Boulder, Colo.: Westview.

Sobel, Mechal. 1987. *The World They Made Together: Black and White Values in Eighteenth-Century Virginia.* Princeton, N.J.: Princeton Univ. Press.

Solana, Juan Joseph. 1759. Report to the Bishop, 22 April. Manuscript, AGI, 86–7–21/41; transcription, Historic St. Augustine Preservation Board, St. Augustine, Fla.

South, Stanley. 1974. *Palmetto Parapets: Exploratory Archaeology at Fort Moultrie, South Carolina, 38Ch50.* Anthropological Studies 1. Institute for Archaeology and Anthropology, University of South Carolina, Columbia.

——. 1977. *Method and Theory in Historical Archaeology*. New York: Academic Press.

South, Stanley, Russell K. Skowronek, and Richard E. Johnson. 1988. *Spanish Artifacts from Santa Elena*. Occasional Papers of the South Carolina Institute of Archaeology and Anthropology, Anthropological Studies 7. Columbia: University of South Carolina.

South Carolina Archives. 1954. *The St. Augustine Expedition of 1740: A Report to the South Carolina General Assembly*. Reprinted from the Colonial Records of South Carolina with an introduction by John Tate Lanning. Columbia, S. C.

Speck, Frank G. 1928. "Chapters on the Ethnology of the Powhatan Tribes of Virginia." *Indian Notes and Monographs* 1 (5): 227–455.

Spencer, Linda. 1972. Site History, Archaeology, and Ceramics at Fort Mosé. On file, Florida Museum of Natural History, Gainesville.

Sprinkle, John H. 1991. "The Contents of Charles Cox's Mill House Chest." *Historical Archaeology* 25 (3): 91–93.

Stafford, Cornelius William. 1797. *The Philadelphia Directory for 1797*. Philadelphia: Woodward.

——. 1798. *The Philadelphia Directory for 1798*. Philadelphia: Woodward.

Stampp, Kenneth M. 1956. *The Peculiar Institution: Slavery in the Ante-bellum South*. New York: Alfred A. Knopf.

Staski, Edward. 1990. "Studies of Ethnicity in North American Historical Archaeology." *North American Archaeologist* 11 (12): 121–45.

Stearns, Richard E. 1940. *The Hughes Site: An Aboriginal Village Site on the Potomac River in Montgomery County, Maryland*. Proceeding no. 6. Baltimore: Natural History Society of Maryland.

Stephenson, Robert L., and Alice L., L. Ferguson, with sections by Henry Ferguson. 1963. *The Accokeek Creek Site: A Middle Atlantic Seaboard Culture Sequence*. Anthropological Papers 20. Ann Arbor: Museum of Anthropology, University of Michigan.

Stern, Theodore. 1951. *Pamunkey Pottery Making*. Southern Indian Studies 3.

Stewart, T. Dale. 1954. "A Method for Analyzing and Reproducing Pipe Decorations." *Quarterly Bulletin of the Archaeological Society of Virginia* 9 (1).

Stine, Linda Francis, Melanie A. Cabak, and Mark D. Groover. 1996. "Blue Beads as African-American Cultural Symbols." *Historical Archaeology* 30 (3): 49–75.

Stobel, Arnulf. 1984. *Afrikanische Keramic*. Munich, Ger.: Hirmer Verlag.

Street, Margaret. 1980. *Ashanti and Hausa Pottery*. Birmingham, Eng.: School of Art Education, Birmingham.

Stuckey, Sterling. 1987. *Slave Culture: Nationalist Theory and the Foundations of Black America*. Oxford: Oxford Univ. Press.

Sudbury, Byron. 1977. "History of the Pamplin Area Tobacco Pipe Industry." *Quarterly Bulletin of the Archaeological Society of Virginia* 32 (2): 1–35.

Sutch, Richard. 1976. "The Care and Feeding of Slaves." In *Reckoning with Slavery*, ed. Paul A. David. New York: Oxford Univ. Press.

Swem, Earl Gregg. 1934–36. *Virginia Historical Index*. 2 vol. Roanoke, Va.

Tafuri, Manfredo. 1980. *Theories and Histories of Architecture*, trans. Giorgio Verrecchia. New York: Harper and Row.

Tate, Thad W. 1979. "The Seventeenth-Century Chesapeake and Its Modern Historians."

In *The Chesapeake in the Seventeenth Century: Essays on Anglo-American Society and Politics*, ed. T. W. Tate and D. L. Ammerman, 3–50. New York: W. W. Norton.

Tepaske, John. 1975. "The Fugitive Slave; Inter-Colonial Rivalry and Spanish Slave Policy, 1687–1764." In *18th Century Florida and Its Borderlands*, ed. S. Proctor. Gainesville: Univ. Presses of Florida.

Thomas, David Hurst. 1988. "Saints and Soldiers at Santa Catalina: Hispanic Designs for Colonial America." In *The Recovery of Meaning*, ed. M. Leone and P. Potter, 73–140. Washington, D.C.: Smithsonian Institution Press.

Thompson, Robert Farris. 1981a. "Kongo Civilization and Kongo Art." Chap. 1 in *The Four Moments of the Sun*, R. F. Thompson and J. Cornet. Washington, D.C.: National Gallery of Art.

———. 1981b. "The Structure of Recollection: The Kongo New World Visual Tradition." Chap. 2 in *Four Moments of the Sun*, R. F. Thompson and J. Cornet. Washington, D.C.: National Gallery of Art.

———. 1983. *Flash of the Spirit: African and Afro-American Art and Philosophy*. New York: Random House.

———. 1993. "Round Houses: Mande-Related Architecture in the Americas." In *Art in Small-Scale Societies: Contemporary Readings*, ed. R. L. Anderson and K. L. Field, 357–65. Englewood Cliffs, N.J.: Prentice Hall.

Tilley, C. 1989. "Interpreting Material Culture." In *The Meanings of Things*, ed. I. Hodder, 185–94. London: Unwin Hyman.

Trimingham, J. Spencer. 1978. *Islam in West Africa*. Oxford: Clarendon Press.

Trowel, Margaret. 1960. *African Design*. New York: Praeger Publishers.

Tyler-McGraw, Marie, and Gregg D. Kimball. 1988. *In Bondage and Freedom: Antebellum Life in Richmond*. Richmond: Valentine Museum.

UNESCO. 1987. Feasibility Study for Conservation and Restoration of Cultural Heritage in Jamaica, vol. 2, The Case of New Seville. Final Report to UNESCO, Kingston, Jamaica.

United States Direct Tax of 1798. Philadelphia City Archives (PCA). Philadelphia.

Upton, Dell. 1978. "Board Roofing in Tidewater Virginia." *APT Bulletin* 8:22–43.

———. 1980. Early Vernacular Architecture in Southeastern Virginia. Ph.D. diss., Department of Anthropology, Brown University.

———. 1982a. "The Origins of Chesapeake Building." In *Three Centuries of Maryland Architecture*, 44–57. Annapolis: Maryland Historical Trust.

———. 1982b. Slave Housing in Eighteenth-Century Virginia. Report prepared for the Department of Social and Cultural History, National Museum of American History, Smithsonian Institution, Washington, D.C.

———. 1985. "White and Black Landscapes in Eighteenth-Century Virginia." *Places, a Quarterly Journal of Environmental Design* 2:59–72.

———. 1986. "Vernacular Domestic Architecture in Eighteenth-Century Virginia." In *Common Places: Readings in American Vernacular Architecture*, ed. D. Upton and J. M. Vlach, 315–35. Athens: Univ. of Georgia Press.

———. 1990. "Imagining the Early Virginia Landscape." In *Earth Patterns: Essays in Landscape Archaeology*, ed. W. M. Kelso and R. Most, 71–86. Charlottesville: Univ. Press of Virginia.

———. 1991. Landscape and Imagination. Paper, Eighth Conference on Restoring Southern Gardens and Landscapes: The Southern Vernacular Landscape, Winston-Salem, N.C.

———. 1996. "Ethnicity, Authenticity, and Invented Traditions." *Historical Archaeology* 30 (2): 1–7.

Valdez, Geronimo. 1729. Manuscript, AGI 58-2-16/25 (Bishop of Cuba to the Spanish Crown, 14 Jan.). Photostat, Stetson collection, University of Florida.

Valentine, C. 1968. *Culture and Poverty: Critique and Counter-proposals.* Chicago: Univ. of Chicago Press.

Van Dantzig, Albert. 1978. *The Dutch and the Guinea Coast, 1674–1742: A Collection of Documents from the General State Archive at the Hague.* Accra: Ghana Academy of Art and Science.

———. 1980a. *Forts and Castles of Ghana.* Accra: Sedco.

———. 1980b. *Les Holladais sur la côte de Guinée à l'epoque de l'essor de l'Ashanti et du Dahomey, 1680–1740.* Paris: Société Française d'Histoire d'Outre-Mer.

Vanderpool, Frank C. 1986.Telephone interview by William E. Rutter. 11 Feb.

Van Ness, Margaret. 1987. Personal communication. Letter report on analysis of coprolite specimen from 20IO58.

Van Sertima, I. 1985. "Nile Valley Presence in America B.C." In *Nile Valley Civilizations*, ed. I. Van Sertima, 221–46. Atlanta: Journal of African Civilizations.

Vaughan, Alden T. 1972. "Blacks in Virginia: A Note on the First Decade." *William and Mary Quarterly*, 3d ser., 29 (3): 469–78.

Vlach, John M. 1978. *The Afro-American Tradition in Decorative Arts.* Cleveland: Cleveland Museum of Art.

Walker, Alice. 1983. "In Search of Our Mothers' Gardens." In *Search of Our Mothers' Gardens: Womanist Prose*, 231–43. San Diego: Harcourt, Brace, Jovanovich.

Walker, Iain C. 1977. *Clay Tobacco Pipes, with Particular Reference to the Bristol Industry*, vols. 1–4. Ottawa: Parks Canada.

Wallerstein, Immanuel. 1991. "The Construction of Peoplehood: Racism, Nationalism, Ethnicity." In *Race, Nation, Class: Ambiguous Identities,* ed. Etienne Balibar and Immanuel Wallerstein, 71–85. New York: Verso.

Waselkov, Gregory A. 1983. "Indians of Westmoreland County." In *Westmoreland County, Virginia, 1653–1983*, ed. W. Norris, Jr., 15–33. Montross, Va.: Westmoreland County Commission for History and Archaeology.

Washburn, Wilcomb E. [1957] 1972. *The Governor and the Rebel: A History of Bacon's Rebellion in Virginia.* New York: W. W. Norton.

Washington, Booker T. 1965. *Up from Slavery: An Autobiography.* New York: Dodd, Mead & Co.

Watters, David. 1987. "Excavations at the Harney Site Slave Cemetery, Montserrat, West Indies." *Annals of Carnegie Museum* 56 (18): 289–319.

Webb, Steven Saunders. 1985. *1676: The End of American Independence.* Cambridge: Harvard Univ. Press.

Weisiger, Benjamin B., comp. 1980. *Charles City County, Virginia, Court Orders, 1687–1695.* Richmond: Benjamin B. Weisiger.

Weld, Issac. 1807. *Travels through the States of North America.* London.

Wells, Camille. 1987. "The Eighteenth-Century Landscape of Virginia's Northern Neck." *Northern Neck of Virginia Historical Magazine* 37:4217–55.

Wells, John. 1971. "Mussel Shell Island, Mecklenburg County, Virginia." *Quarterly Bulletin of the Archaeological Society of Virginia* (25) 3: 141–86.

Wenger, Mark R. 1986. "The Central Passage in Virginia: Evolution of an Eighteenth-Century Living Space." In *Perspectives In Vernacular Architecture II*, ed. C. Wells, 137–46. Columbia: Univ. of Missouri Press.

———. 1991. "Thomas Jefferson, Tenant." *Winterthur Portfolio* 26:249–65.

Wertenbaker, T. J. 1940. *Torchbearer of the Revolution: The Story of Bacon's Rebellion and Its Leader*. Princeton, N.J.: Princeton Univ. Press.

Wesler, Kit W. 1987. West African Perspectives on Afro-American Archaeology. Fifth Annual Symposium on Ohio Valley Urban and Historic Archaeology, Paducah, Ky.

Westmacott, Richard. 1992. *African-American Gardens and Yards in the Rural South*. Knoxville: Univ. of Tennessee Press.

Wheaton, Thomas, Amy Friedlander, and Patrick Garrow. 1983. *Yaughan and Curiboo Plantations: Studies in Afro-American Archaeology*. Marietta, Ga.: Soil Systems Inc.

Wheaton, Thomas R., and Patrick H. Garrow. 1985. "Acculturation and the Archaeological Record in Carolina Lowcountry." In *The Archaeology of Slavery and Plantation Life*, ed. T. A. Singleton, 239–59. Orlando, Fla.: Academic Press.

Wheeler, R. E. M. 1940. *Medieval Catalogue*. London Museum.

Whiffen, Marcus. 1984. *The Eighteenth-Century Houses of Williamsburg: A Study of Architecture and Building in the Colonial Capital of Virginia*. Williamsburg, Va.: Colonial Williamsburg Foundation.

Wilkie, Laurie. 1995. "Magic and Empowerment on the Plantation: An Archaeological Consideration of African-American World View." *Southeastern Archaeology* 14 (2): 136–48.

———. 1996. "Medicinal Teas and Patent Medicines: African-American Women's Consumer Choices and Ethnomedical Traditions at a Louisiana Plantation." *Southeastern Archaeology* 15 (2): 119–31.

Willett, Frank, and Graham Connah. 1969. "Pottery Making in the Village of Use near Benin City, Nigeria." *Baessler-Archiv*, Neue Folge 17:133–49.

Williams, B. F. 1989. "A CLASS ACT: Anthropology and the Race to Nation across Ethnic Terrain." *Annual Review of Anthropology* 18:401–44.

Williams, Eric. 1942. *The Negro in the Caribbean*. Bronze Booklet no. 8. Washington, D.C.: Association of Negro Folk Education.

Willis, W. S., Jr. 1972. "Skeletons in the Anthropological Closet." In *Reinventing Anthropology*, ed. D. Hymes, 121–52. New York: Vintage.

Wilson, George. Plantation Diary, 1853–1855. Swem Library Special Collections, College of William and Mary, Williamsburg, Va.

Wilson, J. S. 1860. "The Peculiarities and Diseases of Negroes." *American Cotton Planter and Soil of the South* 4.

Winfree, Westwood R. 1967. "The T. Gray Haddon Site, King William County, Virginia." *Quarterly Bulletin of the Archaeological Society of Virginia* 22 (1): 2–26.

———. 1969. "Comparative Material: A Comment upon Indian Brown Clay Pipes." *Quarterly Bulletin of the Archaeological Society of Virginia* 24 (1): 79.

Wittkower, Rudolph. 1983. *Palladio and English Palladianism*. New York: Thames and Hudson.

Wolf, Eric. 1982. *Europe and the People without History*. Berkeley: Univ. of California Press.

———. 1990. "Distinguished Lecture: Facing Power—Old Insights, New Questions." *American Anthropologist* 92:586–96.

———. 1994. "Race, Culture, People." *Current Anthropology* 35 (1): 1–12.

Wolff, Norma. 1987. Personal communication, Department of Sociology and Anthropology, Iowa State University, Ames, 28 June.

Wood, Peter. 1974. *Black Majority: Negroes in Colonial South Carolina from 1670 through the Stono Rebellion*. New York: Alfred A. Knopf.

———. 1989. "The Changing Population of the Colonial South: An Overview by Race and Region, 1685–1790." In *Powhatan's Mantle: Indians in the Colonial Southeast*, ed. P. Wood, G. Waselkov, and M. T. Hatley. Lincoln: Univ. of Nebraska Press.

Wood, Peter H., Gregory A. Waselkov, and M. Thomas Hatley, eds. 1989. *Powhatan's Mantle: Indians in the Colonial Southeast*. Lincoln, Neb., and London: Univ. of Nebraska Press.

Woodward, C. Vann. 1955. *The Strange Career of Jim Crow*. New York: Oxford Univ. Press.

Work Projects Administration. [1940] 1986. *Drums and Shadows: Survival Studies among the Georgia Coastal Negroes*. Rept., with introduction by Charles Joyner. Athens: Univ. of Georgia Press.

Wright, Irene. 1924. "Dispatches of Spanish Officials Bearing on the Free Negro Settlement of Gracia Real de Santa Teresa de Mosé." *Journal of Negro History* 9:144–93.

Yarwood, John, ed. 1991. *Master Plan for Seville Heritage Park*. Report to the Jamaican Urban Development Corporation. Kingston, Jamaica.

Yentsch, Anne. 1991. "A Note on a 19th Century Description of Below-Ground 'Storage Cellars' among the Ibo." *African American Archaeology* 4:3–4.

———. 1994. *A Chesapeake Family and Their Slaves: A Study in Historical Archaeology*. Cambridge: Cambridge Univ. Press.

Zierdan, Martha, Lesley Drucker, and Jeanne Calhoun. 1986. Home Upriver: Rural Life on Daniel's Island, Berkeley County, South Carolina. Report (Contract No. FA1-526-41[63]) pprepared by Carolina Archaeological Services and the Charleston Museum. Submitted to South Carolina Department of Transportation, Federal Highway Administration, Columbia.

# Contributors

**Douglas V. Armstrong,** Associate Professor and Chair, Department of Anthropology, Syracuse University, Syracuse, New York.

**Beverly E. Bastian,** Ph.D. candidate, Department of History, of California, Santa Barbara.

**Edward A. Chappell,** Director of Architectural Research, Colonial Williamsburg Foundation, Williamsburg, Virginia.

**Thomas E. Davidson,** Chief Curator, Jamestown-Yorktown Foundation, Jamestown, Virginia.

**Kathleen A. Deagan,** Distinguished Research Curator of Anthropology, Florida Museum of Natural History, University of Florida, Gainesville.

**Christopher R. DeCorse,** Associate Professor of Anthropology, Syracuse University, Syracuse, New York.

**James Deetz,** Professor of Anthropology, University of Virginia, Charlottesville

**Matthew C. Emerson,** Assistant Professor, Department of Anthropology, Southern Illinois University, Edwardsville.

**Terrence W. Epperson,** Vice President of Research, CHRS, 403 East Walnut Street, North Wales, Pennsylvania.

**Leland G. Ferguson,** Professor and Chair, Department of Anthropology, University of South Carolina, Columbia.

**Barbara J. Heath,** Director of Archaeology, Corporation for Thomas Jefferson's Poplar Forest, Forest, Virginia.

**Mary Ellen N. Hodges,** Archaeologist, Virginia Department of Transporation, Richmond.

**Jane Landers,** Associate Professor, Department of History, Vanderbilt University, Nashville, Tennessee.

**Martha W. McCartney,** Historian Consultant, Williamsburg, Virginia.

**Larry McKee,** Director of Archaeology, The Hermitage, 4580 Rachel's Lane, Hermitage, Tennessee.

**L. Daniel Mouer,** Associate Professor, Department of Sociology and Anthropology, Virginia Commonwealth University, Richmond.

**Ivor Noël Hume,** Director, Department of Archaeology (Retired), Colonial Williamsburg Foundation, Williamsburg, Virginia.

**Robert Paynter,** Professor, Department of Anthropology, University of Massachusetts, Amherst.

**Warren Perry,** Assistant Professor, Department of Anthropology, Central Connecticut State University, New Britain, and Associate Director of the African Burial Ground Project, New York, Howard University.

**Dennis J. Pogue,** Director of Restoration, Mount Vernon Ladies' Association, Mount Vernon, Virginia.

**Merrick Posnansky,** Professor Emeritus, Departments of History and Anthropology, University of California, Los Angeles.

**Stephen R. Potter,** Regional Archaeologist, National Park Service Capitol Region, Washington, D.C.

**Susan L. Henry Renaud,** Senior Planner, National Park Service, Washington, D.C.

**Theresa A. Singleton,** Curator of Anthropology, National Museum of Natural History, Smithsonian Institution, Washington, D.C., and Associate Professor, Department of Anthropology, Syracuse University, Syracuse, New York.

# Index

Italicized page numbers indicate illustrations.